Reform and transformation in Eastern Europe

Reform and transformation in Eastern Europe

Soviet-type economics on the threshold of change

Edited by János Mátyás Kovács and Márton Tardos

London and New York

IN ASSOCIATION WITH THE INSTITUT FÜR DIE WISSENSCHAFTEN VOM MENSCHEN, VIENNA

First published 1992
by Routledge
11 New Fetter Lane, London EC4P 4EE

Simultaneously published in the USA and Canada
by Routledge
a division of Routledge, Chapman and Hall, Inc.
29 West 35th Street, New York, NY 10001

© 1992 János Mátyás Kovács and Márton Tardos
Typeset in Times by Selectmove
Printed and bound in Great Britain by
Mackays of Chatham PLC, Chatham, Kent

British Library Cataloguing in Publication Data

Reform and transformation in Eastern Europe:
  Soviet-type economics on the threshold of change.
  I. Kovács, János Mátyás II. Tardos, Márton
  330.9470853

ISBN 0–415–06630–1

Library of Congress Cataloging in Publication Data

Reform and transformation in Eastern Europe: Soviet-type economics on the
  threshold of change / edited by János Mátyás Kovács and Márton Tardos.
      p.   cm.
  Includes bibliographical references and index.
  ISBN 0–415–06630–1
  1. Europe, Eastern – Economic conditions – 1989– 2. Europe, Eastern –
Economic policy. 3. Soviet Union – Economic conditions – 1985– 4. Soviet
Union – Economic policy – 1986– I. Kovács, János Mátyás. II. Tardos, Márton.
HC244.R3757   1992
338.947–dc20
                                                                91–25207
                                                                    CIP

Contents

List of Contributors

Petr O. Aven, Deputy Minister of Foreign Affairs, Russian Federation, International Institute for Applied Systems Analysis, Laxenburg, Austria.

Aleksander Bajt, Economic Institute of the Law School. University of Ljubljana, Yugoslavia.

Leszek Balcerowicz, former deputy Prime Minister and Minister of Finance, Poland. Research Institute of Economic Development, Central School of Trade, Warsaw, Poland.

Włodzimierz Brus, St Antony's College, Oxford, England.

Ellen Comisso, Department of Political Science, University of California, San Diego, USA.

Robert W. Davies, Centre for Russian and East European Studies, University of Birmingham, United Kingdom.

Raimund Dietz, Vienna Institute for Comparative Economic Studies, Austria.

Irena Grosfeld, DELTA, Centre National de la Recherche Scientifique, Paris, France.

János Mátyás Kovács, Institute for Human Sciences, Vienna, Austria; Institute of Economics, Hungarian Academy of Sciences, Budapest, Hungary.

Tadeusz Kowalik, Institute of the History of Science, Warsaw, Poland.

Helmut Leipold, Institute for Comparative Systems of Economic Control, University of Marburg, Germany.

Deborah Duff Milenkovitch, Institute on East Central Europe, Columbia University, New York, USA.

John Michael Montias, Institution for Social and Policy Studies, Yale University, USA.

Alec Nove, Centre for Development Studies, University of Glasgow, United Kingdom.

Jerzy Osiatynski, former Minister of Planning (Poland), Institute of the History of Science, Warsaw, Poland.

Leon Podkaminer, Polish Academy of Sciences, Warsaw, Poland.

Pekka Sutela, Department of Economics, University of Helsinki, Finland.

Márton Tardos, head of the parliamentary faction of the Alliance of Free Democrats (Liberals) in Hungary. Institute of Economics, Hungarian Academy of Sciences, Budapest, Hungary.

Xiao-Chuan Zhou, Ministry of Foreign Economic Relations and Trade, Beijing, China.

Prologue

Prologue

Crossing the threshold

János Mátyás Kovács and Márton Tardos

We recommend this book to the reader at a time when nearly every week offers a new surprise to the students of Eastern European economics. The old system, euphemistically called 'real socialism', is dead or dying in most countries of the 'other Europe', and a new one is emerging in its place. We do not see clearly why the agony, which we were ready to study for many years to come, has suddenly accelerated, and we are only trying to guess what kind of economic institutions will fill the vacuum left behind by the Soviet-type system. Nevertheless, we may predict with great exactitude which are those economic concepts which will certainly *not* prompt the scholars and politicians of these countries to make new experiments in the near future. Although, realistically, one cannot expect Eastern Europe to reach the 'end of history' in the form of a liberal market economy soon or ever, that is, one must not remain unprepared for relapses to state interventionism and authoritarian rule, it is also most likely that Communist ideas will not be instrumental in economic change during the first stages of the transition from socialism.

These ideas have become discredited *en bloc* because they were – justifiably – associated with repeated attempts to force such institutional arrangements (state ownership, overcentralization, party interference, and so on) on economic agents, which in the last analysis proved not only Utopian but also inhuman due to their inherent links to the various forms of political dictatorship. In other words, the Mises–Hayek thesis of the impossibility of rational economic calculation under collectivism appears to be justified even in the case of the most recent efforts to implement 'market socialism', a pragmatic reform concept that has increasingly compromised the original Marxian dream of a non-market-non-state economy or its Stalinist mutant of the centrally-planned state economy. Undoubtedly, even the most radical reform programmes in the 1970s and 1980s, which have been based on less and less simulated projects of deregulation, but have not touched directly the taboo of one-party rule, were not able to solve (or even aggravated) the crises caused by the previous drives of ultra-regulation by the party-state. By 1989, there remained no more promises to make and break. The Soviet-type economies of Eastern Europe not only multiplied their backwardness as compared to the advanced western countries and the newly-industrialized nations, but also dispelled every illusion about the economic merits of socialism (macro-planning, rapid growth, innovativeness, focusing on the consumer, distributive justice, and so on). Furthermore, the Soviet-type systems proved unable to maintain the military-political position of the Eastern bloc as a whole, and the ruling elite has gradually lost its confidence in the possibility of attaining even this pragmatic goal.

The successive economic reforms initially helped prolong the life of the Soviet-type societies in Hungary, Poland and Yugoslavia. In the other countries of Eastern Europe, however, market socialism had been aborted before it could have proven its ultimate inability. Although the reformers in Bulgaria, Czechoslovakia, the Soviet Union, and so on, have also become finally aware of the fact that, after a certain point, genuine marketization is inconceivable without large-scale privatization, and the latter without the dismantling of the party-state, they did not put much hope in essential political change even on the eve of the 1989 landslide. In any event, the *ancien régime* was far more vulnerable than expected and the peoples of Eastern Europe were not patient enough to wait until each of their national economies totally exhausted their reformist reserves and went bankrupt – in this way irrevocably demonstrating the truth of the Mises–Hayek school.

Reform-making was interrupted or prevented both by the disintegration of the ruling elites and organized political action (civil disobedience, bargaining, open revolt) from below. As a consequence, socialist reform-ation remained unfinished, but the reform-minded theoretical economists, the overwhelming majority of the representatives of economic science in Eastern Europe of the late 1980s, showed no sign of frustration. On the contrary, they were convinced that the two principal political limits of reformism (the predominance of state ownership and one-party rule) would no longer constrain their imagination either in economic science or in policy. The romantic trust in the possibility of finally launching genuine liberal reform programmes without the usual real-socialist political compromises has in the meantime been offset by the realism of the transition process. The former reformers are on the way to realize that marketization and privatization cannot only have 'dictatorship limits' but also 'democracy limits'; that the harmonization of the simultaneous tasks of the transition, such as stabilization, deregulation, modernization, and so on, can be blocked by their technical and logical incompatibilities as well, and not exclusively by built-in political brakes; and also that these political brakes are only partly deactivated by the new regimes.

Consequently when, in the early 1990s, the economists in Eastern Europe are searching for fixed points in economics and political science during the first phases of the transition from socialism, the long-awaited rediscovery of liberal thought cannot satisfy all their needs. In light of the surprising facts of continuity within revolutionary change, they cannot avoid re-examining the intellectual luggage they carry along when crossing the threshold between the repeated reforms and the final transformation of the Soviet-type system. We would like our volume to show what is to be found in that luggage.

REFORMERS: COMMUNISTS IN DISGUISE OR CLOSET CAPITALISTS?

Ever since Bukharin was discovered in Soviet studies, historians of economic thought have filled libraries with papers written about the 'economics of reform' in Soviet-type socialism. As yet, however, no comprehensive and comparative work on the history of socialist reform thinking has been published either in the west or in the east. After three major waves of economic reform in Eastern Europe and the Soviet Union between Stalin's death in 1953 and the 1989 collapse of real socialism, we are still not equipped with appropriate instructions for disentangling the ambiguous theoretical attitudes, sociological positions and political roles of the reformers. This may in turn disturb the understanding of the current changes in Soviet-type economics, where we see the former reformers rapidly become 'transformers', that is, economists who conduct research and make policy proposals on the transition from socialism rather than searching for partial improvement in the framework of the old regime.

Whenever in the past an impartial spectator looked at a socialist reformer, he encountered a peculiar mixture of liberal and collectivist ideas in his discourse. In order to comprehend this hybrid of principles, the observers have made fragmented attempts at classifying reformist thought, either in terms of its political radicalization, or in terms of the technical details of economic deregulation. Nevertheless, the underlying theoretical questions whether: (a) liberalism and collectivism can be harmonized at all within the framework of the Soviet-type economy; (b) reform thinking can be separated from the Stalinist political economy of socialism; and (c) a genuine theory of transition to a market economy can be constructed along the lines of reformist principles, have usually been ignored.

The scholarly literature has been full of journalistic truisms, for example, about the reform economists who – as Communists in disguise – help legitimize the survival of Stalinism; or, on the contrary, who – as 'closet capitalists' – strive to undermine real socialism. Meanwhile, many reformers cherished an idea in between, contending that they were on a way to create a new social-liberal paradigm (the 'third way') of economic science. Sometimes there were surprising similarities between western liberal views on and the neo-Stalinist critique of socialist reformism: both parties were willing to exaggerate the liberal features of reform thinking. In any case, labels such as naïve and radical reformers, étatists and those favouring self-management, technocratic and syndicalist reformers, and so on, proliferated without thorough explanation, causing a lot of confusion.

Now, in the light of the quick fall of real socialism, the problem of misinterpreting the reformers seems at first sight outdated. One may even ask whether it is reasonable to put much effort into refining the notion of socialist reformism after 'really existing socialism' has been replaced by a sort of 'really emerging capitalism'. The former reformers of Eastern Europe are experimenting with genuine liberal transformation programmes – why should we bother ourselves with the retroactive clarification of the concepts of simulated liberalization?

TEMPORA MUTANTUR . . .

When, in 1987, we started to think about a research programme on comparative reform concepts in Soviet-type economies, the logical framework of the project seemed relatively clear. At that time few would have challenged the view that the definition of reform should be linked to that of the Soviet-type economy. By and large, economic reform thinking was then considered a combination of controversial attempts at making scientific discoveries and setting up policy proposals for limited economic change; attempts that were made *within* the limits – even if gradually eroding limits – imposed by the Soviet-type party-state. Intellectually, the reformers diagnosed certain malfunctions of the economy, as well as recommending moderately strong remedies, in a language that was traditionally based on the soft categories of 'plan' and 'market'. Sociologically, the reform-minded economists tried to link research work with political bargaining within the labyrinth of the party-state.[1]

Those observers who ventured to determine where the boundaries of socialist reformist thought lay, had a hard time disentangling the varied plan-market combinations (from Langeism and 'computopia', through the concepts of 'regulated market' and 'self-managing market' all the way to 'managerial' or to 'entrepreneurial socialism') in the reform blueprints. In other words, it often seemed impossible to classify the many dozens of liberalization scenarios which all aimed to prove why markets cannot (and how they nevertheless should) work in an economy integrated by the party-state. What if this party-state ceases to be a constant in the definition? What if the party-state starts not only to relax its grip on the economy but even to disintegrate?

In the last phase of their power, Communist party leaders were initiating large-scale privatization drives, reconciling themselves to parliamentary pluralism, and even calling the idea of communism a Utopia. Finlandization, Austrianization, mixed economy, civil society, rule of law, human rights, private property, self-regulating market, and so on – these terms became elements of the economic discourse of the radical reformers, being as indispensable as were, decades ago, the phrases 'socialist law of value' or later the 'regulated market'. After leaving the world of market socialism ('socialist market economy'), the reformers of yesterday march hand in hand with the members of the old and now of the new elite towards *Soziale Marktwirtschaft* ('social market economy').

That is why a Hungarian friend of ours said, with a smile: 'You wanted to construe an up-to-date typology of socialist reform concepts; now you should write the obituary of reform thinking as a whole instead.' Well, the re-emergence of liberal thought in Eastern Europe may in the near future dull the *political* edge of such questions as 'What is a reformer like?' or 'How to compare reform concepts?'. None the less, in the future textbooks of the history of socialist economic thought, reform thinking, will occupy a large place. Together with Marxism as well as with the Bolshevik and Stalinist types of political economy, it will most likely be depicted (to rephrase the familiar joke) as the longest path from nineteenth century *laissez-faire* liberalism to twentieth century social liberalism.

The fact that a current issue is partly becoming a *historical* one before our very eyes, lends the observer the unique possibility of making a dynamic survey. Until recently, we could only be aware of where the *Dogmengeschichte* of socialist reform started. Now we can also explore where it may end up. This can help delimit the field in which reform concepts should be discussed. In addition, after having crossed the threshold, we may have the emotional distance from the stage, expected from an unbiased historical audience, while still being familiar with the behavioural nuances of the main actors.

Nevertheless, socialist reformism has not become a *par excellence* historical problem yet. (Not only because in some countries of real socialism – from China to Cuba – reformist thought has not exhausted all its reserves thus far.) Undoubtedly, economics in Eastern Europe is on its way to cross the threshold between reformist thought and the various schools of western economic science. The first steps that have been taken in the last two years towards *Soziale Marktwirtschaft* are promisingly quick. The widely-expected neo-liberal turn, however, is not likely to take place during the initial stages of transition. What we are witnessing in most countries of Eastern Europe is a kind of 'social democratization' of radical reform thinking (though often with Christian democratic undertones), a triumph of social liberalism on the ruins of the Soviet-type economy, rather than a neo-liberal breakthrough. The pendulum has begun to swing in the liberal direction (especially in rhetoric) but – after leaving the point of suspension – it has not gone very far yet. At this juncture one cannot predict the real dimension of change in economic theory under post-socialism. Until recently, the obstacles to change were primarily political and ideological in nature. Now they are rather practical. The events of 1990–1 in all Eastern European countries clearly show how painful are the starting moves of the transformation, and how difficult is their conceptualization in a liberal fashion (cf. the Epilogue).

This 'long moment' of crossing the threshold offers a good chance for getting rid of the hasty typologies of reform thinking, as well as of our illusions concerning the new liberalism of the transformers. In the 1980s, thousands of economists (scholars and politicians) in the east confessed to belong to the 'parish' of the reformers. Reformism even became a sort of state religion in Hungary, Poland and Yugoslavia, while its representatives already began to work on the first scenarios of the transformation. Now at the turn of the decade, the leading figures of the economic profession in Eastern Europe (Brus, Kornai, Šik, and so on) are looking back at their own intellectual prehistory in order to find their common roots and explain the recent changes in their discourse. Would we forgive ourselves if we missed this unique – and maybe ultimate – chance for a comprehensive study of the evolution of late reformist thought from the perspective of the emergence of a theory of post-socialist transformation?

REFORM ECONOMICS: PLAN-AND-MARKET VERSUS PLAN-OR-MARKET

When our research programme on 'plan and/or market' was launched at the Vienna Institute for Human Sciences, and simultaneously at the Institute of Economics, Hungarian Academy of Sciences, Budapest,[2] we used the value-free term of '*reform economics*' to denote comprehensively – the way we do in Hungary – such concepts as 'optimal planning', 'socialist commodity production', 'planned market', 'regulated market', 'market socialism', and so on. (Similarly, the words 'reform economist' and 'reformer' were applied interchangeably.)

The research project envisaged both an *external* and an *internal* classification of the reform concepts. Externally, reform economics was to be compared with the main currents of liberal economic thought, as well as with other schools of socialist (collectivist) political economy. Internally, we planned to construct a historical taxonomy of the reform ideas through their real types, while naturally not rejecting a substantive definition of the ideal type(s). Quite understandably, the members of our research group regarded the preliminary category of reform economics as empty, and tried to fill it according to their own intellectual traditions.

This is how we formulated *the specifics* of our research programme at the outset:

1 Economic reform thinking in Soviet-type societies is considered, by the project participants, a sovereign scientific problem in the history of economic thought and not – as conventionally – an obscure political and ideological corollary of research into practical reform processes.

2 Comparison is made, not only between the individual reform concepts, or between reformist thought and the Stalinist political economy, but also between reform economics and western economic theories (a field of research completely ignored so far).

3 The project goes beyond the comparative description of the evolution of reform thinking in the selected countries of Eastern Europe and the Soviet Union (which is also lacking in the literature); its final objective is to construe an analytical typology of reform concepts in Soviet-type

economies, and to answer the ultimate question 'Is reform economics possible at all?' Is it reasonable to expect the birth of a new paradigm of economic science based on the harmony of 'plan' and 'market'? Or in the last analysis, do 'plan' and 'market' rather exclude each other in Soviet-type economies?

4 The research group is multi-cultural and interdisciplinary by purpose: it consists of scholars living in the countries concerned (Czechoslovakia, China, Hungary, Poland, the Soviet Union, Yugoslavia) and of western experts (often émigrés of these countries); they are economists, historians, sociologists and political scientists. The group has been organized for long-term research work.

Since, in the meantime, reformist thought has reached the limits even of the most radical concepts of market socialism in Eastern Europe, the project participants have also started to focus on the intellectual *challenges* the transformers now have to face (see the corresponding three chapters in the volume). In order not to get lost in the labyrinth of the transition trajectories, the transformers:

(a) have to study what has been offered by western schools of economics in the field of the theory of reform and transformation;
(b) have to examine critically what reform economics has still retained from the Stalinist political economy;
(c) have to find out how a genuine transformation theory can be constructed on the ruins of the Soviet-type economy.

The papers in this collection demonstrate not only the cumulative radicalization and professionalization of reform thinking in the past decades, but also the seamy side of reform economics, that is, the imperfect understanding on the part of the reformers of modern economic science in the west, the inhibited separation from Stalinism, and the built-in obstacles to designing a sophisticated theory of transformation. As one member of our research group put it,

> while our project is not likely to cause a revolution, it is at least going to serve as something like a confessional, after leaving which we may go on committing the same sins, but perhaps with less self-assurance than before.

FROM REFORM TO TRANSFORMATION

The first stage of our research project included two international conferences in Vienna (December 1988, June 1989), and a conference in Noszvaj, Hungary (April 1989) with Hungarian participants only.[3] At these meetings we laid the theoretical foundations of the project by discussing more than forty papers on reform economics.[4] Then we embarked upon writing case studies of reformist thought according to countries, periods of time and fields of economics. Understandably, however, the year 1989 has completely reorganized our research agenda. Many of us grew interested in the rediscovery of liberalism in Eastern European economics;[5] some of our colleagues (Balcerowicz, Gligorov, Klaus, Osiatynski, Tardos, *et al.*) have got involved with the daily tasks of practical transformation; and those who remained in academia have begun to work on the exciting new theoretical problems of economic transition (primarily on those of privatization) rather than preparing historical case studies of reform thinking. (Unfortunately, the contacts with our Chinese colleagues have in the meantime been disturbed.)

This volume represents the last words said by the project participants about reform economics before (or at the beginning of) its transition to a kind of social-liberal transformation theory. The reason why we decided to publish the results of the 'reformist' part of the project separately is twofold. On the one hand, we wanted to grasp the moment of crossing the threshold, and on the other, we would like to hope that the next volume that we have already started to compile, will appear under new headings.

Instead of '*Reform and Transformation*', the title may be simply '*Transformation*' to indicate the end of the reformist discourse and also the emergence of an original theory of liberalizing the Soviet-type economy, which may well prove in the future much more significant from a scholarly point of view than the birth of reform economics decades ago. Nevertheless, for the time being we would not venture to anticipate the optimistic subtitle: '*Eastern European Economics: Beyond the Threshold*'. True, real optimism would also require us to abandon the adjective 'Eastern European' for good, in the hope that our countries will join the liberal mainstream of economic science fairly soon, and geographical distinctions will become irrelevant . . .

NOTES

1 It would be too much to say (if we may inject a personal note) that, in the spring of 1987, we could foresee one of us, Márton Tardos, becoming a few months later the general director of an independent research institution (joint stock company) and a political leader of the Hungarian Free Democrats. He had for a long time been a member of the group of the radical reformers in Hungary. Formerly a full-time research director at the Institute of Economics of the Hungarian Academy of Sciences, and a non-party adviser to the Central Committee and the government, Tardos became a free entrepreneur, and two years later, the deputy chairman of the Economic Commission of the new Parliament.
2 We wish to express our gratitude to the Vienna Institute for Human Sciences, the Budapest Institute of Economics, Hungarian Academy of Sciences, the George Soros Foundation, New York, the Fritz Thyssen Stiftung, Köln and the National Scientific Research Foundation (OTKA), Budapest, for funding the project.
3 Thanks are specially due to the following colleagues for their valuable comments at our conferences: László Antal, Abram Bergson, Karel Dyba, Henryk Flakierski, János Gács, Stanislaw Gomulka, Agota Gueullette, John Hall, Stefan Hedlund, Annamária Inzelt, Pál Juhász, Jan Klacek, Kazimierz Kloc, Peter Knirsch, Vojislav Kostunica, Karel Kouba, Mihály Laki, Kamilla

Lányi, Kazimierz Laski, Marie Lavigne, Boris L'vin, Gennadii Lisichkin, Aladár Madarász, Iván Major, Paul Marer, András Nagy, Mario Nuti, Vilen Perlamutrov, Boris Rakitskii, Tamás Réti, István Rév, Gábor Révész, Gabor Rittersporn, Vladimír Rudlovcak, Ladislav Rusmich, Tsuneaki Sato, Erich Streissler, László Szamuely, Iván Szelényi, Aleksandar Vacic, Éva Voszka, Hans-Jürgen Wagener, Jing-Lian Wu, Jianhua Yang, Józef Zieleniec, Albert Zlabinger.

4 The following papers were submitted to our conferences in addition to those which are included in this volume: Karel Dyba and Karel Kouba, 'Czechoslovak attempts at systemic changes (1958, 1968, 1988)'; Henryk Flakierski, 'The economic system and income distribution in Yugoslavia'; Agota Gueullette, 'Soviet concepts of foreign trade: 1917–1945'; John Hall, 'Comparison of Hungarian and Chinese reform concepts'; Stefan Hedlund, 'The role of Soviet man in reforming real socialism'; Jan Klacek, 'A scenario methodology for appraising economic reforms'; Kazimierz Kloc, 'The NEP and the economic controversies of the twenties in the light of current economic reforms'; Marie Lavigne, 'Is the French theory of regulation relevant to reform economics?'; Gennadii Lisichkin, 'Some theoretical thoughts about the principles of perestroika in the Soviet Union'; Paul Marer, 'Hungary's reform and performance in the Kádár era'; Jan Mujzel, 'Reformability of real socialism'; Mario Nuti, Perestroika: the economics of transitional reforms in the centrally planned economies'; Boris Rakitskii, 'Market laws in a distorted socialist environment'; István Rév, 'Uncertainty as a technology of power. Approaching the transition'; Gabor Rittersporn, 'Soviet reform attempts in historical perspective'; Ladislav Rusmich, 'A Long Path to the concept of socialist economy'; László Szamuely, 'The Marxian concept of socialism and the present-day reforms of the socialist economies'; Iván Szelényi, 'Eastern Europe in an epoch of transition. Towards a socialist mixed economy?'; Aleksandar Vacic, 'Open issues of the political economy of socialism'; Éva Voszka, 'Reform economics: role and oeuvre'; Jing–Lian Wu, 'The strategic options of reform and the evolution of economic theories. China's example'.

5 See 'Rediscovery of Liberalism in Eastern Europe' (*East European Politics and Societies*, Vol. 5, no. 1 Winter 1991); a special issue including the papers of Ellen Comisso, Vladimir Gligorov, Irena Grosfeld, Tomás Jezek and Václav Klaus, János Mátyás Kovács, Mihály Laki, Oleg Rumiantsev, George Schöpflin, Jadwiga Staniszkis, Erich Streissler and Gáspár Miklós Tamás.

Part I

Reform economics and economic theory and the west – missed opportunities

Introduction to Part I

According to a widespread view, reformism is tantamount to moving away from Stalinist orthodoxy in the direction of liberal economics. But what kind of liberalism? Vienna? Cambridge? Chicago? – they are all 'more liberal' than Moscow. What could the reform economists borrow from their western colleagues? Were the reformers able to profit from the position of being a 'newcomer'? Was it worth while expecting a new synthesis (a 'third way') in reform economics, and a *rapprochement* of east and west in economic thought on the basis of this synthesis? The papers included in this chapter seek answers to these questions.

The socialist calculation debate which began more than half a century ago has not yet been digested by the reformers (and the transformers), whereas the Mises–Hayek thesis of the impossibility of rational economic calculation under collectivism seems to be proven by the decline of Soviet-type economies – a fact that has otherwise been thoroughly diagnosed by the reform economists themselves. The liberal message of the critics of collectivism about the dangers of extreme étatization and centralization – reads Balcerowicz – did not lead to radical changes in the world outlook of the reformers. They accepted the warnings about the distortion of information in hierarchical organizations, the lack of incentives for risk-taking and innovation, and so on, but ignored for a long time the private entrepreneur as the *conditio sine qua non* of marketization.

Duff Milenkovitch, Grosfeld, Leipold, Montias and Nove all focus on another missed opportunity in the intellectual communication between liberals and reform-minded socialist economists: they point to the apparent inexperience of the reform economists in new institutional economics. While the protracted rediscovery of the Austrian tradition prevented the reformers from building their programmes on a sophisticated dynamic theory of the market (Leipold), the fragmented knowledge of the new institutionalist concepts, such as property rights and transaction cost economics, the theory of the bureaucracy, constitutional economics, and so on, limited the understanding of the existing Soviet-type economic institutions (cf. the notion of institutional equilibrium with Montias), as well as impeded the comparison of market versus government failures in formulating the reform proposals (Grosfeld). The property rights idea will reappear in the papers of Bajt, Comisso and Tardos in the following chapters.

Nove argues with great passion that socialist reformers and post-socialist transformers cannot learn much from general equilibrium theory; they had better consult the neo-institutionalist critique of the neo-classical paradigm if they prefer realism to sophistication. Duff Milenkovitch lists a series of alternative concepts of socialist economic organization to conclude that the theory of non-profit organizations – coupled with the new concepts of bureaucracy – could have served as an adequate model for comprehending Soviet-type economic institutions. Finally, Dietz combines Simmel, Hayek and Luhmann to arrive at a market theory, based on the concepts of 'exchange' and 'communication', which could have helped the reformers lose their illusions concerning the symmetrical mix of plan and market.

There are, of course, a couple of related questions of great importance, which could not even be superficially dealt with in this chapter. Why did the reformers at a certain point become suspicious with regard to general equilibrium theory? How does this affect their expertise in economic science? Why have they remained uneducated even in welfare economics; a discipline that, in principle, must best meet their 'taste'? How do the reform economists mix Keynesian-type and monetarist economic policies in their reform blueprints? Which are the typical limits to the rediscovery of the liberal tradition by the reform economists? These problems were widely discussed at our conferences and are also reflected upon in the chapters of Bajt, Brus, Comisso, Kovács, Kowalik, Podkaminer and Tardos.

1 The 'socialist calculation debate' and reform discussions in socialist countries

Leszek Balcerowicz

INTRODUCTION

The 'socialist calculation debate' (SCD) has been discussed in the economic literature many times (see, for example, Hoff 1949; Bergson 1948, 1967; Ward 1967; Delhaes 1983; Schoppe 1982; Neck 1982; Dore and Kaser 1984; Lavoie 1985; Bernholz 1987). It is known that before the Second World War, the participants on the 'anti-socialist' side included Ludwig von Mises, Boris Brutzkus and Friedrich A. Hayek, and on the opposite side Fred A. Taylor, H. D. Dickinson, Oskar Lange, Joseph A. Schumpeter and Maurice Dobb.[1] The debate continued in the post-war period. Various mathematical procedures for decentralized planning, partly based on the previous proposals of the 'socialists', were then elaborated by Arrow and Hurwicz, Malinvaud and others (for a comprehensive analysis of these schemes, see: Heal 1973). Some of the issues discussed during the SCD were generalized by Hurwicz (1960) in his concept of the 'allocation mechanisms'. The literature on this topic and on the related problem of 'incentive compatibility' has been growing very fast in recent years (for a review, see Radner 1987).

Many participants of the SCD focused on the problem of rational calculation, or in other words, on the issue of the allocative efficiency of socialism. This is even more true of the commentators on the SCD. But it would be improper to reduce the SCD to the 'calculation debate' because some of the protagonists (mostly on the anti-socialist side) raised other issues as well.

In what follows, I will try to relate the SCD to the reform discussions in the socialist countries after the Second World War, that is, to investigate what kind of relationship (if any) exists between these two streams of economic thought. As far as the SCD is concerned, I will concentrate on the writings of the above-mentioned authors. With regard to the reform discussions, I shall focus my attention on those which have taken place in

Poland and Hungary. I will disregard the question of to what extent the reform proposals (or the reform practice) in these countries have influenced the theoretical literature belonging to the SCD.[2] Finally, I will not try to trace the actual flow of ideas from the participants of the SCD to the reform economists, that is, to establish which of the latter were familiar with the SCD and which were not.

The relevant question is therefore this: Did the contributions to the SCD contain anything of potential value to the reform economists?

The writings of the latter typically consist of two parts. One is a critical examination of the established (that is, Soviet-type) economic system. This may be called a diagnosis, as it aims at identifying the main weaknesses in the economic performance and at linking them to some aspects of the system. The second part is a description of the proposed new system, which, if established, would hopefully eliminate the indicated weaknesses.[3]

I will first discuss the relevance of the SCD for the diagnostic part of the reform concepts and then for the reform proposals proper. One should, of course, remember that the diagnoses of the system may have an indirect impact on the reform proposals, as they influence the direction of the search for a better system.

THE 'SOCIALIST CALCULATION DEBATE' AND THE DIAGNOSIS OF THE FAILURES OF SOCIALISM

The problem of economic calculation

This problem can be broken down into two broad issues:

1 the availability of proper economic data for comprehensive central planning.
2 The informational capacity of the centre, that is, the capacity to assimilate and process the data in such a way as to arrive at rational decisions with regard to the allocation of resources.

The original challenge of the anti-socialist critics centred on (1). One can distinguish here two problems. Brutzkus (1922b:167–70) was one of the few authors who pointed out that identifying the consumer preferences and, consequently, determining the correct structure of the production of consumer goods in the absence of the market for these goods, may be a relatively easy task only at a very low level of economic development.[4] With income per capita rising, there would be, however, an increasing differentiation of consumer preferences and the problem would become very complex. Physiological norms as the basis for consumption planning would not do. Similar points were made by Hoff (1949:74–5, 182–3). In contrast, Mises, widely perceived as the main protagonist on the anti-socialist side of the SCD, did not pay much attention to the difficulties in the central determination of the structure of the production of consumer goods. He even stated (1935:107) that 'the economic administration [in the socialist state] may know exactly what goods are most urgently needed'.

The second problem, which lay at the very heart of the calculation debate, was the alleged lack of proper economic data for identifying the optimal combination of resources to produce a given output, that is, to establish which production technique is the cheapest. This point was emphasized both by Brutzkus and Mises. Both authors derive this assertion from the lack of markets for the means of production in socialism (as envisaged by the Marxists), and both try to show why the free market prices are the indispensable informational input for rational calculation. There is, however, one difference between them. Mises goes one step further and maintains that only the institutions typical for capitalism can ensure that proper market information will be generated,[5] while Brutzkus admits the possibility of an efficient 'market socialism' and even provides its outline (see the third section).

On the other hand, Mises emphasizes that the problem of calculation only arises under the inherently dynamic, changing conditions of the real world:

> if we assume that the socialist system of production were based upon the last state of the system of economic freedom which it superseded, and that no changes were to take place in the future, we could indeed conceive a rational and economic Socialism. But only in theory. A stationary economic system can never exist. Things are continually changing, and the stationary state, although necessary as an aid to speculation, is a theoretical assumption to which there is no counterpart in reality.
>
> (Mises 1951:122)

Thus, contrary to the opinions of many later commentators, Mises's challenge as to the impossibility of rational calculation in socialism referred to the real world and not to the imaginary world of economic theory (cf. Lavoie 1985:48–77):

The main response on the socialist side to Mises's challenge was to propose procedures of iterative, price-guided planning, whereby the Central Planning Board takes the place of the Walrasian auctioneer by fixing the prices by trial and error and the enterprises' and industries' managers are instructed to follow the rules of welfare economics. Oskar Lange (1938) is widely considered to have elaborated the fullest non-mathematical version of these procedures. It was later formalized by Kenneth Arrow and Leonid Hurwicz (1960). Another version was elaborated by Malinvaud (1967). These economists concentrated on the convergence property of the proposed schemes and demonstrated that under some restrictive assumptions (for example, no incentive problem, no externalities, no increasing returns to scale) there is within the framework of their mathematical models, a convergence to Pareto-satisfactory equilibrium.

However, as soon as one leaves the realm of pure theory and tries to visualize the operation of these schemes in the real world, many doubts come to mind.[6] Most of them were formulated already in 1940 by Hayek (1949:181–208). First, without dismissing the problem of the availability of proper data to the planning board, he emphasized its insufficient informational capacity, while referring to central price fixing by trial and error:

> when . . ., one proceeds to consider the actual apparatus by which this sort of adjustment is to be brought about, one begins to wonder whether anyone should really be prepared to suggest that such a system will ever even distantly approach the efficiency of a system where the required changes are brought about by the spontaneous action of the persons immediately concerned.

Hayek adds, following Mises, that the difficulty arises out of the dynamic nature of the real world:

> If in the real world, we had to deal with approximately constant data (. . .), then the proposal (. . .) would not be so entirely unreasonable. But this is far from being the situation in the real world, where constant change is the rule.

Other issues raised by Hayek include the omission of price expectations in the Lange-type schemes, and thus the disregarding of the problem of who is to bear the responsibility for the consequences of the decisions based on erroneous forecasts; the difficulty of identifying the marginal costs by the managers who are required to produce until these costs are just equal to the price of the good; the inability of the centre to set the prices in accordance with the differences in the quality of the goods, and so on.[7]

Hayek did not pay much attention to the question of why the socialist managers should follow the rules specified in the Lange-type schemes, which does not mean that he did not consider it as a problem. He rather wanted to show that *even if* the managers were perfectly willing to obey these rules, the procedure still could not work properly. Some other authors discussed *the incentive problem* related to these rules at greater length (see, for example, Bergson 1967; Ward 1967; Schoppe 1982; Pickersgill and Pickersgill 1974; 310–14). The general point they make is that as soon as we abandon the unrealistic assumption of the harmony of interest between the managers and the centre, new difficulties emerge: the former may (a) misrepresent the input needs and production possibilities; (b) behave in a monopolistic way by limiting production and thus creating artificial shortage in order to get higher prices; (c) pressure the centre for more investment outlays than is economically rational; and so on.

Taking into account the conflict of interests means that one passes from the analysis in terms of the team-theory (in the Marschak–Radner sense) to the game-theory approaches. Indeed, such approaches to the analysis of central planning have been intensively developed in recent years. However, as John Roberts (1987:350), who made a significant contribution to the formulation of this line of analysis, points out, the positive results in game-theory approaches to planning have been achieved by using at least one of a pair of unpalatable assumptions: 'a myopia assumption, that postulates that agents, in choosing their messages at any iteration, care only about the change in their utilities at that iteration', and the assumption of complete information. With regard to the latter he rightly comments: '. . . in reality one believes that individuals are not perfectly informed about one another; indeed, if they were, it is not clear why we would need any decentralized procedure'. This reminds us to some extent of the objections of Mises and Hayek to analysing the calculation problem in a static framework, which assumes away the informational complexities.

Initiative, risk-bearing, innovation

What would happen to actions involving risk, if the competitive market system based on private enterprises were replaced by comprehensive bureaucratic planning linked to the state ownership of the means of production? One difficulty noted both by Brutzkus (1922a:53–4; 1922c:57) and Mises (1935:116–18) is how to make the socialist managers responsible for the losses incurred by their enterprises. Both predicted that the lack of appropriate mechanisms of managers' financial responsibility would lead to a tendency to fill this gap by detailed bureaucratic regulations, constraining the initiative of the managers. The tendency for bureaucratization was also emphasized by Hayek (1949:198–9) in his analysis of the Lange-type schemes, whereby the managers are required to follow some centrally determined rules:

> From the point of view of the manager, it will be much more important that he should always be able to prove that in the light of knowledge he possessed the decision actually taken was the right one than that he should prove to be right in the end. If this will not lead to the worst forms of bureaucracy, I do not know what will.

The bureaucratic restrictions on the managers' initiatives were considered by Brutzkus (1922c:57) to lead to poor innovative performance of the socialist economy to 'technical inertia and conservatism'. He considered bureaucratization a sufficient reason for this, but also pointed out another potential barrier: the lack of sufficient material rewards for the would-be inventors and innovators.

With regard to innovation, Hayek (1949:196–7) emphasized that it is competition that brings about the discovery of the new production techniques which result in the lowering of the level of costs. The socialist economy, based on planning that replaces the market, would therefore be deprived of the major innovative force. A somewhat related point was made by Hoff (1949:89). He noticed that in a capitalist society there is always a number of persons 'irresistibly attracted' by risky investment in new technical developments. Such persons will also be found under socialism 'but it will not be possible to make use of their peculiar attributes and self-sacrifice, as the socialist community does not allow commercial activity on one's own account'. Hoff thus pointed out the direct link between the type of property rights and the innovative performance of the economy.

And what were the views of the prominent representatives of the social side of the SCD? Lange (1938:109–10) admitted that the bureau-cratization of economic life may indeed be a danger under socialism, but he claimed that he couldn't see 'how the same, or even greater, danger can be avoided under monopolistic capitalism'.[8] It is also this allegedly growing monopolization which was responsible, in his view, for capitalism's increasing inability to exploit new technological opportunities (pp. 112–15).[9]

Schumpeter (1962) was no less confident about the relative innovative possibilities of socialism. He assumed that industrial managers would be instructed to produce as economically as possible, and as a result they would introduce new and more efficient pieces of machinery (p. 178). He also thought that 'in the socialist order every improvement would theoretically spread by decree and substandard practice could promptly be eliminated' (p. 196).[10]

Consequences of the centralization of investment

In Lange's model, the centre was to determine only the overall volume of investment while its allocation among the various industries and plants was to be left in the hands of lower-level managements. Hayek (1949:200–1) pointed out that any attempt at practical application of this model would most likely result in a widespread central control of investment. Lange himself changed his position and advocated that the centre should directly determine the allocation of investment. Hence, he joined his socialist critics (for example, Dobb, Baran and Sweezy) in the belief that direct central control over investment is the source of the basic superiority of socialism over capitalism. Such a control was thought to lead to a better co-ordination of investment (that is, avoiding the 'duplication' of the productive capacities). The centre was also regarded as being capable of foreseeing the technological developments and of ensuring that the selected investment projects would reflect the 'general interests' of the economy. Besides, the central determination of the rate of accumulation was to ensure a higher rate of growth,[11] for the individual consumers were considered notoriously short-sighted.

It was left to the anti-socialist critics to point out the dangers of the centralization of investment. Brutzkus (1922b:170–2) emphasized that the investment decisions taken by the centre would be politically motivated and, therefore, of poor economic quality. He also predicted that the central distribution of the investment outlays would induce the lower levels, unconstrained by any fear of bankruptcy, to put enormous pressure on the centre in order to get as many means allocated as possible. As a result, the overall co-ordination of investment will be so poor as to make the 'capitalist anarchy' appear a perfect harmony (Brutzkus 1922b:173). A similar point was made by Hoff (1949:206), who also questioned the ability of the central authorities to display a greater foresight with regard to technical developments and the future preferences of consumers than the 'autonomous concerns in the capitalist society where managers and owners are more or less dependent for their living on the correctness of their judgment'. Hoff also contended that 'if a central authority should prove unwilling to admit to mistakes, the development will continue in the same false direction, so that final readjustment will be more painful than the trade fluctuations of the capitalist society'.

How to explain these differences in the views on the consequences of the centralization of investment? They stem, it seems, from the profound divergence in the assumptions on the nature of the socialist state. The proponents of socialism implicitly assumed that central decision-makers would have no informational problems[12] and that they would only be interested in serving the 'social interest'. The anti-socialist critics had much more realistic views on the nature of the socialist state (and on all states, for that matter).

Shortages

This phenomenon, characteristic of socialist economies, was not in the centre of the SCD. One can find, nevertheless, some penetrating observations on this topic, mostly made by the anti-socialist critics. Brutzkus (1922c:57) stated, for example, that comprehensive planning replacing the market mechanism would lead to price rigidity and to the unresponsiveness of the supply of consumer goods to the changing demand for them. The resulting shortages of these goods would in turn weaken the incentives to work. Brutzkus (1922b:172) also predicted that the administrative rationing of inputs would generate massive misallocation.

The issue of shortages was also raised by Hayek (1949:193) in his critique of central price-setting, proposed in the Lange-type models. Hayek pointed out that, because of inevitable delays in this process, and due to the inability of the centre to fix prices in accordance with the differences in the quality of goods '. . . a great many prices would be at most times substantially different from what they would be in a free market'. In other words, the administrative prices would often diverge from the market-clearing level. One should, therefore, not confuse a 'simulated' market with the real one.[13]

Comments

Anyone familiar with the experiences of the socialist economies easily recognizes that the problems of socialism identified by its critics during the SCD[14] overlap, to a large extent, with the weaknesses of the Soviet-type economic system. These were pointed out during the reform discussions in the socialist countries and provided the rationale for the reform proposals.

In contrast, some of the prominent participants on the socialist side of the SCD formulated predictions as to the beneficial effects of socialist schemes, which from the perspective of real socialism appear rather naïve. Apart from the aforementioned belief in the advantages of the centralization of investment, one may recall Lange's (1938:48–107) claim that socialism would solve – thanks to the elimination of private entrepreneurship, and central price-setting – the problem of externalities, or that only socialism can reap the benefits of free competition. Schumpeter (1962) was even more optimistic in attributing to socialism the possibilities for more rapid technical change, higher workers' discipline, quicker structural change and lower administrative expenses – as compared to capitalism.

THE 'SOCIALIST CALCULATION DEBATE' AND THE REFORM PROPOSALS

In taking up this issue, we may first recall that the main response on the socialist side to Mises's challenge was the elaboration by Taylor, Lange and others of the price-guided schemes of central planning, or, in other words, of the 'simulated' market. However, these schemes have never been adopted by the economists in the socialist countries as the basis for their reform proposals. This was very well put by Marschak (1973:47):

> The practitioners of economic reform in socialist countries attempting to decentralize a command economy have rejected any idea of adopting in some practical way the classic proposals for a socialist economy in the western literature. The scheme of Lange and Lerner, with market-clearing price-setting by a central agency and profit maximizing production decisions by managers, and the many later schemes which are its offspring, appear to be treated with amusement, disdain, or total neglect.

We may add that this attitude of the practically-minded reformers is understandable. (Marschak himself names some of the reasons for this.) For these schemes, being the offshoots of orthodox neo-classical economics, disregarded essential complexities of the real world.[15] An attempt at applying them in practice was bound, therefore, to end up in complete failure or in the creation of an economic system very different from that envisaged in the schemes and quite similar to the traditional centralized planned economy (for more on the latter see Schoppe 1982).

Hence, what has been considered the main socialist solution put forward during the SCD did not find any counterpart in practically-oriented reform thinking in the socialist countries. On the other hand, for a long time the reformers seemed to be in basic agreement with the socialist critics of Lange-type models as to the desirability of the centralization of basic investment decisions. This is clearly visible in the influential book by Włodzimierz Brus (1961), who proposed a decentralized model' whereby the decisions regarding the current operations of the firms would be largely decentralized but the central authorities would retain direct control over new investment. This kind of a model appears to constitute a basic 'reform paradigm' in the 1960s and 1970s in Poland and Hungary.[16] However, in the late 1980s not many reform economists in these countries believed in the merits of the centralization of investment.[17] (This scepticism is also shared now by the author of the 'decentralized model' – cf. Brus, in this book). Thus, neither Lange-type schemes, nor those of his socialist opponents, are to be found nowadays among the reform proposals in the former socialist countries. The prevailing view presently is that economic reform must involve the introduction of the genuine market mechanism.

Interestingly enough, this idea of economic reform can be found in Brutzkus (1922b:180–1), one of the most outspoken critics of Marxian and Soviet socialism. He envisaged a system in which natural resources and fixed assets were national property, but were placed at the disposal of independent groups of employees against payment of interest and rent. The community was to collect all non-labour incomes.[18] This was, in Brutzkus's view, not only desirable from the point of view of social equity, but also economically necessary because socialism, as he pointed out, reduces the propensity of individuals to save. The proposed system was to be based on the genuine market mechanism, comprising both consumer goods and the means of production. This vision of market socialism reminds us to some extent of the Tibor Liska's concept of 'entrepreneurial socialism' (see Bársony 1982). Leasing the state enterprises also constituted one of the preferred directions in recent economic reform proposals in the Soviet Union (Muzhin 1989). Leasing the state land to the farmers has been the backbone of the 'responsibility system' in Chinese agriculture since 1979 (see Erling 1984).

Some participants on the socialist side of the SCD also sketched out schemes of 'market socialism' (see Hoff 1949:139–46, 153–63). For example, Roper (1931:60–2, quoted in Hoff 1949:140), after a critical examination of the system based on central price-fixing by trial and error, arrived at the following conclusion: 'the best chance for success of a socialist community lies in a decentralized organization which retains, so far as possible, the strong features of capitalism.'

This general proposition reminds us of the recent search in socialist countries for the models of – what one could call – *'simulated capitalism'*, that is, an economic system with capitalist institutions but without private capitalists. The main idea here was to transform the present state enterprises into joint-stock companies exclusively, or predominantly, owned by some non-private institutions. There would also exist a stock exchange on which the latter could buy and sell shares. Depending on what institutions are to become shareholders, we get some more specific models. One of them heavily emphasizes the role of the state holdings. Another proposal additionally admits non-administrative institutions like banks, pension funds, municipalities, universities, and so on. One can envisage still another variant where each enterprise would be predominantly owned by some other enterprises, a minority share belonging to its own personnel as represented by the workers' council.[19]

Such proposals were often accompanied by demands to lift the restrictions on the founding and developing of private firms. Indeed, liberal laws with respect to the domestic private sector were passed in Poland and Hungary before 1989. There was also a considerable liberalization of foreign investment in these countries.

All these were signs of a – so much needed – economic pragmatism. But a student of the SCD cannot help but recall Mises's assertion (1951:217–20) that the effective reform of the socialist economic system entails, in fact, a return to capitalism. In any case one can – somewhat pointedly – subsume the development of the reform concepts in the countries of real socialism as 'the imitation of capitalism under increasingly relaxed constraints'.[20] The original Marxian model of socialism resembled one huge capitalist factory with all operations being centralized. Then there appeared the proposal for the decentralization of current operations with the basic investment decisions remaining in the hands of the centre, that is, there was no capital market included in the system. This resembles the large capitalist corporation. The next step was 'simulated capitalism', which allows for capital market but bans or heavily restricts private shareholders. Freedom to establish private firms and the privatization of state enterprises are the final point in the whole process, thus fulfilling Mises's ironic prediction.

NOTES

This paper was partly written when I was the beneficiary of the Friedrich Ebert Foundation in West Germany. The financial assistance of the Foundation is gratefully acknowledged.

1   For brevity, I will sometimes refer to the two sides of the SCD as 'anti-socialist' and 'socialist', respectively. These expressions denote the position taken during the debate and not necessarily the political sympathies of the participants.

2   We may, however, mention some examples of this impact. The Soviet economic practice has heavily influenced the thinking of Dobb (1933). The quantity-guided planning schemes of Kornai and Lipták are theoretical models of the actual Soviet-type planning. The 1965 change in the system of material incentives in the Soviet Union spawned a sizeable analytical literature in the west (see Koont and Zimbalist 1984)

3 Some reform concepts also contain the description of the transition path from the existing system to the reformed one. This is an issue of great practical importance, one that is relatively neglected in the literature on economic reforms.

4 Brutzkus obviously assumed that socialist production is to be adapted to the consumers' preferences. This was an assumption that only few socialist participants of the SCD would contest. One of them was Dobb (1933,591).

5 Mises argues that capitalist ownership is indispensable for rational calculation because it provides the necessary autonomy and the necessary incentives for the economic subjects to try to forecast correctly the future economic data, including future prices. Capitalist institutions are also important for rational calculation because they separate – through the mechanism of bankruptcy – those which are especially competent in this forecasting activity from those who are not. Mises thus considers the capitalist institutions, which generate correct expectations, and in turn shape the current market data, public goods (for more on this, see Murrell 1983).

6 This is not meant to be a critique of the post-war authors in mathematical planning, as if they were only interested in pure theory and refrained from making any claims as to the practical applicability of their models. This, however, cannot apply to Oskar Lange, who was directly responding to Mises's challenge. For Mises explicitly referred to the real world, and Lange responded with a proposal placed in the Walrasian world, thus assuming away most of the practical problems. Lange, it seems, either misread or ignored Mises's challenge (see Murell 1983). In an early critique of Lange's scheme, Hoff (1949) stated that '. . . Lange ought in any case, to have said that his alleged solution was not of practical value' (p. 188).

7 In some other writings, including an earlier one (1935), Hayek also pointed out the problem of inarticulability of knowledge. He stressed that some of the knowledge possessed by the managers and relevant for decision-making cannot be articulated by them and, hence, communicated to the centre. This point has been recently developed by Lavoie (1986) (see also Sowell, 1980:218–20).

8 For more on Lange's views on bureaucratization under socialism, see Kowalik's chapter in this book.

9 In comparing socialism with capitalism, Lange was thus using two different paradigms. While describing his proposed socialist system he was operating most of the time (except for the rare moments of realism as in the case of bureaucratization) within the Walrasian framework, where the most important practical problems of socialism were assumed away. However, in describing capitalism he was using the Marxian paradigm, according to which capitalism was inevitably developing into a monopolistic phase.

10 It is not clear what Schumpeter meant by 'theoretically'. The following passage implies, however, that he had in mind a real possibility, that is, a possibility of socialism operating in the real world.

11 Thus, even if allocative efficiency and consumer sovereignty suffered from the centralization of investment, the sheer volume of the investment outlays was thought to be sufficient to ensure that, in a relatively short time, the consumers would be better off than under the capitalist system starting from the same level of development.

12 Hayek (1949:201) observed, with respect to the seemingly – decentralized schemes of Lange and Dickinson, that their authors console themselves, while describing the advantages of central control over investment, with the hope for the 'omnipresent, omniscient organ of the collective community'.

13 This is why the term 'market socialism' should be used, in my view, only with

respect to those models that envisage a genuine market, which includes free
price-setting.
14 The critics also raised other issues. Brutzkus (1922:58–61), for example,
argued that the state ownership of the means of production and centralized
planning are incompatible with civil and political liberties, a point developed
later by Hayek. Brutzkus (1922c:62) also contrasted two approaches to social
problems: one which advocates a total overhaul of the existing institutions of
capitalist society in the belief that the new system would ensure universal
happiness, and another, more modest approach, which aims at combating
concrete social evils. This reminds us of Hayek's critique of 'constructivism'
and of Popper's critique of 'holistic' social engineering.
   Mises (1951:202) has some interesting thoughts to offer to those reform
economists who think that the main economic problem of real socialism lies in
the lack of political democracy and not in the nature of property rights, and
who thus advocate a 'democratization' or 'socialization' of central planning. For
Mises envisaged such a 'democratic socialism' and argued that in such a system
'the opposition will always be ready to prove that more could be assigned to
immediate satisfactions and the government will not be disinclined to maintain
itself longer in power by lavish spending'.
15 For the critical assessment of the relevance of neo-classical economics to the
comparative analysis of the real-world economic systems (and therefore, to
reform economics), see Nelson 1981; Neck 1982; and Nove, in this book.
Some newer developments in western economic theory might be, however,
more relevant to the reform economists (see Grosfeld and Kovács in this
book). This does not mean that these new concepts provide detailed blueprints
for better systemic arrangements, but that they indicate in what directions one
should look for them.
16 This paradigm was also popular in Yugoslavia (cf. Ellman 1971:20)
17 This scepticism is well founded. Besides the aforementioned doubts as to the
economic rationality of central investment decisions, one could note the fact that
the centralization of investment precludes the free entry by new competitors and
makes difficult, if not impossible, the delineation of the financial responsibility
of enterprises. For the latter can always claim that their financial difficulties are
due to the mistaken investment decisions of the superior bodies.
18 The payments for the entrepreneurial services were, however, to be included
in labour incomes.
19 For various proposals of 'simulated capitalism' see, for example, Tardos in this
book; Antal *et al* (eds) (1987); Swiecicki (1988); 'Privatising in China' (1989).
20 The main departure from this trend is the model of the labour self-managed
economy. But it has its own problems as the vast literature on 'Illyrian socialism'
shows.

BIBLIOGRAPHY

Antal, L., Bokros, L., Csillag, I., Lengyel, L. and Matolcsy, G. (eds) (1987)
'Turnaround and reform' *Közgazdasági Szemle* 6.
Arrow, K.J. and Hurwicz, L. (1960) 'Decentralisation and computation in resource-
allocation', in R.W. Pfouts (ed.) *Essays in Economics and Econometrics in Honour
of Harold Hotelling*, Chapel Hill, NC, University of North Carolina Press.
Bársony, J. (1982) 'Tibor Liska's concept of socialist entrepreneurship', *Acta
Oeconomica* 3–4.
Bergson, A. (1948) 'Socialist economics', in Howard Ellis (ed.) *Survey of Contemp-
orary Economics*, Philadelphia, Blakiston.

Bergson, A. (1967) 'Market socialism revisited', *Journal of Political Economy* 5, 655–73.

Bernholz, P. (1987) 'Information, motivation, and the problem of rational calculation in socialism', in Svetozar Pejovich (ed.) *Socialism. Institutional, Philosophical and Economic Issues*, Dordrecht, Kluwer Academic Publishers, 147–75.

Brus, W. (1961) 'Ogolne problemy funkcjonowania gospodarki socjalistycznej', Państwowe Wydawnictwo Naukowe Warszawa. (English version (1972) *The Market in a Socialist Economy*, London, Routledge & Kegan Paul).

Brutzkus, B. (1922a) 'Problemy narodnogo khoziaistva pri socialisticheskom stroie' ('Problems of the national economy in a socialist system'), *Ekonomist* 1, 48–65 (Moscow).

Brutzkus, B,. (1922b), 'Problemy narodnogo khoziaistva pri socialisticheskom stroie' ('Problems of the national economy in a socialist system'), *Ekonomist* 2, 163–83 (Moscow).

Brutzkus, B. (1922c) 'Problemy narodnogo khoziaistva pri socialisticheskom stroie', ('Problems of the national economy in a socialist system'), *Ekonomist* 3, 54–72 (Moscow).

Delhaes, K. (1983) 'Zur Diskussion über die Funktion der Preise im Sozialismus', *Arbeitsberichte zum Systemvergleich* 4, Marburg, Forschungsstelle zum Vergleich wirtschaftlicher Lenkungssysteme.

Dobb, M. (1933) 'The economic theory and the problems of a socialist economy', *Economic Journal* 43, 588–98.

Dore, M.H.J. and Kaser, M.C. (1984) 'The millions of equations debate: seventy years after Barone', *Atlantic Economic Journal* 3, 30–44.

Ellman, M. (1971) *Soviet Planning Today*, University of Cambridge Department of Applied Economics, Cambridge University Press.

Erling, J. (1984) 'Reformen in der Chinesischen Landwirtschaft', in T. Bergmann, P. Gey and W. Quaisser (eds) *Sozialistische Agrarpolitik*, Köln, Bund–Verlag, 214–31.

Hayek, F.A. (1935) 'The present state of the debate', in F.A. Hayek (ed.) *Collectivist Economic Planning*, London, Routledge, 201–43.

Hayek, F.A. (1949) 'Socialist calculation III: the competitive "Solution"', in *Individualism and Economic Order*, London, Routledge & Kegan Paul, 181–208, reprinted from *Economica* VII (26) (1940).

Heal, G.M. (1973) *The Theory of Economic Planning*, Amsterdam, North Holland.

Hoff, T.J.B. (1949), *Economic Calculation in the Socialist Society*, London, William Hodge & Co. (Norwegian original published in 1938).

Hurwicz, L. (1960) 'Optimality and informational efficiency in resource allocation mechanisms', in K. Arrow, S. Karlin and P. Suppes (eds) *Mathematical Methods in the Social Sciences*, Stanford, Calif., Stanford University Press.

Koont, S. and Zimbalist, A. (1984) 'Incentive and elicitation schemes: a critique and an extension', in A. Zimbalist *Comparative Economic Systems: Present Views*, Boston, Kluwer – Nijhoff Publishing, 159–75.

Lange, O. (1938) 'On the economic theory of socialism', in B.J.Lippincott (ed.) *On the Economic Theory of Socialism*, Minneapolis, University of Minnesota Press, 55–120.

Lavoie, D. (1985) *Rivalry and Central Planning. The Socialist Calculation Debate Reconsidered*, Cambridge, Cambridge University Press.

Lavoie, D. (1986) 'The market as a procedure for discovery and conveyance of inarticulate knowledge', *Comparative Economic Studies* 28(1), 1–19.

Malinvaud, E. (1967) 'Decentralised procedures for planning', in E. Malinvaud and M.O.L.Bacharach (eds) *Activity Analysis in the Theory of Growth and Planning*, London, Macmillan.

Marschak, Th.A. (1973) 'Decentralizing the command economy: the study of a pragmatic strategy for reformers', in M. Bornstein (ed.) *Plan and Market. Economic Reform in Eastern Europe*, New Haven, Yale University Press, 23–64.

Mises, L.von (1935) 'Economic calculation in the socialist commonwealth', in F.A.Hayek (ed.) *Collectivist Economic Planning*, London, Routledge, 87–130 (German original published in 1920).

Mises, L.von (1951) *Socialism: an Economic and Sociological Analysis*, New Haven, Yale University Press (German original published in 1922).

Murrell, P. (1983) 'Did the theory of market socialism answer the challenge of Ludwig von Mises? A reinterpretation of the socialist controversy', *History of Political Economy* 92–105.

Muzhin, A.B. (1989) 'Arenda gosudarstvennykh predpriatii v SSSR', mimeo, Sopron.

Neck, R. (1982) '"Die Sozialismusdebatte" im Lichte ausgewählter neurer Entwicklungen der ökonomischen Theorie', *Jahrbuch für Sozialwissenschaft* 2, 242–64.

Nelson, R.R. (1981) 'Assessing private enterprise: an exegesis of tangled doctrine', *Bell Journal of Economics* 12(1), 93–111.

Pickersgill, G. and Pickersgill, J.E. (1974) *Contemporary Economic System: A Comparative View*, Englewood Cliffs, New Jersey, Prentice-Hall.

'Privatising in China' (1989) *The Economist*, 11 February, 62.

Radner, R. (1987) 'Decentralization and incentives', in T. Groves, R. Radner and S. Reiter (eds) *Information, Incentives and Economic Mechanisms. Essays in Honour of Leonid Hurwicz*, Oxford, Basil Blackwell, 4–47.

Roberts, J. (1987) in T. Groves *et al.* (eds), *Information, Incentives and Economic Mechanisms. Essays in Honour of Leonid Hurwicz*, Oxford, Basil Blackwell, 349–74.

Roper, W.C. (1931) *The Problem of Pricing in a Socialist State*, Cambridge, Mass.

Schoppe, S.G. (1982) 'Das Problem der Wirtschaftsrechnung in einer Zentralverwaltungswirtschaft aus neuer burokratietheoretischer Sicht', *Jahrbuch für Sozialwissenschaft* 2, 225–41.

Schumpeter, J.A. (1962) (1st edn 1942) *Socialism, Capitalism and Democracy*, New York, Harper & Row.

Sowell, Th. (1980) *Knowledge and Decisions*, New York, Basic Books.

Swiecicki, M. (1988) 'Reforma wlasnosciowa', mimeo, Warsaw.

Ward, B. (1967) *The Socialist Economy. A Study of Organizational Alternatives*, New York, Random House.

2 The reform of Soviet socialism as a search for systemic rationality

A systems theoretical view

Raimund Dietz

Given complete centralization, the planner confronts his task not like an omniscient auctioneer, but like a dumb ox, facing a great heap of unconnected things. People learn to connect things through exchange. Without this there is neither economy nor reason.

INTRODUCTION: THE ASYMMETRIC MIX OF PLAN AND MARKET

Bolshevik socialism stepped on to the stage of history with a knapsack filled with historic optimism. The optimism rested on the misconception that the elimination of the market, and its replacement by central control of society, would end anarchy and establish a more rational order. The provender has largely been consumed. We know the symptoms of socialism's decay, but the causes of that decay are not sufficiently understood: because we have no adequate understanding of what, exactly, is the market.

The assumption, that deregulation and decentralization would lead to higher efficiency and faster innovation in the economy may be correct, but it is not, or not sufficiently, supported by economic theory. In economic theory one cannot even find support for the following, and, I believe, 'reasonable' propositions explicitly or implicitly held both by 'realistic conservatives' and 'enlightened socialists'.

1 Every modern society depends on the interplay between the market and bureaucratic (and central) control by the state.
2 These two forms of co-ordination cannot be mixed arbitrarily, if the mix is to function properly. The market must be the basis. State intervention which is necessary – and may become even more so – must depend on signals of the market as an autonomously working subsystem of society. In other words, a socialism with 'market elements' is functionally inferior to a market economy controlled by an interventionist welfare state. That means that centrally-planned economies equipped with

'commodity-money relations' are less rational than market economies controlled by state.

In other words, plan and market are not co-ordination mechanisms capable of being symmetrically mixed – a little less of the one, a little more of the other, but they are systems which – comparable to the interplay between consciousness and bodily functions in man – execute completely different, yet mutually interdependent tasks. Man's mental activity must rely on the vital forces of the body, which can in no way be directed by strong will – in which case neither the forces of digestion could function, nor his brain, centre of his mental activities. Yet, on the other hand, it is decidedly advantageous if man acts consciously when ingesting his food: he can advance both his bodily and mental forces. Along the lines of this analogy we can proceed from an asymmetrical relation between plan and market.

The asymmetry thesis recommends itself in a different aspect, too, in that it corresponds to the indubitably asymptotical convergence of the systems: the reforms in East Europe lead to a transformation of the centrally planned into market economies, whereas in the western societies, despite substantially expanded state involvement in the past, the market forces retained unimpaired vitality.

REFORM VERSUS THEORY

Taking a look at the reform process of Soviet socialism from a greater distance, the observer will note that: (1) despite very great differences in the pace of the reforms in the various socialist countries the direction of the reform process is, by and large, unequivocal; (2) the reform process manifests very considerable thrust; (3) great advances were and are achieved without reliance on any consistent (economic) theory.

Direction

The thesis propounded here states that the reforms must lead to a transformation of Soviet socialism into western industrial-type societies (socio-economic orders). This means that they correct Soviet socialism until it has been transformed – irrespective of the labels attached to it – into a socio-economic state that is no longer distinguishable in principle from the formerly incriminated 'model' of western civilization. Minor differences will probably persist: but they will probably be assessed as being rather socialist burdens and leftovers than persisting socialist achievements.

In this we do not propound any historic determinism. The history of civilization does not progress straight and smooth; it may suffer delays and even setbacks. But after setbacks, invariably and tirelessly, society has subjected centralist power to its civilizing tutelage (Burckhardt 1874).

Thus the process of reform proceeds in a certain direction but without a clear view of the actual goal; it is rather like an advance, in a fog, with a compass: the goal is invisible, but the direction is unmistakable. Yet it is very hard to guess at the distance that must still be covered.

Thrust

The reforms of Soviet socialism are comprehensible only if we assume the existence of a very powerful evolutionary thrust; without this it could not overcome the manifold kinds of resistance. The evolutionary thrust derives its force from the contradiction between the functional requirements of a modern society and the Soviet system as a command economy: not only does the Soviet socialist system get increasingly into contradiction with these requirements, it is from the outset at loggerheads with the functional contexts of a modern society. To survive, it was obliged to make such concessions to society, which, from the beginning, called its basic assumptions in question.

In the New Economic Policy (NEP) period, and since Stalin (and even under Stalin), systemic changes have been taking place in the USSR and other socialist countries which – given that changes are supposed to make any sense at all – can only be interpreted as the system's searching for systemic rationality.

Step by step, with promises of increased efficiency, the reformers wrested policy concessions from the ruling parties, and the changed conditions, piecemeal softened up and legalized, gave the reformers scope for new demands. With these tactics the reformers managed to avoid open conflict with the rulers of the moment: politics is the art of doing what is possible – 'a little reform is better than no reform at all' (Kovács 1988).

What distinguishes the Stalinist state socialism from other despotisms is the fact that it is a secularized state. As in other despotisms, state authority, ideology – and in its case also the economy – are centralized, but its aims are materialistic. It wants to create a modern society – but in usurping society through centralization it comes into direct conflict with its claim to modernity.

Reform without theory

In advancing their cause the reformers are largely left in the lurch by their theory. This applies quite obviously to traditional Marxist thought, basically opposed to market-type reforms, but also to the so-called mainstream economics of western derivation: whereas the economists, out of their predominantly liberal sentiment, welcome reforms, economic theory proves excessively unyielding. It is all too significant that the academic socialism debate following after the neo-classical equilibrium models (Barone,

Lange/Lerner, and so on) remained in effect without any influence on the reform discussion going on in the socialist countries (Lavoie 1985). Anyway, the reformers, in supporting their reform proposals, did not even bother to find a theoretical foundation. Even Kornai, who may be considered East Europe's foremost economic theorist, has quite deliberately dispensed with using western mainstream (equilibrium) models, apparently under the impression that this could only have obstructed him in his purpose (Kornai 1971 and 1980). The fact that the sympathizers of reform abstain from theorizing may be understandable, yet it is a pity, since the complexity of the problems would require not less but rather more theoretical application.

Quite similar to the Keynesian 'revolution' in the west, it may be said that the reforms in the east have come along, not because of, but despite theory. The reality of reform in East Europe and in the USSR displays a dynamics that leaves mainstream economics more or less speechless.

The thesis of asymmetrical mix or asymmetrical convergence is easily pronounced, but hard to prove. All our economic thinking opposes that thesis with all its weight. I see the reason for the block against scientifically substantiating the asymmetry thesis in the fact that economic thinking is ruled by the concept of substantial rationality (Simon 1978).

Most economists assume the existence of an equilibrium, or optimum, for the whole economy or for society. In consequence, economics is defined in textbooks as the study of the allocation of scarce resources to unlimited and competing needs (Simon 1978,1). Hence economic reasoning is devoted to the question as to what is 'economical', that is, whether any allocation may be classified as optimal. This approach presupposes the assumption that there exists a state of rational affairs – from which, as we all know, reality will always stray. But this state, hypothetical though it may be, is nevertheless a fixed point in our reasoning (Kirman 1987). We call the degree by which we approach this hypothetical state 'substantial rationality'.

These models encourage clear thinking within the framework of given premises. But 'When policy conclusions are drawn from such models, it is time to reach for one's gun', says Hahn (1982a,29). Well this may apply to the plan/market debate.

The concept of mainstream economics that there exists an equilibrium, or an optimum in the economy as a whole, must lead, whether we like it or not, to consequences which, from the point of view of modern systems theory, are unacceptable:

1 The framework of substantial rationality renders it impossible to assign to systems a productive role of their own: the rationality of any system is reduced to its contribution to reaching the equilibrium. So that, seen from that perspective, one is only left to examine to what extent

a co-ordination mechanism is able to bring about this equilibrium (substantively visualized rationality). From this lofty point of view both central planning and the market appear in principle as being capable of doing the same thing, that is, as if the development of modern industrial societies could be brought about either by this or that way, or any mix between them. It is known that from the classical Walrasian model the thesis can be derived that the ideal plan and the ideal market are totally equivalent. To neo-classical welfare economics the perfect market, or the perfect plan, is defined as a system that guarantees friction-free equilibrium. This thesis of absolute equivalence, sustained until the 1960s, has in the meantime been replaced by the assumption of relative equivalence of the market and of bureaucratic control. In comparative economics imperfections for both forms of co-ordination (better communication systems) are diagnosed relative to perfect (hypothetical-substantive) solutions. Thus suspicion of insufficiency is cast on both these forms of co-ordination: The market's hypothetical shortcomings in performance are offset against plan performance shortfalls (see Grosfeld's paper in this book). However, such comparisons lack reality because they are acted out before the background of fictive ideals. Tied to concepts of substantive rationality the economist will assign only a secondary role to the co-ordination mechanisms.

2 The concept of substantive rationality willy-nilly leads to a centralistic anti-market position – to Hayek this is the fatal intellectual conceit of our century. Useful as the concept of substantial rationality (*homo economicus*) may be for the (normative) analysis of decision-making of individuals who face given environments, this concept is grossly misleading for the inquiry into economic systems. Unfortunately, economic literature is full of inappropriate transpositions of the logic of rational men on to societies. Most economists, though being centralists, will believe that they are true liberals – wasn't it proved by Arrow, Debreu and others that the 'competitive market equilibrium' is the best of all imaginable worlds?

Unfortunately, this proposition was proved on premises which are not only unrealistic but inappropriate since they are rather an application of a mathematical construction *à la* Bourbaki (Ingrao/Israel 1985,90) than a reflection of a world of free contracting (exchange socialization). The Walrasian model of general competitive equilibrium (and the Lange model of market socialism) is an auctioneer model and has therefore a centralistic structure: the price vector is established by a centre that acts in lieu of society. It forbids, *inter alia*, 'false' contracting. The model presumes that agents know their preferences and techniques. Agents do not communicate and exchange on their own. The model is a-societal, and the agents are unfree.

The history of reforms and of reform thinking seems to prove that only painful experience with Soviet-type socialism can correct the economists' natural propensity for seeking central (rational) solutions in favour of the market.

3   Within the concept of substantial rationality, decentral co-ordination mechanisms derive their justification from the recognition of the fact that it is impossible to know all the conditions that determine equilibrium, and especially, that central allocation cannot keep pace with quickly-changing conditions. If that is so, then decentralization is nothing more than the centre making allowance for the informational deficiences of complete centralization, but not, as will be argued, an intrinsic requirement of complex systems.

SYSTEMS-THEORETICAL ELEMENTS OF A THEORY OF MODERN SOCIETY

Society is communication

The concept of substantial rationality must lead to a totally distorted view of the creative achievements of the market, since it proceeds from the normative conception that it is the specific function of every market to establish equilibrium. Consequently, failure to achieve equilibrium is declared a market failure. This approach would only make sense if one could assume that an equilibrium exists, and that it is independent of the process of the market. But that, as admitted by the theoreticians of general equilibrium, is not the case (Fisher 1984).

Now, to assess the systemic superiority or inferiority of a system – there cannot be an absolute measure – one must not proceed from a fictional ideal but must, to put it simply, proceed from the assumption of the participants' total ignorance concerning the economic-societal environment, that is, from zero. Next, the question arises as to which system (the market or central-bureaucratic control) can work its way into a complex and constantly changing (natural, psychic and societal) environment in such a manner that complexity is reduced (for example, by price signals), and that new complexity can be built up by that reduction? Only by starting out from that zero perspective will one be able to make apparent what is the real achievement of the market.

Most economists project the relating potential into the world of things: they search for equilibria in commodity spaces specified by production possibilities and preference sets. This implies full information and cost-free co-ordination. Social (and economic) reality, however, does not exist before communication. It is – and can be – generated only by communication. Not only must opportunities be discovered by communication, they do form only in a societal context. Communication gives wants and techniques operational specificity. 'The limits of my language are the limits of my world', said Wittgenstein. That is also true for societies (economies). They consist of, and build up by, communication.

Basing myself on Georg Simmel (1907) and (partly in his succession), on modern systems theory (Luhmann 1984, 1988; Baecker 1986), I would like to indicate how the most complex structures in a modern society grow from the simplest elements of communication. On this path 'up from below' the market presents itself as a system that produces information and that organizes and reproduces itself. Modern economies are, according to Luhmann (1988) 'autopoietic' systems.

Exchange as the basic element of economic communication

According to Simmel (1907), exchange is the basic act of communication in a (modern) society's economy. Exchange is a simple systems element, from which very complex forms and structures are derived, such as money, prices, modern private ownership, organizations. Conversely, the abolition of exchange communication and its replacement, for example, through central commands, is connected with immeasurable economic and social consequences.

The market economy owes its systemic efficiency to a simple basic principle. It depends on the fact that the real world's interdependence, which must always be understood as global and simultaneous – everything somehow depends on everything – is dissolved into singular successive acts of exchange between two subjects. That dissolution into single steps according to the principle of utilitarianism is absolutely necessary, because total interdependence as such is quite incomprehensible (this applies to other, for example, biological, systems also). Only by bilateral step-by-step communication are economic agents able to realize (in a very reduced form) a part of these real interdependences by substitution. One acquires A, B, C, and so on, by paying pA, pB, pC, thus substituting, for A, B, C, certain quantities of a (money-) commodity, from which certain ratios derive between A and B, A and C, B and C and so on. Other prices and other ratios were seen elsewhere and at other times. For those prices one could obtain the goods, though maybe one might have been willing to pay other (higher) prices, or one might have been able to obtain the goods at lower prices. And at the same time one expects such and such prices and attempts to adjust to these prospects. Thus by exchange communication – a network of actual and hypothetical ratios and relations between commodities come into existence; economic agents substitute commodities by trading and for this they prepare by constant comparing, that is, by evaluating. Simultaneously, money emanates as an embodiment of these relating processes and as a means (code) of communication (Simmel 1907).

Other than by this step-by-step relation forming, no evaluating connection in the world of things is imaginable. The planner, were he to attempt allocation of resources directly, would confront his task, 'not like an omniscient auctioneer, but like a dumb ox, facing a great heap of unconnected things'.

To exchange communication the following properties or structures of systems can be connected:

(a)   Information and observation

Exchange is the prerequisite for making observation and gathering information. While mainstream economics assumes known commodity spaces (defined by convex sets and the distribution of quantities) and practically excludes exchange communication, systems theory underlines that exchange actions are a prerequisite for making observation possible (Baecker 1986). This means that, for example, an offer to exchange must have been made to enable one to observe at what conditions something may be obtained. Other agents' preferences and production functions cannot be directly observed. One receives indications at the points of junction of the net of exchange communication. Without these the subjects act in a no man's land.

(b)   From exchange emanates money as a general communications code

With its help, information concerning the degree of scarcities of goods is enormously simplified. Thereby the set of choices available is immeasurably enlarged. Thus money is the most productive social 'invention': only money enables man to shorten the long chain of technical connections, thereby dramatically easing his access to all goods, services and knowledge (Simmel 1907,206). It is a prerequisite to fashioning, out of a primitive society, an 'extended order' (Hayek 1988). A change of money supply may be nearly neutral as affecting the real variables' structure; but money *per se* is anything but neutral. It is the medium that makes socialization possible.

(c)   Money economy is profit economy

Being the most general means of economic activity, money inevitably becomes the immediate target of human actions. The producer/investor pays only to enlarge his payments potential (Luhmann 1984). Where the question is one of satisfaction of derived needs – and the more highly developed an economy, the more men depend on them – there the economy can only orient itself by reference to profit (as a price difference).

(d) The monetary sphere controls the real sphere

In a money economy all production factors are nothing but the material that is used by the self-augmentation mechanism of value – represented by money as an accounting unit (*Selbstvermehrung des Werts* – Marx). In other words: the sphere of reality is harnessed to the reproduction process of money (better: capital) and thus subsumed under the monetary sphere (as its control sphere).

(e) As a communicative action exchange is autonomous

It has a rationale of its own, its rationality needs no reference to other actions. Subjects *A* and *B* exchange in the expectation that by exchanging they shall be better off. On the other hand, a planning act *p* alludes to planning acts *x, y, z*, and so on. Its rationality is only secured if the activity triggered by *p* is reconciled with all the other imaginable consequences.

To avoid conflict among economic agents on the allotment of scarce resources, the centre must have recourse to secrecy. Exchange, quite to the contrary, pacifies, competition is depersonalized, and there is no need to fight battles for the resources. Hence the civilizing role of exchange (Simmel 1907; Luhmann 1988). In a society based on exchange, maintaining secrecy in order to avoid conflict is less necessary than elsewhere.

(f) Exchange and boundaries

The autonomy of the exchange act is a characteristic of supreme importance for the structure of complex systems. Modern systems theory reminds us that complex systems are not governed from one centre, but they are decomposed systems. They consist of subsystems and systems, the systems in their turn are possibly subsystems of other systems. Subsystems and systems must be separated from each other by clear boundaries, the boundaries being the system's self-generated elements. Boundaries, according to Luhmann (1984) are among the most important components of complex systems. For one, clearly drawn boundaries enable clear identification of the subsystems, and also the evolvement of clear environments. This is equally valid for all complex, that is, self-organizing systems. In the economy, to delimit, or to draw boundaries, means clear identities of organizations (enterprises) and clear environments (markets). Both emanate from exchange.

(g) Exchange generates enterprises' environments

Systems theory designates markets as intra-economic environments. They are of quasi-'parametric' nature: the quasi-parametric character of markets derives from exchange: the partner can accept or reject. He is dependent, but autonomous. Sociologically speaking, the markets obtain a more 'objective' character, the more extensively and exclusively communication takes place by way of exchange, and, economically speaking, markets function the better, the finer meshed the net of actual opportunities wherein the transactors act. One can best observe the connection between sociological objectivation and economic functioning in black markets: due to the sporadic and badly-organized exchange, only a very coarse network can come into being, where price formation is also influenced – constantly varying frictions aside – by very personal factors. Accordingly, the price disparities encountered in black markets are appropriately large.

Prices thus acquire social objectivity, not because of their 'rightness', as being, say, in accordance with a (fictitious) equilibrium or with other criteria as might be applied by an external observer (for example, Pareto), but out of the societal exchange communication. According to Simmel, values can be expressed only through exchange. Only through exchange do values obtain a statable amount. Another kind of objectivity in economics, Simmel (1907,44) points out, we cannot attain. To Simmel (to Marx, too) prices are more than mere reflections of scarcities as ratios of quantities (for example, demand/supply); they are embodiments of social relations which have their own reality: they may be unjustifiably high or low, but transactors face them as given or as conditionally alterable. Prices are as they are, and if they are changed, one must reckon with possible consequences.

According to welfare economics, parametric prices are essential to safeguarding Pareto-efficient allocation. They are, however, not at all a prerequisite for the proper functioning of the market. Markets are important just where prices are non-parametric (Hayek). Further, the concept of parametric prices – that is, prices, which the actor cannot influence and to which he will have to adapt his quantities – is useless in our context. So, for example, centrally-set prices may be parametric without contributing to 'objectifying' the economic environment of the enterprise, that is, to clear boundaries. For if the state sets a price, it will also have to stand good for the enterprise's losses. Objectivation of prices, then, is a sociological event: it happens by communication between subsystems (agents) who act, based on their own observations, independently of the centre.

(h)   Exchange allows the identification of enterprises

In addition, exchange gives enterprises their goal: to earn a profit, in other words, to participate in exchange communication and to create chances for further participation. Thereby exchange contributes decisively to the identification of economic organizations (enterprises). In the product markets the enterprise communicates with its environment about price/performance ratios, in the money and capital markets about the public's expectations concerning the success of its portfolio management. In that participation in exchange, communication is dictating its goal to the enterprise, it becomes largely independent of the management's personal motives.

From a purely exchange-theoretical view, organizations (hierarchies) are superfluous: every exchange act is an action out of its own reason. It means offering up a value in order to obtain another (greater) value. The sense of gathering numerous exchange acts in one organization lies in giving the discontinuous flow of exchange acts a joint addressee (firm) and to mitigate the technical and financial indivisibilities (indirect costs, overheads) by creating a unified enterprise budget.

(i)   Exchange creates modern private property

Owners, in a modern economy, no longer dispose directly of physical assets but only of nominal representations of such physical assets. One can only use them (*usus fructus* and *abusus fructus*) if exchange communication goes on in society. (If it stops, all the owner holds is printed paper.) Exchange communication thus also makes organizations largely independent of owners, thereby increasing the economy's systemic efficiency. Enterprises are more independent, owners are freer.

THE REFORM

We have thus assembled the theoretical component parts needed for our purpose. They help us to a better understanding, not only of the vitality of modern market economies, but also of the system-specific problems of socialist economies. The theory of exchange tells us what direction the reforms take: they are a transformation of the bureaucratic centrally-regulated system into a system based on exchange communication. They are propelled by an evolutionary force that rests on the immense superiority of exchange communication *vis-à-vis* the command economy. The progress of reform may be gauged by how far and how broadly the readjustment to exchange communication has succeeded.

Systems specific problems

Shortages

In all centrally-planned economies we encounter a bundle of difficulties which can, in Kornai's terms, be ascribed to one common denominator: Socialist economies are shortage economies. With inimitable accuracy Kornai describes the various shortage phenomena, analyses the enterprises' and households' behaviour under conditions of shortage and enquires after the causes of changes in shortage intensity (this presupposing a sort of shortage equilibrium) – yet the prime cause of shortages (more precisely: that of the normal degree of shortages) remains in the dark. There is no operable definition (Hare 1986).

Shortages, just like other system-specific phenomena, must also be capable of being explained by means of system-specific communication. In the first place it is useful to keep in mind that all hierarchies are internally quantity controlled. Organizations report the economic restriction internally in the form of quantities, and participants in organizations can become aware of scarcities only in the form of quantities. But that is precisely the state of affairs under shortage: physical resource constraints hit first. Within hierarchies the participants' scope of action is always constrained by quantities.

Only then do scarcities not appear, or do not seem to be shortages, if, before the selective resource restraint, the monetary restraint takes effect. In this view scarcity can only be eliminated by enhancing the role of money, not by increasing quantities. Thus systems can 'outwit' scarcity only by a communications code which now signals scarcities in its own language. And that is money; but money presupposes, as we have already pointed out, extensive exchange communication. Therefore the following thesis must be spelt out: as long as systems suppress exchange communication, they remain – despite actually achieved wealth – shortage economies. But never fear: they do not grow wealthy, for they are wasteful; and they are sluggish innovators.

This takes us to the material consequences of hierarchic-quantity versus decentrally money-controlled systems. Let us enumerate some of them here. With Simmel (1907) and Luhmann (1988) I hold that money, far from being neutral, is extremely productive with reference to the system.

(i)   Money facilitates the search for opportunities

A money economy compels economic agents to search permanently for new opportunities. At the same time money also facilitates that search. To obtain a good, the buyer needs only pay, and so he has 'free' energy to search for new opportunities. In a quantity-controlled or semi-monetarized economy the economic agent must muster – beside money – a number of other prerequisites, which may well differ, depending on the type of desired good, on the seller, or time of sale. To get meat he'll maybe have to get an exhaust for the butcher's car, to acquire a book maybe he'll have to organize some rolls of wallpaper. One condition will have to be met today, tomorrow maybe another. In such ways the system absorbs energy and for innovative search there's hardly any energy left.

(ii)   The more active the money, the more unequivocal the signal function of prices

Only in a developed money economy are scarcities made manifest by prices. In socialist economies, conversely, costs and opportunities are reflected by a bundle of signals in which price is only one and not necessarily the most prominent element. Non-price scarcity indicators are: queueing, forced substitution and so on (Kornai 1980). The more intense the shortages, the weaker is the signal function of prices – and the lower are price elasticities. Therefore the producer or seller must be offered disproportionately large amounts of money to dispose him to produce. Historically-cumulated money overhangs (USSR) aggravate the problem. In developed money economies, on the other hand, both the prices' information function and their incentive function are far stronger: if I know the price, I know opportunities, and if I have money, I can realize them.

(iii)   The more generalized the money code, the tighter the tie up between the markets

Money is an exchange medium. Its activity depends on the intensity of the economic society's communication by exchange. Only when it is generally used really as a means of exchange, can a connection of the markets be effected. The restriction of the exchange communication to the consumer goods market results in the socialist countries in the existence of, side by side, consumption money and investment money. Consumption money cannot be used to buy investment goods, nor does investment money buy consumer goods. Money's fragmentation hinders, not merely communication between the various markets, but also within them. So do, for example, systems of direct distribution of inputs prevent the emergence of genuine consumer goods markets. The obstruction of exchange communication inhibits the mobility, and with mobility the commensurability of the resources. Shortages (and, simultaneously, unjustifiably high slacks) are the consequence. For in this context, shortages only mean that money cannot, or can only with undue difficulty, be converted into goods.

In the light of this, one may be tempted to reduce the contrast of slacks and shortages, set down at the beginning of Kornai's book, *Economics of Shortage* (1980), to the simple formula: Must money wait for the goods, or goods for money? Who is in stronger position, the money owner or the owner of goods? If the question is thus posed, it is wrongly posed. For in that case a symmetry is assumed (regrettably, it runs right through Kornai's book) which does not exist.

For money, like language, is an additional element, generated by society's communication and eminently enhancing society's systemic rationality. True, though, it also involves the economy's tendency to slacks. A centrally-controlled economy, where the money sphere is subsumed under the real sphere, simply lacks this dimension – or it is underdeveloped – and therefore the communications system is more primitive. The 'full employment' of resources, such a bright feather in the socialist countries' cap, was very dearly paid for.

Soft budget constraints

If the analysis of chronic shortages in socialist countries calls for a theory of economic communication, then that applies even more so to the concept of budget constraints. The concept of soft budget constraints plays a key role in Kornai's explanation of shortages. Soft budget constraints lead to an almost insatiable hunger for current inputs, including for labour, as well as for investments (Kornai 1980).

For Kornai there exist two groups of factors that make the budget constraints soft. One is price behaviour in the markets. Firms are usually not price takers, therefore they can increase their revenues by increasing prices (Kornai 1980). This explanation provoked among others the view that chronic shortages might be eliminated by a price mechanism (Gomulka 1985). It was an opinion Kornai was unable to share (Kornai 1985). He argued that shortage conditions are resistant and not removable by price adaptation alone. That is why, in later studies, Kornai emphasized the second group of factors, which he sums up under the blanket term of paternalistic behaviour, referring to mutual arrangements and behavioural relations between enterprises and the state: budget constraints are soft because taxes are levied flexibly on enterprises; enterprises may receive gifts from the state; or loans may be made available in circumstances when ordinary considerations of creditworthiness would argue against them (Kornai 1980, 1985).

But these are precisely the kind of situations that would be summarized by systems theory under the concept of unclear boundaries between the enterprise (subsystem) and the economy (system). In centrally-planned economies the enterprises are not clearly distinguished from the overall economy. Hard budget constraints exist only on the level of the national economy. There, distribution cannot permanently exceed production. But within the national economy resources are shifted this way and that, with the consequence that the enterprises, without knowing it, are constantly living at society's expense. Early Soviet socialism had expected enhanced systemic rationality precisely from the removal of boundaries by converting the economy into one single giant enterprise. Today it is broadly recognized that clear boundaries are the prerequisite for the functioning of a modern society. Precisely in that sense must Kornai's demand for a hardening of the budget constraints of enterprises be understood. Hard budget constraints are, in fact, nothing but the financial expression of boundaries. The softness of budget constraints indicates that the boundaries are blurred.

We have seen above that exchange communication leads to clear boundaries, that is, to a hardening of the budget constraints. Other forms of communication are less, or not at all, able to achieve this. The more intense and pervasive the exchange, the clearer will be the boundary lines: exchange leads to the genesis of intra-economic environments, and with the profit aim it gives identity to the enterprises. They operate in clear environments and they have their own autonomy (see above, the third section).

Start, destiny and the long march of the reforms

It is the long-term destiny of socialist reform to put the process of communication back into the hands of society, who had never completely lost it, since otherwise the system would have become utterly ungovernable. In the meantime, the Communist Parties are in the process of explicitly renouncing the claim to leadership monopoly in society. That is a big step forwards. With it the reform can really get into its stride, because the old system is bereft of its ideological basis. But, Rubicon crossed, the country beyond, alas, still awaits being conquered. This conquest consists in the setting-up of a new communicational system from within society, now liberated from totalitarian tutelage.

That is a long and tedious process, because between system (*qua* communication) and material structure – or, to put it in Marx's terms, between production relations and productive forces – there is a substantial discrepancy. On the one hand, the structure of socialist societies is highly complex: industries are developed, the percentage of urbanized population is high, national and international division of labour is extensive (though, not sufficiently), all sectors are dependent on all others, and so on – the degree of material integration is high. On the other hand, we see that in the socialist countries communication systems are too primitive to fit more complex structures.

That discrepancy embodies considerable difficulties for the reform process. In capitalism both material structure and communication grew up hand in hand. Socialism was launched with a communication's breakup, and was able, up to a certain degree (not in small measure with the help of the capitalist environment), to build-up the material structure. At this stage, with its systemic deficits apparent, socialism must get the old communications system – the commodity system – going again to resuscitate the colossus. Communication can be constructed by communication only, not by legislative decree. Administrative regulations or institutional creations can merely facilitate the process.

The setting up of the 'bourgeois' exchange communication may, in principle, be started from inside the system, that is, by reforming the state economy, or else by admitting a competing private economy, confronting it with a new environment from outside.

In reforming their state economy, the strategists of reform are faced with the difficulty indicated above, namely that the economy's structure is complex whereas exchange communication needs a time-consuming build-up period. In this endeavour the socialist state economies face the well-known egg-and-chicken problem: where to begin? On the one hand exchange presupposes clear boundaries which the system must generate. Without clear boundaries exchange communication may lead to socially and economically intolerable consequences. As long as the boundaries are not sufficiently clear – for which objective criteria are impossible to name since boundaries are elements derived from social communication – the centre will tend directly to intervene in the process. On the other hand, exchange communication alone is capable of generating boundaries (identities and environments).

First of all, it must be realized that exchange communication de-etatizes state ownership because enterprises cannot enter into exchange relations unless they have a power of disposal over the products. Nor can they carry responsibility for the exchange of products if their right to make exchanges does not include such rights over investment goods. And finally, if the rights of the state enterprises are also extended to being entitled to acquire enterprises or parts of enterprises – this is a prerequisite of capital markets – then that must lead to a withdrawal of the state – even if, formally, state ownership is retained – from operative control of the economy through quantities (physical indicators). State property, like any other property, would then also be 'separate' property; and the state, as an economic agent, would act as a civil law agent. The state, which in several countries today still acts as the economy's collective (or overall) entrepreneur, might, in its function as owner (not in its political function), be transformed into a large-scale capitalist. This, acting through relatively independent organizations (banks), can manage various assets.

What militates against this prospect is not the systemic logic of a capitalist money economy (which would be dominated by the major shareholder, the state), but the difficulty of initiating modern communication within a socialist state economy where there are neither clear identities for enterprises, nor clear environments (markets). True, certain start-up possibilities exist. First, there is the capitalist outside world which constitutes sufficiently clear environments for the socialist economies, although these environments are system-relevant only if the socialist enterprises are not cut off from foreign trade. Second, in socialist countries economic agents also communicate with each other by exchange. But it is apparent that exchange communication, factually and regionally limited by state patronage, does not suffice for 'hardening the limits'. Every draught of state paternalism is poison for clear boundaries. (The longer economic mentality had been exercising loyalty towards bureaucracy, the less poison would suffice).

The efforts of reforming the state sector have not been very encouraging so far. It must be admitted, however, that until recently, the political prerequisites were non-existent. With the creation of a constitutional state and a multi-party system, people may gain confidence in the progress of reform and gradually revise their economic mentality from loyalty *vis-à-vis* the bureaucracy to market behaviour. Seen from the system-theoretical point of view, the reform of the state economy – that is, a reform from within – remains a difficult undertaking, since it cannot fasten on to clear environments, nor clear identities.

And so the socialist countries are forced to get going with exchange communication also 'outside' the state economy by admission of private ownership. Individuals, families, small groups, and so on, get active as 'simple commodity producers' and they build 'family' enterprises (unincorporated firms).

Superficially, support for a petty-bourgeoisie in socialist countries might be considered a relapse into the nineteenth century. But from a system-theoretical view, the admission and promotion of private ownership makes sense: true, initially the 'environment' (market) is equally obscure to them as it is for state enterprises. But small producers of goods or entrepreneur capitalists, as natural persons or groups of persons, are at least unequivocally identifiable actors. Their identity does not derive only – as with modern enterprises – from exchange communication within the system but from their physical and psycho-social setting. In principle this applies also to group ownership: it should facilitate identification of the group (as a social unit) with the enterprise's functions (as a participant in exchange communication). Even when the exchange system is destroyed, it is easier to initiate exchange communication by means of units that have a natural identity. In addition to this, the admission of private property has a political and economic meaning. Politically, it makes sense because it liberalizes society and a bourgeois stratum (class) may, in the long run, come into being again. The economic significance is the welfare contribution: private ownership can contribute decisively to improving the supply situation if it is not ostracized, discriminated against and thus constantly imperilled in its existence. It must grow beyond being able to set up street bazaars: trade must emit positive effects on production. That will be the easier, the less the discrepancy between structure and communication.

That is exactly why privatization in agriculture and the promotion of private industry are so successful in underdeveloped China: small family enterprises are able to keep up with state industry. In more developed socialist countries the starting conditions are less favourable. There the level of consumers' expectations and the productivity level are already so high that it is very difficult for private industry to compete with state industry. As a consequence, private business concentrates mainly on exploiting existing bottle-necks in order to achieve high profits. No wonder therefore that private businessmen are soon tarnished by the smears that have always been levelled at them by socialist doctrinaires. Even in early capitalism, exchange communication had been initiated by natural persons (or groups of persons). That is repeated today in socialist countries. But of course, reform must not stop at permitting 'simple commodity production'. If communication were to stop at that simple level, it would be unable to cope with the complexity of the existing real structures. Simple commodity production must be able to progress into a modern money (= capitalist) economy.

That is necessary because in simple commodity production the productive assets are still withheld from evaluation by exchange communication. Consequently, productive assets cannot double into finance capital. Considerable functional disadvantages stem from the absence of that dimension of communication, especially once enterprises have outgrown a certain order of magnitude and the economy has already become very complex.

Exchange communication tends in that direction quite on its own: all direct connections (between owner and property, investment and saving, production and consumption, and so on) dissolve, and that enhances the economy's system-rationality. The system's elements – private property, prices, money, markets, organizations – result from communication.

Only the state's authority would be able to suppress by sheer force the evolutionary process in the direction of exchange communication. But it would be an ideologically ill-advised thing to do, were one to restrict exchange communication in a highly complex society. For the factual interdependence in a modern economy can only be coped with by communicational relations appropriate to these interdependences. There is no cause, either economic or moral, for involving products and means of production only, but not also enterprises or parts of enterprises into exchange communication. For only by such practical substitution can products and assets be valuated and can new opportunities for substitution be realized. The exclusion of productive assets from exchange communication leads – that is persistently demonstrated by the example of the socialist countries – not only to their being wasted, but also to severe distortions of competitive positions in the commodity market.

SUMMARY

The reform process is understood as a transformation from a bureaucratic-centralistic control system to a system based on decentralized exchange communication. If this process is not obstructed, it leads to a modern money (capitalist) economy. This is the direction in which the reform proceeds.

The process is driven by an evolutionary force, without which the reform could not surmount the resistance of the system (vested interests). The force derives from the systemic superiority of exchange communication over the command system in finding practical solutions to problems.

The reform process will only be understood by radically departing from concepts of substantial rationality (commodity space-based models), and by conceptualizing the systemic rationality of modern (western) societies by means of exchange communication. Exchange is the basic communicative element from which all other modern economic institutions (prices, money, private property, organizations, and so on) emanate.

Etatist, that is, anti-capitalist, socialism is not workable, it is doomed to fail, like any other intellectual blueprint forced on to society. If socialism is to have any meaning, then it is because it rests on a political organization of a society that deals more consciously and more circumspectly with the vital forces emanating from exchange: capitalism means economic life, and socialism could mean more conscious life.

POSTSCRIPT

True, the market as a subsystem may have only limited rationality since it interferes with its (natural, mental and social) environments – it lives at their cost – and since it is largely unable to reflect these costs and reintroduce them into its own communication (Luhmann 1988:39). Nevertheless, it generates signals which other social subsystems (polity, and so on) may observe and react to in various ways: they may utilize or modify them, for example, by levying taxes, granting subsidies for production of goods and knowledge, organizing the supply of public goods, introducing safeguards to protect the environment, and so on. From all this it follows that the centre must not attempt to determine what the future is to be like, but it may try to influence it. All further-going claims of the centre boil down to the inhibition, or at least to the curtailment, of authentic communication in the economy, and will inevitably lead to the suppression of the very potentialities on which the productivity and vitality of modern societies rest.

NOTE

For helpful comments I am in particular indebted to Prof.K. Laski, Linz. My friend, Fred Prager, has translated the text with his usual care.

BIBLIOGRAPHY

Baecker, D. (1986) *Informationen und Risiko in der Marktwirtschaft*, dissertation, Bielefeld, University of Bielefeld.

Brus, W. (1988) 'Utopianism and realism in the evolution of the Soviet economic system', *Soviet Studies* 40 (3), 433–43.

Burckhardt, J. (1874) *Weltgeschichtliche Betrachtungen*, Kroener, 12th edn, 1978.

Clower, R. (1963) 'The Keynesian counterrevolution: theoretical appraisal', *Schweizerische Zeitschrift für Volkswirtschaft und Statistik* 99, 8–31.

Csaba, L. (1989) 'Some lessons from two decades of economic reforms in Hungary', *Communist Economies* 1(1), 17–29.

Deutscher, I. (1954) *Trotzki: Der bewaffnete Prophet*, Stuttgart, Kohlhammer, 1962.

Dietrich, P. (1987) 'Geheimbund oder totalitäre Partei: Zur "Geheimbund-Verfassung" kommunistischer Parteien bei Peter C. Ludz', *Ideologie und gesellschaftliche Entwicklung in der DDR*, Deutschland Archiv, 1985, 133–42.

Dietz, R. (1976) *Sowjetökonomie: Warenwirtschaft oder Sachverwaltung – Ein Beitrag zu einer alternativen Theorie des Sozialismus*, Achberg, Achberger Verlagsanstalt.

Fisher, F.M. (1984) *Disequilibrium Foundations of Equilibrium Economics*, Cambridge, Cambridge University Press.

Gomulka, S. (1985) 'Kornais's soft budget constraint and the shortage phenomenon: a criticism and restatement', *Economics of Planning* 19(1), 1–11.

Hahn, F. (1982a) 'Reflections on the invisible hand', *Lloyds Bank Review* 144.

Hahn, F. (1982b) *Money and Inflation*, Oxford, Basil Blackwell.

Hare, P. (1986) 'Theoretical foundations: models of shortage', in C. Davis and M. Charemza (eds) *Models of Disequilibrium and Shortage in Centrally Planned Economies*, Florence, European University Institute.

Hayek, F.A. (1945) 'The use of knowledge in society', *American Economic Review* 35(4), 519–30.

Hayek, F.A. (1952) *Individualismus und wirtschaftliche Ordnung*, Erlenbach-Zürich, Eugen Rentsch Verlag.

Hayek, F.A. (1988) 'The fatal conceit: the errors of socialism', in *The Collected Works of F.A. Hayek*, 1, London, Routledge.

Ingrao, B. and Israel, G. (1985) 'General equilibrium theory. A history of ineffectual paradigmatic shifts', Part II, *Fundamenta Scientiae* 6(2), 89–125.

Kirman, A. (1987) *The Intrinsic Limits of Modern Economic Theory: The Emperor Has No Clothes*, European University Institute, Working Paper no. 87/323, Florence.

Kornai, J. (1971) *Anti-Equilibrium. On Economic Systems Theory and the Tasks of Research*, Amsterdam-Oxford, North, Holland.

Kornai, J. (1980) *Economics of Shortage*, Amsterdam-New York-Oxford, North, Holland.

Kornai, J. (1985) 'Gomulka on the soft budget constraint: a reply', *Economics of Planning* 19(2), 49–55.

Kornai, J. (1986a) 'The Hungarian reform process: visions, hopes, and reality', *Journal of Economic Literature* 24, 1687–744.

Kornai, J. (1986b) 'The soft budget constraint', *Kyklos* 39 (1), 3–30.

Kornai, J. (1989) 'The affinity between ownership and coordination mechanisms – the common experience of reform in socialist countries', Paper prepared for the Round-Table Conference on 'Market Forces in Planned Economies', Moscow, 28–30 March.

Kovács, J. M. (1988) 'Reform economics: the classification gap', Paper presented to the Institut für die Wissenschaften vom Menschen (IWM) 'Plan and/or Market' Conference, Vienna.

Kowalik, T. (1986) 'On crucial reform of real socialism', Research Report no. 122, The Vienna Institute for Comparative Economic Studies.

Laidler, D. and Rowe, N. (1980) 'Simmel's philosophy of money: a review article for economists', *Journal of Economic Literature* 18, 97–105.

Lavoie, D. (1985) *Rivalry and Central Planning. The Socialist Calculation Debate Reconsidered*, Cambridge, Cambridge University Press.

Luhmann, N. (1984) *Soziale Systeme. Grundriß einer allgemeinen Theorie*, Frankfurt a.M., Suhrkamp Verlag.

Luhmann, N. (1988), *Die Wirtschaft der Gesellschaft*, Frankfurt a.M., Suhrkamp.

Marx, K. (1968) *Das Kapital* 1, *Collected Works of Marx and Engels* 23, Berlin (Ost).

Masuch, M. (1981) *Kritik der Planung – Naturwüchsigkeit und Planung im relaen Sozialismus*, Darmstadt, Luchterhand, Soziologische Texte.

Mises, L. von (1920) 'Die Wirtchaftsrechnung im sozialistischen Gemeinwesen', *Archiv für Sozialpolitik* 47, 86–121.

Nuti, D. (1988) 'Perestroika: the economics of transition between central planning and market socialism', Paper presented to the Institute für die Wissenschaften vom Menschen (IWM) 'Plan and/or Market' Conference, Vienna.

Samuelson, P.A. (1968) 'What classical and neoclassical monetary theory really was,' *Canadian Journal of Economics* 1(1), 1–15.

Schroeder, G. (1988) 'Property rights issues in economic reforms in socialist countries', *Studies in Comparative Communism* 21 (2), 175–88.

Simmel, G. (1907) *Die Philosophie des Geldes* (6th edn), Berlin, Duncker & Humblot, 1958.

Simon, H.A. (1978) 'Rationality as process and as product of thought', *American Economic Review* 68 (2), 1–16.

Stigler, G.J. (1961) 'The economics of information', *Journal of Political Economy* 49 (3), 213–25.

Tardos, M. (1982) 'Development program for economic control and organization in Hungary', *Acta Oeconomica* 28, 295–315.

Wagener, H.-J. (1979) *Zur Analyse von Wirtschaftssystemen. Eine Einführung*, Berlin-Heidelberg-New York, Springer–Verlag.

Williamson, O.E. (1981) 'The economics of organization', *American Journal of Sociology* 87 (3), 548–77.

3 An organizational theory of the socialist economy

Deborah Duff Milenkovitch

INTRODUCTION

We sometimes proceed as if we had a theory of socialist economic organization. There is, for example, little disagreement concerning the general nature of the economic problems of centrally-planned socialist regimes. There also seems to be a consensus among experts that the Soviet-type model (despite all our premature predictions) is now finally about to prove correct our expectation of economic collapse. After all, the socialist economies have continued on a long-term low-growth trajectory which sharpened the internal contradictions.

I do not believe we have such a theory. The standard centrally-planned socialist system is breaking down and we are witnessing the disintegration of a world view which has dominated since Yalta, in which the Soviet Union remains immutable and Eastern Europe is both its pale carbon copy and its appendage. While our theories anticipate the dysfunctional pressures of classical socialist economic organization, our theories did not predict the responses to them in terms of changing property rights structures, development of a legitimized opposition, or the increased diversity of solutions across socialist states. This view is shared by Jerry Hough (1989). At the Kennan Institute on 24 April 1989, he stated that 'Soviet studies have become totally nontheoretical'. We have 'simply reversed our conventional views of the Soviet Union over the past fifteen years, without any analysis or self-awareness'.

What could constitute the basis for a theory of socialist economic organization in retrospect? What would such a theory have to do? Such a theory, to be fully useful, would have to account for the range of the features of socialist economies observed across historically-different states: Yugoslavia, Hungary, Poland, Germany, Czechoslovakia, Rumania, and Bulgaria.

These are questions of both substance and method. Eastern Europe still offers a stunning opportunity to observe states with similar – though eroding – ideologies, property rights and political structures, and strikingly different

– old-new – national identities. The task is not unlike that which Marx faced in looking at capitalist development in Germany, France, Great Britain and the United States. In order to understand what was similar about capitalism in its different manifestations he attempted to identify the internal logic of capitalist systems. Marx located this logic in the institution of private property which enables the capitalists to obtain control of the economic surplus. Capitalists seek to maximize the economic surplus and to reinvest it. From this simple behavioural logic, Marx developed a theory of capitalism which explains specific phenomena (for example, deskilling of the labour force, characteristics of technological change, business cycles), the similarity of capitalism in different countries and a dynamic of capitalism in development over time.

We are far from having a theory of socialism on a grand scale paralleling Marx's theory of capitalism, although Fehér *et al.* (1983) identify the task and make important contributions in this direction. The approach taken here aims to make a partial contribution to that goal. In order to understand better the internal logic of socialist economic organization (taken as the entire system of socialism) I propose to focus on one point I believe has been underdeveloped: the process of relegitimation of system leaders and goals. I will look, not just at democratic and non-democratic governments, but at a broader set of social organizations, distinguishing between those with mechanisms for external evaluation and relegitimation of system leaders and goals, and those without. Organizations without external mechanisms have certain characteristic patterns of behaviour that differ from those of organizations with such mechanisms. Elected governments and for profit organizations (fpos) have mechanisms for external relegitimation. The stockholders of the fpo annually elect the directors of the corporation and approve the acts of the officers. A democratically-elected government stands for election at periodic intervals. Other organizations (macro and micro) such as monarchies, the Roman Catholic Church, military dictatorships, socialist economic organizations and large non-profit organizations such as Harvard University, lack mechanisms for routine external relegitimation. I propose to explore the behavioural consequences of the absence of such mechanisms for large, bureaucratic organizations. Large bureaucratic organizations which require legitimacy and lack external mechanisms have to become self-legitimating bureaucracies.

This chapter will proceed as follows. The first section will identify the phenomena that a theory of socialist economic organization would need to explain. The second section will review some existing theories of socialism. The third section will articulate the rationale for looking at the socialist economic organizations as self-legitimating bureaucracies. The fourth section will develop a preliminary theory of self-legitimating organizations drawing from the theory of non-profit organizations. The fifth section will assess the usefulness of the theory of self-legitimating organizations for understanding socialist economic organization. The last section will present some conclusions. The approach throughout will be skeletal rather than fully articulated, impressionistic rather than rigorously explicated. The analytical intention is to provoke thought as to whether the notion of a self-legitimating bureaucracy affords useful ideas and insights.

TASKS OF THE THEORY

Socialist (Soviet-type) economies have several structural characteristics which serve to define them and differentiate them from other types of economies. Certainly three of these (very similar to the characteristics established by Brus 1986) include:

- state ownership and management of the important means of production exercised on behalf of society by the state apparatus, under general direction from the party apparatus;
- central administration of the system of financially self-sufficient firms, typically but not exclusively by ministries;
- a monopoly political party which controls the government and the economic apparatus.

According to the doctrine, state ownership and management should ensure that resources are used for the benefit of the (universal) working class. Central planning and management of the system of enterprises is intended to eliminate the well-known defects of capitalist market systems (exploitation, inequality, market failure, micro-imbalances, macro-imbalances, sectoral imbalances, inattention to environmental issues, inappropriate incentives for investment and innovation, and so on). In practice, however, the ability of socialism to improve upon capitalist market economies is mixed. Socialist economies have usually speeded industrialization (although at very high economic and human costs) and have often improved employment opportunites and the general availability of education and health care. More important for our purposes than any comparison of capitalism and socialism are the emergence of five problem areas that are common to socialist economic systems. I would argue that these outcomes are consequences of the system, and not of policy. (Some aspects of this point will be developed more fully in the second section under 'Ideology' – pp. 48–9.)

1   Microeconomic inefficiencies

- focus on quantity, not quality or assortment
- inflexible prices, disequilibrium, rationing
- excess use and stockpiling of labour and materials
- low productivity increase
- insensitivity to the requirements of customers
- resistence to innovation

2   Macroeconomic imbalances

- taut planning
- investment cycles
- large foreign debt
- high rates of investment
- low incremental capital-output ratios
- repressed inflation

3   Sectoral imbalances

- chronic difficulties in agriculture
- lagging quality and quantity of consumer goods
- overdevelopment of heavy industry
- pollution and environmental decay
- underdevelopment of the service sector

4   Motivational problems

- unattractive product mix for worker-consumers
- dominance of political over professional qualifications for jobs
- absenteeism, turnover, theft, alcoholism, slowdown on the first job
- hierarchy in the workplace
- absence of means for bottom-up input

5   Problems of equality

- suppression of data on income distribution
- multiple channels for distribution of goods and services
- conflict between egalitarianism and meritocracy

These phenomena erode the elite's claim to legitimacy based on economic performance and social justice. Thus, one task of any theory of socialist economic organization is to understand how the system has consistently, over long periods of time and across many countries, produced these outcomes which would appear to be contrary to those desired and which undermine the regime's legitimacy. Further, since these phenomena appear to be dysfunctional, by undermining the regime's legitimacy, a second task is to determine what the systemic response may be to these dysfunctions.

Further, although our countries have a number of common features:

- a common set of socialist institutions imposed by the common local hegemon after the Second World War;
- the countries of Eastern Europe are all mid-sized countries (from 10 million to 50 million);

- they are at middle levels of development
- the culture is European, although with important sub-differences between a Catholic, an Orthodox and a Protestant tradition;
- these nation-states assumed their approximate present form only in the last seventy years,

They also differ amongst themselves in important and relevant respects:

- the degrees of worker alienation and citizen dissatisfaction – the degree of political repressiveness;
- the degree of decentralization of the market economy and the freedom of the second economy;
- the degree of integration into CMEA and the world market economy;
- the degree to which the regime tolerates independent institutions.

None of these differences are explained well by the two dimensions in which East European states clearly differ from one another: (a) the degree of economic development (historic pre-Second World War rankings are unaltered in the socialist era); (b) the degree of ethnic homogeneity.

A third task of a theory must be to account for such differences across countries. Of course, no theory can explain all these pheonomena, but the theory must be able to account for this range of outcomes on the basis of historical factors without simply dismissing them as anomalies. We have now proposed a test for a successful theory of socialist economic organization. Of course, to accomplish all three tasks simultaneously is an ideal, and in reality any theory will be imperfect in fulfilling this standard.

EXISTING THEORIES OF SOCIALIST ECONOMIC ORGANIZATION

We consider below several traditional theories of socialism, drawn with broad strokes and necessarily oversimplified. This section expands on the analysis of Comisso (1986). These theories are not mutually exclusive and often overlap. Each selects out certain properties and elements to emphasize, to the potential exclusion and neglect of others. Our purpose is to search for the insights they capture successfully, in order to incorporate them at the next stage of our argument.

Totalitarian regime

According to early theories of the socialist system (Friedrich and Brzezinski 1965), the party (somehow embodying the will of the masses) exercises monopoly control over the state apparatus and all forms of productive and non-productive organizations. The total character of the system atomizes society, isolates individuals and precludes any non-sponsored groupings. The party does so in the name of a militant vision of the good, which requires this total control to eliminate anarchy and enemies of the people. Charismatic leadership, terror, coercion, or material benefit induce obedience, compliance or collaboration.

This notion correctly emphasizes the key goals of the leadership (that is, to achieve its vision of the good and the rationalization for maintaining itself in power against anarchy and enemies of the people and the principal means (that is, the system of political appointees and the monopoly on all organizations).

The relationship of the rulers to the ruled in totalitarian theory includes both nearly total repression of the entire population as in the USSR, and the active manipulation of subgroups in the masses to accomplish the leaders' goals, as in Nazi Germany. The totalitarian model is consistent with either state ownership and management of resources or with irresistible political intervention in private ownership in a Fascist framework. There is much of value in the totalitarian model in understanding contemporary socialist economic organization, especially if not taken in an extreme, static, all-or-nothing version (Hough 1989).

Ruling-class theories

Totalitarian and ruling-class theories are both state versus society conflict models, with conflict within the state and party by and large limited to factional struggles. Whereas totalitarian theory underscores the conflict between the rulers and the ruled and the commitment of the leaders to a vision of the good, and points to the role of the monopoly on organizations and the political control of all important appointments, ruling-class theories elaborate how the top leaders manage society through their appointed *nomenklatura*.

Ruling-class theories (Djilas 1957) show how the ruling class appropriates a large portion of the surplus product from its citizens, through its monopoly/monopsony relationship as the only employer and the only store in town, as well as owning the sheriff, the bank, and the newspaper and having the only key to the city gates. It also determines the uses of the surplus product and uses Marxist ideology to rationalize its policies (Djilas 1989).

The burden upon ruling-class theories is to identify who belongs to the ruling class and what constitutes the class interest (Comisso 1986; Nove 1975). The *nomenklatura* is the leading candidate for the definition of the ruling class. The distinguishing characteristic of the *nomenklatura* is that all members are political appointees, subject to removal from the class by the personnel committee of the secretariat of the central committee of the Party or other high Party organ. Thus, the first loyalty must be to the Party apparatus. Members of the *nomenklatura* have a sense of commitment. They are performing a key function for the top leadership in maintaining its power and in carrying out its mission; this, combined with the ample rewards for successful loyalty, helps us understand why they behave like members of a ruling class in their relations with ordinary members of society and why, like ruling classes everywhere, they believe they are entitled to their status, power, perks and privileges. But the *nomenklatura* appear to be the instrument of a higher ruling group and not the ruling class itself.

To be more useful, ruling-class theories need to be expanded or elaborated in several directions:

(1) They need to take into account the relationship of the *nomenklatura* to the top political leadership which both appoints them and is recruited from their ranks (the internal job ladder), as well as the party and administrative structure serving the leaders, the technocratic levels supervizing the workers, the professional interest groups, and the workers, consumers and citizen-beneficiaries of the system.

(2) They also need to explore more fully the interests of the leadership. Presumably, like the top leadership of any political organization, these include money, perks, power and prestige, but primarily revolve around power itself. Power makes it possible to command human and material resources to carry out the leaders' vision of the future of socialism.

(3) They need to take account of the problem of relegitimation.

Interest group theories

Interest group theories (Skilling 1966; Kanet 1978) posit the existence of value-oriented semi-autonomous groups between the state and society. These groups are not homogeneous and have potentially conflicting values and interests both with one another and with the top leadership. These occupational and opinion groups (*apparatchiki*, industrial managers, economists, writers, environmentalists, human rights activists, national, ethnic and religious groups) are members of the intelligentsia, but represent only a small portion of the intelligentsia.

Interest group theory assumes that the major power of decision-making is in the hands of a few top leaders, and it does not see policy formulation as the mechanistic result of pressures and counterpressures of rival groups. While not always decisive, the interest groups are more than epiphenomena. They are useful in drawing attention to essential complexities in socialist societies. While at times manipulated by the leaders in their own struggles for power and factional disputes, they none the less have remained not only cohesive over time, but existing and new groups (including new political organizations) have grown to the point where they have begun to challenge the state's monopoly on all organizations. This has occurred because of the need of the leaders for these groups, but we do not understand fully why this need has evolved.

Organizational-bureaucratic politics paradigm

This approach highlights the role of established organizations (Rigby 1976) as opposed to interest group theories which are based on agglomerations of individuals. It represents conflicts for survival and expansion among the organizational elites as a central factor in policy choices. This approach does account for the bargaining and haggling that are endemic to *vertical* relations (as between enterprises and ministries) in socialist systems. Various factors will influence the vertical bargaining process, such as informal personal connections and the capacity of the bargainer to withhold. Each of the major bureaux and departments is a major political constituency in its own right (defence, secret police, producers of important outputs, exports, and so on) which has the capacity to bargain by withholding certain outputs from the leadership (Csanádi 1989). This approach also accounts for the necessary *horizontal* competition between existing bureaux for budgetary resources, prestige, access and power. The absence of an active price system, and an unambiguous objective function according to which performance can be measured, make this kind of competition endemic in non-profit organizations and in government.

Comisso (1986) has pointed out that the theory does not explain how vertical conflict and horizontal competition are resolved. By focusing on the bargaining, it detracts attention from the determination of the boundaries within which the bargaining occurs. It deflects attention away from the role of the political leaders both as the *necessary* mediators of conflict between subordinate organizations and as the establishers of boundaries. It also ignores the fact that organizational interests very often originate at the top because that is where strategies are selected, structures are reorganized, and where appointments are made. While no theory can explain the particulars in each country, the task is to determine whether there are some generalizations that can be made about the handling of vertical conflict and horizontal competition in self-legitimating systems.

Soviet hegemony theories

In its strong form, this theory argues that the power of the hegemon was complete, and national economies were wiped out following the imposition of Soviet-type institutions and Soviet-supported leadership. In its weaker form, these economies of Eastern Europe remain national economies, but are compelled to use the institutions, ideology, and language of the local hegemon, while essentially following national goals and objectives in national and traditional ways, within the (variable) constraints imposed by the hegemon (Clemens 1976). The former case allows no room for national diversity; the latter case denies any explanatory power to the notion of socialism and reduces Soviet influence to mere *Realpolitik*. The current shift from the strong form to the weak form is a necessary corrective

(Rothschild 1989), but what is ultimately required is rethinking of the premise that either there is no diversity within the socialist paradigm, or that the existence of diversity nullifies the explanatory power of a theory of socialist economic organization. Instead, it may be that substantial diversity can even be predicted within a common organizational framework. In addition, attention must be paid to how the surviving national values have been affected by forty years of externally-imposed socialist experience, how the external constraints and opportunities for diversity have changed (the changing role of Western Europe), how the Soviet perceptions of its goals, constraints and risks have changed.

Ideology

Another explanation of socialist organization focuses on the Marxian heritage: revulsion at the exploitation inherent in private ownership of the means of production, distrust of the anarchy of the market, belief in the rationality of planning and in the appropriateness of prices based on the value of labour inputs, the priority of heavy industry. Adherence to these tenets has been offered to explain both the economic *goals* (high levels of investment, sectoral priorities) and the *structure* of the economy (elimination of independent economic activity, the domination of the plan and the use of labour-cost-based prices). As ideology has seemed more mutable in recent times (socialist states have reintroduced private property, the right of private individuals to employ other individuals, the possibility for foreign investors to own from 51 per cent to 100 per cent of domestic companies, the possibility for individuals to buy stocks in socialist corporations, and so on), the appeal of ideological explanations of socialist economies has faded.

Furthermore, an alternative and more persuasive explanation can be offered for the same phenomena. The bureaucratic organization explanation would argue that although all ministries compete for investment and other scarce resources, ministries integrally connected with one another in the production process (by virtue of being customers of, or suppliers to, other ministries) will also have a common interest. Thus, iron, coal, steel, metalworking, machine tools, investment goods, and defence goods would all benefit from a policy favouring heavy industry and high rates of investment, and the basis for a powerful coalition is likely to exist. Here, for the reasons given, I would argue that the choice of development strategy (or policy) was not independent of the interrelations between the relatively powerful groups. The chemical industry, much of whose output goes to fertilizers, which goes to farms and ultimately benefits consumers, would not have as many allies in the inter-bureau competition for scarce investment resource. This coalition would also explain why, when there are increases in consumer goods, consumer durable goods are much more likely to increase than foods or consumer services, and similarly, why the service sector in production is also underdeveloped. Again, the selection of a strategy or policy which underemphasizes certain sectors can be seen as not just a policy choice, but as a result of the specific system. The use of labour cost pricing undervalues the cost of heavy industry and thus obscures the real opportunity cost of investment in these sectors. Further, if prices have no meaning, it is difficult to have any independent evaluation of the policy choices of the elite, a point Trotsky recognized fifty years ago:

> The obedient professors managed to create an entire theory according to which Soviet price, in contrast to market price, has an exclusively planning or directive character. That is, it is not an economic but an administrative category, and thus serves the better for the redistribution of the people's income in the interests of socialism. The professors forgot to explain how you can 'guide' a price without knowing the real costs, and how you can estimate real costs if all prices express the will of a bureaucracy.
>
> (Trotsky 1937: 75)

Thus, in my judgement, ideology as an abstractly given set of goals provides an unconvincing explanation for the organization or strategy choices of socialist societies. As Marx might have observed, a more accurate characterization of the role of ideology is that it evolved in such a way as to constitute a rationale for the policies preferred by the governing elite, policies which focused on their maintenance of monopoly control of all important economic and political organizations. As Marx would have been aware, the process of developing an ideology which supports the interests of a ruling estate or class is not a purely instrumental process, nor is ideology, once developed, without a guiding and moral force. What Marx might have understood, however, is that ideology is never independent of the interests of the ruling elite.

Summary

Each of these theories, two of which (totalitarian and ruling class) are grand theories and the rest of which are partial theories, is useful in explaining some facts and each has important insights about socialist economic organizations. Totalitarian and ruling-class theories are both state versus society conflict models. Totalitarian theory underscores the conflict between the rulers and the ruled and the commitment of the leaders to their vision of the good. It reminds us of the centrality of staying in power and of the willingness of leaders to use whatever measures are necessary. Ruling-class theories elaborate how the top leaders manage society through their appointed *nomenklatura*. Organization theories point to the horizontal competition between bureaux and departments, the vertical bargaining, and the need for top leaders to channel and mediate the conflict. Hegemonic theories remind us of external constraints. Interest group theories point to utility to the leaders of semi-autonomous, value-oriented groups. Finally, ideology-based explanations underscore the role of ideology in justifying the mission and interests of the top leaders. In my judgement, the grand theories need to be enriched by taking into account the partial theories. However, there is one partial aspect which appears to me to be underdeveloped. This is the part that can be contributed by an analysis of the problem of legitimacy, and development of a theory of behaviour of self-legitimating bureaucratic organizations. That is the task of this paper.

SOCIALIST ECONOMIC ORGANIZATIONS AS SELF-LEGITIMATING ORGANIZATIONS

How shall we begin the construction of a theory of socialist economic organization (seo)? At first glance it might appear that the theory of governmental bureaucracies provides us with an adequate theory (Jackson 1983; Niskanen 1971; Wildavsky 1964). Certainly, in a full development of a theory of seo's one would want to formally incorporate many insights of that body of theory. However, theories of governmental bureaucracies have been developed within the framework of elected governmental organizations (egos), with the bulk of the theoretical and empirical work drawn from the US and the UK. What we are dealing with in the case of socialist economic organizations is a non-elected bureaucracy.

There are two major consequences. The first is that in the absence of election, the bureaucracy is in a monopoly situation. More precisely, the bureaucracy is, as suggested above in the discussion of the ruling class, a monopolist/monopsonist in a company town. Under such circumstances repression and coercion have little cost to the system managers. Second, there is no external means of evaluating and relegitimating systems goals and leaders.

It seems to me that relegitimation is a very important problem for socialist regimes. The evidence of the last decade points to the increasing centrality of legitimacy, as judged by internal efforts to increase that legitimacy and as judged by the observation of knowledgeable analysts (Djilas 1989; Fehér *et al.* 1983 among others). The importance of legitimacy also captures a key distinction between different types of non-elected governmental organizations (negos). There are many non-elected governments or fraudulently-elected governments throughout the world for which legitimacy does not appear to be as big a problem as in socialism. Although socialist economic organizations may share with all negos a willingness to use repression and bribes to remain in power, seos have an additional need for legitimacy because their claim to govern rests not on brute force but on representing themselves as trustees of the national resources for the workers.

Ordinary bureaucratic theory is of limited help here, as indicated above. I propose to consider here a body of theory that has not normally been used in this connection, namely, the theory of non-profit organizations (npo). Despite obvious differences, in one key respect, non-profit organizations are similar to seos. Both npos and seos lack mechanisms for routine external evaluation and relegitimation of the goals and attainments of top management. Both accomplish self-legitimation by establishing goals and by evaluating their own accomplishment of the goals. Both are governed by self-perpetuating boards of directors.

This structural characteristic distinguishes both of them from for profit organizations (fpos) and elected governmental organizations (egos) and is the source of their functional similarity with respect to the problem of legitimation. Fpo shareholders elect the directors who appoint management. The shareholders can evaluate management on the basis of profit performance, which can be compared with performance of other enterprises in the same industry. (Obviously, if the fpo is a monopoly, the ability of shareholders to evaluate management becomes more difficult, for there is no obvious point of comparison.) Even if the shareholders are diffuse, corporate take-over specialists can accomplish the same end (Manne 1965). There should be a correlation between managerial efficiency (resulting in profits) and the price of shares. If the enterprise is poorly managed, the price of its shares declines relative to those of other firms in the same industry. The lower the stock price, relative to what the take-over group believes it could be with better management, the greater the incentive for a corporate take-over to replace existing management and reap the capital gain.

In elected governmental organizations (egos), there is no single standard such as profit according to which managerial performance can be evaluated. Indeed, it is the nature of governmental organizations that both the costs and the benefits of the government services provided have to be estimated in circumstances in which precise estimation is impossible (for example, the 'value to the nation' of defence, and so on). Government services are most often provided because there are imperfections in the markets for such items (not all the costs or benefits of a given service can be charged to each individual). Not only is there no single standard according to which managerial performance can be evaluated, in most instances governmental organizations cannot be compared because there are no fully comparable bodies. None the less, the management of egos face the test of the electorate, at specified intervals.

Unlike the top management of fpos and egos, the top management of npos (defined as Board, CEO and top professional staff, following James 1983) and seos are not subject to either the routine test of the market nor the routine test of the electorate. (Of course, both are subject to objective constraints and can lose legitimacy or position in a number of ways.) Table 3.1 will help summarize the similarities and differences.

Table 3.1 Non-profit organizations governed by a Board of Directors

Governing board		Objective function	Source of funds	Evaluation of goals leaders
npo	self-perpetuating	self-defined	donations/sales/ cross-subsidizations	self-evaluation
fpo	elected directors	profit maximization as interpreted by directors	profits	evaluation by shareholders
ego	elected parliament/ president	social welfare as defined by elected officals	taxes; user-fees	evaluation by voters
seo	self-perpetuating	self-defined	taxes/sales/ cross-subsidization	self-evaluation

With this initial understanding of the structural similarities and differences between npos, fpos, egos and seos, we are now ready to move to a fuller specification of the behaviour of the non-profit organization as a step on our way to understanding self-legitimating organizations.

THEORY OF NON-PROFIT SELF-LEGITIMATING ORGANIZATIONS

The defining legal characteristic of the non-profit organization (npo) is not that it cannot earn profits, but that it is barred from distributing its profits to shareholders. There are several types of non-profit organizations (membership- or board-governed, with and without entrusted assets (Hansmann 1980)). The kind of non-profit organization closest to a socialist economy is one governed by a Board of Directors which manages entrusted assets, continues to seek donations, may have members, and produces goods and services for sale. Harvard University, Planned Parenthood, Columbia Presbyterian Hospital or the Catholic Church would be examples of this type.

This kind of non-profit organization has certain characteristics:

- The governing body (Board of Directors) is self-perpetuating.
- The board may be recruited from inside or outside the organization.
- The organization faces a hard budget constraint with respect to the external world.
- The board is entrusted with administering the resources placed under its trusteeship.
- Subject to fulfilling its public trust, it defines for itself the objective function which it pursues.
- The organization may earn profits in some market transactions or through user fees and use these to subsidize other activities.
- The board is not routinely scrutinized or evaluated by any outside body with respect to either the definition of the objectives or the administration of the resources.

- Challenges to the trusteeship can be made by appeal to an independent judiciary, or the board may lose its legitimacy with its membership, clients, donors, or the public at large.

The traditional literature on non-profit organizations addresses three issues: why do npos come about, how do they behave (James and Rose-Ackerman 1986). Npos come about for a variety of reasons, among which two are most germane here: as an autonomous provider under significant government funding (schools and hospitals); and because individuals are willing to donate resources to provide certain services, and entrusting them to the non-profit organization governing boards to translate their donations into the desired activities.

The portion of the literature on non-profit organizations most relevant here concerns the behaviour of the non-profit organization. While comparisons of performance that have been made of npos, for profit organizations (fpos) and governmental organizations (especially in health care and in education, sectors in which all three forms coexist in the US) may be of interest, our concern here is the inner logic of the npo.

To understand that inner logic, we need to understand the motives of the system leaders. Models of npos have been developed assuming a variety of motives on the part of the leadership: altruism, faithful trusteeship and self-interest (defined in several ways). While it seems reasonable for some purposes to use altruism or faithful trusteeship (missionaries in dangerous territories; church wardens), there is nothing inherent in the notion of a non-profit – the absence of distribution of profits to shareholders – that requires such altruism. Indeed, in the United States, large and quite entrepreneurial non-profit organizations operate our principal universities, hospitals, museums and opera companies, with very high entrepreneurial rents going to the Chief Executive Officers (CEOs). It seems likely that for these kinds of institutions (as opposed to churches, and so on) which hire people from the same pool of labour as the for-profit and the governmental organizations which may operate in the same sectors, that ordinary self-interest is more appropriate than altruism. It is true, of course, that people who work in government or the non-profit sector may have somewhat different utility functions from those who work in the for-profit sector, as do actors, dancers, musicians, artists and writers, but altruism does not seem to be the distinguishing characteristic.

Self-interest has several components: monetary income, non-pecuniary perks, power to command human and material resources to accomplish preferred programmatic objectives, and prestige. Power and prestige are especially important in npos and in governmental organizations, elected or non-elected. Alternatively stated, monetary income, non-pecuniary perks, power and prestige can all be seen as a function of discretionary control over the economic surplus. The question is what conclusions about behaviour follow from the structural and behavioural characteristics of npos? What follows below is a set of propositions about such behaviour. The intuitive logic for these propositions is given, or appropriate reference, but no rigorous proof.

Organizationally simple npos

1 *The proximate objective of management of a non-profit organization is to maximize the economic surplus and discretionary control, subject to the external hard budget constraint.* The discretionary income will be used to maximize the utility of the top leadership.

2 *The leadership will justify its preferred uses of discretionary image through a rationale, mission, or ideology.* The npo will be very concerned with its image. The definition of and packaging of its mission become quite important public relations activities. If the npo seeks to continue to grow and expand, it does so both by being a good manager of resources and cultivating potential donors (James 1983). The top echelons of the non-profit will use a variety of techniques to mediate the relationship between itself and the donor world.

3 *An npo will maximize its discretionary funds by generating profits from some of its activities which can be used to cross-subsidize other preferred but unprofitable activities* (James 1983).

4 *Ordinary poor performance will not normally result in a change of management. There is a lower minimum threshold of performance for npos than is true for fpos and egos.* This occurs precisely because there is no mechanism for their evaluation by either stockholders or voters. Due to the strict profitability test, fpos in a competitive environment have relatively little discretion about sustaining objectives or policies that do not pay off. (A well-protected fpo monopoly may resemble an npo more closely than it does a competitive fpo.) Egos face periodic elections. Npos, facing neither the test of the stockholders nor the test of the voters, will have less pressure to evaluate either programme or means. Further, the value of the outputs of npos, like those of egos are often inherently hard to measure. In the case of egos the voters can express dissatisfaction with the mix; in the npo case, future donors may not support a mix/quality package not to their liking, but previously entrusted funds are already committed. In the case of socialist economic organizations, there is no mechanism for the workers/citizens/consumers to express their support for the mix/quality package, at least not any direct mechanism.

5 *There will be more variety in the behaviour of similarly situated organizations of this type than in similarly situated fpos.* Because the affected public is not offered clear-cut choices about policies and objectives, both npos and seos have a wider degree of latitude in defining their objectives than egos or fpos. There will be a wider margin of entrepreneurial discretion covering a spectrum of motivations,

objectives and resulting behaviours in npos than in fpos (Young 1981; James and Rose-Ackerman 1986, Part IIe), and thus greater variety than in competitive fpos which typically have a narrowly-defined objective and sharp accountability standards enforced by market forces, as discussed above.

Complex economic organizations

Let us now build up a more layered notion of the npo. We can envision a complex npo with a Board of Directors, a Chief Executive Officer, staff officers, line officers, professional staff, skilled and unskilled workers and all the features of hierarchic bureaucratic organizations.

The complex npo will differ from the simple npo in three respects: (1) there are now many players with different interests; (2) the structure is now too complex for any single individual to possess all the relevant knowledge and to implement all decisions personally; (3) the absence of an objective, unambiguous measure of performance affects the representation of interests and the evaluation of performance.

6 *Different interests among the members of the top leadership lead to factional disputes over goals and means*. Factional disputes will be characteristic, unless the CEO is strong enough to dominate the board. Often there is a dominant coalition on the board.

7 *Factional disputes are usually resolved internally, without public airing of the issues*. Sometimes, however, the disputes go public in order to garner public support for one side or to challenge the legitimacy for the other. The presence of deep factional disputes under conditions where no faction dominates could lead to the appeal to outside groups and public support to tip the balance.

8 *A strong and successful CEO may dominate the board*. In the fpo, the Board of Directors is elected by the stockholders, and appoints the CEO. The existence of large institutional shareholders and corporate take-over barons limit the influence of the CEO on the board because the board is externally elected and can be changed, and institutional investors and take-over specialists are willing to do so. In the npo, the relationship between the board and the CEO is more one of mutuality than of hierarchy. The board of an npo will be as fast as an fpo to fire a CEO who is not successful in holding its confidence. An npo CEO who can deliver will be in a better position than the fpo CEO to have a major voice in selecting future board members because the board composition is internally determined. Such a CEO may bargain for an agreeable board as the price of his remaining with the organization.

9 *As in all hierarchies, there is vertical conflict*. Vertical conflict arises because the top leadership is now in conflict with subordinates over

the selection of goals and over the maximization of the discretionary surplus – for example, over wage rates, supervision and evaluation.

10 *Vertical conflict in a complex npo is more ambiguous than in a complex fpo.* First, the relationship between the npo board and CEO and its employees is more ambiguous than in an fpo because there is no explicit capital/labour struggle over profits. Second, it is more ambiguous because there is an alleged shared, socially-useful goal. The ambiguous relationship between employers and employees is most clearly expressed in the conflict over wage rates and supervision. Here the difficulty in measuring performance enters also.

11 *Employer–employee conflict will be consciously obscured by management.* In the npo, as in an fpo, management attempts to *isolate* the group of workers seeking to unionize and to ally itself with all other workers in pursuit of the shared goal. The unionizers are cast as hindering the organization in carrying out its essentially collectivist or altruistic mission. However, in the fpo case, the conflict of the interests of workers versus owners is sharp and serves to reduce the ability of management to isolate the workers. In the npo case, the solidarity of workers is attenuated, because there is no clear set of owners.

12 *Top management claims to have the unique 'disinterested' view of the socially-useful task.* All other views about goals and means are labelled as the self-serving articulation of interest groups, professional groupings or opinion groupings. This claim obscures the fact that they have a very direct interest: maximization of the surplus and of their control over its uses.

13 *As in all bureaucratic systems, peripheral units will edit the information and implement directives in their own best interests.* In npos, however, as a consequence of the absence of unambiguous goals and standards, the manipulation of information becomes central in both the vertical conflict and horizontal competition.

14 *As in all bureaucratic systems, there will be favoured departments.* As a consequence of the absence of objective, quantifiable goals or measures of goal attainment, management defines the criteria for evaluation and reward, and for resolution of horizontal competition. The bases for evaluation can change more readily than in fpos and allow more opportunity for favouritism. Npos, because they define their own objectives and evaluate their own performance, have a greater margin here than public bureaucracies.

15 *There will be more politicking and attention to the definition of standards and objectives, and less attention to efficiency, than in complex fpos.* The lack of internal prices for non-marketed outputs renders cost accounting impossible or arbitrary. This makes cost-cutting less important than political battles over the budget (plan).

16 *Groups with non-competing interests will form coalitions, in order to conduct politicking more effectively.* This point was discussed in the second section under 'Ideology' (pp. 48–9).

17 *As in all hierarchical organizations, the self-interest of individuals depends on both their present location in the hierarchy and on their aspirations and prospects for rising in the hierarchy*. The ambitious will seek upward mobility. The capacity to rise will have all the familiar qualities from complex fpos and egos: the ability to understand both the formal and the informal distribution of decision-making authority. But the process is more insidious in self-perpetuating hierarchies (as is abundantly clear in court intrigues) than in fpos and egos.

18 *Horizontal competition, vertical conflict and difference of interests and opinion will generate internal critics*. Because there is no external 'vote' in which voters can be offered clear alternatives among ends and means, differences and conflicts will be articulated out mainly internally through criticism of goals and means, systems of evaluation, and side effects of selected policies.

19 *Top management must disarm the critics. This is one of its central strategic functions*. Criticisms that do not threaten the top leadership may be accepted. Otherwise, the critics must be disarmed. They may be ignored, trivialized, fired, isolated, ostracized by counter-attacks on their character. Management may attempt to disarm them by creating new structures that appear to solve the problems without making any significant concessions, such as inviting their participation in an advisory capacity. They may attempt to co-opt them, or to bribe them.

THE SOCIALIST ECONOMY AS A SELF-LEGITIMATING BUREAUCRACY

The next step is to identify the similarities and differences between the self-legitimating bureaucracy as exemplified by the non-profit organization and socialist regimes.

The following principal structural characteristics of an npo, with little change, could apply to socialist economic organization:

- a self-perpetuating governing body;
- absence of external evaluation and relegitimation of the governing body;
- a hard budget constraint with respect to the external world;
- administration of resources placed under governing body's trusteeship;
- self-definition of the objective function, subject to fulfilling its public trust;
- challenges to the trusteeship (legitimacy) possible by appeal to an independent judiciary, membership, clients, donors, or the public at large with minimal modification could also describe a socialist economic organization – equally, the behavioural characteristics;
- maximization of economic surplus and discretionary control subject to external hard budget constraint;

- lower minimum threshold of performance for npos;
- more variety in the behaviour of similarly-situated npos;
- high concern with image and packaging of 'mission';
- cross-subsidization pursued to fund preferred activities;
- factional disputes over goals and means;
- factional disputes are usually resolved internally;
- vertical conflict exists, is ambiguous, and is obscured;
- top management's 'disinterested' view;
- peripheral units' exercise of informational and implementational discretion;
- politicking over standards and objectives displaces attention to efficiency;
- coalitions of groups with non-competing interests;
- existence of favoured departments;
- self-interest a function of money, perks, power, prestige and future prospects in the organization;
- strong and successful CEO may dominate the board;
- conflict, competition and differences of opinion will generate critics;
- centrality of capacity to disarm critics, the substitute for defeating the opponent in elections.

Nevertheless, there are important differences. A major difference between the non-profit organization and the socialist economic system is that the socialist economic system is a monopoly. In a monopolist/monopsonist relationship, as indicated above, there is the potential for coercion and repression that does not exist otherwise. At the same time, history points to the fact that socialist economic systems have over time become less coercive, have reduced their monopoly role in production and employment, and have liberalized exit from the system. A major question is why the regimes have voluntarily reduced their monopoly/coercive power, but that question will not be addressed here. But monopoly and repression have become less important characteristics of these countries over time, and the quest for legitimation more important. For this reason, I have deferred the introduction of the monopoly element to the end, in order to develop more fully the argument about characteristics of self-legitimating bureaucracies.

20 *Where an organization has a monopoly right to secure the economic surplus, top management will most likely pursue that goal more vigorously than otherwise*. The capacity to extract and control the surplus is not without limit, however, as it can sufficiently alienate the workers/customers that they cease to work effectively.

21 *The breadth of the monopoly in socialism reduces options for 'voice' or 'exit' (Hirschman 1970) and makes loyalty, or legitimacy, even more important than in the case of the npo*. The legitimacy of capitalism rests on public belief in its efficiency, liberty and equal opportunity. The legitimacy

of an elected government comes from the voters. The legitimacy of the church is rooted in religious belief. For the npo, its past record or the public reputation of its board members induces individuals to entrust additional resources. Socialist economic organizations may once have had the trust of the working class, but this trust appears to have eroded.

22 *Only those employees who have been appropiately socialized will be able to rise in the organization, and there is only one organization in town.* People who are aiming to achieve personal well-being have to learn how to observe and play the rules of the game (Narojek 1986, Rychard 1988).

23 *Seos will resist price reform.* A fourth important difference between the npo and the socialist economy is that for the former, the prices of inputs and outputs are to some extent determined independently of the non-profit organization itself. The very existence of units of measure that are logically relevant and independent of the control of the bureaucrats, such as prices, reduces their power and provides the basis for critics to challenge goals and means. The absence of such units makes that task harder.

24 *On the one hand, in the absence of democratic elections to renew the mandate of the government, the claim of the seo to legitimacy rests almost solely on outcomes: the ability to deliver. On the other, the capacity to deliver credible legitimate performance is hindered by the characteristics of the system itself.* This is the fundamental tension of the self-legitimating bureaucracy.

CONCLUSIONS

What can we learn from the theory of the self-legitimating bureaucracy? First, the behaviour of socialist economic organizations is similar in many respects to another, quite different self-legitimating bureaucracy, the large non-profit corporation. The organizational form of a self-perpetuating board entrusted with resources produces some predictable outcomes. I have tentatively identified over twenty such outcomes. Second, it is perhaps unsettling to see many aspects of the behaviour we associate with seos is also found quite close to home and is not only the product of totalitarian revolution. Third, this approach does help us understand the diversity we observe, since self-legitimating organizations have a wide range for discretion (especially when external hegemonic constraints are eased). Fourth, by approaching the socialist economic organization from this point of view, we are able to grasp more clearly their inner logic. The inner logic derives from three factors: a self-perpetuating elite which controls the productive resources of society, is not subject to formal review and relegitimation, and its members are motivated by self-interest. That logic accounts reasonably well for observed dysfunctional behaviour.

Finally, it makes crystal clear the dilemma in which self-legitimating organizations find themselves. On the one hand, in the absence of democratic elections to renew the mandate of the government, the claim of the seo to legitimacy rests almost solely on outcomes: the ability to deliver. On the other, the capacity to deliver credible legitimate performance is hindered by the characteristics of the system itself. This is the fundamental tension of the self-legitimating bureaucracy. What it must deliver to legitimate itself, it cannot do without external validation (in the form of elections of review boards composed of persons with integrity and expertise) which requires surrendering some control, unless a new broom. If bureaucracy is the routinization of a charismatic system, then the self-legitimating bureaucracy ultimately is an oxymoron.

BIBLIOGRAPHY

Brus, W. (1986) 'Institutional change within a planned economy', in M. Kaser (ed.) *The Economic History of Eastern Europe, 1919–1975* vol. 3, Oxford, Clarendon Press, chs 23–6.

Clemens, Walter (1976) 'The European alliance systems: exploitation or mutual aid?', in Charles Gati (ed.) *The International Politics of Eastern Europe*, New York, Praeger, 217–37.

Comisso, Ellen (1986) 'Introduction: state structures, political processes, and collective choice in CMEA states', *International Organization* 40 (2), 195–238.

Csanádi, Mária (1989) 'Party-state interlocking directorates: economic and political decision making in Hungary', manuscript.

Djilas, Milovan (1957) *The New Class*, New York, Praeger.

Djilas, Milovan (1989) 'The crisis in communism', *Telos* 80, 117–21, Summer.

Fehér, Ferenc, Heller, Ágnes and Márkus, György (1983) *Dictatorship over Needs*, New York, St Martin's.

Friedrich, Karl and Brzezinski, Zbigniew K. (1965) *Totalitarian Dictatorship and Autocracy*, New York, Praeger.

Hansmann, Henry (1980) 'The role of the non-profit enterprise', *Yale Law Journal* 89, 835–98, reprinted in Sue Rose-Ackerman (ed.) *The Economics of Nonprofit Institutions: Studies in Structure and Policy*, New York, Oxford University Press.

Hirschman, Albert (1970) *Exit, Voice, and Loyalty*, Cambridge, Mass., Harvard.

Hough, Jerry (1989) 'Totalitarianism revisited', talk delivered at the Kennan Institute for Advanced Russian Studies, The Wilson Center, 24 April, Washington, DC.

Jackson, P. M. (1983) *The Political Economy of Bureaucracy*, New York, Barnes & Noble Books.

James, Estelle (1983) 'How nonprofits grow: a model', *Journal of Policy Analysis and Management* 3, 350–63, reprinted in Sue Rose-Ackerman (ed.) *The Economics of Nonprofit Institutions: Studies in Structure and Policy*, New York, Oxford University Press.

James, Estelle and Rose-Ackerman, Sue (1986) *The Nonprofit Enterprise in Market Economies*, vol. 9, in *Fundamentals of Pure and Applied Economics*, New York and London, Harwood.

Kanet, Roger (1978) 'Political groupings and their role in the process of change in Eastern Europe', in Andrew György and James Kuhlmann (eds) *Innovation in Communist Societies*, Boulder, Westview, 41–58.

Manne, Henry (1965) 'Mergers and the market for corporate control', *Journal of Political Economy* 73, 110–20.

Niskanen, W. (1971) *Bureaucracy and Representative Government*, Chicago, Aldine.

Nove, Alec (1975) 'Is there a ruling class in the USSR?' *Soviet Studies* 27 (4), 615–35.

Rigby, T. H. (1976) 'Politics in the mono-organizational society', in Andrew Janos (ed.) *Authoritarian Politics in Communist Europe*, Berkeley, University of California Press, 31–81.

Rose-Ackerman, Sue (ed.) (1986) *The Economics of NonProfit Institutions: Studies in Structure and Policy*, New York, Oxford University Press.

Rothschild, Joseph (1989) *Return to Diversity*, New York, Oxford University Press.

Rychard, Andrzei (1988) 'Social and political preconditions for and consequences of economic reform in Poland', Research Report no. 143, The Vienna Institute for Comparative Economic Studies.

Skilling, H. Gordon (1966) 'Interest groups and Communist politics', *World Politics* 18, 435–61.

Trotsky, Leon (1937) *The Revolution Betrayed*, New York, Doubleday Doran.

Wildavsky, A. (1964) *The Politics of the Budgetary Process*, Boston, Little, Brown.

Young, Dennis R. (1981) 'Entrepreneurship and the behavior of nonprofit organizations: elements of a theory', in M. White (ed.) *Nonprofit Firms in a Three-Sector Economy*, Washington: Urban Institute, 135–62, reprinted in Sue Rose-Ackerman (ed.) *The Economics of Nonprofit Institutions: Studies in Structure and Policy*, New York, Oxford University Press.

4 Reform economics and western economic theory
Unexploited opportunities

Irena Grosfeld

INTRODUCTION

A western economist looking at the literature on the economic reforms in the centrally-planned economies (CPEs) would have some trouble to find familiar currents and references. It is indeed striking how isolated the reform thinking is from western economic theory. Of course, the repeated attempts at transforming the economic system were not based on fundamental choice of institutions in conformity with some theoretical considerations but were rather determined by a continuous streams of *ad hoc* policies under the pressure of actual political constraints. However, East European economists and policy-makers do refer to 'economic theory' and, particularly in the recent period, complain that the supply of the theory does not follow the demand of the practice quickly enough.

Until now the economists in the east and the west have worked separately using their own languages and terminology. The East European economists stress the specificity of their problems and experience and do not try to fit them into the general framework of western economics. Surely there are good reasons for it and we can imagine a rationale behind such an attitude: the scale of their problem is different (western economists were never confronted with the challenge of designing the whole economic system); the separation of political and economic spheres is more difficult; many of the theorems of the traditional economic analysis are based on assumptions facilitating the formalization procedure that make the theory irrelevant for empirical problems; until the 1960s the economic literature was dominated by the general equilibrium approach on the one hand, and by the theory of market failure on the other – neither of these two currents could attract the attention of East European reformers.

However, it seems that the reformers did not notice the evolution of classical economics to a more socially and politically-relevant political economy. They often dismissed economic theory as if it were still limited to the case of perfect competition. The origin of this misperception was probably ideological but with time this kind of resistance disappeared. The inability to recognize that the extensions of the economic analysis and dynamically-developing new fields were concerned with similar problems and might have been usefully exploited by reformers seems to be due in a large extent to the specific training of East European economists and their lack of interest in western economic science. It is also a linguistic problem. As long as they are convinced about the particularities of the issues they face and, consequently, use specific language and terminology, the perspective of common themes and questions remains difficult.

The fundamental economic issues are certainly different in the west and in the east (employment and inflation versus shortages and lack of technological progress). But reform economics is concerned with the optimal mix of centralization and decentralization, of market and hierarchy, of autonomy and control, and – more recently – of public and private. All these issues have been extensively treated in western economic literature.

Since the 1970s some western authors[1] have argued that the concepts and tools of conventional macroeconomics may be applied to study particular problems of the CPEs; that systemic differences notwithstanding, the issues of economic policy in the CPEs may be comparable (with some modifications) to equivalent issues in mixed economies. Although on a macroeconomic level this view is defendable (but it has never been accepted by the East European economists), we shall adopt here a different perspective, that of the reform economists who look for a new institutional order, and not only for adequate policy instruments.

In what follows we shall try to indicate those fields in contemporary economics which could offer the East European reformers an enlightening perspective and useful tools for their particularly challenging enterprise. We shall also suggest incidentally some developments in economic theory for which observing the East European experience more closely might have been stimulating and instructive for western economists. This will be a very tentative list of themes which should be developed in further research.[2] Also references to the literature will be necessarily incomplete and given for illustrative purposes.

The question of unexploited opportunities is not only of historical value. It is also of immediate importance and interest. We are witnessing an unusually far-reaching wave of redesigning the economic system in the Soviet Union and Eastern Europe. More thorough understanding of the real possibilities and limits of western economic theory is probably now more urgent than ever.

MARKET FAILURES AND NON-MARKET FAILURES

For long, economists have been divided roughly between two schools of thought: there were those who believed that markets work best if left to themselves and that the function of the state should be limited to the establishment of a legal framework ensuring that markets work properly, and those who believed that the government should be an active agent concerned with the maximization of some social welfare function which can significantly improve the operation of the economy. Since the Keynesian revolution in the 1930s and for the next thirty years the second trend remained the mainstream of macroeconomic theory and largely dominated the literature. To remedy the unquestionable market failures (externalities and public goods, increasing returns, informational imperfections) two solutions have been envisaged and applied: first, government intervention in the allocation of resources through regulation and taxes, and second, nationalization. The existence of any market inadequacies was considered as a necessary and sufficient condition for the government's intervention as if it involved no social costs.

Welfare economics – which contributed to rapid growth of the public sector – was not interesting for central planners and reformers. They knew only too well the arguments for central planning but also its dysfunctions. Their experience could be rather enlightening for those western economies who for long remained fascinated by the idealistic vision of the welfare state. Since the mid-1960s, however, the non-market (government and bureaucracy) failures have been carefully examined. It became largely accepted, following Demsetz (1969) that it would be a fallacy ('a Nirvana-form of analysis') to suppose that perfect government can replace an imperfect market, and, consequently, to compare an unrealistic optimal system with a real non-optimal one.

A huge literature has been devoted to the unintended and unexpected consequences of government intervention and to the social costs that it implies. Several critiques of the involvement of public authorities in economic life have been formulated, underlining different aspects of the problem: the public choice school and the economic theory of bureaucracy, political business cycles literature, the theory of property rights and the theory of incentives.

The public choice school and the economic theory of bureaucracy[3] study the performance shortfalls of different non-market organizations, including governments. They stress the fact that public organizations, developed in order to guarantee the law, to provide public goods, to stabilize and control the economy, fail in several respects to fulfil their original tasks. Bureaucrats are not disinterested men totally devoted to the public interest, they are ordinary men trading off (at best) between their own private interests (defined as the three 'p's: more pay, power and prestige) and the public interest. Moreover, because they are not submitted to budgetary constraints and systematically checked by 'hard facts' in the same way as market firms, the correction of the distorted information (and action) may be long in coming. The resulting inefficiency of the public sector has been studied extensively.[4] This large literature, considered often as weak from the theoretical point of view, marked an important breakthrough; it pointed out that the respect of optimal rules cannot be taken for granted and that the actual implementation should be carefully scrutinized; it also stimulated the development of rigorous models of behaviour of public firms.

The economics of public enterprises providing private goods, first more normatively oriented and looking for the optimal behaviour rules, switched to positive studies of bureaucratic behaviour, analysing allocative inefficiencies due, not only to government objectives, but also to difficulty of control, incorporating the dimensions of imperfect and asymmetric information (for example, on unobservable productivity parameters), and the question of incentives. The key issue became the distortion of information by the self-interest-seeking behaviour of different groups. Then came the theory of property rights, the theory of agency and the theory of incentives (which will be treated in the fourth and fifth sections).

Constitutional economics is another extension – a strongly normative one – of the public choice school. It underlines the importance of political and economic institutions and of the long-term constitutional constraints on government. It goes beyond the usual concern of economic analysis (efficiency) and looks for such institutional design that will allow for social improvement (in terms of increased individual freedom).[5]

Both the public choice school and the constitutional economics approaches seem to be particularly close to the reform economists' preoccupations. Critiques of government involvement in economy and the search for viable political and economic reforms are indeed the very essence of their endeavour.

An important qualification is, however, in order. The positive theory of public enterprises supposes that the system of control of public enterprises operates within a market framework; that public enterprise is subject to constraints arising out of market conditions (and technology and government control). This is obviously different from the CPE context in which market sanctions do not exist.

Also political business cycles' literature stresses the unintended consequences of government intervention. It is based on the observation that politicians are driven by short-term electoral considerations and their policies can destabilize the economy. Indeed, in democratic systems there is an incentive to policy-makers running for re-election to use stabilization policies to win popular support. Before elections, democratic governments are inclined to adopt expansionary policy actions with immediate visible benefits and hidden, delayed costs.[6] Although in the CPEs there is no real electoral checks, social discontent can manifest itself through decline in productivity, withdrawal from the labour market, visible accumulation of frustrations, or even revolt. In several East European countries planners proved to be sensitive to this kind of 'vote' and reacted to consumer dissatisfaction by stopping investment expansion. Therefore, instead of western democratic government destabilizing *ex ante* before elections (applying popular measures), and stabilizing *ex post*, we can expect East European planners' investment policy to overheat the economy *ex ante* (using unpopular measures), and to equilibrate *ex post*, when a growing dissatisfaction of the population forces them to adjust.[7]

Since the end of the 1970s, a sketchy reconciliation and synthesis of these two opposite traditions in economic policy thinking – enthusiasm of welfare economics and scepticism of public choice school – emerges in several works stressing the necessity of comparing relative costs and advantages of different institutions. Between public economics (assuming perfect control of public firms by the government) and the economic theory of bureaucracy (fundamentally distrustful of public intervention), it comes to be more and more accepted that, in terms of allocative Pareto efficiency, the theory of market failure has to be confronted with the theory of non-market failure;[8] that the economy can be moved by the policy-makers only along the frontier of the social opportunity set, trading off one good for another (for instance, externalities for more costly administrative structure, or employment for real wages); that dynamic efficiency and the incentive for technological innovation may remain in conflict with the static, allocative Pareto efficiency (for instance, patent regulations restricting access to technological information in the interest of long-run efficiency reduce competitive pressure and the short-run efficiency).

This way of looking at economic issues might have been extremely useful for reform economists. Their search for a new system combining central planning with some elements of the market was usually based on one of two presumptions: some viewed central co-ordination of the economic life as basically beneficial and were looking for a limited injection of a market mechanism, others were convinced that 'the market was a marvel' and would like to graft as much of it as possible into the 'real socialism' (the second tendency has been particularly alive for the last few years). Pragmatic evaluation of the actual working of different institutions was rarely undertaken.[9]

Transaction cost economics adopts this comparative institutional approach, views each organization as a package of distinctive strengths and distinctive weaknesses, and examines the choice between market and non-market organization in terms of assessing comparative advantages of different institutions.[10] It is based on the presumption: 'in the beginning there were markets' and tries to explain why and when transactions are removed from markets and organized internally. Contrary to the common-sense explanation according to which vertical integration has technological origins,[11] transaction cost economics attributes it basically to the opportunity of economizing on the 'costs of running the system', equivalent to friction in a physical system. However, the gains offered by a hierarchy may be offset by the monitoring costs: for instance, in a firm, the costs of negotiating separate contracts for each exchange are reduced, but the control loss may exceed this gain. Therefore, transaction cost economics is concerned with the reasons for which firms exist but also with the limits on their growth. It favours the vertical integration as long as the marginal costs of transaction are smaller than those of completing transactions through the market.

If we think of the CPE's institutions in terms of transaction cost economics, the point of departure is 'in the beginning there was a big organization' but the internally-organized transactions broke down and have to be shifted to the market. If in the case of the market economy the main question is when a hierarchy can be expected to internalize a part of the market successfully,[12] in a CPE it will probably be how far the hierarchy (the national economy) should be transformed into the market. To answer the first question the experience of the planned economy may be relevant, and vice versa, the operation of the market economy gives some arguments in favour of not overly reducing the size of the firm.

The concept of transaction costs, stressing the importance of the contract execution stage, is quite appealing for the analysis of the centrally-planned, shortage economy. For example, in the course of exchange between firms, specific informal costs should be taken into account: formal monetary costs are not of primary importance for the enterprise (cost-based prices allow the incorporation of the cost into the higher price for the product and money hoards are relatively useless); what counts most are goods and services in short supply which are at the firm's disposal and which have to be exchanged for other goods and services, necessary but in short supply (a 'vector price' for each deficient good might be established for such a barter exchange). Other informal transaction costs should include bribing the supplier, sending him employees of the firm as workers, accepting his demand for credit.[13]

COMPARATIVE ECONOMIC SYSTEMS

Reform economists were familiar with concepts of comparative economic system analysis and sometimes used them. However, the deep sense of the systemic approach does not seem to be widely assimilated nor applied. Beyond a meticulous description of various aspects of economic systems and an attempt to create a common conceptual framework allowing for the comparison of different systems, the systemic approach is a way of seeing different elements of an economic system as necessarily and inevitably interrelated. If we agree – as most of us do – that any economic system can be characterized by its decision-making structure, information structure and incentive structure, the normative conclusion of comparative economic systems is that any change in one part of the system necessitates adequate adjustment in other elements. The neglect of this principle may render futile or even harmful any apparently rational measure aiming at overcoming some imperfections of a given system. For example, it is useless to create strong incentives encouraging economic agents to make some decisions that, according to the authority structure, will not be in the area of their competence.

The history of economic reforms in Eastern Europe gives several examples of the incompatibility of reform proposals with this basic tenet of comparative economic systems. Since 1956 most of the successive reform proposals touched upon all three subsystems: decision-making had to be decentralized to lower entities; the number of plan indicators had to be reduced and financial indicators had to replace direct physical allocation of resources (information structure); incentives had to be associated with the performance of the enterprises. However, the lack of coherence of different blueprints was notorious: failure to take into account conflict between any incentive system and basically unstable rules of the game (the limits of the centre's decision-making power being ill-defined, some theoretically good incentive systems proved to be inefficient because of the enterprises' expectation of change); contradictions between the incentive systems at different levels of the economic hierarchy (modifications of the success indicators on the level of the enterprise without adequate changes on the level of intermediary units, for example, industrial association); lack of adaptation of the information structure and incentive structure (the search for an increased autonomy of the enterprises did not bring about consequent substitution of orders by financial parameters); incompatibility between the decision-making structure and the incentive structure (incentives have often been changed to make managers more sensitive to efficient use of resources and to stimulate innovations, but this had not been accompanied by adequate modifications of the decision-making structure, giving them, for instance, the right to buy and sell the capital of the firm).

Related, although somehow different, is the problem of the relationship between the economic policy and the economic system. The economic policy is different from and external to the economic system, although it influences in a significant way its performance (for instance, the policy of full employment or of a strong progressive taxation inevitably weakens any incentive system). Given strong interdependence between the two, it is admitted that they should be carefully adjusted one to the other: a particular economic policy may be compatible only with a limited set of organizational solutions and, conversely, a particular economic system imposes some constraints on the set of policies which may be implemented without challenging the logic of the system.

In writings about the CPEs, the awareness of these subtle relationships is not always present (but, for example, Kornai 1986 distinguishes carefully between the two). In practice there is often a tendency to consider the economic policy as a substitute for institutional changes (for example, Gierek's period in Poland). Another confusion, more characteristic of the western perception, is to speak about reforms when what we have to deal with is merely change in economic policy (there are several exceptions, for example, Hewett 1988 stressed forcefully this distinction). In situations of profound disequilibria, the problem of priorities between the economic policy and the economic system is discussed: some argue that if there is strong excess demand, an appropriate macroeconomic policy should be the precondition of the reform; others say that it is only a deep reform which can bring about the equilibrium. Empirical evidence suggests that as long as disequilibria are relatively weak and the economic system relatively coherent (even if inefficient), adequate economic policy can be successful; but beyond some threshold of decomposition of the economy (Poland), profound systemic changes seem for many economists to be the necessary preliminary step (with adequately-adjusted economic policy measures).

Looking back at over thirty years' experience of reforming the CPEs, it appears that this misperception had a harmful effect on the reform process. As soon as the conflict appears between the goals of the economic policy and the (temporary?) effects of the reformed system, the new rules of the game are abandoned: if, for instance, the profit-oriented incentive scheme creates differences of revenues incompatible with a wage policy expressing distributions preferences, the former is sacrified to the advantage of the latter.[14] Because of this substitution effect, and the fundamental instability of the rules of the game, it is often difficult to disentangle the impact of the system itself and of the economic policy on the performance of the CPE. This can probably explain some contradictory theoretical statements about the CPEs. For instance, according to Granick (1987), many malfunctions in the CPEs, which have been commonly attributed to the existence of a central-planning system, can be attributed to the centres' preference for a job rights overfull employment objective. Granick argues that this has the highest priority in the planners'/government's eyes and that the choice of policies and institutions is subordinated to it. This contradicts Kornai's conviction that overfull employment is the *result* of the distinctive systemic features of the CPEs: permanent disequilibrium, overheating and soft-budget constraint. Needless to say, the choice of one hypothesis or another will strongly influence the reform economics and policy thinking.

THEORY OF INCENTIVES

Comparative system analysis puts an accent on the informational, incentive and decision-making properties of an economic system and stresses the complex and delicate relations between these three subsystems. There is, however, a normative extension of this approach that studies feasibility, implementability and efficiency of different organizational solutions.

Decentralized procedures for planning may be considered as the first works in this field. Their focus on the *ex ante* contracting stage and the informational aspect of an allocation mechanism probably discouraged CPE economists and planners from considering them as a serious alternative solution to the CPE problems. The neglect of the motivational side and of the implementation stage was one of the reasons for the distrust of Lange-type schemes.

However, since the beginning of the 1970s, there has been a boom in the literature stressing the strategic aspects of the economic agents' behaviour which have come to be considered by many economists as the key problem of economic organization.[15] It appears in different forms: theory of agency, principal-agent problem or theory of incentives.

The problem of incentive is formulated as follows: the principal, who engages agents and delegates to them some decision-making authority, has his own objectives which do not coincide with those of the agents. Moreover, some of the agents' private information is not known to the principal (which may lead to adverse selection) and/or the principal cannot observe the agents' actions perfectly (moral hazard). So the principal must choose an incentive scheme which specifies in advance how he will react to the agents' information and action (that is, what will be the agents' reward for each possible observed outcome), and which induces the agent to reveal truthfully its characteristics and to behave as if he were maximizing the principal's welfare (or at least which limits a divergence from his interest). The principal-agent theory has several applications: to the relationships between government and managers of public firms,[16] between shareholder and managers of privately-owned firms, between employer and workers and between insurer and insured.

The theory proposes several procedures (transfer functions) possessing desirable incentive properties in different frameworks – static or dynamic, under moral hazard and/or adverse selection, with or without commitment – and with a variety of behavioural assumptions: firms maximize profits, or value-added per worker (Ward 1958), or a combination of 'effort' and money, or some more complex objectives. These transfer functions, composed usually of a fixed transfer (higher for low-cost agents than for high-cost agents) and a bonus (or penalty), which depends on the difference between expected and observed outcomes (Picard 1987), assure that the truthful revelation (of endowments or of a marginal rate of substitution) and the optimal effort are a dominant strategy.[17]

The problem which reformers face in the CPEs may be also formulated in terms of the incentives theory: is it possible to design a contract between the planner and the state enterprises which will guarantee that the firms do not use their informational power and that will induce them to work hard? It is a particularly complex problem of a dynamic incentive scheme, combining adverse selection (hidden information) during the working out of the plan (the planner does not know the firms' production functions), and moral hazard (hidden actions) during the carrying out of the state plans (the planner cannot observe how far the firms' choices are guided by the search of a maximum input/output ratio and of a quiet life). The complexity of the problem is increased by the fact that there is no credible warranty that the planners will respect the agreement (an incentive scheme without commitment). As far as we know, no incentive scheme has been proposed until now allowing for such a complexity.

So, very abstract and mathematically sophisticated, the theory of incentives may not be applicable directly to the real CPE's world. Besides the extreme complexity of the CPE's principal-agent problem, there is the question of a basically non-market environment for the state firms in a CPE. The distinguishing mark of any firm is that it supersedes the price mechanism, but in a market economy (or in a mixed economy) the firm remains related to an outside network of relative costs and prices. The implicit hypothesis of the theory of incentives is the presence of this strongly-motivating factor. The firms in the CPEs are free from this constraint. The second objection concerns the lack of commitment. Without a minimal guarantee that planners will respect the terms of contract, the whole incentive problem is meaningless.[18] The firms will not reveal information if it may be used against them. Constant modifications of the regulation system of enterprises make problematic even the assumption of short-term commitment. The 'success indicators', and the bonus system of a CPE enterprise, change very often and the prediction of this change is part of the firms' rational expectations.[19] This shows the limits of the possible utilization of the principal agent as a positive theory of the CPEs. But, at the same time, it suggests that the stabilization of the rules of the game and the building up of trust are necessary preliminary conditions of any efficient incentive scheme. This is another way of arguing the importance of constitutional economics. However, even at a positive level the theory of incentives may provide some instruments allowing the assessment of different incentive schemes actually used or proposed in the CPEs.

THEORY OF PROPERTY RIGHTS AND THEORY OF AGENCY

If the incentive theory takes the organizational structure of the economy as given and tries to design an optimal incentive scheme, the theory of property rights goes another way around and studies the impact of the distribution of property rights on the economic agents' performance.

In a broad definition, property means not only 'ownership', but also various rights (regulation) enforced by legal means.[20] Ownership is defined as the right to use the assets (*usus*), the right to appropriate returns from the assets (*usus fructus*), and the right to bear the consequences (positive or negative) of the changes in the value of those assets (*abusus*).[21]

The property-rights approach maintains that private property is the best institutional arrangement creating incentives to channel individual economic effort into activities that bring the private benefits (or costs) close to the social benefits (or costs). It claims that in order to use economic resources in the most productive way, it is necessary to develop property rights completely: they should be individual, exclusive and freely transferable. In all non-private institutions, like public firms, different non-profit institutions, mutual associations, co-operatives, the discrepancies can be expected between private and social rates of return. The argument is based on the absence of capitalizable, saleable property rights and, consequently, the lack of incentives for the 'owners' to move resources from a less productive to a more productive use and to exercise adequate pressure on X-inefficient management.[22]

This is obviously directly relevant to the CPEs. It came to be widely acknowledged by reform economists that the enterprises should have the right to participate in profits from current use of assets (*usus fructus*) and all reform projects were sensitive to this issue. In recent years the problem of ownership has been openly discussed in Hungary, Yugoslavia, Poland and China. The long-term lease of land to peasants has been decided in China and in the USSR. In Hungary several proposals have been made to redefine property rights in order to create incentives in accordance with those of an owner. Looking for the personification of the state ownership, Tardos (1986), for instance, proposed the creation of special bodies – state holding companies – to supervise the enterprise management, as stockholders do in a modern corporation. However, the role of *abusus* seems to be undervalued. And still the possibility for the owner to split up, merge and sell the firm by capturing its market value provides a stimulus of primary importance. Although the utility function of a manager of a private firm in a market environment and that of a manager of a state enterprise in a CPE may be similar (that is, a combination of income, effort level, growth rate of the firm and the level of discretionary managerial expenditure), the first one is constrained in the pursuit of his own objectives by the fact that, ultimately, the shares of his firm are marketable (every shareholder can transfer his property rights to another investor). The empirical evidence suggests, and particularly the analysis of the Yugoslav experience, that the absence of transferable property rights is a powerful disincentive for enterprises to care about the net worth of assets.

The property-rights school also studies extensively the consequences of what is called the separation of ownership and control in a modern corporation:[23] managers who are not the firm's security holders can be expected to appropriate perquisites out of the firm's resources for their own consumption and to devote a smaller effort to creative activities (learning about new technologies, and so on) than in the case of an owner-managed firm. The problem of control is, however, limited, according to the economics of property rights, by the fact that the price of a share in the capital market reflects the expectations about the firm's prospects (it rises if the performance of a manager is good and vice versa) and shares can be bought and sold: every shareholder can transfer his property rights to another investor.

So the property-rights literature attributes to the entrepreneur (the risk-bearer) a central role in disciplining managers. The threat of outside take-over is considered as providing a discipline of the last resort.[24]

The theory of agency, related to the property-rights school, is also concerned with the incentive problem when the decision-makers (managers) do not bear a major share of the wealth effects of their decisions, but its approach is different: if the theory of property rights suggests how to make *ex ante* evaluations of the impact of alternative institutional structures on economic behaviour, the theory of agency views the separation of ownership security and control as an efficient form of economic organization and tries to explain *ex post* the survival of organizations in which shareholders cannot exercise real power to oversee managerial performance.[25] It dispels the notion of ownership and the key role of the entrepreneur in monitoring the managers for two reasons: (1) security holders diversify their portfolio between the securities of many firms and, consequently, are less sensitive to the information about inefficient managerial decisions and less interested in overseeing any of the firms, and (2) managers do care about the performance of the corporation; although they do not suffer immediate gain or loss from current performance, it influences the value of their managerial services on the labour market. So, management and risk-bearing are treated as naturally separate factors of production, the first being constrained by the managerial labour market, the second by the capital market and the possibility of take-over.[26]

Therefore, the theory of agency does not argue that ownership is unimportant, but that the agency costs resulting from the separation of ownership and control are limited by the existence of three markets: the capital market, the market for corporate control, and the managerial labour market. If these markets do not exist the agency costs increase significantly. They will be higher – all else being equal – in public firms than in private firms: in the public sector the lack of a capital market and of a market for corporate control weakens the managerial incentive system.

This presumption must be, however, qualified: it depends strongly on the market structure (degree of competition) and regulation in the market. This shows the limits of the theoretical arguments and the need for empirical evidence about the impact of ownership arrangements on performance.

The empirical studies comparing the actual performance of private and public firms are still very few. The basic reason for this is probably the difficulty in finding comparable firms in the same product area.[27] The recent wave of privatization offers, however, an opportunity to assess the performance of nationalized versus privatized firms. Some conclusions are already available.

Several authors[28] studying the experience of privatization (particularly in the UK) agree that the implications of changes in the structure of ownership depend heavily on the effectiveness of regulatory policy and the degree of product market competition. In other words, privatization and deregulation proved to be satisfactory cures to the inefficiency of public enterprises if there were no important market failures. In the case of firms with important market power subject to regulation the arguments *pro* and *contra* privatization should be carefully scrutinized: unless competition is expanded and/or adequate regulatory policy applied, privatization of a monopoly may not produce expected results.[29] The role of competition appears to be particularly important, both as a powerful incentive system, and as a mechanism for the discovery, revelation and diffusion of information.

The relevance of all this for the CPEs is not straightforward. In a socialist economy there is no capital market, no managerial labour market and no market for corporate control (no threat of take-over). Managers are free from the market pressure; they are monitored by direct control. But all reform projects attempt to increase the independence of managers and limit the scope of central control. The theory of property rights and the theory of agency suggest, however, that without a competitive market environment, this can only increase the agency cost: with the relaxation of the principals' control and without the discipline of the market, the agents' (directors of state enterprises) behaviour may be supposed to diverge still more from an 'optimal' one.

CONCLUSIONS

What could reform economists learn from western economics? Was their scepticism justified as far as the utility of economic theory for reform thinking is concerned, or did they miss something important?

It is true that in looking carefully through different branches of economic theory, a reform economist might feel embarrassed. On the one side there is an overwhelming empirical evidence of the bankruptcy of central planning and of state ownership, on the other economic theory seems to be unable to provide clear-cut well-founded arguments in favour of private enterprise. It says rather that there is no perfect solution; that there are market failures and non-market failures which have to be compared; that a particular institutional set-up does not determine univocally the results because tacit knowledge is important. Economic theory can merely suggest what are the possible trade-offs (for example, between increasing returns to scale and diminishing returns to management, or between uncertainty due to strategic behaviour and uncertainty due to the lack of communication) and where to look for the comparison of costs and benefits. In western thinking about the economy, such an approach seems to be more and more accepted and takes the place of ideal models. Everyday experience shows the ubiquity of intermediary solutions, the coexistence of markets and hierarchies, the eclectic use of advantages of organization and of individual entrepreneurship.

However, crucial for this analysis, and for the operation of various organizations in the west, is that they operate in the framework of a market system with private property as the means of production. This assumption, self-evident in the west and unrealistic in the east, seems to be the key obstacle in making the economic theory relevant to the CPEs.

The role of a market environment is strongly underlined by the theory of economic evolution and economic selection (which may be considered as an extension of the theory of property rights). They also give the most powerful argument in favour of private enterprise. The evolutionary theory of economic change accepts private enterprise because of its sensitivity and responsiveness to unforeseen changes and its capacity to stimulate technological innovations.[30] The theory of economic selection views the pluralistic market economy as favouring the selection of organizations which have the best combination of error-elimination and trial-generation capacities.[31] Both put an accent, not on the resource allocation mechanism (including incentives for truthful information), but on the dynamic aspect of the search for efficient organization, including incentives for entrepreneurship. So the argument is different from the orthodox claim for superior static efficiency. Without a pluralistic market environment, a sophisticated comparison of markets and hierarchies, or of private enterprise and central planning, becomes a totally different problem, both theoretically and empirically.

In a socialist economy with state ownership of the means of production, as in a public economy, selection and evolution do not operate in the same way as in a market economy. Bureaucracies struggle for accommodation with superiors, not for survival. 'Hard facts', such as a budget bottom line, do not play a discriminatory role. Subtle strategies against selection develop; uncorrected errors accumulate.[32] In the reformed CPEs it was more and more recognized that a kind of market pressure is necessary for the market-oriented reforms to produce expected results. Consequently, several interesting institutional proposals have been formulated in the attempt to reproduce market pressure in the framework of a basically state-owned economy.[33] The question remains whether it is possible to create a market environment with all its blessings maintaining state property of the means of production. In other words, is it possible to *simulate* the market?

If we agree that the market must be *real* in at least a large part of the economy, the question is, of course, how large should it be to make its logic spill over onto the non-market sector? The question is common to contemporary market economies and to socialist economies. In mixed economies the question is: how far can we go in enlarging the public sector without losing the main advantages of a private economy; what deviations are acceptable before the system becomes unworkable? In the east the question is: is it possible to get an 'optimal mix' of private and public, coming from a centrally-planned economy with state property of the means of production; can it be done by partial privatization in a 'hostile' (non-market) environment, or is a full switch to the free private economy necessary? (In the first case the positive results may be too long in coming, in the second the social costs and resistance may be prohibitive.)

This points out the fundamental problem that the reform economists face today – the problem of transition. To this economic theory has no answer. It is a political question. The limited tolerance of the population for a radical, painful change may be an argument for the progressive experimentation with different property rights set-ups, institutional frameworks, and so on.

In any case, *'the theory of economics does not furnish a body of settled conclusions immediately applicable to policy. It is a method rather than a doctrine, a technique of thinking which helps its possessor to draw correct conclusions'* (John Maynard Keynes).

NOTES

I wish to thank Pierre-André Chiappori, Ellen Comisso, Roger Guesnerie, János Mátyás Kovács, Pavel Pelikan, Richard Portes, Kazimierz Poznanski and Gérard Roland for useful comments on an earlier draft of this paper.

1 Particularly Richard Portes in his several articles.
2 The positive examples of the application of western economic theory, and particularly of the incentive system, to the study of the Soviet-type economies, do exist but we shall not present them here. The authors of such works are western economists (see, for example, Loeb and Magat 1978; Mougeot 1988).
3 Standard references are Buchanan and Tullock (1962); Niskanen (1971).
4 Some stress the fact that the behaviour of public managers is influenced by political pressure (for example, Fiorina and Noll 1978; others concentrate their attention on bureaucrats' use of informational monopoly to influence the government (Niskanen 1971).
5 Cf., for instance, McKenzie (1984); Buchanan (1987).
6 Cf., for example, Lundberg (1962); Nordhaus (1975); Lindbeck (1976); Frey (1978). Recent empirical evidence is mixed. For interpretation of CPE's fluctuations and adjustment in terms of political business cycles see Grosfeld (1986).
7 In a threshold model of planners' investment behaviour the planners' sensitivity to the evolution of real wages has been confirmed (Cf. Grosfeld 1987).
8 Wolf (1979) proposes a typology of non-market failures analogous to that which exists for market failures: internalities and private goods (due to internal structure of rewards and penalties unrelated to external prices system), redundant and rising costs ('X-inefficiency'), derived externalities (unintended side effects of non-market intervention) and distributional inequity (in terms of influence and power as compared to income and wealth in the case of market 'failure').
9 Kornai (1983) stresses the inevitability of trade-offs between different economic 'diseases' but not between different organizational structures.
10 The fundamental reference is Williamson (1975).
11 Cf. Alchian and Demsetz (1972) who view technological non-separability as primarily responsible for the appearance of the 'classical capitalist firm'.
12 The question has been first asked already by Coase (1937): why is all production not carried on in one big firm?
13 To regulate the flow of capital the central bank in a CPE applies a lower rate of interest for trade enterprises than for industrial enterprises. However, in the situation of shortages, the position of the latter is so strong that it can and does impose conditions on deliveries to the former. Credit (with the low interest rate) is one of these conditions.
14 Recent developments in China are a good example of this phenomenon: after a decade-long period of economic restructuring and market-oriented reforms,

the Chinese government found growing inflation, inequalities and corruption to be unbearable. It decided (as is the typical reflex of CPE's government) to sharply reduce the role of the free market: the control of the prices of many goods will be reimposed, the number of private firms will be limited, and the capital spending by local authorities will be scaled down (*International Herald Tribune*, 18 October 1988).

15 Cf. seminal paper by Groves (1973).

16 In fact, in democratic countries there is a double principal-agent relationship: the government acts as a principal in its relations with managers, but as an agent in its relations with citizens (voters) (cf., for instance, Caillaud *et al.* 1988). The political business-cycle phenomenon may be explained in these terms.

17 A dominant strategy is the best strategy for the enterprise independently of other enterprises' choices. Some authors develop the Bayesian solution defined in terms of an agent's beliefs about others' behaviour.

18 See Guesnerie (1988).

19 For the analysis of a dynamic game with a ratchet effect between the government and the firm see Freixas, Guesnerie and Tirole (1985).

20 Cf., for instance, Pryor (1973).

21 *Abusus* implies, of course, the ability to sell or exchange the share of rights.

22 See Alchian (1969); Demsetz (1967); Furubotn and Pejovich (1972); Alchian and Demsetz (1972). Of course, private property rights are never absolute: they are always restricted by the political order of the society (see Nutter 1974).

23 The issue has been stated first by Berle and Means (1932). One of the most illuminating contributions is Jensen and Meckling (1976).

24 See Manne (1965).

25 Such an approach is similar to Hirschman's search for hidden rationalities. Studying the Colombian reality, instead of stressing various disequilibria and deviations from the path followed by industrial countries, Hirschman looked for possible rational uses of shortages, bottle-necks, unbalanced growth, and so on. He looked for processes that did work although in an unfamiliar way (see Hirschman 1986).

26 See Fama (1980).

27 Cf. M. Marchand, P. Pestieau and H. Tulkien (1984).

28 For instance Yarrow (1986); Vickers and Yarrow (1988).

29 See Vickers and Yarrow (1988).

30 This goes back to Schumpeter's idea of creative destruction (see also Alchian 1950; Nelson 1981).

31 For an excellent presentation see Pelikan (1985).

32 See Forte (1982).

33 See Nuti (1988); Tardos (1986).

BIBLIOGRAPHY

Alchian, A.A (1950) 'Uncertainty, evolution and economic theory', *Journal of Political Economy* 58(3).

Alchian, A.A. (1969) 'Corporate management and property rights', in H. Manne (ed.) *Economic Policy and Regulation of Corporate Securities*, Washington, DC, American Enterprise Institute.

Alchian, A.A. and Demsetz, H. (1972) 'Production, information costs and economic organization', *American Economic Review* 62, 777–95.

Berle, A. and Means, G.C. (1932) *The Modern Corporation and Private Property*, New York, Macmillan.

Buchanan, J.M. (1987) 'The constitution of economic policy', *American Economic*

Review 77(3).

Buchanan, J.M. and Tullock, G. (1962) *The Calculus of Consent*, Ann Arbor, Mich., University of Michigan Press.

Caillaud, B., Guesnerie, R., Rey, P. and Tirole, J. (1988) 'Government intervention in production and incentives theory: a review of recent contributions', *Rand Journal of Economics* 19(1).

Coase, R.H. (1937) 'The nature of the firm', *Economica* 4, 386–405.

Demsetz, H. (1967) 'Toward a theory of property rights', *American Economic Review* 57, 350.

Demsetz, H. (1969) 'Information and efficiency: another viewpoint', *Journal of Law and Economics* 12.

Fama, E. (1980) 'Agency problems and the theory of the firm', *Journal of Political Economy* 88, 288–306.

Fiorina, M. and Noll, R. (1978) 'Voters, bureaucrats, and legislators: a rational choice perspective on the growth of bureaucracy', *Journal of Public Economics* 9.

Forte, F. (1982) 'The law of selection in the public economy as compared to the market economy', *Public Finance* 37(2).

Freixas, X., Guesnerie, R. and Tirole, J. (1985) 'Planning under incomplete information and the ratchet effect', *Review of Economic Studies* 52(2).

Frey, B.S. (1978) *Modern Political Economy*, London, Martin Robertson.

Furubotn, E. and Pejovich, S. (1972) 'Property rights and economic theory: a survey of recent literature', *Journal of Economic Literature* 10.

Granick, D. (1987) *Job Rights in the Soviet Union: Their Consequences*, Cambridge: Cambridge University Press.

Grosfeld, I. (1986) 'Endogenous planners and the investment cycle in the centrally planned economies', *Comparative Economic Studies* 28(1).

Grosfeld, I. (1987) 'Modeling planners' investment behavior: Poland, 1956–1981', *Journal of Comparative Economics* 11(3).

Groves, T. (1973) 'Incentives in teams', *Econometrica* 41.

Guesnerie, R. (1988) 'Regulation as an adverse selection problem', *European Economic Review* 32(2–3).

Hewett, E.A. (1988) *Reforming the Soviet Economy*, Washington, DC, The Brookings Institution.

Hirschman, A.O. (1986) *Rival Views of Market Society*, New York, Viking.

Jensen, M.C. and Meckling, W.H. (1976) 'Theory of the firm: managerial behavior, agency cost and ownership structure', *Journal of Financial Economics* 3.

Kornai, J. (1980) *Economics of Shortage*, Amsterdam, North Holland.

Kornai, J. (1983) 'The health of nations. Reflection on the analogy between the medical sciences and economics', *Kyklos* 36.

Kornai, J. (1986) 'The Hungarian reform process: visions, hopes, and reality', *Journal of Economic Literature* 24, 1687–737.

Laffont, J.J. and Maskin, E. (1982) 'The theory of incentives: an overview', in W. Hildenbrand (ed.) *Advances in Economic Theory*, Cambridge, Cambridge University Press.

Lavoie, D. (1986) 'The market as a procedure for discovery and conveyance of inarticulate knowledge', *Comparative Economic Studies* 28(1), 1–19.

Lindbeck, A. (1976) 'A stabilization policy in open economies with endogenous politicians', *American Economic Review* 66(2).

Loeb, M. and Magat, W. (1978) 'Success indicators in the Soviet Union: the problem of incentives and efficient allocation', *American Economic Review* 68(1).

Lundberg, E. (1962) *Instability and Economic Growth*, New Haven, Conn. and London, Yale University Press.

McKenzie, R.B. (1984) 'Introduction', in R.B. McKenzie (ed.) *Constitutional*

Economics, Lexington, Mass. and Toronto, Lexington Books.

Manne, H.G. (1965) 'Mergers and the market for corporate control', *Journal of Public Economics* 73, 110–20.

Marchand, M., Pestieau, P. and Tulkens, H. (1984) 'The performance of public enterprises: normative, positive and empirical issues', in M. Marchand, P. Pestieau, and H. Tulkens (eds) *The Performance of Public Enterprises*, Amsterdam, North Holland.

Mougeot, M. (1988) 'Les mécanismes incitatifs dans une économie centralement planifiée', *Revue d'Etudes Comparatives Est–Ouest* 19(1).

Nelson, R.R. (1981) 'Assessing private enterprise: an exegesis of tangled doctrine', *Bell Journal of Economics* 12(1), 93–111.

Niskanen, W. (1971) *Bureaucracy and Representative Government*, Chicago, Aldine-Atherton.

Nordhaus, W.D. (1975) 'The political business cycle', *Review of Economic Studies* 62(2).

North, D.C. and Thomas, R.P. (1973) *The Rise of the Western World: A New Economic History*, Cambridge, Cambridge University Press.

Nuti, D.M. (1988) 'Competitive valuation and efficiency of capital investment in the socialist economy', *European Economic Review* 32(2–3).

Nutter, G. Warren (1974) 'Markets without property: a grand illusion', in E. Furubotn and S. Pejovich (eds) *The Economics of Property Rights*, Cambridge, Mass., Ballinger.

Pelikan, P. (1985) 'The formation of incentive mechanism in different economic systems', The Industrial Institute for Economic and Social Research, mimeo.

Picard, P. (1987) 'On the design of incentive scheme under moral hazard and adverse selection', *Journal of Public Economics* 33.

Polanyi, M. (1967) *The Tacit Dimension*, Garden City, NY, Doubleday Anchor.

Pryor, F.L. (1973) *Property and Industrial Organization in Communist and Capitalist Nations*, Bloomington and London, Indiana University Press.

Schroeder, G.E. (1988) 'Property rights issues in economic reforms in socialist countries', *Studies in Comparative Communism* 21(2), 175–88.

Tardos, M. (1986) 'The conditions for developing a regulated market', *Acta Oeconomica* 36(1–2), 67–89.

Vickers, J. and Yarrow, G. (1988) *Privatization: An Economic Analysis*, Cambridge, Mass. and London, The MIT Press.

Ward, B. (1958) 'The firm in Illyria, market syndicalism', *American Economic Review* 48(4), 566–89.

Williamson, O.E. (1975) *Markets and Hierarchies: Analysis and Anti-trust Implications*, New York, The Free Press.

Wolf, C. (1979) 'A theory of nonmarket failure', *Journal of Law and Economics* 22.

Yarrow, G. (1986) 'Privatization in theory and practice', *Economic Policy* 2.

5 Some institutional failures of socialist market economies – a dynamic market and institutional theory approach

Helmut Leipold

STATIC VERSUS DYNAMIC THEORETICAL APPROACHES

In socialist countries several attempts were made to combine market relations with socialist ownership. The emerging systems can be labelled as socialist market economies, a synthesis of plan and market or a decentralized socialist economic system. When such systems exist over a longer period, as for example, in Hungary or Yugoslavia, the economic results do not line up to the expectations of reformers. Characteristic deficiencies are low levels of innovation, labour productivity and international competitiveness as well as relatively high inflation rates. These results indicate imperfections of market competition in these systems.

There is no consensus in diagnosing the causes of these imperfections. One cause may be the lack of an adequate theory of a socialist market economy. Most theories are slight modifications of the neo-classical market theory. One deficiency of this type of theory is its static nature; another one is the absence of any institutional dimension to the economic processes. Basic assumptions are, for example, a given number of existing markets and firms, where all data, such as demand and costs, are known. Hence, the only problem is to find the optimal market equilibrium, which includes the maximization of utility within the households and of profit within the firms (cf. Lange 1938). In reality neither the institutional structure of enterprises or markets, nor the economic data are given, at least not within a workable and competitive market society. Hence, the adoption of the static neo-classical theory cannot provide a sufficient explanation of economic reality. What is needed is a dynamic theory of markets and a dynamic theory of institutional change, with special reference to the institutional peculiarities of socialist societies.

The necessity of a dynamic theory has already been stressed by Mises and Hayek in the socialist calculation debate. According to Mises 'the problem of economic calculation is of economic dynamics, it is no problem of economic statics' (1936:139). Mises specified the dynamic problem as one of 'dissolving, extending, transforming, and limiting existing undertakings, and establishing new undertakings' (Mises 1936:215).

Although Mises stressed the importance of a dynamic theory of markets and institutional change, he did not offer a sufficient explanation for it. Presently, modern economics provide such dynamic theories. The most important proponents of a dynamic theory of market competition were Schumpeter (1964) and Clark (1961). Their works paved the way for the construction of a dynamic market theory. An excellent example is the *General Market Theory* of the German economist Heuss (1965). Together with the 'new institutional economics', such as the theory of property rights or the transaction costs economics, the general market theory offers a fruitful theoretical base for analysing the problems and peculiarities of a socialist market economy (cf. Leipold 1983a).

DYNAMIC MARKET THEORY AND INSTITUTIONAL CHANGE

The general market theory of Heuss integrates the product life-cycle theory, along with various types of entrepreneurs, taking into consideration different market structures and changing degrees of market uncertainty. The integration of these theoretical elements assumes the development of the market processes reflecting the activities of diverse types of entrepreneurs. Heuss divides these entrepreneurs into innovative and conservative types. Innovative types are creative, thereby enforcing new products and new organizational arrangements, incorporating character-istics similar to the Schumpeterian entrepreneur (cf. Schumpeter 1964). Conservative entrepreneurs on the other hand, distinguish themselves by an inflexible attitude to external pressures.

The starting point of every market is the innovation of a new product by a pioneer entrepreneur, who establishes the experimental phase. This entrepreneur may, but need not be, identical with the inventor. Innovation is essentially an entrepreneurial task. Since neither demand nor supply conditions are given, the innovation resembles an open-end experiment. The establishing of new, or the extending of given, productive and marketing capacities entails high economic risks. Therefore it is difficult to activate or tap the requisite venture capital. To stimulate ventures, investors as well as pioneer entrepreneurs must be paid a risk premium. Generally, innovations require a readiness to take risks, an entrepreneurial spirit and creativity. Concerning the institutional environment, decentralized rights of establishing or reorganizing firms and of allocating venture capital are necessary.

If the product innovation has been successful, the experimental phase is then followed by the expansion phase, that is, by an expansion of saales turnover. Although this expansion provides the pioneer entrepreneur a chance to realize profits, further market development involves high economic and technical risks. There is still uncertainty on the demand-side as well as on the supply-side. For example, production techniques are not fixed, so costs are not given. Technical improvements have to be discovered and the development of demand remains uncertain. A further source of uncertainty is the market entry of new competitors. According to Heuss (1965), the spontaneously imitating type of entrepreneur appears, attracted by the expanding market with profit opportunities. Product modifications and/or licences are ways to imitate the new product and to participate in the market. Technical improvements enable firms to reduce costs which in turn lowers the prices. The degree of price reduction depends on the degree of competition. One of the most important preconditions is free market entry, which requires rights to market-oriented allocation of resources, that is, of labour and capital. The expansion phase is not only the field of intensive product and price competition, but also of institutional innovation. New organizational structures of production and marketing have to be invented and tested.

With time, demand and supply conditions stabilize and the market enters into its mature phase. Market turnover now corresponds to the average growth rate of the whole economy. Since technological and product improvements are largely exhausted, the margin for cost and price reductions is rather limited. Competition shifts increasingly from prices to other variables, such as advertising, product modifications, packaging, marketing services, and financing. In this phase innovative entrepreneurs retire and conservative ones become dominant.

Next, the market enters into the stagnation phase. Due to rising costs on the one hand and low price and income elasticity of demand on the other, profit opportunities diminish. This situation creates incentives to restrict competition by ways of concentration, cartels, or other forms. It is now the task of anti-trust policy to prevent these practices.

Finally, demand diminishes and the market thus enters its declining phase. In this phase, the reduction of production capacities is inevitable, which leads to bankruptcies and the elimination of some existing firms.

The dynamic market theory stresses the significance and role of the competitive entrepreneurial activities in the development of market processes. Innovation, imitation and diffusion of new products are necessarily accompanied by the creation, change and adaptation of new organizational structures of production, contract, employment and trade or credit relations. These institutional changes cannot be separated from market processes (cf. also Nelson and Winter 1982). In both cases, the existing institutional framework determines the dynamics of the market structure and market performance.

The institutional framework consists of property rights and organizational arrangements, emerging from these rights. In accordance with the economics of property rights (Furubotn and Pejovich 1974), institutional change can be interpreted as a change of property rights structures. In addition, transaction costs represent an ever present force influencing the choices and changes of institutions. Transaction costs consist of the costs incurred by individuals defining, negotiating, and enforcing resource rights and organizing transactions of these rights. According to Coase, every institution operates with these costs. In his seminal article, 'The nature of the firm', Coase (1937) tried to answer the question why transactions are removed from markets as a mode of bilateral exchange and organized within a firm. He stated that because significant costs are attached to markets, firms emerge to reduce costs. Therefore the firm is only another way to organize economic transactions under a contractual arrangement that differs from ordinary markets (cf. Cheung 1983). The firm incorporates more hierarchical and unspecified contractual relations between the entrepreneur on the one hand, and the owners of specific resources on the other. Dynamic market processes demand the entrepreneur to decide whether to organize transactions through markets or within firms. This decision is as important as the innovation or imitation of products (cf. Leipold and Schüller 1986).

Transaction costs are higher when institutional options, available to entrepreneurial decisions, are fewer, and when incentives to find efficient solutions are weaker. Both conditions depend on the structure of property rights. A system of exclusive and transferable property rights offers a wide range of institutional choices; it ensures contractual freedom and the decision whether or not to sell rights. Private stock companies and capital markets are two examples explaining the simple logic behind this theory.

In terms of the theory of agency, stockholders as principals engage managers as agents. Because both principals and agents are self-interested actors and because it is costly to monitor the behaviour of agents, it is most likely that the interests of managers will not comply with those of the owners. Additionally, small stockholders in large corporations have little influence over management. However, they have the right to sell their shares when displeased with managerial performance. This gives the managers an incentive to control costs and to be innovative. Increased costs or reduced market shares come at the expense of profitability, acting as a condition to attract capital. The right to sell shares of corporate stocks creates capital markets which generate information for many self-interested owners as to the performance of firms. Stock markets, for example, bundle different expectations of owners about future profits and reflect the capitalized value of current managerial decisions. This institution reduces the power of managers to pursue their own objectives at the expense of profits. Another monitoring effect stems from the market of corporate control, the transfer of control from less efficient management to managers who utilize the assets more efficiently. Finally, the market for managers provides an additional control institution (cf. Jensen and Meckling 1976; Fama 1980; Leipold 1983b).

These spontaneously-grown institutions operate only within an institutional framework providing exclusive and transferable property rights.

In the absence of these rights the transaction costs of monitoring managers or other agents increase significantly.

The brief survey of the interrelations between the development of market processes, the role of entrepreneurs and the evolution of institutional devices to reduce transaction costs, leads to the conclusion that a competitive and efficient market order cannot be assumed as given or as self-evident. It is rather the result of a complex interplay between entrepreneurial activities and a related structure of property rights. A workable market order can only be achieved if an economic system provides sufficient rights and incentives for economic activity.

On the whole, both dynamic market theory and institutional economics affirm the thesis of Mises that the key problem of an efficient economy is one of establishing, extending, transforming or limiting enterprises, or – abstractly formulated – institutions. To what extent do socialist reform concepts meet these requirements?

INSTITUTIONAL RESTRICTIONS TO MARKET COMPETITION

The following reflections on the institutional peculiarities of socialist market systems refer to systems that really existed, such as Hungary or Yugoslavia, as well as to theoretical concepts such as the reform proposals of the Polish Economic Society (cf. Delhaes and Peterhoff 1981) or the *Feasible Socialism* of Nove (1983). The basic institutional conditions can be summarized as follows:

1 The state organs, which are dominated by the Communist Party, are responsible for the elaboration of central plans. These plans determine the macroeconomic and structural development and are implemented by indirect methods. A more or less extensive bureaucratic apparatus is responsible for the elaboration, implementation and control of the plans.
2 The enterprises have decision-making autonomy. They are legally categorized into socialist and small-scale private enterprises.
3 There are two basic forms of socialist enterprises: state-owned and socially-owned self-managed enterprises. The key feature of state-owned enterprises is the division of ownership rights between state organs, which retain the basic disposal over assets (establishing, merging, dissolving firms), and the enterprises. The alternative is the self-governed enterprise, which represents a form of group ownership. The co-operative enterprise representing a third form, lies somewhere in between the two basic forms. A common feature of both basic forms is the lack of exclusive and transferable property rights, and thus the absence of capital and stock markets.
4 Private enterprises are permitted, but they are subject to state control and clearly-defined limits such as the number of employees or the value of capital assets.

5 The markets are divided into a controlled-price sector and a freely-negotiated price sector, corresponding to the degree of monopoly power and competition.
6 The banking system is also socialized, either in the form of state ownership (as in Hungary) or of group ownership (as in Yugoslavia).
7 Foreign trade is no longer a state monopoly, but it is still extensively regulated. The entry of potential foreign suppliers is restricted. Only special forms, such as joint ventures, are allowed.

What are the consequences of this institutional framework for the market processes? Our analysis focuses on the incentives and limits of establishing new enterprises or taking over existing enterprises in response to market pressure.

As stated, the basic rights of disposing over state-owned assets belong to state organs. These organs can exert their rights of establishing, reorganizing or dissolving enterprises either directly or indirectly through credit management, licensing or other monitoring forms.

In each case, the economic theory of bureaucracy (Roppel 1979) provides an explanation of the characteristic motives. According to this theory, the official state bureaucrats are not interested in establishing and controlling a great number of independent enterprises. They prefer instead to control larger and fewer enterprises. This structure reduces transaction or monitoring costs of control over management in state-owned firms. State bureaucrats are furthermore not interested in maximizing profits. Rather, they tend to maximize their own bureaucratic utility function. In the case of sectoral organs, such as branch ministries, the expansion of branch turnover is a characteristic goal. In the case of regional organs, the main goal may be the expansion of employment or investments within the region. In any event, capital allocation is not motivated by profitability that would involve cost-reducing considerations. This is one reason why state-owned enterprises have higher costs and lower labour productivity than profit-oriented private enterprises (for empirical evidence, see Blankart 1980: 153 ff). Innovation is also weaker, because the maximization of enterprise or branch turnover can be realized merely by using approved technologies and selling market-approved products. This strategy is facilitated by the lack of competition, and also by state support in the case of losses. The managers of state-owned enterprises have an interest in keeping up paternalistic relations with state organs, since such relations secure employment, financial subsidies and other regulative privileges.

The managers, furthermore, are not efficiently controlled by the capital market, especially by the stock market or the market of corporate control. None of these monitoring forms operate efficiently within the state-owned sector, since the absence of exclusive and transferable property rights and the restrictions on the development of a capital market. As a consequence, there are no effective incentives and controls within the state-owned sector for innovation or imitation of new products or new institutional structures. Because state organs have no motivation to establish or reorganize new enterprises, there exist only weak impulses for the development of new markets. Hence, competition is stifled and cannot yield the desired economic results. The extent to which it is stifled is proportional to the extent of the state-owned sector and the competence of state bureaucracy.

As regards Yugoslavia and the self-managed enterprises, it can be said that the basic principles of self-management also provide no efficient incentives to stimulate competitive market processes. The most important obstacle is the weak incentive to establish independent enterprises (cf. Leipold 1988). Legally permissible founders of self-managed enterprises are state or government units on different levels, existing enterprises, groups of individuals and single entrepreneurs. When self-managed enterprises are founded by state organs or governmental units, the incentives and limitations are similar to those of state-owned enterprises. Concerning the interests of existing enterprises or individuals, self-management seems to be a restrictive condition. According to its principles, there exists a forced separation between founders on the one hand, and employees as subsequent decision-makers on the other, since the founders are not entitled to control their investments. Once an enterprise is founded, decision-making competences must be transferred to the collective of employees according to the one man – one vote – principle. This means that the collective, through its elected body, the worker's council and the director, takes all decisions, such as the rate of output and investment, the level of employment and the distribution of income. The restriction of some or all of these rights by a founder or an entrepreneur would be equivalent to a re-establishment of exclusive property rights or capitalist principles, and thus an attenuation of self-management and socially-owned property rights.

These conditions discourage potential founders from establishing independent firms. The prospect of having to share the management of a newly-founded enterprise with a collective, which has not shared in the strenuous founding activities and the related risk, will necessarily inhibit the dynamics of foundation. This becomes obvious in the case of a private founder. A private entrepreneur has strong incentives for keeping the size of his enterprise below the limit of conversion into self-management. Even generous limits inhibit the growth of small-scale enterprises, that is, of successful and innovative firms in the experimental and in the expansion phase of the market.

Similar limitations apply to the existing self-managed enterprises that are establishing new ones. The compulsory principle of sharing the management rights and the potential income of newly-established firms, or even of capital investments within the firm, with the collective of new employees deters the existing collective from initiating such activities. This principle stimulates either discriminating practices toward the new employees, or, if this is not possible, labour-saving capital investments within the existing enterprise.

The deeper source of such practices is evident within the existing structure of property rights, which does not allow exclusive and alienable shares of the assets with corresponding rights to use and to appropriate returns from them. The introduction of such exclusive property rights would inevitably lead to a modification of the self-management principle towards more or less hierarchical relations between the owners or founders, on the one hand, and dependent employees with fixed salaries, on the other. As long as the basic principles of self-management and socialist ownership remain untouched, the foundation and evolution of independent and flexible economic units will be hampered.

The consequences for the dynamics of market structures and competition are similar to those already mentioned for the state-owned enterprises. The establishment and the growth of efficient small-scale enterprises are hampered and large enterprises dominate the market. The resulting negative effects on competition, innovation and prices are evident.

As long as socialist property rights dominate, markets tend to stagnate longer. Within this extented stagnation phase, monopolistic and quasi-monopolistic market structures prevail. The traditional price theory explains that monopolists are able to maximize their profits by supplying smaller quantities of goods at higher prices in comparison to competitive market structures. Institutional economics and the consideration of transaction costs provide further evidence that state or socially-owned enterprises operate with higher costs compared to private enterprises. Under the condition of socialist property rights, the collective of owners, that is, state organs or employees, do not feel the full benefits and costs of managerial decisions. This is one reason why the incentives to control managerial behaviour, and especially costs, are weak. Second, control efforts are costly. Since owners cannot acquire exclusive shares of public-owned enterprises, and/or cannot sell their shares, the spontaneous evolution of capital markets as a means of the indirect monitoring of management behaviour is inhibited. The remaining possibilities of direct managerial control involve high costs of detecting, monitoring and delimiting shirking and other inefficient managerial practices. In addition, direct control has to deal with the free-rider problem, where everyone seeks to enjoy the benefits of efficient management, although only a few are prepared to contribute to the related control efforts.

The structure of socialist property rights and the emerging organizational arrangements to control management provide not only weak incentives, but also high costs of disciplining the behaviour of managers. The non-competitive attitudes of managers also effect the lower levels within the firm, resulting in low productivity and high costs. The lack of market competition adds to these economic deficiencies. The combination of economic and political interests characterizing socialist ownership especially contribute to the domination of monopolistic market structures which offer rent-seeking opportunities to the enterprises (cf. Tollison 1982). An obvious example is the subsidizing of unprofitable enterprises. It is common to legitimate such practices as a means to ensure continual employment. In reality, this is a comfortable method to secure a permissive environment for rent-seeking at the expense of consumer interests. Within this environment, incentives to improve efficiency and profitability are small, due to the fact that bankruptcies are not allowed.

The combination of economic and political interests and the resulting competitive shortcomings form a vicious circle. Poor economic conditions, such as inflation and low real incomes, nurture discontent, adding to a strong resistance towards reform policies and creating a demand for additional market regulations. The bureaucratic interference in the market mechanism has unintended consequences which are well-known and which create additional intervention. The state bureaucracy has an elementary interest in regulating markets, since it makes bureaucracy both indispensable and strengthens its economic and political role. As the theory of economic regulation shows, regulation normally leads to an interplay between regulatory agencies and special enterprise interests. Both sides gain by it: the regulation secures jobs and the influence of the bureaucrats; for managers it provides soft budget-constraints that are much more comfortable than the competitive challenge (cf. Stigler 1971; Peltzman 1976).

The interplay between state bureaucracy and the enterprises further weakens market competition. Market phenomena, such as prices, costs, incomes, profits or losses cannot be interpreted as objective indicators of market performance. As the Hungarian, Yugoslav or Chinese experiences show, the vicious circle between deficient competition and intensive regulation cannot be broken by partial institutional reforms. The dissolution of some ministries or state agencies, the breaking up of trusts or large enterprises, the loosening of the foreign trade monopoly of the state, the introduction of various new price systems or the reorganization of the banking and credit system while important, are insufficient to stimulate innovation and competition in socialist market economies.

Compared to these measures, the promotion of more exclusive and transferable property rights, that is, of private activities, co-operative enterprises or leasing, would be more effective.

CONSEQUENCES FOR THE REFORM POLICY

The dynamic market theory and institutional economics provide a theoretical foundation, identifying the institutional failures of socialist economies, which impede the development of a competitive market order and also indicate necessary reform measures. It can be concluded that the idea of a workable market economy requires a broad scope of entrepreneurial freedom and spirit, full autonomy of enterprises, especially of capital formation and the creation of proper economic interests, which include interests in the profitability of firms.

The structure of socialist property rights cannot satisfy these require-ments. Under the condition of state or socially-owned property rights, political interests influence the economic system and tend to dominate the development of market processes and of institutional choice. The combination of political and economic interests evolving out of socialist property rights, represents the most crucial institutional failure of reformed socialist economies. As long as this combination exists, the implementation of reform ideas will remain extremely difficult. The introduction and development of a competitive market order and a pluralistic ownership structure must result in a redistribution of vested incomes, rents and privileges. Hence, privileged groups try to resist or to modify economic reforms. It is obvious in the case of Communist Party officials and state bureaucrats that these negative attitudes towards reform ideas exist. Managers are also possible victims of reforms. They are forced to bear more risk and to behave more actively. The rewards, however, remain limited. When controls within state or self-managed enterprises are strengthened, workers are also added to the list of possible victims. They may be unable to act as free riders and engage in second economy activities. Lastly, they are faced with a new phenomenon, unemployment.

The path of economic reform is not straight. It involves high costs of institutional change. Taking into account the vested interests, the introduction of more exclusive and transferable property rights seems to be the most promising measure to implement economic reform. This adds to the reduction of state involvement in the economic processes, ensuring contractual freedom as a prerequisite to stimulate entrepreneurial activity and institutional change.

Above all, the creation of a sort of capital market – however imperfect – seems to be necessary. The functions of state organs and the state budget must be taken-over in commanding capital formation and controlling managerial performance. This also requires changes in the banking system, which has to operate on a commercial basis, and a high degree of openness to the world market.

Epilogue

Recent developments in Hungary, Yugoslavia and other socialist countries support our analysis. The demise of socialism provides ample evidence that institutions do matter. The failure of both centrally planned as well as of socialist market systems demonstrates the economic impor-tance and impact of property rights. The transformation of all socialist economies into a workable market economy demands a transformation of ownership rights. Liberalization of prices, trade, exchange rates and a prudent stabilization policy are also necessary steps. For crossing the Rubicon towards a functioning market economy, however, a fast and mas-sive policy of privatization enjoys priority.

BIBLIOGRAPHY

Blankart, Ch. B. (1980) *Ökonomie der öffentlichen Unternehmen*, München, Vahlen Verlag.

Clark, J. M. (1961) *Competition as a Dynamic Process*, Washington, DC, The Brookings Institution.

Coase, R. (1937) 'The nature of the firm', *Economica* 4, 386–405.

Cheung, St N. S. (1983) 'The contractual nature of the firm', *Journal of Law and Economics* 26, 1–21.

Delhaes, K. V. and Peterhoff, R. (1981) *Zur Reform der Polnischen Wirtschaftsordnung. Arbeitsberichte zum Systemvergleich*, 1, Forschungsstelle zum Vergleich wirtschaftlicher Lenkungs systeme, Marburg/L.

Fama, E. F. (1980) 'Agency problems and the theory of the firm', *Journal of Political Economy* 88, 288–306.

Furubotn, E. G. and Pejovich, S. (eds) (1974) *The Economics of Property Rights*, Cambridge, Mass., Ballinger Publishing Company.

Heuss, E. (1965) *Allgemeine Markttheorie*, Tübingen and Zürich, J.C.B. Mohr.

Jensen, M. G. and Meckling, N. H. (1976) 'Theory of the firm: managerial behaviour, agency costs and ownership structure', *Journal of Financial Economics* 3, 305–60.

Lange, O. (1938) 'On the economic theory of socialism', in B. J. Lippincott (ed.) *On the Economic Theory of Socialism*, Minneapolis, University of Minnesota Press, 55–120.

Leipold, H. (1983a) 'Der Einfluß von Property Rights auf hierarchische und marktliche Transaktionen in sozialistischen Wirtschaftssystemen', in A. Schüller (ed.) *Property Rights und ökonomische Theorie*, München, Vahlen Verlag, 185–218.

Leipold, H. (1983b) *Eigentum und wirtschaftlich-technischer Fortschritt*, Köln, Otto A. Friedrich-Kuratorium.

Leipold, H. (1988) *Wirtschafts- und Gesellschaftssysteme im Vergleich*, 5th edn, Stuttgart, Gustav Fischer Verlag.

Leipold, H. and Schüller, A. (1986) 'Unternehmen und Wirtschaftsrechnung: Zu einem integrierten dynamischen Erklärungsansatz', in H. Leipold and A. Schüller (eds), *Zur Interdependenz von Unternehmens- und Wirtschaftsordnung*, Stuttgart and New York, Gustav Fischer Verlag, 3–40.

Mises, L. von (1936) *Socialism*, New Haven, Yale University Press (German original published in 1922).

Nelson, R. and Winter, S. (1982) *An Evolutionary Theory of Economic Change*, Cambridge, Mass., Belknap.

Nove, A. (1983) *The economics of feasible socialism*, London, Allen & Unwin.

Peltzman, S. (1976) 'Toward a more general theory of regulation', *Journal of Law and Economics* 19, 211–40.

Roppel, U. (1979) *Ökonomische Theorie der Bürokratie*, Freiburg i. Br., Haufe.

Schumpeter, J. A. (1964) *Die Theorie der wirtschaftlichen Entwicklung*, 6th edn, Berlin, Duncker & Humblot.

Stigler, G. J. (1971) 'The theory of economic regulation', *Bell Journal of Economics and Management Science* 2, 3–21.

Tollison, R. D. (1982) 'Rent seeking: a survey', *Kyklos* 35, 575–602.

6 On firms, hierarchies and economic reforms

John Michael Montias

My remarks are focused on the partially reformed Soviet-type economy to which Gregory Grossman has given the apposite name of half-way house. In this economy, described in further detail in the first section, the hierarchy that transmits orders from the centre all the way down to the lower levels is still intact, but the centre no longer has the power to impose its unchallenged will on producing-enterprises: Bargaining on output levels and input allotments goes on at all times between 'higher-ups' and their subordinates, who wield more countervailing power than in the classical Soviet or East European economy of the 1950s. Orders from the centre, usually based on imperfect and distorted information, are often disregarded or carried out in a manner more convenient to the subordinate than pursuant to the centre's goals and preferences. Producers' prices systematically deviate from relative scarcities *and* fail to equilibrate supply and demand in producers' markets. I will concentrate on the role of the enterprise in this mixed system and on the possibility of substituting 'indirect control' for 'petty tutelage of enterprises' in guiding the economy from the centre.

FIRMS

There has been an upsurge in interest lately, prompted in part by the work of Oliver Williamson, on the Janus-headed relation of firm managers, in partially-reformed economies, towards their hierarchic superiors and towards client-firms constituting their 'market'. Among other questions, students of this problem ask themselves, which costs to society, as they are assessed by hierarchic superiors, are likely to be 'internalized' by firms in such economies, and which are not?

'Costs to society' here are meant to cover far more than the harmful impact of production on the environment or the health of employees. They may comprise the socially-undesirable effects of unemployment or even of excessive disparities in wages. Thus state-owned firms, forced to carry out government employment or incomes policies, may have to internalize the costs associated with these policies, including the employment of workers exceeding their needs or restraints on wage and salary differences despite their efficiency-promoting incentive properties. Firms may even, in case of public disorders, have to fulfil security functions which elsewhere would be carried out by specialized organs. It is ironic that as firms in socialist economies undergoing reform are gradually allowed to unburden themselves of some of these social costs, their counterparts in the United States and Europe are expected to bear more of them: from keeping redundant workers to hiring handicapped employees at wages exceeding their expected contribution.

David Granick, in a recent essay (1988), argues that property rights in the 'existing job' and in 'equal earnings for equal work', which are institutionalized in the rules to which firms are subject, are among the most serious impediments to reform in the economies of Eastern Europe. To the extent that firms are obliged to implement governmental full-employment policies, he is probably right as far as job tenure is concerned. But there is such a clear efficiency gain in guaranteeing every worker *some* job (in one or another firm) over guaranteeing him his *existing* job that I cannot believe enlightened reformers would stop short of exposing workers to the possibility of dismissal if they could ensure them jobs elsewhere. The rub here is that a reforming economy may not have enough forward momentum to provide for full employment altogether. The enormous social waste in Yugoslavia associated with the overstaffing of worker-managed firms, under the prodding of local authorities, is perhaps an unavoidable consequence of the output stagnation of recent years, and of the associated failure to create new firms. As to the institutionalization of 'equal pay for equal work', I can see little evidence for it. Haven't workers in heavy industry earned quasi-rents in many 'socialist' countries for decades? The Hungarian economist, Tamás Bauer, wrote the following words on this issue:

> Any reasonably observant surveyor of labor relations in Eastern Europe must realize . . . that labor is at least as much subject to market conditions as are the means of production. Wages . . . are important regulators of labor allocation. . . . Branch and wage differentials became particularly evident during the 1950s, the 'heroic' age of industrialization . . . in the practice of the USSR and Hungary.
>
> (Bauer 1984:39)

The point cited by Granick that wages in the Shchekino combinat, where enterprise managers were given a larger measure of autonomy with respect to hiring, firing and wage-setting than in other Soviet firms, only rose 6 per cent more than average between 1966 and 1970 seems to be a very weak reed to hang such a weighty proposition on. In my view, it would be more accurate to say that there have been strong equalitarian values, both among the Communist elites and the population at large in Eastern Europe, that militated against excessive wage differentiation (not motivated by differences in education and training). But unlike legal rights, values are subject to trade-offs. A central question of reform is whether these elites and the population at large are willing, in any given country, to accept perceptible gains in average wages at the expense of greater income differentiation. Even the poorest paid workers may support such an option if it ensures them a rise in *their* wages. (John Rawls, who certainly cannot be faulted for his lack of commitment to income equality, would consider such a trade-off reasonable.)

Granick claims that the combination of rights 'in the existing job', and in 'equal earnings for equal work' would appear to dictate the organization of the economy along hierarchical lines . . . rather than into a system dominated by horizontal communication', of a market or quasi-market variety. The reason is that the authorities, in order to give these rights full effect, must (1) retain centralized controls on firm financing, and (2) appoint most of the managers. The first is needed to allow the state to subsidize firms in financial difficulties that would otherwise be forced to dismiss their workers (soft-budget constraint). The second because otherwise the state could not guarantee the principle of 'equal pay for equal work'. These arguments are fairly compelling, but they depend critically on their premises: that the right to a job in a particular factory is so inviolable that no reform can weaken it and that the principle of 'equal pay for equal work' will be protected come what may. The second premise was probably not valid for any economy of Eastern Europe or for China. The first might be valid in several centrally-planned economies, but it has been eroded in the Soviet Union and elsewhere as the Communist elites and the population at large became more conscious of the inefficiencies it engendered.

Before delving further into the 'ins' and the 'outs' of socialist firms, I need to make a few general propositions on the nature of the pre-reform systems and of the place that firms occupied in the decision-making structure.

We have been talking for over thirty years about 'overcentralization' of the centrally-planned economies (for example, Kornai 1959). But we would not necessarily agree on how centralized they really were. Raymond Powell (1977), Ed Dolan (1970) and others have shown that the pre-reform Soviet economic system was far more decentralized in practice than might appear from standard descriptions, by reason of the impossibility of micro-managing a complex economy from the centre. A close inspection of the Polish débâcle of the mid- to late 1970s reveals that the excessive bargaining power of ministries – intermediate organs in the hierarchy – and the incapacity of the 'centre' (the Planning Commission) to enforce its co-ordinating decisions had much to do with the deterioration of the economic system in these years (Montias 1982).

In my view, any analysis of the place of firms in reformed systems must begin from a recognition of the following basic features of all centrally-planned economies that have evolved from the original Stalinist model: (1) At each level of the hierarchy, which plans and manages the economy, bargaining takes place with regard to the tasks that subordinates are expected to perform and the resources that will be assigned to them to carry out these tasks; (2) the information available at successively higher levels of the hierarchy is more aggregated and distorted; (3) because subordinates have more detailed information about the environment than do their superiors; they have a bargaining advantage that they can use to elicit easier tasks and/or pry out more resources to fulfil them; (4) the extent of this opportunistic behaviour (to use Oliver Williamson's terminology) depends on elements of the broadly-defined environment in which the hierarchy is embedded, including the ideological cohesion (*esprit de corps*) of its members and their managerial qualities; (5) the partial *de facto* autonomy of subordinates (greater in terms of a finer grid of information than of a coarser nomenclature) may be beneficial or deleterious for the system as a whole, in terms of the preferences of the highest authorities, depending on the incentives motivating subordinates, the degree to which producer prices may diverge from relative scarcities, and the ability of superiors to intervene to check lower-level decisions that seriously diverge from what they may consider desirable.

Certain economic reforms of the moderate type may be regarded as a legitimation of the state of affairs in the pre-reform economy.[1] Their principal beneficial effect may reside in a clearer demarcation of the autonomy sphere of subordinates, with more limited prerogatives of superiors to interfere in their decisions, thus reducing lower-level uncertainty.

If we think of sub-hierarchies (ministries, *glavki*, *Kombinaten*, firms, and so on) as dependent on the centre for the good things of life (financial resources, credits, promotions, perquisites, higher salaries) in the existing system, then we can see how a reform that would sever or even fray these ties may threaten the well-being of the functionaries who run them, unless they can assure themselves access to equivalent benefits. The inability of reforming legislation to guarantee them equivalent benefits may induce lower-level functionaries, including enterprise directors, to press for recentralizing measures. During the 1957–64 period in which a regionalized system superseded the old functional, product-defined, hierarchy in the Soviet Union, complaints emanated from firms that they had become 'orphans', cut off from their lifeline to Moscow.

Oliver Williamson's paradigm forces us to think about the firm as a component part of the hierarchy within which activities go on that are *not* co-ordinated by the centre; it has also impelled us to ask what activities are undertaken 'inside' and what activities are undertaken 'outside' such firms. This is essentially how Sacks poses the problem in a recent essay (1988). My objection to his approach is that it confounds interdependent activities that are assigned to a firm by the hierarchy because this is thought to be the most expedient thing to do and those that are taken up by firms, beyond those initially assigned to it by superiors, because it is to their advantage to do so. The accretion of new production activities to guard against the risk of unreliable deliveries has long been a familiar aspect of the analysis of centrally-planned systems (among many citations of this phenomenon in the literature, see Koopmans and Montias 1971,73). Williamson's approach suggests another reason cited by Sacks (1988): the integration of separable activities reduces the opportunistic exploitation by the parties who formerly ran these activities independently because 'the parties to the transaction are not able to claim for themselves the increased profits that would come from opportunistic behaviour'.[2] The reason, presumably, is that two activities under one 'shell' (to use Sacks's metaphor) will contribute to a joint pay-off that cannot be individually exploited.

Another useful idea, partly due to Williamson, is that information circulates better and is less apt to be distorted among participants covered by a separate shell, again providing that their pay-off is joint, thus attenuating the incentive for each individual to exploit the information he/she may possess for selfish uses. I say 'attenuating' rather than 'eliminating' because individuals always have the option of slacking: the pay-off function in an organization, no matter how few individuals it may comprise, is never fully joint if we include in it such arguments as leisure and an 'easy life'. In fact, the larger the organization with a joint monetary pay-off, the weaker the incentive to contribute to the organization's success for each individual because these incentives are 'diluted', and the more opportunistic behaviour in the form of slacking comes into play. Workers frequently hide their full productive potential from their foremen, who are members of the same sub-organization to which they belong, both in centrally-planned and capitalistic economies. These and other moral-hazard problems explain in part why firms embedded in market economies cannot grow beyond certain bounds (Ben-Ner and Neuberger 1988,6).

For Sacks, the primary reason why there are merged enterprises and industrial associations in the Soviet Union and Eastern Europe is to allow co-ordination of interdependent activities without meddlesome interference (Sacks 1988,2). He lays emphasis on the benefits of integrating sequential activities, on the basis of the principle that efficient sequences under uncertainty cannot be fully planned from the centre. It is better to 'cross each bridge when you come to it' than to follow a rigid sequence, imposed with limited knowledge from above, irrespective of the states of the environment that actually occur. This is a good and valid reason for integrating upstream or downstream activities in a hierarchic unit which can then be co-ordinated on the basis of local, detailed information. However, the argument, which is akin to the one developed some time ago by Herbert Simon for the advantage of hierarchic decision-making in 'The architecture of complexity' (1969), does not really apply to associations made up of firms with the same or a similar production profile. Here we have to resort not to 'bounded rationality', which underpins the above reasoning, but to the 'law of averages' and the experience that may be garnered from observing the behaviour of technologically-related firms in a more or less identical environment. Sacks's argument is also too general to justify the existence of 'firms', at least as the concept is understood by Ben-Ner and Neuberger, since it applies equally well to sequences of interdependent activities at all levels of the hierarchy: not only do firms have such sequences, but ministries, establishments, shops and even intra-firm work groups.

Ben-Ner and Neuberger define a firm as an organization that has (1) legal existence and responsibility, (2) separate financial accounting, and financial responsibility, and (3) some degree of autonomy (Ben-Ner and Neuberger 1988,4). They argue that firms exist in Soviet-type economies, under conditions of uncertainty, bounded rationality, and information impactedness, where controls and monitoring are necessarily imperfect, because it is efficient to have, at some tier in the hierarchy, units with separate boundaries, within the confines of which members internalize the consequences of their actions and can be rewarded for so doing. I am not entirely persuaded by this argument. The US Army is hierarchically structured but has no 'firms'. Responsibility is vested in the commanders of units at each tier (regiment, battalion, company, and so on). The incentive structure – a combination of threats for non-compliance and promotion prospects – is centred on the unit's commander who internalizes the actions of his subordinates. (The quartermaster corps performs production and distribution tasks that are sufficiently similar to those in an economic hierarchy to make the comparison plausible.)

What distinguishes the firm in centrally-planned economies from units at other levels of the hierarchy is that it stands on its own financial bottom (the second of the properties listed by Ben-Ner and Neuberger). The question arises why this may be thought to be an advantage in an economic hierarchy. Here also uncertainty and the limits to information can be invoked. It is useful for superiors in the hierarchy to be able to collect information on the aggregate performance of their subordinates (output or value of tasks performed, net resources consumed, valued at *some* set of prices). This measure is unavailable in a military hierarchy because, for a variety of reasons, the output of units cannot be evaluated. How do you assess the value of ground gained in battle and aggregate it with the value of enemy soldiers killed or taken prisoner? The 'firm' is usually the only unit in the hierarchy where such a net valuation takes place for, if it is made at more than one level (say, the association and the firm or the firm and the establishment), neither the superior nor the inferior unit will be able to micro-manage its affairs autonomously. The superior will intrude in an inefficient manner into the detailed management of its subordinate units. In point of fact, the extension of *khozraschet* to units above the firm in centrally-planned economies has been vexed with problems.

The advantage of having a level of the hierarchy where measures of aggregate perfomance are generated also emerges in the workings of the credit mechanism. Such a mechanism is needed, incidentally, because if firms, or any other units in the hierarchy, had unlimited working capital to finance their inventories, whose level and composition could not be accurately monitored by superiors, they would be under no pressure to keep them under control and the performance of the entire economy would deteriorate. Given the fact that inventories are frequently of a seasonal nature and are affected by unpredictable changes in the environment, short-term crediting decisions cannot be taken centrally. It makes eminent sense, in my view, to have local branches of the mono-bank award short-term credit to firms on the basis of detailed transfer documents (bills of lading, invoices, and so on), checked more or less perfunctorily against the *Promtekhfinplan*, as has been the practice in the Soviet Union for decades. Here the comparison is between a centralized and a regionally-decentralized mode of decision-making. A more profit-oriented credit mechanism with really autonomous sources of credit might be even more efficient, but that is another matter. It is inconceivable, in any case, that local branches of the mono-bank could perform this function if there were no 'firms' as defined by Ben-ner and Neuberger.

DIRECT AND INDIRECT CONTROLS

The advantages of indirect control over petty tutelage have been given wider currency ever since 'reform-mongering' began in the late 1950s. Yet I have seen little or no economic analysis of the system change involved.

A simple example illustrates the direct and the indirect modes of control. A hierarchic supervisor controls two firms A and B, each producing two goods X and Y with outputs x and y. The firms each have decided on, or have been allotted, their inputs so that their production possibilities sets (A) and (B) can be drawn as in the Figure 6.1(a) and 6.1(b). To make the example interesting, I have assumed that the two firms have substantially different capabilities of producing X and Y. Firm A can produce X and firm B can produce Y with relative ease, that is, at relatively low per-unit cost. The third diagram (Figure 6.1(c)) is constructed as the sum of the sets A and B and is denoted $(A + B)$. It shows all the combinations of X and Y that are jointly possible (provided A and B do not share any inputs).

We assume that the managers of A and B are pursuing goals that may be represented as linear objective functions of X and Y with price weights P_x and P_y. (These may be sales or profits or any other value aggregate.) They maximize the value of these functions at S and T, which are tangent to straight lines with the same slope Px/Py. Point R (7.5, 1) in the third diagram is the sum of S (5.0) and T (2.5,1) (where the co-ordinates of each point are added up). From the viewpoint of the supervisor's preferences, the outputs at R are in the wrong proportions: he would like firms A and B to produce jointly a combination of outputs such as at point Q, where X and Y are produced in equal proportions. How does he get to *induce* point Q?

If the supervisor knew the shape of the set $(A + B)$ and, in particular, the

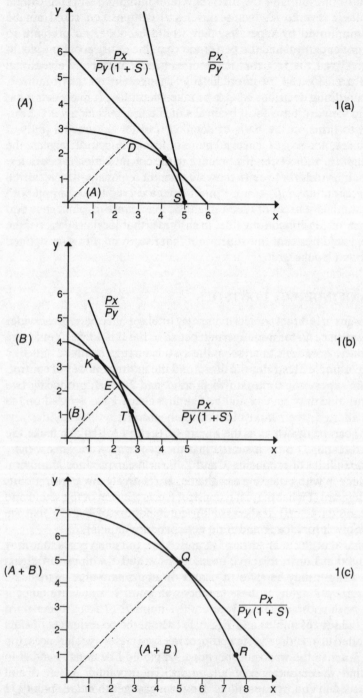

Figure 6.1   Direct and indirect control of firms

slope of the frontier at Q, his problem would be solved. He would offer a per-unit subsidy s for the production of Y such that the ratio of the effective prices confronting A and B, that is, the ratio of Px to Py $(1 + S)$, would be equal to the slope of the tangent at Q. Given these prices, A would produce at J (4, 1.5) and B at K (1, 3.5) and their joint outputs would be (5.0, 5.0) at Q. This would be the ideal indirect control: a single number s, the per-unit-of-Y subsidy, would cause both A and B to produce the right quantities of X and Y that would sum to Q, the desired combination of outputs on the efficiency frontier of $(A + B)$.

But there is not a ghost's chance, even in this highly-simplified planning situation, that the supervisor would have sufficient information about the shape of $(A + B)$ to come up with the right number s.[3] The only information he can have about $(A + B)$ comes from what he knows about (A) and (B) separately. And here he is very unlikely to know much more than one or two combinations of feasible outputs for each firm from previous experience. The problem would even be more difficult if there were more than two firms and two goods. So what to do? If he knows little or nothing about the shape of (A) or (B), he can issue direct orders to each firm to produce as much X and Y as possible in equal proportions. This 'petty tutelage' option will result in the combination of outputs at D (2.4, 2.4) for A and E (2, 2) for B. The sum of these outputs is (4.4, 4.4), which falls short of the efficient combination (5, 5) by 12 per cent. The reason for this shortfall is that the production orders failed to take advantage of the comparative advantage of A in X and B in Y. If he had observed that the relative production cost of X was lower in B than in A, he might have ordered B to produce most of the desired increase in Y. But he could only have hit on the right quantity targets for both A and B to arrive at the mix of joint outputs at Q by chance.

To what sort of indirect controls could the supervisor have resorted to cause firms A and B to produce the mix at Q? He would certainly have wished to subsidize Y (and possibly to tax X to achieve a financial balance). But by how much? He would have had to be able to locate the optimal points J and K to figure out what the relative prices (including subsidies) should be from the ratios of the marginal costs of X and Y at these points. But then he might just as well have *ordered* A and B to produce at J and K.

It is of course correct, as Abram Bergson observed in a verbal comment on this essay, that a supervisor may grope his way toward a superior solution – one providing more output of X and Y in equal proportions than the petty tutelage option – by issuing a higher or a lower level of subsidy of Y depending on the observed behaviour of the enterprise. This trial-and-error procedure, which resembles a Lange-type scheme of price-setting, differs from it in that it would converge, if it converged at all, not on a clearly identifiable point of equilibrium between supply and demand, but on an optimum that was unascertainable *a priori*. There would be no way of figuring out when the process should be brought to a halt. Moreover, I should think that an official supervising several firms producing a variety of products would be hard put to even guess at the combination of subsidies and taxes required, at each iteration, to induce a more desirable mix of outputs, not to speak of the disruption caused by the frequent manipulation of subsidies if the process were to take place in reality rather than on paper.

These arguments suggest that the instruments of indirect control (taxes-and-subsidies) cannot be more aggregated than the instruments of direct control (production targets and input allotments). Detailed accounting information about costs may be just as hard to collect and process as information on production capacities for individual products.[4]

In all fairness, however, two important arguments in favour of indirect controls should be invoked: (1) the substitution of indirect for direct instruments of control may give the firms more room to display their 'initiative' (explore a new range of inputs and outputs of which the official was unaware, change the mix between the resources they devote to production, sales, exports and R and D, and so forth); (2) the new set of net outputs for this subsystem of the economy may, even though it deviated more than before from the net output targets in the plan, be preferable, even from the viewpoint of the co-ordinating official, to this set of targets or at least to the set of net outputs that would emerge as a response to detailed orders (because the quality mix may be improved, or because the firms' knowledge of the demands of consumers may be better than the co-ordinator's). Unfortunately, there is no way to predict on the basis of theoretical argument the balance of advantages and disadvantages of the change in the mode of control. In my view, the net advantages of introducing more aggregated controls have frequently been exaggerated. This simplified example failed to consider other reforms, particularly in the price system or in the degree of competition that could be calculated to achieve better co-ordination simultaneously with the introduction of 'indirect' controls. But, in my view, these reform measures represent an analytically separate issue.

CONCLUSIONS

I argued in the first section that the *modus operandi* of firms after a reform may not be much different from what it was before. This is in part because the indirect controls discussed in the second section cannot possibly work in the absence of other deep-reaching reforms, and higher authorities must resort to detailed controls if they want to bring about any co-ordination at all. In part it is also due to the pressures of firm managers on superiors who prefer centralized co-ordination to production anarchy because it enables them to have a more orderly access to the inputs they need. This suggests that there may be a sort of institutional equilibrium keeping a semi-centralized system from either moving too far in the direction of petty tutelage ('overcentralization') or in the direction of granting firms a very wide degree of autonomy. This in-between state is characterized by bargaining among the decision-makers in the system that is probably more intense and covers a greater scope of decisions than in the original Stalinist system with its rigidly maintained discipline. The situation described here applies to all the economies of member-states of CMEA where the production hierarchy, from the Planning Commission or Council of Ministers down to the individual firm, has been maintained. Whether or not the reform legislation in any of these economies intended to shield firms from arbitrary interference by officials at any level of this hierarchy, interference is always possible and is indeed often resorted to. Moreover, as Márton Tardos has observed, because promotions and demotions are still determined by the decisions of officials in the hierarchy rather than by survival in the market, firm managers continue to act as the agents of the 'principals' above them rather than as agents of the market. They not only comply with the direct orders of their superiors: they often seek to satisfy what they know to be their superiors' preferences before these preferences have been transformed into commands.

Yugoslavia was the only Eastern European economy in 1989 where the industrial hierarchy had been dismantled (as early as 1952–3). The lesson of the Yugoslav experience in recent years is that an economy characterized by pervasive bargaining between political authorities at federal, republican, and local levels on credits, foreign exchange allocations, investments, employment, and a host of other variables may work less well than either a free market economy, where managers are not subject to political interference, or a semi-centralized economy of the type summarily described in the first section. It was this spectre of a 'paralyzed economy' operating at a low-level institutional equilibrium that hovered over the valiant but unsuccessful efforts of the reformers in Eastern Europe in 1989.

NOTES

1 In 1963 I was assured by the head of an economic institute attached to the Ministry of Food-Processing in Czechoslovakia that the mini-reform of 1958–61, which I thought had gone fairly far towards decentralization of decision-making, had made no difference whatever to the way the enterprises in this industry were operating.
2 I take it that Sacks means by 'profits' any advantages, pecuniary or otherwise, that opportunistic behaviour can generate.
3 Note incidentally that if the price weights of the objective function pursued by A and B are not the same, a different rate of subsidization would have to be set for each firm, and a basic advantage of indirect controls would be lost. Each firm would bargain for a higher rate of subsidization with its superior authorities, which would be the equivalent of bargaining for lower output targets.
4 Martin Weitzman's 'Prices versus quantities' (1974) compares the two modes of subordinate control with regard to the production of a single product. He assumes that the subordinate maximizes profits on a convex production set, which leads him to equate marginal cost to price in the price mode. If the supervisor has poor information on the marginal cost of his subordinate, the latter may choose an output significantly deviating from the target he wants him to achieve. The negative

welfare effect, from the supervisor's point of view, of this deviation will depend on the derivative of the supervisor's loss function or, equivalently, on the slope of his marginal benefit curve. On the other hand, if he issues a quantitative target and he has poor information on the marginal cost of meeting that target precisely, the loss will depend on the slope of the producer's marginal cost at the target output. The balance of advantages and disadvantages of the two modes depends critically on the relative slopes of the supervisor's marginal loss (or benefit) function and of the supervisee's marginal cost schedules. Neither mode is superior prima facie.

BIBLIOGRAPHY

Bauer, Tamás (1984) 'The second economic reform and ownership relations', *Eastern European Economics* 22 (Summer), 33–87.

Ben-Ner, Avner and Neuberger, Egon (1988) 'Towards an economic theory of the firm in the centrally planned economy: a transaction costs internalization, and externatization', *Journal of Institutional and Theoretical Economics* 144(5), 839–49.

Dolan, Edwin G. (1970) 'The teleological period in Soviet economic planning', *Yale Economic Essays* 10 (Spring), 3–41.

Granick, David (1988) 'Property rights vs. transactions costs in comparative systems analysis', *Journal of Institutional and Theoretical Economics* 144(5), 871–8.

Koopmans, Tjalling and Montias, J.M. (1971) 'On the description and comparison of economic systems', in Alexander Eckstein (ed.) *Comparison of Economic Systems*, Berkeley, 27–78.

Kornai, János (1959) *Overcentralization in Economic Administration*, London, Oxford University Press.

Montias, J.M. (1982) 'Poland, roots of the economic crisis', *Bulletin of Association for Comparative Economic Studies* Fall, 1–19.

Powell, Raymond (1977) 'Plan execution and the workability of Soviet planning', (manuscript).

Sacks, Stephen R. (1988) 'Transaction costs in non-market economies', *Journal of Institutional and Theoretical Economics* 144(5), 865–71.

Simon, Herbert A. (1969) 'The architecture of complexity', in *The Sciences of the Artificial*, Massachusetts Institute of Technology, 84–118.

Weitzman, Martin (1974) 'Prices versus quantities', *Review of Economic Studies* 41, 477–91.

7 Soviet reforms and western neo-classical economics

Alec Nove

It is known that Marx and Engels held that socialism and commodity production [that is, production for the market] were not only contradictory but also incompatible. Lenin adopted the same position. Even today no one would have the 'theoretical cheek' to claim that Lenin was the founder of the theory of commodity production under socialism. Was the theory of Marx, Engels, Lenin, about socialism then incorrect, or was their theory on commodity production incorrect?

This was said by Professor A. Sergeyev at a conference devoted to a draft of a new textbook on political economy (*Voprosy ekonomiki* 7, 1988,40). The former director of the Institute of Economics, Abalkin, declared at the same conference that

> for historical reasons we are facing the necessity to reassess anew many of our conceptions of socialism, . . . to take into account phenomena which could not have been foretold in the nineteenth century, when Marx and Engels worked, and which Lenin could not observe or investigate in the first years of Soviet power.
>
> (Ibid.: 59)

The editor of *Voprosy ekonomiki*, G. Popov, stated: 'We lack a decisive break-through towards the elaboration of a contemporary theoretical model of socialism . . .' (ibid.: 5).

What could they learn if they were all to attend a course in neo-classical economics? Having read the standard textbooks, what could they apply to their reality? Needless to say, the phrase 'neo-classical economics' or 'the neo-classical paradigm' covers a wide range of different writers, and all would freely admit that their theories do not and cannot pretend to 'realism' in the assumptions, with respect to any real, functioning economy. All theories involve abstractions. This is as true of Marx as of Milton Friedman. Thus the assumption in *Das Kapital* about the rate of profit is an equilibrium assumption; in real life, as Marx well knew, rates of profit vary widely. In his definition of productive labour under capitalism he abstracted from the existence of the self-employed, and so on. As will be seen, part of my critique of the relevance (to *any* economy) of the neo-classical paradigm lies, not in what the theory or its interpreters say, but in what is left silent, or not emphasized. For example, no one denies that what appears to be profitable to do depends in some degree on the area of responsibility of the decision-maker – but no one says so either.

Let us begin with the question of shortage, the *defitsit* which worries Soviet economists and managers in equal measure. The same issue of *Voprosy ekonomiki* (7, 1988) carries a full and fair account of János Kornai's interpretation of its causes. But Kornai, whether he be right or wrong, is not a neo-classical economist, and is the author, among other things, of a book entitled *Anti-equilibrium*. The neo-classicals generally assume that 'markets clear', or would do so if there were not some imperfections, such as price controls, trade unions and the like. If some labour or materials remain unused, then this cannot be 'Pareto-optimal', as more could be produced without diminishing anyone's income. In general equilibrium everything is fully utilized, and this is the *optimum optimorum*.

Yet this view is, I submit, false. False because it is inconsistent with the assumption of competition. For competition actually to be occurring there *has* to be spare capacity, at the very least among the less successful. Competition must mean losers as well as gainers, and this is already inconsistent with the 'Pareto' principle which speaks of gainers with no losers. (I once said to a neo-classical: 'Surely you cannot envisage a situation in which any innovation or indeed any major act would cause no loss to anyone!' He replied: 'In that case the situation is already Pareto-optimal' . . .). Equally important, a situation in which aggregate supply equals demand with full employment of material and human resources will guarantee the existence of shortages at the micro-level, and all experience shows that fear of shortages generates a mode of behaviour (hoarding, overapplication for resources, concealment of capacity) which makes shortages more acute. The basic reason is simple, and applies to all systems: precise knowledge of the future does not exist, the unexpected always happens, there are millions of variants of goods and services when fully disaggregated. Since these are not and cannot be perfect substitutes for one another, spare capacity must exist if demand is to be satisfied, to cope with the unexpected. It cannot be achieved by price manipulation (or fluctuation) alone, because of innumerable instances of complementarities in production. Long ago Kornai correctly observed that, for user demand to be satisfied, it must be difficult to sell, one needs a buyers' market. He had in mind, among other things, the psychological effect on the would-be seller: he may not bother to adapt the product to new requirements if there is a sellers' market.

It follows that – except in a static world confined exclusively to textbooks – markets not only do not clear, they *should* not clear. A smoothly functioning system requires excess production capacity, competition presupposes its existence. Unless, that is, one assumes perfect micro foresight, that is, a situation never encountered anywhere at any time.

The neo-classical paradigm lays overwhelming stress on the concept of equilibrium. There are some good theoretical and pedagogic reasons for this. It is, as Frank Hahn likes to say, a 'beautiful' theoretical construction. No alternative can match its beauty and its completeness. Economics has become highly mathematicized, and important elements of reality tend to be excluded because they are not amenable to mathematical techniques. Everyone, including the authors of equilibrium models, are well aware that the real world is full of disequilibrium. There are indeed disequilibrium models, but they are, so to speak, equilibrium-disequilibrium models. To quote Henry Wu: 'disequilibrium (becomes) a merely reconciliating expedient employed to reconstitute the disequilibrating concepts within the equilibrium framework' ('What's wrong with formalization in economics?', p. 91). Similarly, uncertainty is recognized, but, as G. Shackle and others have been pointing out, the models incline many users to imagine insurable, actuarial uncertainty, to which one can apply theories of probability or game theory and in the end it becomes (almost) certain uncertainty, as in the case of 'rational expectations'. It is clear, of course, that people (east and west) adjust their behaviour to expectations and try to be rational, but this is no excuse (to quote Keynes) for 'reducing uncertainty to the same calculable status as that of certainty itself'. Furthermore, to cite Brian Loasby (*Choice, Complexity and Ignorance*, Cambridge University Press, 1976, 26), 'equilibrium models cannot explain, since they specify no causal process'. Phyllis Deane, in her *Evolution of Economic Ideas* (Cambridge University Press, 1978, 223) points out that 'it was the notion of taking uncertainty into account that proved most difficult to absorb into the neo-classical paradigm. For a world of uncertainty is a world of perpetual disequilibrium'. Three quotations from Frank Hahn, an intelligent *defender* of 'neo-classicism':

(a) We have no good reason to suppose that there are forces which lead the economy to equilibrium. By that I mean we have no good theory. If indeed there is order we do not understand how it is brought about.

(b) It is a fair question whether it can ever be useful to have an equilibrium notion which does not describe the termination of actual processes.

(c) If price changes are themselves the outcome of the rational assessment of their consequences for the agent making the change, then we can no longer take the neo-classical axiom for granted.

Hahn, F. (1973) On the Notion of Equilibrium in Economics,
Cambridge University Press, pp. 10–11, 48, 85.

The so-called 'new classical economics' is far worse. One of its principal creators, Sargent, wrote: 'It's very hard to do disequilibrium work . . ., the reason being that the possibility of disequilibrium complicates agents' decision problems. One reason in favour of equilibrium models is that it solves a lot of technical problems' (quoted from Klamer (ed.) (1984) *The New Classical Macroeconomics*, 68). So much the worse, therefore, for the real world. Solow noted that 'new classical economists wonder why rational people do not always see that a 10 per cent increase in the money supply is equivalent to a 10 per cent increase in every price overnight and that all real things remain in the pre-existing equilibrium' (ibid.: 139). Instantaneous adjustment is assumed, and for Lucas all things are by definition in equilibrium. Thus he denies the very possibility of involuntary unemployment: since everyone does what he or she prefers, they must prefer leisure! (Opponents of this school refer mockingly to the fact that fifteen million Americans happened to have 'preferred leisure' in 1933!). I will not pursue these ideas further, but it is wrong not to note (and deplore, with amazement) the very considerable spread of 'new classical economics', explicable only by its elegant mathematics, at least in my view, and its helpfulness to extreme *laissez-faire* ideologists (they claim that the doctrines prove that government intervention can achieve nothing), but also because it is a species of *reductio ad absurdum* of formal neo-classicism, 'an admirably consistent and logical outcome of the neo-classical assumptions of rational maximizing behaviour', to cite Prychitko (*Critical Review* 1).

I pass to two attacks directed from 'ideologically' very different quarters. One comes from the unjustly-neglected Oxford economist G.B. Richardson, the other from the 'Austrian school'. Both are highly relevant to East European reform models.

The essence of Richardson's critique also concentrates on uncertainty, with special reference to *investment decisions*. He shows that, paradoxically, uncertainty and imperfect knowledge are not regrettable imperfections, as implied by neo-classical theory. To cite an admirer of Richardson, Brian Loasby:

> The conventional view, of course, is that in perfect competition the price and output of every unit within the economy is precisely determined, whereas under oligopoly they are indeterminate. Richardson demonstrates that, in the absence of the (Walrasian) auctioneer, formal perfect competition provides no basis for expectation, whereas oligopoly does at least define the apparently relevant set of competitors and may well promote the exchange of information which gives firms the confidence to make commitments. It is perfect competition that is indeterminate. The imperfections are what makes the system work.
>
> (Loasby, *Complexity, Choice and Ignorance*, Cambridge University Press, 1976)

Richardson argues that

under perfect competition it would be impossible for any firm to know how much of any good to produce . . . Presumably, firms are supposed to equate future marginal costs with future prices. But how is a producer to predict future prices, depending as they do on the demands of the consumers and on the supply plans of all his competitors? This the textbooks do not tell us . . . If the future price of a good were known to be greater than the current cost of making it, then a profit opportunity may be said to exist; but if there are an unlimited number of firms able to respond to the opportunity, no individual firm will know what to do. A profit opportunity equally available to everyone is in fact available to none at all.

(Richardson, G.B. 'Planning versus Competition', *Soviet Studies* January 1971, pp. 456–7. His full argument is set out in his *Information and Investment,* London, Oxford University Press 1960)

Neo-classical textbooks do not, as a rule, handle investment satisfactorily. They appreciate, of course, that investment raises the question of time, of *future* prices, interest and exchange rates. But most neo-classical models are of their nature static. To cite Hahn again, investment 'is profoundly mysterious under perfect competition' (*Oxford Economic Papers*, July 1986: 360). Investment involves risk, an estimate of what the future might bring. It involves estimating the future actions of actual or potential competitors, the plans of the providers of complementary inputs. In the real world, as Kornai pointed out long ago, no one takes a major decision on the basis of price information alone, yet many models (including the Lange model of 1938) assume that they do. The theoretical gap is visible also in some of the Soviet reform models, with their emphasis on 'self-financing' and on decentralized investments. These are, in themselves, desirable, since the system has suffered from overcentralization. However, one does not see in the reform proposals an adequate stress on the availability of information on the basis of which investment should be made. In Richardson's universe, which is the real world, investment takes place because of so-called imperfections: imperfect knowledge (one firm knows something the others do not), collusion, market domination, government-sponsored co-ordination (Japan's Ministry of Trade and Industry undertakes this), or long-term links with large customers. The greater the anticipated competition, the less the incentive to invest. (The British government's economic advisers seem quite unable to understand this.)

Now to the Austrians, typified by Lachmann. He too believes that the real market 'maintains itself through a divergence rather than a convergence of expectations, and this cannot be defended as a strictly equilibrating process' (I quote this from Prychitko (1987) *Critical Review* 1: 65). He too follows Shackle in stressing 'true uncertainty', which he counterposes to 'late classical formalism', formalism under which 'the economist's focus on functional relationships between the prices and quantities of things' elimates 'human intentionality' and 'learning by doing'. It is assumed that 'the probabilities of certain outcomes are given and known', and this is needed for formal mathematical modelling. *Different* expectations, disequilibrium, actual or anticipated, are the bases for entrepreneurship, which itself can disequilibrate. 'Austrians', such as Hayek, have been pointing out that the standard neo-classical model of competitive price '*assumes* the situation to exist which a true explanation ought to account for as the effect of the competitive process'. Israel Kirzner, a New York 'Austrian', stresses 'the extraordinary assumptions concerning availability of information' which underlie standard theory. This

> simply assumes that firms know the nature of 'given' preferences and supply perfectly appropriate products. I wanted a theory that could be practically applied and did not assume out of the way all the interesting informational issues in order to reach determinate solutions in a highly formalized manner.
>
> (Peter Earl, *Economic Imagination*, 8)

But back to the 'Austrians' and to Kirzner (I am quoting from an unpublished paper of his, entitled 'Some crucial implications of the socialist calculation debate', prepared for a 'Capitalism and Socialism' conference in Florida in 1987). He pointed out that L. von Mises, in trying to show that Lange's socialist model was inadequate, 'emphasized with unsurpassed clarity how important it is to see the market as an entrepreneurial process rather than a state of equilibrium affairs'. Again, 'markets work, in the Austrian view, because they are characterised by a continual process of entrepreneurial discovery', and profits are a consequence of actions under disequilibrium. Indeed, in the formal general equilibrium theory profits tend to zero, since there is no function for an entrepreneur and so no reward for entrepreneurship. The German economist Helmut Arndt made a similar point in his *Irrwege der politischen Ökonomie* (München, Beck, 1979, 217–18): 'The manager or entrepreneur, and also the purchaser, are in fact almost totally deprived of function . . . What they "do" could just as well be left to a robot!' W. Baumol wrote: 'The entrepreneur has virtually disappeared from the theoretical literature' ('Theories of the firm . . .', *American Economic Review* 67 (1963)).

Richardson and the 'Austrians' are surely more relevant to Soviet reforms than is the neo-classical paradigm (even if the Austrians may idealize the 'entrepreneur' in an age of corporate bureaucracies). One need not accept their conclusions, but one must take their arguments seriously. In the USSR, too, the investment decision and the managerial function relate to the world of disequilibrium and uncertainty. Socialist entrepreneurship involves risk in a dynamic world, with imperfect (but not non-existent) information. One thinks too of Schumpeter, who linked large-scale research and innovation with large firms which possessed or hoped to possess market domination, for in its absence the risk involved would be too great. (Yet an excessively protected monopoly may not wish to innovate, . . . so the conclusion is controversial.)

This brings me to the theory of the firm. The general equilibrium perfect-competition model has problems with the firm, and, to cite M. Shubik ('A curmogeon's view of micro-economics', *Journal of Economic Literature* June 1990, 413) , sees no difference between a giant like General Electric and the corner ice-cream store. The question of the internal organization of firms was left unexplored: a firm is a 'black box'. ('Outsiders' such as H. Simon and H. Leibenstein have tried to enter the box.) Efforts to fit the firm into the neo-classical world have been made by R. Coase, and more recently by O. Williamson. In the latter's book, *Markets and Hierarchies*, he explored the reason why some activities are undertaken under hierarchical orders and not through the market. He centred his analysis on the concept of 'transaction cost'. Indeed, markets are not costless, nor is the obtaining of information. If a given transaction costs less if under the authority of the firm (and 'cost' includes the cost of ensuring that contracts are observed), then the answer is 'hierarchy'. Soviet reformers should indeed devote more attention to the role and logic of hierarchy in capitalist market economies. However, in doing so they should bear in mind the incompleteness of Williamson's interesting and valuable analysis.

In my view, the problem arises from overconcentration on 'the trans-action' as the basic unit of the analysis. It is true that, in deciding whether to perform a *given* task oneself, or to use a subcontractor in the market, the considerations advanced by Williamson do indeed apply. But this leaves out of account the factors guiding the decision-maker to undertake that transaction. It is silently assumed that all transactions are profitable *as such*, and that the firm's overall strategy and role do not contribute to the decision.

This is connected with another lack in conventional neo-classical theory, which in fact inspires the title of Leijönhufvud's book, *Information and Coordination* (New York, Oxford University Press, 1981). Let me quote him:

> In Walrasian general equilibrium theory, all transactors are regarded as price takers. As noted by Arrow, 'there is no one left over whose job it is to take a decision on price'. The job is in fact entrusted to a *deus ex machina*: Walras' auctioneer is assumed to inform all traders of the prices at which all markets are going to clear. This always trustworthy information is supplied at zero cost.
>
> (p. 6)

There are no situations conceivable at which 'demand and supplies do not mesh', since firms face 'perfectly elastic demand and supply schedules without ever having their trading plans disappointed' (ibid. :6). He, too, points out that 'the model leaves no room for the production manager, product designer, distribution expert, etc.'. In the neo-classical model there is no need for conscious co-ordination. There is also a problem with time. Hahn agrees that the Arrow-Debreu neo-classical model is 'careless in its treatment of time', collapsing the future into the present, or else assuming that intertemporal market signals exist, so that future equilibrium prices are somehow known. In another of his articles ('Capitalism and the factory system', in Langlois (ed.) *Economics as a Process*, Cambridge) Leijönhufvud points out that the use of production-function analysis predisposes the analysts to seeing the actual process of production as an instantaneous combination of production factors. Yet in fact production takes place in a series of interrelated *sequences*, through time. The separate marginal or incremental assessment of the contribution of each of the sequences is thereby complicated, sometimes rendered impossible. Furthermore, firms have strategies, choose a role in the market, and the profitability or otherwise of a specific transaction is judged *within* a wider whole. In identical situations firm A may act when firm B does not, because of where the given transaction fits into the more general pattern. This aspect, which is prior to a decision whether to do it oneself ('hierarchy') or hiring a subcontractor ('market') is missing from Williamson's analysis, and from the neo-classical textbooks generally.

In my own critique of conventional theory I referred to 'myopic', or 'one-dimensional' marginalism. This analytical deficiency can be illustrated with numerous examples. Neo-classical theory silently assumes that every transaction is directly market-related and earns a profit as such. Yet a large number of marginal decisions, whether on current production or on investment, can only make sense if seen as part of the larger whole. Thus, given the prior decision to invest in the oil industry in northern Siberia or Alaska, a large number of choices must be made: on the routing and diameter of pipe-lines; location and equipment of pumping stations; and a great deal else. These are margins *within* a hierarchy of margins.

Another and very different example. A shop, like Fauchon in Paris, Fortnum and Mason in London, Eliseyev in old Moscow, bases its profitability on its reputation for a very large assortment of foods. In Glasgow 'myopic-marginalist' accountants destroyed a similar shop by removing from its shelves those products that did not 'pay', thereby destroying that shop's raison d'être; eventually the shop closed. Common-sense says that in all businesses the part must be related to the whole, that is why there *is* a whole, yet conventional neo-classical theory fragments. Textbooks are full of references to margins, but the nature of marginal decisions are not discussed or defined. Yet the 'marginal' pumping-station or *pâté de fois gras* in the two above examples must be judged in relation to their effect on the oil project and the food store respectively. In the real world, decisions are marginal, but within a *hierarchy of margins*, to which there is a corresponding *hierarchy of decision-makers*, whose task is to relate the part with the whole. In neo-classical models the issue of optimal organizational and decision-making structures seldom arises, yet it is a vital, decisive aspect of the Soviet reform process. An American economist,

Harold Demsetz, pointed out that the so-called perfect competition model has 'little to say about competition, or the inner organization of firms', since,

> What is modelled is not competition, it is extreme decentralization; real competition and real firms require at least a modicum of authority in the allocation of resources . . . The framework necessary for understanding most competitive activities, the very possibility of which depends on superior knowledge and real time lags and which is motivated by a desire to best others, is lacking in the perfect decentralization model.

He also stresses that 'the real roles of management . . . to devise or discover markets, products, production techniques and actively to manage the actions of employees, have no place' in such a model. It cannot handle 'managed coordination'. He rightly criticizes the 'transaction costs' approach as 'much too narrow', as it ignores the positive importance of co-ordination. 'Prices, and the markets in which they are revealed, simply provide information about the value others place on resources, they do not themselves "allocate" or "coordinate" the uses made of these resources', (quoted from 'The theory of the firm revisited', UCLA discussion paper, paper, 1987).

Hahn (1973, op. cit. p. 50) touched on a related point when he wrote: 'There are theoretical difficulties for accounting for the existence of firms unless we allow there to be increasing returns of some sort.' Yet, most neo-classical models find increasing returns a problem, since they are inconsistent with equilibrium, which requires firms to be on a diminishing returns curve. (Otherwise they would already have expanded . . . But this again is a static concept; in real time *some* firms are expanding, others not.)

A similar critique of 'one-dimensionalism' was made by Brian Loasby:

> Even in economics, where the proliferation of multi-level interdependence is the conceptual base on which the subject has been built, very drastic simplifications are the rule. Highly complex sub-systems, such as firms or even whole sectors of the economy, containing within themselves many layers of great complexity, are regularly treated as simple elements, while components of a complex system are analysed as isolated units.
>
> *Complexity, Choice and Ignorance*, p. 30.

Kornai (1971) made the same point more briefly in his *Anti-equilibrium* (Amsterdam, North Holland, p. 84): 'It is surprising that economics should have neglected for so long the problem of multi-level phenomena.'

Two illustrations of error caused by incorrect approach to multi-level problems, one from the UK and one from the Soviet Union, follow.

The British government has decreed the privatization of all municipal bus services, allowing free competition and outlawing 'cross-subsidization', that is, the covering of losses on one service with profits from another. Apart from the confusion and congestion such a decision has caused, its inherent unsoundness rests on the implied belief that, conceptually, each bus line or metro service, perhaps even each bus or train, is a separate profit-making or *khozraschyot* unit, to be evaluated separately. The *system or network* aspect disappears. In no other civilized country is this example being followed: in every European, American and Canadian city known to me there is a publicly-operated *network*, with the subsidy (if any) paid to the network, which inevitably implies cross-subsidization between parts of the whole.

The Soviet example relates to service enterprises in agriculture. Decrees promulgated in 1982 and in 1985 set up an 'agro-industrial' hierarchy, *Agroprom*, to resolve the problem caused by the tendency of the service organizations (for example, for repairs, drainage, 'chemicalization'), to fulfil their own turnover plans in roubles rather than to serve the farms economically. It was decided that they should be rewarded in relation to their contribution to the 'final result', for example, the harvest. There was a fallacy here, which the student of neo-classical economics would not be able to spot (but Leijönhufvud would!). Of course, in a tidy formal model a service organization *would* be paid in relation to its marginal productivity contribution. However, this overlooks a very important aspect of reality. The reason why Soviet 'service' organizations could not be paid in relation to their contribution to the final result is that *no one could know what it was*. We can know that the harvest on a given land area was a thousand tons or bushels, but how to discover what proportion of this was due to insecticides, or drainage work, or repairs? The key to the answer, as Soviet reformers do now realize, is to place decision-making and co-ordination in the hands of whosoever is in charge of *all* the sequential operations. Thus an American or British farmer makes estimates about the need to use insecticides or for tractor repairs and can also decide whether to do the job himself or hire a subcontractor in the market, but in both instances *he is in command*, he decides, in relation to the entire sequence of tasks. The area of responsibility of the decision-maker, as well as his success criteria, *matter*. As Demsetz pointed out, the task of co-ordination is itself productive.

This brings me to another vitally important aspect of real competitive economies, *goodwill*. Firms find it important to maintain or improve quality, to undertake actions which *in themselves* may not pay, because reputation pays, and to maintain reputation it is worth spending time and effort. Obvious? Then I suggest that sceptics should look at any ten economics textbooks and look for the word 'goodwill' in the index. It is almost invariably missing. (Samuelsen does mention that it is a saleable asset, but without examining its nature or stressing its importance.) I have never seen the word used in Russian. Yet here is a vital missing ingredient in the Soviet system: under conditions of monopoly or a sellers' market bad service or poor quality cannot be 'punished' by the customer going elsewhere, so loss of goodwill does not matter, and nor do the customer's requirements. Why is goodwill missing from most neo-classical textbooks? Because under so-called perfect competition and in equilibrium the firm can by definition sell all it produces at the equilibrium price, *and* because of the analytical simplification that quality is *given* (a different quality is a different product. Incidentally, 'quality' is also almost invariably absent from the index to a neo-classical textbook). Under pure monopoly, of course, goodwill does not matter either. It matters under *real* competition. But goodwill raises another analytical complication: it links together different transactions by the same firm, they react upon one another, whereas theory prefers to separate them, linking them only with the market. (Analysts do sometimes discuss brand names and product differentiation, under the heading of 'imperfect competition', and do note that it does have some effect on quality. But this is another example of so-called 'imperfections' being in fact necessary, and so not imperfections.)

The neo-classical view of human behaviour, whether of capitalists, or managers, or workers, is quite remarkably narrow. Firms maximize profits, individuals maximize utility. This approach is frequently linked with so-called methodological individualism: the whole is but the sum of its parts. (Mrs Thatcher has said that 'society' does not exist, only persons and families do.) If this implies that the separate pursuit of profitability by parts of a firm is necessarily and always consistent with the interests of the firm as a whole, that is surely nonsensical: why, then, is the firm large, why does it maintain a head office and an expensive corporate bureaucracy? This too is highly relevant for Soviet reformers. In the west there are a multitude of firms of all sizes, and within large ones there are different degrees of financial and operational autonomy of the parts. I would refer back to what I wrote earlier about hierarchy of margins and also the co-ordination of sequential or interrelated operations. It is by no means a matter of technological economies of scale; Du Pont operates nearly a hundred factories and plants, so the economy must be informational and/or arises out of the interconnections between the parts. Some Soviet reformers have frequently sought to devise a model within which the interests of the parts are always consistent with the interests of the whole. We must realize that this can never be completely achieved in any system. There are bound to be contradictions, conflicts of interest, to resolve by higher authority, whether this be within the corporation or within the state. These dilemmas are in no way illuminated by the neo-classical paradigm, which, as we have noted, assumes 'perfect decentralization'. But back to human motivation. Simon has properly reminded us of its complexities: capitalists or managers do not 'maximize profits' in any meaningful way, it is an axiom which can neither be proved nor refuted, any more than it can be shown that individuals maximize utility, except in the purely tautological sense that whatever the firm or the individual does *is* maximizing behaviour. Suppose a capitalist takes a holiday in Honolulu, or I address a conference in Vienna; is he 'maximizing profits' when he could be in his office? Do I prefer talking to a conference to taking a holiday with a magnificent blonde in Capri? (This is pure theory, of course.)

Out of these oversimplifications have emerged so-called theories of 'public choice', which can serve (in the west) the ideological purpose of denigrating public services. However, they also have a basis in reality. Relevant here also are theories of bureaucracy, including those of Marx and Weber. It is wrong to counterpose to an imperfect market a perfectly-motivated government. Public servants are human, have their own interests and careers to think of. It is, undoubtedly, useful to be reminded of the fact – well-known also in the USSR – that some politicians, public officials and bureaucrats feather their own nests, pursue power and privilege, but quite another to assert that this is the rule throughout the public sector. Officials in charge of kindergartens, public parks, hospitals or artillery tend to identify with, and desire improvements in, the areas of their respective responsibilities. The problem, much discussed in the USSR, of 'departmentalism' (*vedomstvennost*), arises out of such identifications.

This is neither purely personal selfishness, nor altruism. Thus (to take another example) the librarian of Moscow or Glasgow University desires to acquire more books, periodicals and shelving space because he is morally committed to his (or her) work, and not because he is 'maximizing his personal utility'. Unless, of course, we adopt the tautology that everyone prefers whatever he prefers, in which case we will be unable to distinguish between the devoted and honest librarian and one who secretly sells off books in the black market! Both would be 'maximizing' . . . There are two serious dimensions to this over-simple approach. First, it is used to justify privatization, because it is held that in pursuing profit the capitalist will be compelled to be efficient (which is true subject to two conditions: that there is competition, and that profitability is the appropriate guide to efficiency, and, as we shall see, neither is necessarily the case). Second, it abstracts from pride in work done, loyalty, and commitment, which affect performance of management and labour alike. The maximizing robot may 'fit' mathematical models, but is a poor substitute for real 'economic men', who pursue a whole number of sometimes inconsistent objectives, in the USSR, Austria, Britain, everywhere.

Neo-classical theory does recognize the existence of 'public goods', where the market cannot function effectively, though there are disagreements as to where to place the 'boundary' between public and private, for example, in health, education, garbage collection. Water, electricity, gas, posts, are seen by many to be 'natural monopolies', where competition is either impossible, or wasteful (competing water pipes down the same street?). In most countries such considerations would apply also to urban public transport. Important, too, are *externalities*, positive or negative. This applies particularly to infrastructure, a point duly noted already by Adam Smith, who advocated public expenditure on roads, canals and ports, and, of course, there are external *dis*economies, such as congestion and environmental pollution. In such instances the profit rate is a misleading guide, state intervention or a subsidy may be appropriate.

In the UK there have been debates for many years concerning efficiency criteria for public or private monopolies. They, and the controversies surrounding privatization, are directly relevant to the present Soviet discussions on what they call 'full *khozraschet*', profit-and-loss accounting, wherever considerations of monopoly, externalities and public service are important. I read years ago of a Soviet town where each bus driver *en route* to suburban destinations was instructed to turn his passengers off the bus if their number fell below a minimum figure, as the rest of his journey was unprofitable! If there were competition, this would be 'bad for business' through loss of goodwill; where competition is absent then there must be an obligation, a duty to the public, which may require to be enforced. It is, by the way, another example of the fact that, in the real world, firms (even profit-oriented private firms!) find it necessary to undertake some loss-making activities to maintain goodwill, under competitive conditions.

There are useful lessons to be learnt, positive and negative, from western discussions on efficiency criteria for enterprises providing public goods and/or which are natural monopolies. This is a subject to which I have made some contribution (for example, *Efficiency Criteria for Nationalized Industries*, London, Allen & Unwin, 1973, and also an article published in EKO, Novosibirsk, 9, 1988). There is a real problem in reconciling financial success criteria with social obligations, under conditions when profits can be enhanced by raising prices and reducing quantity and quality. What should be the nature and the powers of the regulatory authority, and what effect do its powers have on managerial responsibility? This kind of institutional economics is outside or on the fringes of the neo-classical main line, but of undoubted relevance to the evaluation of performance of, and the devising of incentives for, those Soviet sectors where competition is weak or undesirable.

Neo-classical price theory in 'perfect competition' models suffers from the assumption that all firms are 'price takers', that prices are given. It is of course recognized that real firms frequently 'administer' prices, the range of choice being limited by what they believe their competitors will do. This acts as a restraint in both directions: price cuts may involve a price war, in which they and the competitors could both lose; ruthless use of opportunities for price increases afforded by a degree of monopoly could attract competing firms. Very useful here is Baumol's notion of 'contingent competition'. A firm may be dominant in the market, and the cost of entry (the investments needed) may be high, but if it raises its prices and profit rates too much it may well attract a competitor. (This is one reason why 'profit maximization' is so vague and indefinable a term. Loasby wrote in *Complexity, Choice and Ignorance* that it 'has no unequivocal meaning outside of economists models' (p. 122).) This, too, is a point worth pondering in the context of Soviet reforms. In some sectors there are real economies of scale, a dominant producer, who could raise prices excessively; one solution is price control, another is to provide the means for a competing enterprise to be created, and thereby influence price behaviour.

In discussing Richardson's challenge to orthodoxy, we already raised by implication the 'cobweb' problem. This is most evident in agriculture, but is of wider application, whenever time is involved. Suppose prices of (say) onions or pork go up. Producers expand output. The price then goes down. Producers reduce output. The resultant shortage causes the price to go up. Fluctuations can be severe, and no tendency to equilibrium can be discerned. It is not only political considerations ('the farmers' vote') that cause agricultural prices to be controlled in virtually all the countries of the world. A similar phenomenon can be envisaged as occurring in industrial investment: prices rise, many invest in new productive capacity, there is then overproduction, prices and output fall, and so on. It is the risk of such an outcome that could discourage investment, or alternatively lead to overinvestment. Such a danger exists even if prices were wholly free and there were a smoothly-functioning capital market. My reading of Soviet writings on self-financed investments suggest that this has not been taken sufficiently into consideration, though the problem of the absence of a capital market has been discussed. In this whole area there is little in neo-classical economics that could help. The cobweb does not 'belong' in the paradigm, in which 'the future is collapsed into the present'.

Finally, what *is* there that Soviet reformers should learn, positively or negatively, from neo-classical textbooks? Certainly there are some generally accepted propositions which are valid and important, but nearly all (or even all) of them were already to be found in Marshall almost a hundred years ago, and indeed in the work of early Russian economists, too (I have been reading Shletser and Shtorkh, respectively the first professor of economics in Moscow University and the first economist-academician, who lived in the reign of Alexander I). Prices controlled below the supply-and-demand balancing level ensure shortages and black markets. Budgetary deficits financed by money creation contributed to inflation in 1806 and also in 1986. Credits too freely granted at artificially low rates of interest, or which turn out to be non-repayable grants, have some predictable consequences. The Soviet economy is at this very time in trouble for neglecting the elementary propositions of monetary theory. (Indeed they could have derived much profit from carefully reading the works of two admirable monetary economists, Falkner and Yurovsky, both of whom perished in the Stalin terror.) In his article in *Kommunist* 3 (1989) entitled *Eshchyo ne pozdno* (It is not yet too late), B.Bogachev calls on his fellow economists to study Wicksell, Hawtrey, Keynes and Friedman, to pay much greater attention to the need for macroeconomic balance. A few dozen young men 'who are not totally bemused by propaganda about a gold rouble and similar medieval relics' should be sent to work for a while in western finance ministries, central and commercial banks.

Indeed, he is right. They would learn a lot about what to do, and what not to do.

People in Russia, as elsewhere, try to improve their material position, subject to constraints, which must be taken into account in wages policies. Arthur Koestler (in his book *Janus*) warned against two opposite excesses: seeing the parts *only* in the context of the whole, or seeing the whole as *only* the sum of its parts. In the USSR the individual was surely for too long subordinated to the collective, to 'society', to 'needs' defined by the party leadership. A corrective is desirable, and here the neo-classical stress on the individual is helpful. However, this is accompanied by neglect of intermediate categories. The firm is accommodated within its paradigm with some difficulty, an industry not at all, and social needs tend to be downgraded. Neglect of institutions causes neglect of the study of what Hahn called 'the invisible hand in action', the way the market actually works, as well as what goes on *within* firms. The general equilibrium framework of analysis seems to me quite irrelevant, and its mathematical refinements equally so, if one is concerned with modifying the functioning of the real Soviet (or any other) economy in a practical way. We must be concerned with *processes*, not with equilibrium.

American institutional economists, cold-shouldered by most of their neo-classical colleagues, express similar views. Thus in his presidential address to their association, William M. Dugger said:

> Institutionalism is a processual paradigm, emphasising social process, not market equilibrium . . . The price system of neo-classical mythology is supposed to create a socially beneficent equilibrium. But the actual prices of a modern industrial economy bear little resemblance to the socially beneficent equilibrium prices of an ideal market economy. Institutionalists have long parted company with such neo-classical myths. We do not even agree that ours is essentially a market economy.

Of course, markets do exist, but 'the real forces operate behind the market in determining whose interests will be benefited and whose actions will be allowed . . . We might be able to save the [economics] profession from impending irrelevance by focussing on the real economic problems of our time' (*Journal of Economic Issues*, 1988, 983). Some Soviet economists may indeed be unable to distinguish the 'textbook' market from the real market processes in western economies, and so should not neglect the institutionalists. Also important are works of Simon and of Leibenstein on the functioning of real and not mythical firms. Also the work of Kurt Rothschild and others (1971) on *Power in Economics* (the title of a Penguin book of readings on this subject); power is all too frequently a factor ignored in neo-classical textbooks. A related subject which has recently been much discussed is that of 'principal and agent', that is, explorations of conflict of interest that can arise between the principal and someone he hires to work on his behalf. Some similar problems arise within Soviet (and other) hierarchies, relationships between the nominal superior and the nominal inferior, in the monitoring and evaluation of performance.

This in turn relates to the now quite large literature on the relationship between management and owners. Within large western corporations, the manager (for example, of a chemical factory or a supermarket) is no more a capitalist owner than is his Soviet equivalent. Furthermore the 'owner', who is supposedly the 'enterpreneur-risk-bearer', may be thousands of shareholders plus a few dozen institutional investors (pension funds, insurance companies) administering funds on behalf of millions of individuals. Western controversies on these subjects, including the positive or negative effects of 'hostile' take-over bids, can help Soviet reformers to see more clearly about the nature of capital markets and the whole issue of property rights.

Another very valuable and original western economist, also well off the orthodox textbook track, is Albert O. Hirschman (1970) with his theories on 'reform-mongering' (Soviet economists need to think most carefully about reform *strategy*), and his *Exit, Voice and Loyalty* (Cambridge, Mass., Harvard University Press) which discusses the ways in which, in various systems and circumstances, errors are (or are not) corrected and grievances and protests dealt with. (Of course, in general equilibrium there are, by definition, no uncorrected errors or unredressed grievances.)

One final observation. In 1958 I was at the London School of Economics, listening to a lecture by Danzig introducing linear programming. I was sitting near to Lord Robbins who, as is known, believed that a socialist economy could not function because of the large number of simultaneous equations that had to be solved. He told me that Danzig's lecture worried him. The USSR, unlike the west, had a political authority which could define and determine an objective function, which could then be realized through a computerized programme, and socialism then could be efficient, a prospect which alarmed him. It is of interest to see why and where he was wrong, for we know that Soviet mathematical economists have for many years sought to devise SOFE (System of Optimally Functioning Socialist Economy), and one reason why it does not exist is precisely that it has not proved possible to define an objective function. One is further reminded of the last work by Norbert Wiener, the inventor of cybernetics: *God and Golem, Inc.* (MIT Press, 1964), translated into Russian as *Chelovek i robot* and published in *Novyi mir* many years ago. He warned against the use of cybernetics in the social sciences and presented an example of how difficult it is to define, for operational purposes, the wishes of just one person (let alone society as a whole). In a story by W.W. Jacobs, a British sergeant returns from India with a magic monkey's paw, which will grant three wishes. Someone steals it and wishes for 200 pounds sterling. Soon a man arrives and tells the 'wisher' that his son has been killed in an accident, and that he will receive £200 in compensation. The second wish was to undo the result of the first wish. Moral: even so simple an objective as £200 is in fact conditional upon a long and almost infinite list of circumstances in which one would prefer not to have it, and all must be incorporated in the computer's programme, or else disaster could befall.

And yet we still have models with clear, simple and unambiguous 'preference functions'. Their authors live in an unreal world. Wassili Leontief (*Science* July 1982) rightly condemned the tendency for 'preoccupation with imaginary, hypothetical rather than observable reality' and complained that the pure theorists 'drive out' of the profession those who study the actual economy; they produce mathematical models 'without any data' (Leontief himself is a fine mathematician). There is a moral here that transcends geographical and ideological boundaries.

So what kind of economics *do* we all need? That is a subject for another paper.

Part II

Reform economics and economic theory and the east – separation from Stalinism incomplete

Introduction to Part II

Reformist thought emerged within the framework of the Stalinist political economy and had to distinguish itself from Stalinism and Marxism under rather repressive political conditions. At the same time, although having incorporated important elements of liberal economics into their discourse, a great many reform economists insisted on a part of their original socialist ideals (for example, self-management). The papers collected in this chapter examine the second-best solutions provided by the reformers to these dilemmas, and raise the question of how far these ambiguities can be maintained at all. Where does Stalinism end and reformism begin? Is Stalinist political economy reformable?

Brus portrays his own 'long march' from revisionism to pragmatism, from Lange and Kalecki to the concept of the mixed economy, although not forgetting the detours (cf. regulated market instead of privatization, poliarchy instead of pluralism). He recalls the first stimuli given by Stalin's works to develop his own 'market orientation'. My reform economics – says Brus – 'shows a gradual, one may even say, reluctant evolution in the direction of marketisation'. Kowalik also draws his conclusions from the evolution of reform thinking in Poland, highlighting the problem of conceptualizing the bureaucracy in reform theories. He denies the widely-accepted view that Lange or his companions among the pioneer reformers ever nourished strong illusions about the coexistence of Soviet-style bureaucracies and the market. On the contrary, they sought institutional guarantees against the excesses of both the market and the state in schemes of industrial democracy. Consequently, reform thinking was not limited to the harmonization of plan and market only: from the very beginning reformers had to cope with the economic and political problems of self-management as well.

The 'objective laws' of the transition from capitalism to communism had been carefully sanctioned by the Stalinist political economy of socialism. Were these laws reformable? – asks Sutela. Could one reasonably expect that this kind of political economy might be modernized from inside to satisfy the requirements of the transition of opposite direction? To the first question he says yes, to the second, however, his answer is strongly in the negative. Although these laws (first of all the law of value) could be given a slightly reformist interpretation at the time of the birth of reformist thought, any improvement in the discourse only helped a *sui generis* conservative body of theory survive.

This body is, however, extremely resistant to change. This is exemplified by the paper of Davies from the aspect of historiography. By pointing to the traditional weaknesses of the Soviet historical profession as far as economic reforms are concerned (rough periodization of the economic systems, idealization of the political leadership and state ownership, and so on), Davies acknowledges that the main assumptions made by Soviet economic historians have become more realistic over the last few years. None the less, in many cases these changes – as radical as they may be from an ideological point of view – remained on the surface (critique of Stalinism, emancipation of the New Economic Policy). Aven would add: the reform economists first of all have to abandon the use of the whole concept of 'command (or administrative) system', which they inherited from the Stalinist political economy via totalitarian sovietology, provided that they want to understand how Soviet-type economies work. In his opinion, planned economies pass through the stage of the 'bargaining economy' in the process of transition to market economies. Bargaining also means that economic reforms cannot really be implemented by legislative acts. The strong belief in normative action demonstrates the Stalinist roots of reformist thought.

Which were the final constraints of the development of reform economics: were they of an external (political) or of an internal (theoretical) nature? What was the typical evolution pattern of reform thinking (did reformist thought develop in cycles)? Which was the safer way of leaving the world of Stalinist ideas: the managerial or the self-management type reformism? How did the institutionalization of reformist ideology affect the refinement of reform thinking? These questions came up many times during the discussions, and are also dealt with in the papers of Comisso, Dietz, Kovács and Zhou.

8 Economic reform in a bargaining economy

Petr O. Aven

INTRODUCTION

The success of economic reform in the former Soviet Union is absolutely impossible without overcoming myths and oversimplifications existing both in economic theory and practice. Surprisingly, these myths can be found, not only in traditional socialist economic thought defending the old economic order, but also in some of the recent critical views of the Soviet economy.

The source of traditional mythology is a belief (or its imitation) in an accordance between economic practice and a Utopian model, described in textbooks of political economy. Therefore, the critique of orthodox views can be based either on the exposure of internal contradictions of the model or on the demonstration of its weak representation of reality. In fact, the latter is also used as a proof of the contradictory nature of any national economic system that is designed according to the pattern of industrial enterprise.

The critique of the apologetic view has a long history. In the Soviet Union a vast number of critical publications have appeared in the last three or four years. Some of them are brilliant (see, for instance, the articles of Chernichenko, Lisichkin, Popov, Seliunin and Shmelev). Although such criticisms perform important political and educational functions, their scientific value tends to zero. The need for market mechanisms, the absurdity of overcentralization and all-embracing price control, and so on, no longer call for any demonstrations (it is not by chance that the majority of the more witty critical publications appeared in socio-political and literary but not in scientific journals). However, the groundlessness of modern myths doesn't seem so obvious. Their disclosure is extremely important – too high a price has already been paid for old delusions.

The new myths and oversimplifications usually stem from the negation of the traditional, 'ideal' model of a socialist economy. They can be divided into three groups. The first group of myths concerns the present state of the economy; especially its institutional structure, motivation mechanism and distribution of power. The second is related to the model of the future economic mechanism. The third is associated with the trajectory and the conditions of transformation.

This paper deals only with the first group of 'non-orthodox delusions'. Its main goal is to demonstrate some essential features of the existing economic mechanism and to expose important regularities of its development, which ought to be taken into account in the process of economic reform.

COMMAND OR BARGAINING ECONOMY?

The main myth about the existing economic mechanism of the Soviet-type system originates in the critique of the orthodox model. One of this model's foundations is the legend of 'sufficient knowledge' which permits an 'economic centre' to control the lower levels of hierarchy effectively. Another foundation is the legend of 'democratic decision-making' under which those on these lower levels take part in planning, profit distribution, promotion of managers, and so on. In realizing the exceptional complexity of modern economy, where no time is left for long-term discussions and the economic centre has no ability for processing all data needed for highly-centralized control, it was usually argued that the economic mechanism in the Soviet Union could be defined as a 'command economy' ('administrative system'), where the centre – possessing no sufficient information – gave almost meaningless orders to the production units without paying attention to their interests and opinions (see, for example, Popov 1987; Yasin 1988). In economic practice there were examples of such command relationships: output planning, directive redistribution of incomes, fixation of prices, and so on. Nevertheless, despite all these examples, the real importance of command management was essentially overestimated.

The reason for this overestimation is the insufficient understanding of the complexity of the economic system. The necessary precondition of a command economy is the transparency of the economic system and the fulfilment of the following requirements:

- the upper levels of the hierarchy have adequate ideas about the economic potential of the lower ones;
- strict responsibility for implementing orders based on these ideas is established.

At the beginning of the 1930s, when the command mechanism was introduced, these two requirements were, at least partly, met. On the whole, this was a result of the limitation of the number of sectors where central management seriously pursued the goals of increasing production and quality. Gradually, however, the ability of the upper levels to collect all the necessary data without permanent 'information help' from the lower sections became more and more doubtful. The growing complexity of the economy and the impossibility to restrict the field of control reduced the possibility of checking the received data, though there were attempts to increase the number of controlling bodies. The complexity of horizontal links between enterprises allows each of them to accuse the partners of derangement of supply, which in turn serves as an explanation for frustrating the plan. Such accusations can rarely be checked. The impossibility to define the real need for investment forces the economic centre to rely on the claims of the production units, while the problem of surplus demand is also solved on the basis of data received from the applicants.

For this reason, decisions made by upper levels of the economy are increasingly based on information 'from below'. The sections presenting this information have their own specific interests, which considerably influence the veracity of data. The opportunistic behaviour (to use Williamson's (1975) terminology) of economic agents is unavoidable. In this respect the Soviet economy does not differ from a market economy. Hence, in the centre conclusions are drawn from permanently and substantially distorted data. However, on the one hand, distortion over a definite size is risky: obvious cheating may be discovered. On the other hand, and more importantly, the economic agents are interested in the preservation and stability of the existing order. Therefore, they usually supply the upper levels with information reflecting not only their specific interests but also goals for sustaining the system. On the level of national ministries, the dominance of opportunistic targets and the sacrifice of public interest manifest more explicitly. This is a result of the greater power of ministries and their readiness to oppose society. However, at lower levels of the hierarchy economic agents prefer co-operation to confrontation. Thus, an atmosphere of 'watchful confidence' emerges.

'Information co-operation' combined with the impossibility to objectively identify 'best and worst' producers (which inevitably conflicts with the second precondition of a command economy, that is, strict responsibility) successively destroy the command order. Not only information but also all other interactions between the levels of hierarchy are subsequently based on collaboration instead of subordination. Each of the partners, while pursuing his own goals, is forced to consider the priorities of the others.

In other words, 'command economy' is substituted by a bargaining mechanism, where equilibrium is reached through numerous vertical and horizontal haggles (Aven and Shironin 1987). In vertical haggles, the resources of the upper sections include material and financial assets, various rates and normatives, possibilities to encourage administration, and so on. Among the resources of the lower levels we find: the fulfilment of plan targets or promises of such fulfilment, participation in meaningless campaigns (especially in agriculture), and so on.

In several rural regions of the USSR 300 leaders of non-private agricultural enterprises were asked to explain why they fulfil (in their view) non-optimal orders concerning the dates of sowing and harvest. The answers include the following reasons (Aven and Grodsky 1988; Aven and Shironin 1987):

- 'orders from above have to be fulfilled';
- the refusal may influence your career;
- the refusal may cost you the party card;
- you have pecuniary (personal) incentives to obey the orders;
- if you accept demands from an upper authority, this authority will help you later on.

The absolute majority of those leaders, who admitted the breach of dates, tended towards the last answer. Therefore, under conditions of low (if any) responsibility, participation in meaningless campaigns is regarded as a resource which may be reimbursed to the enterprise.

The objects of horizontal bargaining are various producer goods and services. In this case, the main difference as compared to a normal market is the absence of a 'common equivalent', that is, universal and absolutely liquid money. Such an absence results in 'fuzzy' prices of resources which, in turn, provoke the introduction of 'black' arguments (bribes, personal favours, and so on) in bargaining. As in the vertical interactions, such phenomena strengthen the informal interdependence of the economic agents, necessitating their inclusion in the network of intimate co-operation.

The idea of 'bargaining economy' or 'quasi-market' is certainly not new. However, there are several points to note. First, until recently the critics have been oriented towards accusations of a harmful 'top' that hinders the successful activity of the 'bottom'. The contraposition of different levels of the hierarchy results in appeals to 'liberate' producers (who often do not want to be liberated). A main cause for the recent worsening of the economic situation in the Soviet Union is the practical implementation of these appeals. (Certainly, some reform economists understood the danger of destroying an existing co-ordination mechanism without adequate substitution. At any rate, the possible consequences of such destruction are essentially underestimated. The desire to switch from one managerial paradigm to another, to begin (again) 'from the very beginning', is still strong enough.)

Second, the concept of command economy includes the conviction that its reform can be carried out through the introduction of 'good' laws and rules, which are created by the economic centre and followed by the subordinates without 'a murmur'. In reality, bargaining results in 'soft legislative constraints', in 'fuzzy' legislation, that is, each new law immediately becomes an object for inter-level haggling. (Thus, the formal independence of collective farms always served as an additional argument in their haggles with local party authorities. In the course of bargaining, rights for autonomous planning, income distribution, and so on, were included in a 'package for exchange'). Hence, the idea of the legal state (rule of law) contradicts the essence of the previous economic system.

The belief in the power of proper legislation allowed some economists, especially those who participated in legislative work, to accuse economic executives of distorting the laws (see, for example, Shatalin 1989). In fact, such distortion is an inalienable feature of the system, which reformers have to take into account when proposing new laws. A reliable forecast of the actual use of passed laws calls for a scrupulous analysis of the bargaining practice. Until recently, only few attempts of such analysis have been made (see Naishul and Konstantinov 1986; Aven and Grodsky 1988). As a result, the real bargaining economy (negotiation procedures, weights or 'prices' of various resources, and so on) is still unknown – that is the third point to note here. (Karagedov (1984) was absolutely correct when he said that in Soviet economic literature descriptions of normative economic mechanisms dominate over careful exploration of the existing system and its shortcomings.)

Superfluous passion for scholastic discussions about 'proper' economic orders and insufficient attention paid to reality result in the emergence of myths. Their disclosure calls for empirical investigations, which are, however, constrained by the lack or closed character of relevant information, by the decision-makers' unwillingness to open their 'bargaining world' for the researchers, and so on. (The difficulties in understanding are doubled by the outwardly unnatural character of some transactions. Thus, bargaining for plan targets in agriculture usually hover around obviously inachievable figures. However, such negotiations also have their own intrinsic logic.)

MYTHS AND OVERSIMPLIFICATIONS

The description of a bargaining economy may be divided into three parts. The first is connected with a structure of the economic system that is characterized by 'top' and 'bottom' elements, their possibilities and priorities. The second is associated with vertical and horizontal flows of financial and material resources and their prices. The third is related to the procedures of bargaining, that is, contracting, 'black' and 'non-material' arguments, and so on. Myths are connected with each of these parts. First of all one general myth must be noted – the 'myth of uniformity'.

If we assume that the lower sections of the economic system are obedient to laws and rules formulated in Moscow, we also admit the homogeneity of 'business life'. So the existing legislation does not include modifications depending on regional or sectoral specifics. 'Soft legislative constraints', however, result in essential differences in actual rules of decision-making and in heterogeneity of roles played by similar institutions under different conditions.

In several rural districts of the USSR we tried to compare real participation of local party authorities in agricultural production. Comparisons were based on estimates made by leaders of state and collective farms. Various 'scales of influence' were constructed – each had to represent the participation of local party leaders in the solution of concrete problems (decision on plan targets, distribution of machinery and fertilizers, and so on). On the scales, nil was associated with the absence of influence; one, with full power of the party. For almost all questions, districts turned out to be ranged between 0.4 and 0.9. Such distribution reflects the presence of districts with permanent party control together with districts without almost any party intervention in agriculture.

Differences between economic mechanisms of rural districts are much weaker than those between various republics or sectors in the economy. Nevertheless, in numerous proposals for the improvement of the economic system such diversity is not reflected adequately – the same measures are suggested for all areas. Moreover, it is often assumed that economic reform can be achieved not only uniformly, but also simultaneously in all regional and sectoral subsystems.

The initial oversimplification concerning the structure of the economic system is connected with its description as a hierarchy of two or three levels (centre – enterprise – worker). In reality, the number of hierarchical levels with their own specific roles and incentives are much greater. (Kordonsky (1986), for example, showed that there are four distinctive levels within a Soviet industrial enterprise only.) The significance of the sectoral level is essentially underestimated. In discussions on reform this level often fused with the economic centre and it is assumed that there will be no place for sectoral ministries in the future, post-reform system. However, in a large-scale economy, tasks of general co-ordination must be distinguished from tasks of sectoral development – the economic centre cannot deal with both. Sectoral problems cannot be solved by the enterprises either.

The perception of the economic system as a two-level structure with a powerful 'top' and an almost powerless 'bottom' does not correspond to the clarification of who these 'tops' and 'bottoms' in the various subsystems of the economy actually are and what their interests look like. An important myth concerning the 'top' is the 'myth of Party leadership'. According to this, party authorities permanently intervene in the production process, forcing meaningless plan targets on the enterprises.

Our empirical study of 'distribution of influence' in rural districts demonstrated significantly less intervention by party authorities in agricultural production than usually assumed. Routine questions (such as the determination of sowing and harvest dates, selection of technologies, distribution of machinery, fertilizers and labour within a farm) were, as a rule, solved by the enterprises without any participation of local leadership. Usually, party bosses also had relatively weak influence on resource allocation within a district.

At the same time party authorities played an active role in solving uncommon and 'strategic' problems:

- the determination of a 'general framework' for business operations;
- making decisions which directly contradict the existing legislation;
- management in extraordinary situations.

The first point is connected with 'fuzzy rules', the interpretation of which is a prerogative of local administration. Thus, until 1988, agricultural enterprises in the Soviet Union could not officially exchange machinery without permission of the district authority. In the absolute majority of districts this rule was never observed, but in some others the necessity to obtain permissions seriously influenced the intensity of exchange.

The second point concerns more serious violations of law, which cannot be made by the enterprises without informal support 'from above'. Decisions are included here which contradict not only legislation, but also the interests of producers. A typical example is the forced purchase of grain produced over the plan figure. An important advantage of the party leadership stemmed from 'oral' or 'telephone' law: the orders and (more often) the requests from party authorities were not fixed on paper. This certainly expanded their flexibility to violate laws. At the same time, such violations made by state or collective farm leaders strengthened their ties with the party leaders.

A typical example of an extraordinary situation: sudden weather change. Though such changes may occur rather frequently, they always call for fast decision-making which is impossible in a bargaining atmosphere.

The last point shows that party authorities performed important functions which simply could not be fulfilled by a quasi-market. Their role had to be played by some (if other) institution.

The party apparatus represents its 'subordinates' in haggles for resources with upper levels of the hierarchy. In some sense it plays the role of a cartel or trading corporation. Another function of the party authorities is the assistance in bargaining between 'their' enterprises and some external agents. Frequently, a collective farm or a small factory has to do business with much more powerful partners, who have the possibility of organizing unfair, non-equivalent exchange, and violating the terms of a treaty. In such cases, only intervention from the party apparatus can help the victim. (Thus, only local party authorities can help a collective farm replace a defective tractor, which has already been paid for and delivered.) Under the conditions of a highly-monopolized economy this function is significant.

The third important function is arbitration. The growing complexity of the economy makes the attainment of agreements in limited time unlikely, therefore the bargaining parties often ask the party administration to serve as an arbitrator. It is necessary to pay for arbitration but the 'price' turns out to be less than potential losses from derangement of the transaction. (A well-known example of arbitration is the day-to-day concordance of prices for repairs of machinery in agriculture.)

Inevitably, all functions mentioned above must be carried out. Otherwise, the efficiency of a bargaining economy (which is anyway too low) would further decrease. Therefore, appeals to exclude the party apparatus from economic management only make sense if a new 'mechanism of quasi-market support' is proposed. The weakening of the traditional, party-based co-ordination system without adequate substitution results in monopolistic price increases and in doubling the shortages.

Among the most important gaps in our knowledge of the existing system is a lack of information concerning the actual interests and priorities of economic agents. In a command economy interests have no importance. But what are the incentives of the various 'tops' and 'bottoms' in a quasi-market? Galbraith's (1967) idea of aspiration for growth and expansion does not look serious under Soviet conditions. (Rural districts have very definite limits to growth, particularly with respect to space. Only for national ministries, an orientation towards expansion can explain peculiarities of behaviour.) The traditional views concerning the managers' desire for making a career, and their fear to lose the party card also do not look very convincing.

Our investigations in the rural sector demonstrated that fear to be punished was almost non-existent, at least for the majority of state and collective farms leaders who are in their forties and fifties. Such leaders already have no career plans, they are not afraid to lose their position (because the level of their salary is relatively low and that of responsibility is sufficiently high), and they pay no attention to the numerous reprimands (without any real consequences) coming from above.

In discussing interests we again have to deal with the problem of uniformity. It is doubtless, that the priorities of managers (even on the same hierarchical level) are quite different. While some of them are oriented towards satisfaction of the demands of their bosses at the 'top', others maximize personal income or pursue some specific goals usually popular within society. Therefore, a system of incentives proposed for post-reform models also must be sufficiently diverse. In conditions of empty consumer and producer markets, monetary stimuli must be supplemented with non-monetary ones.

Diversity of interests is connected with the heterogeneity of priorities relevant to distribution of material and financial resources. In the orthodox Soviet-type model it is assumed that the economic centre has certain criteria for allocation, knows how to optimize these criteria and is capable of implementing the best variant. In a command economy the centre has no idea about the best distribution. Hence, either a conclusion is drawn about the impossibility of 'proper' distribution without market, or various methods are proposed for improving the existing practice. As a rule, such methods are never used, because they do not take into account the real priorities of decision-makers in resource allocation.

According to our empirical study, on district level, the actual 'weight' of marginal productivity usually was less than the 'weight' of well-being. In other words, the desire for 'fair' distribution is stronger than the incentives to increase efficiency.

Oversimplifications concerning the structure of the economy coincide with a lack of knowledge about the vertical and horizontal flows of various resources and their prices. The illegal character of many barter agreements results in insufficiency of data, which reflect such flows. In fact, the amount of exchange in resources is unknown. This causes the 'myth of money'.

In the orthodox model, money is part of the economic mechanism, serving as an important stimulus for greater productivity. ('More and better production means that more profits are received by an enterprise. So it has material incentives for better work' – Rumiantsev *et al.* 1977.) Nevertheless, if money can be withdrawn from an enterprise by an upper authority, it cannot be regarded as a serious incentive. Hence, it is usually concluded that in the existing economic system money 'is not needed at all', 'is not in shortage', and so on. Indeed, in the majority of cases the distribution of physical resources takes place independently from the financial status of recipients. Indeed, loans can be granted without reliable guarantees for repayment. Nevertheless, 'soft budget constraints' (Kornai 1980) are not equivalent to the lack of any constraints at all. Moreover, the strictness of financial constraints is essentially different for various sectors of the economy (absolutely 'soft' for defence industry, and relatively strict for light industry or agriculture).

In economic practice, the availability of money serves as an important argument in bargaining for resources. It is no mere chance that in horizontal haggles the prices of resources exchanged are discussed carefully. So in some sense, money in a bargaining economy can be considered as one of many relatively scarce resources, whose distribution and flows have definite peculiarities.

BARGAINING ECONOMY: REGULARITIES OF DEVELOPMENT

The bargaining mechanism is an unavoidable stage between command and market economies because of:

- the necessity to introduce market tools in the economy (taxes, differential payments, and so on), which do not really work in the first phases of the bargaining model (or work in some specific, non-market way as, for example, individual normatives of profit distribution), but penetrate the minds of economic agents;
- the necessity to generate and promote entrepreneurial activity (which obtains special incentives in the horizontal haggles);
- the necessity to gradually unify the economic legislation (or to create a 'legal economy' which cannot be simply 'switched on').

The regularities of development of a bargaining economy are directly connected with the 'transitional' character of its existence. In some sense, these regularities may be regarded as directions of transformation within a 'bargaining paradigm'. An example of penetration was the concession of equal 'bargaining rights' to the industrial combines and the ministries in the GDR (Shabalin and Tsedilin 1984). Another example is the rights given to labour teams in the majority of East European countries.

The best way to define priorities in the redistribution of rights is to codify already existing and useful, but officially non-legitimate, rules. Codification legalizes bargaining activity. For horizontal haggles it means official permission for any exchange between enterprises, that is, their actual liberation from any control from above of their horizontal links. For vertical bargaining, it means a precise definition of the rights of the enterprises. Codification also results in clarification of existing rules. This promotes the overcoming of 'fuzzy legislation' and its alienation from reality. Besides, obtaining more precise constraints causes economic agents to behave 'economically'.

In the meantime, the object of bargaining changes. In the first stages of the bargaining economy, plan targets in vertical haggles were mainly exchanged for material resources. Later (as the Soviet and the Hungarian experiences demonstrate – see, for example, Nyers and Tardos 1978) economic normatives substitute machinery or raw materials: bargaining for economic regulators begins to dominate. In the process of such substitution the list of regulators is permanently changing – the search for 'the best one' continues. In addition, the legalization of bargaining permits discussion and assessment of the possible consequences of changes in the regulators given to the enterprises. All this serves as a base for the introduction of a system of common normatives necessary for a 'real' market.

An important feature of the Soviet-type economy and, therefore, of a 'young' bargaining one is the lack of any common rules. In order to complete the transition to a market economy, it is necessary to substitute individual regulators (first of all, economic normatives) for common ones. Such substitution cannot be carried out in one step – a temporary use of group normatives is unavoidable (Aleksashenko *et al.* 1989). Nevertheless, a bargaining economy permits co-ordinating their levels, and to 'grind in' the different positions, which is indispensable for the introduction of a market model.

BIBLIOGRAPHY

Aleksashenko, S. *et al.* (1989) 'Nalogovie shkaly: funktsii, svoistva, metody upravlenia' ('Tax scales: functions, specifics and control techniques'), *Economika i matematicheskie metody* 3.

Aven, P. and Grodsky, V. (1988) 'Systema upravlenia raionnim APK: opit sravnitelnogo analyza' ('Controlling the district agro-industrial complex: a comparative analysis'), *Sbornik trudov VNIISI* 4.

Aven, P. and Shironin, V. (1987) 'Reforma khoziaistvennogo mekhanizma:

realnost' namechaemih preobrazovanii' ('Reform of the economic mechanism: the planned transformation in reality'), *Izvestia SO AN SSSR*, ser. ekonomiki i prikladnoi sotsiologii 3.

Galbraith, J.K. (1987) *The New Industrial State*, Boston, Houghton Mifflin.

Karagedov, R. (1984) 'O napravleniah sovershenstvovania khoziastvennogo mekhanizma' ('On the directions of improving the economic mechanism') *Izvestia SO AN SSSR*, ser. ekonomiki i prikladnoi sotsiologii 3.

Kordonsky, S. (1986) 'Nekotorie sotsiologicheskie aspekti khoziaistvennih otnoshenii' ('Some sociological aspects of the economic relations'), *Sbornik trudov VNIISI* 6.

Kornai, J. (1980) *Economics of Shortage*, Amsterdam, North Holland.

Naishul, V. and Konstantinov, N. (1986) *Protsedury ustanovlenia planovikh zadanii* ('Procedures for determining the planning targets'), Moskva, IEP NTP AN SSSR.

Nyers, R. and Tardos, M. (1978) 'Enterprises in Hungary before and after the Economic Reform,' *Acta Oeconomica* 20.

Popov, G. (1987) 'O romane A.Beka "Novoe naznachenie"' ('About A. Bek's novel "New Appointment"'), *Nauka i zhizn* pp. 4, 54–65.

Rumiantsev, A. *et al.* (1977) *Politicheskaia Ekonomiia (Political Economy)*, Moskva, Politizdat.

Shabalin, A. and Tsedilin, L. (1984) *Kombinaty v systeme upravlenia narodnim khoziaistvom GDR (Combines in the Management System of the National Economy of the GDR)*, Moskva, Nauka.

Shatalin, S. (1989) 'Ischem kozla otpuschenia?' ('Looking for a scape goat?'), *Pravda*, 4 May.

Williamson, O.E. (1975) *Markets and Hierarchies*, New York, The Free Press.

Yasin, E. (1988) 'Administrativnaya systema tsen ili ekonomicheskij mekhanizm' ('Administrative system of prices or economic mechanism'), *Ekonomika i matematicheskie metody* 2, 205–20.

9 From revisionism to pragmatism
Sketches to a self-portrait of a 'reform economist'

Włodzimierz Brus

The 'plan and/or market' project raises very difficult and ambitious queries about the 'paradigm' of 'reform economics', its scholarly affiliations, ideological inspirations, political constraints, and so on. For a number of reasons I felt ill at ease to take up these subjects in even the minimally-required detached manner; besides, several other contributors – among them people eminently more competent than myself – made the attempt to locate 'reform economics' in its proper slot. Thus I decided that perhaps the best I could do was to tell a simple personal story which should not be taken as 'true' in the objective sense, but which might provide some input into the discussion of the questions under scrutiny. I should like to make it clear that what I try to sketch below concerns my 'reform economics' evolution on the academic (scholarly?) plane, as reflected in publications, without dwelling on the inevitable compromises of the practical reform struggles of 1956 and later in the first period of activity of the Polish economic council (1957–8) in which I had the chance to participate.

The first signs of my, let us call it, 'reform attitude' came in late 1953 when not only the 'new course' after Stalin's death got under way, but also the first somewhat more genuine picture of the actual economic performance emerged. The stimulus was thus provided by economic reality. Also the direction of the postulated change – modification of the institutional set-up of the 'system' and not only in the economic policy priorities – was derived from the evident inefficiencies at the micro-level (easier observable) caused by informational and motivational failures. Hence the emphasis on better incentive structure and conditions for more rational choice at the enterprise level – through elevation of 'synthetic' indicators (profitability), reduction and later abolition of obligatory target planning and physical allocation of resources, activation of money – price mechanism, and other things known today under Kornai's apt term of hardening the budget constraint. The conviction that these requirements did not stem from specifically Polish circumstances was strengthened by my own experience as an enterprise planner in the Soviet Union during the war, and by gradually developing contacts with economists from other Communist countries (György Péter of Hungary in the first place, then a conference in East Berlin in 1955, first Liberman's articles in the same year, and on).

There were ideological influences too. I was perhaps particularly suscep ible to some sort of 'market orientation' because of the lingering memory of frank discussion of the topic in the Leningrad University during the war (after the publication of the famous article 'Some problems of teaching political economy' in 1943), reinforced later by Stalin's peculiar rehabilitation of the law of value under socialism in 1952. As far as Oskar Lange's celebrated model of 'market socialism' was concerned (I knew it then only from the partial publication in the Polish theoretical journal *Ekonomista*), it was not for me a source of inspiration in any sense – probably both because its neo-classical methodological foundations were far more removed from my own Marxist ones, and because its author clearly underplayed at the time the significance of his essay.

On the other hand I was a firm believer in central planning as an indispensable tool of full utilization of resources, particularly labour, on a macro-scale, harmonious growth with proper anticipation of the necessary structural transformations, development of human and material infrastructure, and so on. This belief was probably strengthened by the influence of Michal Kalecki (both through better acquaintance with his writings and through close direct contacts), but basically it derived from long-standing Marxist convictions, one could say – *Weltanschauung*. That is why, even at the height of the ideological turmoil of the days of the 'Polish October' 1956, when radical reassessments were often the order of the day, I tried to defend central planning (in a reformed system) against those whom I regarded as extreme *laissez-fair*ists. As developed more fully in my 'General problems of functioning of a socialist economy' – ('The market in a socialist economy' in English) written in 1959–60 and first published in Polish in 1961, central planning had to change, had to become planning in a real sense as opposed to detailed management of all actions in the economy, but it had to remain the superior force in resource allocation, with market mechanism indispensable as a tool, a better instrument than commands, but an instrument still.

In conjunction with the view that the state ownership of means of production should retain its dominant position – notwithstanding the recognition of greater scope for genuine co-operatives, some private sector outside agriculture and renunciation of all coercion in developing collective forms in agriculture – this was a clear revisionist stand reflecting the belief in the full viability of socialism as an economic system, provided it would be effectively cleaned of Stalinist deformations. I was aware of the 'Austrian' (Mises/Hayek) criticism, but I accepted that its theoretical thrust was ill-founded, and that the new system of 'central planning with regulated market' would create conditions propitious for solving numerous practical difficulties (which were explicitly acknowledged – so the naïveté pointed out rightly by Kornai in his 1986 article is to be interpreted in relative terms).

The process of my gradual evolution as a 'reform economist' began with the realization of the defeat of the ideas and hopes of the 'Polish October'. The political system of the mono-party-state ('mono-archy' in my preferred terminology) survived and allowed the power elite to push back step-by-step the incipient reform – both in the economic sphere proper (independence of enterprises, profit-based incentives, price reform) and in the sphere of socio-political relations (workers' councils in the first place). It would be wrong to say that political change had at the time not been perceived by myself and others as part and parcel of the economic reform, but too much was taken for granted, and therefore not postulated explicitly. Intra-party democracy, accompanied by radical curbs in the size and power of party apparatus (the idea of merging the departments of party committees and transforming them into representative commissions, apparently pursued much later by Gorbachev, seemed to have been put into practice in Poland then), change in the electoral law, regeneration of the non-Communist parties, wide legal powers of workers' self-management, unprecedented freedom of press and association, and so on – all this made the process of democratization look unstoppable for a while. This – and not any consciously-felt political constraints – provides, in my opinion, the main explanation why in major programmatic documents concerning economic reform, and certainly in my own writings of the time, the political factor had not occupied the place of prominence it deserved.

The defeat of the 'Polish October' profoundly affected my attitude. The interaction between the economic and political change became gradually one of the main concerns in my brand of 'reform economics'. My party membership required from time to time tactical compromises in political activities (including university politics); up to 1966–7 I still regarded the possibility to act 'from within' as an advantage. This, however, has hardly been a factor influencing my intellectual position. Political changes – pluralization of the political system – came to be regarded by me, not only as an obvious condition of introducing meaningful market components into the economic system, but as an indispensable element of a rational economic system of socialism as such. Macroeconomic choices are by their very nature political, and without a pluralist polity they will always remain arbitrary: I tried thus to include the political element into the very notion of rationality of economic decisions, together with the expected impact of democratization on popular attitudes toward centrally-taken decisions scrutinized openly from the viewpoint of social interest as perceived by the people ('disalienation', genuine socialization of ownership of the means of production as opposed to mere statization). This, and only this, could refute in practice the assertions of socialism's inability to solve economic problems, and particularly to secure the necessary balance between responsibility and risk aversion. When I look back now to identify any outside sources of inspiration for this higher politicization of my 'reform economics', first to come to mind are discussions with my Czechoslovak colleagues, among others with Ota Šik – not so much linked to his reform designs of the time, as to his PhD ('candidate') dissertation of *The Economy, Interests, Politics* which was published in full later, during the 'Prague Spring'.

This was the way I moved the ownership problem to the centre of the reform stage: the existing type of ownership of means of production is faulty, not because of its integrated nature, but because integration has been accomplished through an alienated bureaucratized machinery of power instead of through a socialized state. It was from this point of view that I criticized the Yugoslav concept of self-management socialism in 'Socialist ownership and political systems' (1975): its logic leads to unlimited fragmentation of ownership of means of production and to fully-fledged group ownership, whereas I have still advocated the ultimate right of the community as a whole to decide about the level of accumulation, the allocation of the main stream of investment, to determine at least the general rules of the distribution of incomes, and so on. My attitude towards self-management was that it should operate within the confines of a centrally-planned economy with a regulated market mechanism, in which the centre is subjected to popular control through a pluralist political system ('polyarchy' in Dahl-Lindlblom terms). Again, looking back I cannot find any traces of political constraints determining my position. Besides, at that time all remnants of my previous links with any type of establishment in Poland (including the academic one) had been broken, the politicization of my 'reform economics' became the principal target of attacks, and from the end of 1972 I have lived and worked in Britain. Nevertheless, at least until the end of the 1970s I still held on to the ideas briefly described above, as witnessed among other things by the presentation of my 'reform economics' in China during my first visit there in 1979–80. I don't see, therefore, the grounds for a possible 'sociological' explanation of the persistent tendency to keep some elements of the traditional perception of a socialist economic system.

The next stage of the evolution of my thinking came with the absorption of the evidence of the reformed socialist economies – Hungary and Yugoslavia. It was not simply a matter of examining the actual economic performance but mainly of finding a link with the foundations of the system of the functioning of the economy. The nut was very difficult to crack. Take Hungary, for instance: the introduction of the New Economic Mechanism (NEM) brought about (or coincided with?) a number of positive phenomena in the economy, particularly in comparison with other Communist countries. Then came the disappointments, but why? External circumstances – the 1973 oil shock, and so on – could not be easily eliminated from any assessment. As far as systemic factors were concerned, the practice of NEM gave increasingly good reasons for criticism, but was it because the concept itself (the 'half-way house') was wrong, or because it was actually never properly introduced? The Yugoslav case seemed to me even more tricky: apart from the specific national problems and the hypertrophy of self-management, could not the alarmingly growing setbacks in the economy be attributed to excessive marketization of the system, particularly to the decentralization of investment after the 1965 reform? (I must admit that I overestimated the scope of the genuine operation of the market in Yugoslavia after these reforms, especially when the system began to undergo yet another change in the early 1970s). Moreover, both Yugoslavia and Hungary failed to fulfil the political condition: the 'mono-archy' survived intact, despite some degree of cultural liberalization; according to the concept referred to above, this in itself should provide a substantial element of explanation of the malfunctioning of the economic system. As late as 1983 I entertained the possibility that the pressure for more consistent marketization observable among Hungarian economists was a reflection of their pessimistic evaluation of the chances to pluralize the polity: if one cannot bring the centre under popular political control, one is compelled to look for ways of weakening the power of the centre by extending the scope of the market-determined economic decisions to the investment sphere as well.

Closer analysis convinced me, however, that I was wrong. The expectations connected with the introduction of the product market (both for consumer goods and for producer goods) could not materialize for a number of reasons: allocation of the main bulk of investment through a vertical planning mechanism requires necessarily a strong administrative centre which tends to extend its powers into other areas as well; development of competition and entrepreneurial behaviour is unlikely without free entry and exit, requiring in turn the possibility of horizontal movements of capital; the lack of the latter hampers also the disciplining function of the market because it makes it most difficult to distinguish between genuinely unviable firms and those which become unviable owing to closed opportunities to diversify, to acquire new technology, and so on – hence the legitimization of the bargaining process with administrative holders of the keys to resources. This topic could obviously be expanded – both with regard to the capital market and to the labour market – but there is no point in doing it here. What I wanted to show was merely the general direction of the evolution of my thinking under the influence of a closer scrutiny of the experience of the reformed economies. A study stay in Hungary and Yugoslavia in 1983 contributed undoubtedly to a better understanding of the matter.

Letting the capital market into the system represents, in my opinion, an important step on the road from revisionism to pragmatism in 'reform economics'. Of course, it would hardly be warranted to seek a firm watershed between reform thinking within and outside some *a priori* defined socialist framework, but should such an attempt be undertaken, the admission of the capital market would be a strong candidate. (In the past I myself thought it to be *the* watershed.) Capital market impinges upon all the major pillars of a socialist economic system: (1) on central planning as an *ex ante* design of the future physical structure of the economy; (2) on the mechanism of distribution both in the sense of aggregate division of national product into consumption and accumulation, and in the sense of legitimizing the non-work factors of income distribution among individuals and groups; (3) on the ownership relations.

The latter issue becomes particularly complex, as I was soon to recognize. The matter could not be handled any more within the framework of the social nature of the integrated state ownership – the very question of the viability of the integration of property rights on a national scale had to be posed: even apart from the need to separate strictly the state as a political, administrative and regulatory body from the state as the owner of business capital (I leave aside here the area of infrastructure), the distribution of property rights between the state as owner and the enterprises appearing on the capital market, bearing risk and responsibility, must be completely redefined. The separation of the state from the enterprises has to go along with full separation between enterprises themselves. Then the problem arises whether or to what extent state-owned entities are at all suitable for acting in the capital market. Whatever the general answer to this question, I came to share the nowadays widely-accepted conclusion that the change from, using again Kornai's terminology, bureaucratic (direct or indirect) to market co-ordination cannot be based on the absolute and unchallenged dominance of the state sector, even meeting the conditions of separation mentioned earlier. A mixed economy with a sizeable non-state sector of co-operative, private and quasi-private (all kinds of leaseholds, contracting-out, and so on) enterprises competing on equal terms with the state ones seems to be the necessary condition of a consistent reform.

I see now political pluralism not as a factor of rationalization of the superior role of the centre as in my model of 'centrally-planned economy with regulated market mechanism', but as an indispensable element of transition from the old to the new economic system, and as a guardian of the continuous existence of the latter. This does not mean, in my view, that a consistent market-oriented reform excludes the pursuance of values habitually associated with socialism – mitigation of inequalities, major concern for full employment, social care, opportunity for developing talents, and so on. Not all aspects of socio-economic life must be subjected to market co-ordination, and where they would be there is a substantial scope for macroeconomic policy, including such which can even aspire to the designation planning, provided it does not impair the general logic of the operation of the market. In other words, my position is still not identical with the *laissez-faire* one as I retain the belief that the notion of the interest of the society cannot be just reduced to a sum-total of individual self-interests. Whether or not such a system may be called socialism ('market socialism') seems immaterial; it is to be an open-ended system capable of flexible change in line with pragmatically-validated requirements.

This is, in short-hand, the story of my own 'reform economics' over the years. It shows a gradual, one may even say, reluctant, evolution in the direction of marketization under the impact, so I think, of real experience in the first place. The degree of admissibility of this story as evidence, and even more so its wider relevance is – needless to say – subject to discussion.

10 Soviet economic reform in historical perspective

Robert W. Davies

SOCIALISM AND SOCIALISMS

Millions of people wanted to believe . . . that socialism can be achieved easily, that the desire for it is all that's needed, that all natural laws can easily be subordinated to the will of human beings, and paradise will be reached during the lifetime of a single generation: pears will grow on apple trees, wheat will grow from weeds, cows will begin to give all the milk that's required. In that complicated Utopian time the leaders dreamed that production and distribution would be carried out on Communist principles in a country with a declassed proletariat. Remember how, even in the literature of the sixties, not to mention earlier times, we were often told that western specialists had worked out that a building would take five years, but our people got ahead and finished it in a year. We learned how we had refuted the estimates by cautious engineers; how boldly we risked our lives! Social mirages were supported by literary mirages. The last mirage in which the people believed was the solemn promise in the sixties that the present generation of Soviet citizens would live under communism. And they solemnly believed it, as I can testify, as I believed it myself. The *perestroika* is not a revision of the idea of socialism, as some total destroyers think, but a bold return to reality, the elimination of the conflict between the idea and the real human being on earth.

(Vladimir Bondarenko, *Literaturnaya gazeta*, 20 May 1987)

The traditional Soviet view

The existence of several different socialist or semi-socialist economic systems in the course of seventy years of Soviet history is of course a long-established cliché in Soviet thought. The notorious *History of the Communist Party of the Soviet Union (Bolsheviks): Short Course* (Moscow, 1939) distinguished between three systems. First, war communism was 'an attempt to take the fortress of the capitalist elements in town and countryside by assault, by a frontal attack'. Second, the New Economic Policy (NEP) allowed freedom of trade for the peasant and 'a certain revival of capitalism'. Third, in the Soviet economy from the mid-1930s onwards, 'Socialist ownership of the means of production had been established in every branch of national economy as the basis of Soviet society'.

In Soviet textbooks of the 1930s and 1940s there was some analysis of the resemblances and differences between these different stages of the economy. In war communism, all industry was managed by the state; a state monopoly of grain was established, accompanied by the surplus appropriation system; universal labour service was compulsory; individual peasant households continued, however, to predominate in the countryside. Under the first stage of the New Economic Policy, the 'commanding heights' of the economy, especially industry, remained in state ownership, agriculture was largely in the hands of individual peasants, and a market relation existed between them. In the socialist economy from the mid-1930s, state ownership of industry and the agricultural machine-tractor stations was coupled with collective ownership of the collective farms. Much attention was devoted by Soviet economists in Stalin's time to the role of money in the socialist economy and to the role of economic accounting (*khozraschet*) in state industry. By 1936, money was recognized to be an inherent feature of the socialist economy; this overturned the long-established view that socialism as well as communism would already be a moneyless economy.

This Soviet presentation of the major Soviet economic systems of the inter-war years reflected important aspects of Soviet reality. But it suffered from four sets of weaknesses, which dominated Communist ideas outside the Soviet Union and strongly influenced mainstream socialist thinking throughout the world about the transition to socialism.

First, the Soviet images of the three economic systems were one-sided and idealized. Thus the existence of a free or black market during war communism was recognized but it was not treated as an inherent and inescapable element of the system.

The New Economic Policy was defined as coterminous with the whole 'transition period' from war communism to socialism, which was treated as a single stage and a single economic model. On this view NEP was not primarily the market relation with the peasants; it was the struggle to eliminate capitalism and petty capitalism in the USSR. Therefore it did not come to an end until private trade, private industry and private agriculture had all been eliminated, round about 1936. This extremely broad and somewhat bizarre definition of NEP had little influence in the west, and proved very difficult to accept within the USSR. But it remained the orthodox Soviet view until 1987. A Soviet work published in 1982 complained that 'bourgeois authors', including myself, 'date NEP from 1921 to 1928', and explained that the objective of this chronological scheme is clearly to distort the true essence of NEP by separating its first years from the period of the decisive offensive against the capitalist elements in town and country, when the socialist nature of NEP disclosed itself more clearly.

(Yu. A. Polyakov, V.P. Dmitrenko and N.V. Shcherban',
*Novaya ekonomicheskaya politika:
razrabotka i osushchestvlenie*, pp. 228–9)

The economy up to about 1936 was thus included in NEP.

In the description of the socialist economic system, which was held to have been established by about 1936, socialist ownership and planning were treated as the crucial features. The market and quasi-market features of the Stalinist economy, like the similar features of war communism, were treated as merely minor aspects of the system. The partial market for labour, the fixed-price market for retail consumer goods (involving some consumer choice though not consumer sovereignty), and the '*kolkhoz*' market at free prices for part of retail food sales were treated as more or less incidental features of the system. And the unofficial or illegal markets – including barter, deals and prestation within the state sector – were ignored altogether, as was the persistence of repressed inflation. This view of the Stalinist economy influenced – or had common ground with – classic western writings about the Soviet economy (until the classic view was disrupted by the work of Granick, Berliner and others in the 1950s). The Soviet view of their own economy was not vastly different, as far as the economic mechanism was concerned, from the western model of 'planning under a dictator' (later renamed the 'command economy'), and in western writings this concept fitted well with the totalitarian model of the Soviet regime.

The second major weakness of Soviet analysis, closely associated with these oversimplifications, was the assumption that the Soviet leadership almost always acted entirely in accordance with the requirements dictated by the situation in which it found itself; only a few minor exceptions were acknowledged. This was not, however, economic determinism. It is true that the theoretical section of the *Short Course* (Chapter 4, part 2), of which Stalin claimed personal authorship, insisted that in the socialist economy of the USSR 'the relations of production completely correspond to the character of the productive forces' (this formulation was modified substantially by Stalin in 1952). But the *Short Course* acknowledged that war communism was 'necessitated by the exceptionally difficult conditions of national defence, and bore a temporary character'. And Stalin, of course, also insisted that the proletarian state could use its power to pull up the Soviet economy to the level of the advanced capitalist countries: the superstructure transformed the productive forces, rather than being merely determined by them. But all this was treated as an ineluctable result of the application of a correct Marxist strategy to objective circumstances. There was no place for the treatment of the evolution of the Soviet economic system as in part an experiment in the designing of a new and unknown socialist order. The series of fascinating 'false starts' of 1920–2 and 1926–32, for example, from which there is still much to learn today, fell almost entirely out of the picture.

The third weakness of the Soviet analysis was the assumption of a straightforward progression from the market economy to a planned economy, and from private ownership via co-operative ownership to state ownership. On this deeply-held view, under communism, state ownership would prevail universally, collective farms would have given way to state farms, and the household plots of collective-farm families would have been completely eliminated; it would be a moneyless economy, and the collective-farm market would have given way to planned distribution. The further development of the socialist economic system was assumed to involve a steady progression in the general direction of the Communist economic order. This general concept was re-emphasized by Stalin in *Economic Problems of Socialism in the USSR*, a few months before his death.

The fourth weakness in the traditional Soviet approach was its underlying political assumptions. Socialism involved social ownership of the means of production, and distribution of the social product to individuals according to work done. Therefore exploiters and exploitation no longer existed, and, according to the *Short Course*, production was bound to be based on 'comradely co-operation and Socialist mutual assistance'. The analysis did not even consider the proposition that socialist relations of production – whether due to Russian economic backwardness, or to the inherent problems of a certain kind of socialism – could involve the emergence of bureaucratism as a systemic feature or of a bureaucracy as a social phenomenon. And it was taken for granted that 'one-man management', in which managers were appointed and not elected, was not an emergency arrangement due to the shortage of trained politically-trustworthy administrators, but a natural feature of socialism as such. I labour these points about the traditional analysis because its influence has been felt long after Stalin's lifetime, and over areas of the globe far wider than the USSR. In the USSR, even under Stalin, it underwent some modification, and further adjustments were made in the Khrushchev years (see W.Brus (1988) 'Utopianism and realism in the Soviet economic system', *Soviet Studies* xl, 434–43). But the basic traditional framework continued, and in 1970–85 it was strengthened.

In the west the assumptions that socialization meant nationalization, and that socialist planning meant central control, and the centralized appointment of managerial staff, were also predominant. While in the west this view of socialism has complex origins for which the USSR cannot be held entirely or even mainly responsible, it was undoubtedly reinforced by knowledge of Soviet experience. I recall that when I was a student in the late 1940s the bureaucratic arrangements for the newly-nationalized British coal industry and railways seemed to me quite natural in the light of what I knew of Soviet economic history. It is not inconceivable that new Soviet practices in electing foremen and factory directors – if they get anywhere – may in the long run exercise a healthy influence on the industrial practice of the British state.

New Soviet views of socialism

I have suggested in the previous section that there were four characteristic weaknesses in the traditional Soviet view of their own economic history: (1) the images of the economic systems were one-sided or idealized; (2) the policy of the leadership was assumed always to have been more or less correct; (3) state ownership was treated as the highest form of ownership and as the ultimate goal; (4) it was assumed that in an economy with full state ownership, exploitation and class domination were absent, and politics was no longer a problem.

In the course of 1987 and 1988 the new approaches to the Soviet past swept aside the second, third and fourth of these weaknesses (I return to the first weakness later).

Thus in relation to point (2), the policies of the Soviet leadership at every stage in Soviet history have now been called into question. In the first phase of the debate, Lenin was handled with circumspection. But even then Soviet historians argued that during the Civil War he went through a learning process, and in 1921 abandoned earlier assumptions that socialism would exclude commodity production and exclude a role for the state (see, for example, V.Kiselev (1988) in *Nauka i zhizn'* 9, 40–2).

And major and minor policies of all Lenin's successors – Stalin, Khrushchev, Brezhnev, even Andropov – were continuously criticized. The policies of the Soviet Communist party between 1925 and 1985 were described at best in terms of trial and error, and often in terms of a succession of disastrous choices of the wrong alternatives.

In relation to point (3), state ownership was no longer treated as coterminous with full socialism. All forms of social ownership were regarded as of equal status. Great emphasis was placed in particular on the importance of various forms of co-operatives as a major sector in an efficient and democratic socialist economy. The writings of Chayanov, rehabilitated in 1987, received enormous attention. The Director of the Institute of Marxism–Leninism, G.L. Smirnov, asked to define socialism in terms of ownership, referred to 'a multi-coloured spectrum of property relations – state and co-operative property, the property of enterprises, and property as a basis for individual labour activity, and the property of various voluntary organisations' (*Kommunist* 11, 1988, 37–8).

The new view of socialism, coupled with the criticism of Stalinism, led an increasing number of Soviet economists to refuse to categorize Soviet society between the end of the 1920s and 1985 as socialist or as moving towards socialism. According to Kiselev, this was 'a model of state socialism with its extra-economic compulsion, with methods of administrative orders' (*Nauka i zhizn'* 9, 1988, 42), and the prominent Soviet political observer Burlatsky claimed that what took place was not the transition to socialism but 'statization' (*Literaturnaya gazeta*, 20 April 1988). And N.A. Popov, from the Institute of the USA and Canada, declared that Stalin '*created an ideal totalitarian state, in which his personal power extended to everything – economics and science, literature and art*' (*Sovetskaya kul'tura*, 26 April 1988). Academician Bogomolov, prominent economic reformer, noted without comment that the Chinese now describe their past system as a 'feudal-bourgeois fascist dictatorship' (*Sovetskaya kul'tura*, 12 July 1988).

In relation to point (4), a substantial mental revolution took place. At a 'round table' in the Institute of Marxism–Leninism in October 1987 (reported in *Voprosy istorii KPSS* 2, 1988, 110–33), the well-known economic reformer, A.P. Butenko, from Bogomolov's Institute of the Economics of the World Socialist System, argued that after Lenin's last writings 'no one endeavoured to analyse our society from the point of view of the growth and strengthening of the bureaucracy' (Butenko did not mention Trotsky and the Left Opposition). (There is no definite or indefinite article in Russian. '*Byurokratiya*' could be translated 'bureaucratism', that is, the phenomenon, or 'the bureaucracy', that is, the social group. It seems to me that only the latter translation fits with Butenko's argument.) But the bureaucracy was 'a huge danger for socialism':

> At a definite stage in the life of the Soviet state it was not the proletariat and the labouring peasantry which were in power but those who usurped power – Stalin and his entourage. Moreover not only the form of rule (*forma vlastvovaniya*) was established, but also the form of administration (*forma upravleniya*) in the shape of a huge stratum of state and party bureaucracy, torn away from the people and not under its control.

Butenko also asserted that 'the same model of socialism, relying on the state and party bureaucracy', existed in the 1970s and early 1980s as in the 1930s and 1940s.

Butenko's views were strongly challenged. But they were widely accepted in a modified form. Thus V.V. Zhuravlev, deputy director of the Institute of Marxism–Leninism, summing up the discussion on the same occasion, while insisting that the working class and the peasantry remained the social basis of the Soviet system under Stalin, was prepared to concede that Stalin was supported by a bureaucracy, and that Stalin, like Napoleon III, had usurped power.

For our present purposes it is not perhaps the detail of the debate that is important, but the universal recognition in the Soviet discussions that the political economy of socialism must include a free-ranging analysis of social and political relations.

Let us now turn back to point (1). We have seen that the Soviet analysis of past economic systems is now much more flexible and realistic. How far is it nevertheless one-sided? I shall turn to the Soviet treatment of NEP in my third section, and will consider here the recent Soviet view of the command economy under Stalin and after.

In a very searching analysis of the Stalinist economic system, Gavriil Popov, using Aleksandr Bek's novel about the management of Soviet industry as his starting point, depicted what he called the 'Administrative system' of the Stalinist economy ('O romane A. Beka "Novoe naznachenie"' ('About A. Bek's novel "New Appointment"') *Nauka i zhizn'* 4, 1987, 54–65):

> The basis of this system is the centralization of decisions and punctual, undeviating, overriding fulfilment of directives from Above and particularly from Stalin – the Boss.
>
> This is a system of specific and detailed management in kind (*in natura*). It is a system of continuous operational management of the course of production from the centre. This is the Administrative System.

Popov then argued that the 'Administrative System' has continued till the present day: terror and fear have gone, but the system in principle remains. This is a distinction similar to Rigby's between the 'mono-organizational society combined with personal dictatorship' of the Stalin period, and the 'mono-organizational society without personal dictatorship' which followed the death of Stalin (T.H. Rigby, in R.C. Tucker (ed.) (1977) *Stalinism: Essays in Historical Interpretation* 53–76, W.W. Norton & Company, New York). Popov went on to draw sweeping lessons from this for the Soviet future:

> N.S. Khrushchev, and all of us, thought that with the elimination of the cult of personality from the system we would solve all the problems of our future. Now, in the light of historical experience, we see that this is not the case. The System has revenged itself on us.
>
> The problem is to renounce it, to replace it by a new system, corresponding to the contemporary stage of the development of socialism, relying not on administrative but on economic and democratic methods and forms.
>
> The Administrative System is not at all the synonym of the Socialist System, it never included the whole of our structure (*stroi*), it is an ephemeral stage.

This analysis was taken up by Gorbachev in his report on the occasion of the 70th Anniversay of the October Revolution. Gorbachev stated that industrialization and the collectivization of agriculture had been associated with the emergence of the 'administrative-command system of party-state management of the country'. This system, 'firmly established in the economy, also spread to the superstructure, limiting the development of the democratic potential of socialism, and restraining the progress of socialist democracy' (*Pravda*, 3 November 1987).

In spite of its much greater realism, this treatment of the Stalin system has one feature in common with the 'political economy of socialism' in the past: it treats the market and quasi-market elements of the Stalinist and post-Stalinist systems as too trivial to mention in a general description. This is the mirror-image of the treatment of NEP as a socialist market economy with no elements of administrative planning (see pp. 154–60). This one-sidedness is in my opinion an important weakness of the Soviet treatment of the past, because it encourages the dangerous view that everything will be solved if only the administrative system is replaced by the market with sufficient determination.

THE BUMPY ROAD TO REFORM

The nature of the economic mechanism established in the 1930s . . . was determined not only by the transition to socialism, but also by the specific historical forms in which this transition took place, by the variant of the economic and political relations of socialism which was established here in the 1930s and 1940s . . .

Many features of the socialist transformations in Soviet society – particularly the forced development of heavy industry and the precipitous accomplishment of universal collectivization – entered social consciousness as essential features of socialism. Today, considering the seventy years' development of socialism retrospectively, including the experience not of one but of many countries, it is becoming clear that the matter is much more complicated. Socialism can be constructed and developed with less directive methods of planning and with far more widespread commodity-money relations than was the case in Soviet society. In certain conditions co-operation in the countryside takes forms which in no way resemble comprehensive collectivization.

(L.A. Gordon, *Sotsiologicheskie issledovaniya* 4, July–August 1987, 7)

The hopes raised by the 1965 reform have also not been justified. Then we assumed that it was only necessary to limit the scale of administration in the Administrative System, aggregating it, concentrating it on the main issues, supplementing it with economic levers, and we would succeed in solving the problems of our society. The System resisted, it strongly opposed reform. Let us be courageous enough to recognise that it has been victorious and even has strengthened itself to some extent.

(G. Popov (1987) *Nauka i zhizn'* 4, 65)

The limitations of the Soviet understanding of the past outlined on pp. 144–7 were an important factor in circumscribing and slowing down the various attempts at economic reform in the thirty-five years since 1953. The efforts of Soviet economists to understand how their system worked were frequently blocked by powerful ideological and material interests which restricted and censored the discussion. The most far-reaching limitations were imposed in 1968 and after, following the Prague Spring and Summer, and the Soviet military intervention. Ota Šik and other economists, who advocated far-reaching competition between state enterprises on a more-or-less free market – 'market socialism' – were regarded by Brezhnev and his supporters as providing a major ideological justification for the restoration of capitalism; and this condemnation extended to the so-called 'commodity mongers' (*tovarniki*) in the USSR. Those treated as near-heretics included the Central Mathematical Economics Institute, TsEMI, founded in 1963. TsEMI at first advocated the use of 'simulated markets' on computers to plan the economy, but by 1968 prominent economists in TsEMI advocated the use of actual market prices in the economy. In an article in *Kommunist* 9, June 1987, 50–6, Academician N.P. Fedorenko, director of TsEMI for the first twenty years after its establishment, bitterly criticized the treatment in those years of the reform proposals of TsEMI. He described how TsEMI proposed 'self-financing' of enterprises in the second half of the 1960s, with good results in certain experiments carried out at that time. But subsequently in the 1970s 'the very concept of "self-financing" was treated as almost an enemy concept, contradicting the idea of socialism. . . . Twenty years were lost'.

But repression was not the only problem. In the 1950s Soviet economists and economic administrators knew very little about the way in which markets operated. In 1956–7, for example, a vigorous discussion in *Ekonomicheskaya gazeta* about price reform failed to come to grips with the existence of repressed inflation in the USSR; then and later many economists and managers, as in the 1930s, hoped to eliminate centralized supplies, but did not contemplate that this would involve the adoption of planned or market prices which equated supply and demand (see my survey article in *Soviet Studies* VIII, 1957, 426–36). Even if Khrushchev had passionately wanted to reform the price system, not even elementary sound advice would have been available to him on how this could be achieved.

And in 1968, once Czech and some Soviet economists had grasped the price nettle, many of them understood price formation in the terms of an elementary and unrealistic 'perfect competition' model, and did not seriously contemplate how to bring large monopolistic state concerns into a socialist market. Brezhnev was suspicious for the wrong reasons, but he had good grounds for scepticism.

It was different in Hungary. With the development by Kornai and others of their analysis of the planning system, the 1968 Hungarian reform was placed on a better foundation of understanding. Apart from Yugoslavia, this was the first major case of an integrated and substantial reform. Hungary proceeded further than anywhere else along what one of its economists described as the 'bumpy road to cognition of the economic mechanism' (L. Szamuely, *Acta Oeconomica* 29, 1982, 1–24).

In the USSR, where economists and administrators had proceeded only a short distance down the bumpy road, the frequent efforts at reform, involving enormous administrative upheavals, were ingenious, complicated and unsuccessful; they brought about only secondary changes in the operation of the 'Administrative System'. In 1955–6, the State Planning Commission was instructed to transfer some of its decisions to industrial ministries; the ministries in turn were to transfer some of their powers to the enterprises. Little happened, and, in the absence of serious proposals for price reform, Khrushchev launched the thoroughgoing administrative shake-up of 1957: industrial ministries were abolished, and replaced by over 100 regional economic councils, each of which was supposed to manage the whole of industry in its area. The initial impact of the reform was not unhealthy; it cleared away some inefficiencies of thirty years' standing. But it brought little if any access of authority to the enterprise.

Within a year or two of 1957, it proved impossible to do without some of the old ministerial powers. National controls were reimposed step by step, and cut across the new regional administration, to everyone's confusion. In the autumn of 1965, twelve months after Khrushchev's fall (partly brought about by the failure of the 1957 reform, and the hostility to it of the bureaucrats whose lives were disrupted), the industrial ministries were restored and the regional economic councils were abolished.

Like the 1957 reform, the 1965 reform had some positive results. It attempted for the first time to place economic calculation at the centre of the planning system: the profit motive, rather than the administrative instruction, would control the behaviour of the individual enterprise. But no radical change took place in the structure of profits and prices; the price reform of July 1967 eliminated some of the worst deficiencies of the industrial price structure, but made no attempt to use prices to adjust supply to demand. Moreover, the 1965 reform did not deal with the most serious weakness of the traditional system, its failure to encourage innovation: it neither provided economic incentives for the production of new products, nor encouraged competition between state enterprises. Three further attempts were made to remedy these deficiencies in 1969, 1973 and 1979; these minor upheavals, notable mainly for their complexity and their triviality, hardly deserve the name of 'reform'. It is not surprising that Gorbachev, at the XXVII party congress in February 1986, described his new endeavours as 'radical reform' (*radikal'naya reforma*) in order to indicate the seriousness of his intentions. It gradually became obvious that the new reform was indeed intended to be more far-reaching than anything which had preceded it. In preparing the reform, Gorbachev's advisers included Academician Aganbegyan, who was extremely familiar with, and strongly sympathetic to, the Hungarian type of 'market socialism', and G.Kh. Popov, whose forthright attack on the 'Administrative System' is cited above.

The type of reform envisaged in 1987–8 for the Soviet Union corresponded in major respects to the reformed Hungarian economic mechanism after 1968: abolition of the fixing of detailed plans from above; replacement of centralized supply by trade between state enterprises; coexistence of state ownership with genuine co-operative ownership and small-scale private ownership. However, in practice the long series of measures adopted during and after the June 1987 Central Committee plenum were in major respects half-hearted. Some significant developments occurred after July 1987, notably the law on co-operatives (Spring 1988). But many inconsistencies and ambiguities remained.

In consequence of the greater powers acquired by enterprises, inflationary expenditure increased after June 1987. Yet the authorities were unable to introduce financial controls to prevent the growth of inflation; and postponed currency and price reform as politically unacceptable. The first phase of reform was followed by a very grave financial crisis. The second phase of economic reform began in 1990, after a further false start at the end of 1989. In the spring of 1990, the reformer Abalkin had for some months been in charge of economic reform, with the even more reformist Petrakov as his deputy. Their influence was supplemented, once Gorbachev had assumed presidential powers, by the appointment of Shatalin as the most influential economist on the Presidential Council. Shatalin is unambiguously in favour of the gradual conversion of the Soviet economy into a mixed market economy in which the capitalist sector is predominant. In an interview in October 1989 he declared that 'progress in England is associated with the conservative Thatcher', and criticized the French and the English for socializing motor-car and aircraft firms (*Literaturnaya gazeta*, 11 October 1989).

It is probably true to say that the transformation of the Soviet economy into a managed capitalist economy modelled on Sweden or even West Germany is now seen as desirable by most prominent Moscow intellectuals. Joint-stock ownership of most industry would replace state ownership; there would be capital and labour markets as well as a retail market. But opinion is sharply divided about the way forward to a regulated capitalism. Some economists, such as Vasilii Selyunin, favour a rapid transformation, with 'shock therapy' along Polish lines, involving the stabilization of the market and the breaking of the power of the party and state bureaucracy: 'to combine the plan and the market', declared Selyunin, 'is just like putting bits of an hour-glass into a watch; all you do is to ruin them both' (*Literaturnaya gazeta*, 2 May 1990). But Abalkin and Shatalin believed that it was possible to convert the economy by more gradual means. 'One should not be frightened of private ownership, there is nothing terrible in it', Shatalin assured a conference of the Central Committee in October 1989, 'but it is not appropriate today to propose it as a programmatic task' (*Pravda*, 30 October 1989). A few months later he again insisted that there was no alternative to 'the main road of civilization; we shall not switch on the engine of self-development without private property in all its forms, without creating motivation mechanisms which are no weaker than in the west'. But Polish 'shock-therapy' was inappropriate: 'The USSR is not Poland; we are not one nation (and we are certainly not united by the authority of a single church and the colossal authority of the Roman Pope)' (*Literaturnaya gazeta*, 2 May 1990).

The economic reform measures announced at the end of May 1990 undoubtedly envisaged the eventual replacement of the present system by a West European type of mixed economy, and incorporated a serious attempt to stabilize the retail market and public finance through price increases and the abolition of subsidies. But they were again inconsistent and ambiguous, offering the certainty of retail price rises combined with vagueness about the likelihood of substantial changes in the economic system. Yet another attempted reform came to nothing.

In the meantime, a draft law announced, even before the publication of the reform proposals at the end of May, attempts to bring to an end an experiment in socialist democracy which received a great deal of attention in the Soviet press in 1987–9, and played an important part in the development of an independent workers' movement. The draft law proposed to remove from the workers of state enterprises the right to elect their managers, handing it back to the superior state agencies. The announcement of the draft law appeared next to an article entitled 'How to help the unemployed' (*Pravda*, 6 April 1990). In June 1990, the new Law 'On enterprises in the USSR' confirmed this general position, but also left a great deal of room for manoeuvre about the rights of the councils of the enterprises, on which elected representatives were normally to occupy 50 per cent of the seats (*Izvestiya*, 12 June 1990). The fate of socialist self-government in industry remains a matter for future political and social struggle, though technocratic, administrative and even intellectual opinion is biased against it.

The more substantial '500 days' reform programme prepared by Shatalin failed to be adopted in the autumn of 1990. Gorbachev was confronted with a programme from radical reformers which he concluded would have two consequences: the break-up of the Soviet Union and the replacement of its present economic system by a capitalist economy on West European lines. Neither of these developments was he prepared to accept at that time.

THE NEW ECONOMIC POLICY AND CONTEMPORARY ECONOMIC REFORM

The main intention is to open the way to economic methods of management, to extend considerably the independence of collective farms and state farms, to raise their interest and responsibility for the final results. In essence it is a matter of the creative utilization of the

Leninist idea of a food tax applied to contemporary conditions.

(M.S. Gorbachev, report to XXVII Party Congress,
25 February 1986)

Gorbachev's comparison of his new agricultural policy with the food tax (*prodnalog*) introduced by Lenin in March 1921 undoubtedly startled his audience. The food tax replaced the compulsory requisitioning of war communism and led within a few months to the elaboration of the complete model of NEP, in which state industry and individual agriculture were linked through the market. Gorbachev's statement, almost completely ignored by western commentators (perhaps because they did not know enough economic history), was a clear signal that the new party leadership intended to bring about major changes in the economic system. Neither Khrushchev, in advocating his economic reforms, nor Kosygin in introducing the 1965 reform, drew analogies with NEP; at that time Soviet politicians saw NEP as remote and irrelevant. Even among intellectuals little was said about NEP. When G.A. Lisichkin, in his pamphlet *Plan and Market*, published in 1968, argued in favour of market prices which balanced supply and demand, and presented this as a continuation of the tradition of NEP, this was an extreme view among the economists. But by 1988 the view that the present reforms are in an important sense an extension of NEP was almost commonplace. An otherwise conservative article in the party journal *Kommunist* 7, May 1987, while emphasizing that NEP differed from present-day Soviet socialism because petty capitalism was very strong in the 1920s, nevertheless conceded (p. 63) that 'there is of course a direct descent and profound resemblance', because both periods were characterized by the 'uncovering, activizing and maximum utilization of material and economic interest' (*Kommunist* 7, 1987, 63).

A major report on the social sciences on 17 April 1987, by A.N. Yakovlev, a secretary of the Central Committee (subsequently made a full member of the Politburo) presented the whole issue of the transition from NEP to centralized planning as an open question; he told the social scientists that they should investigate why the departure from NEP occurred, how 'administrative-bureaucratic methods of administration' became strong, whether there were alternatives, and why they failed (*Vestnik Akademii Nauk* 6, 1987, 69).

Most Soviet historians and economists who wrote about these questions during 1987 took the view that the economic system of the 1930s was produced by the extraordinary tasks imposed upon the USSR as a backward socialist country threatened by advanced imperialism, though its brutal and repressive aspects were at least partly due to the malign influence of Stalin's personality. Thus L.A. Gordon wrote in the article already cited on p. 150:

The circumstances of the choice made at the time [the 1930s] – the economic and cultural backwardness of the country, the unavoidable military threat, the absence of democratic experience and democratic traditions – speak in favour of the inevitability of forced industrialization and rapid collectivization, and the political arrangements which resulted, rather than of the possibility of a more harmonious development. With a different combination of subjective factors, with a more attentive attitude to Leninist warnings about the political significance of the personal features of I.V.Stalin, no doubt many sacrifices and mistakes could have been avoided.

(*Sotsialisticheskie issledovaniya* 4, July–August 1987, 8)

Other academics and politicians regarded the departure from NEP at the end of the 1920s as unjustified even in the circumstances of the time. Thus the sociologist V.Shubkin bluntly stated (*Znamya* 4, 1987, 183): 'Stalin decided to eliminate NEP prematurely, using purely administrative methods and direct compulsion; this led, speaking mildly, to pitiable results' (*Znamya* 4, 1987, 183).

By the autumn of 1988 the view that the continuation of the market relation with the peasants after the end of the 1920s would have been a viable and superior alternative to the 'administrative-command system' overwhelmingly predominated in the Soviet press and media. On the 100th Anniversary of Bukharin's birth in October 1988, the obituaries were full of praise for the 'Bukharinist alternative' (for example, *Nedelya* 39, 1988, *Pravda, Pravda Ukrainy, Sotsialisticheskaya industriya*, all 9 October 1988). In the course of these discussions there was little serious re-examination of NEP as an economic system, and of its successes and failures. Many economists as well as publicists presented the economy of the 1920s as an unmitigated success. Some writers praised the very high rates of economic growth in the early years of NEP without pointing out that these were largely a result of bringing resources back into use after the collapse of the economy during the civil war. For example, an interviewer in the party theoretical journal *Kommunist*, referring to agriculture, wrote that 'in 1922–8 the average rate of growth per year was about 10 per cent – this is really a very high result' (1, 1988, 55).

Most of the radical critics of the past did not distort the record so crudely. But they often considerably overestimated the economic success of NEP. Thus they frequently exaggerated the speed of recovery of the economy after the Civil War. The economist Vasilii Selyunin enthusiastically declared (*Novyi mir* 5, 1988, 171): 'Within four or five years [that is, by 1925 or 1926] the pre-war level in industry and agriculture was reached. In 1928 it was exceeded in industry by 32 per cent, and in the countryside by 14 per cent'. Otto Latsis, first deputy editor of *Kommunist*, claimed that 'the post-war reconstruction of industrial production was in the main completed by 1925' (*Kommunist* 18, 1987, 18). And Lisichkin even stated that 'the national income reached the pre-war indicator in four years' (*Novyi mir* 11, 1988, 164). The same assessment was made by S.P. Pervushin in *EKO* (10, 1988, 132).

Now the economic achievements of NEP were considerable. But all western specialists agree that neither agriculture nor industry recovered to their pre-war level until 1927; some economists such as Paul Gregory suggest that recovery was far from complete even then. This more sceptical view of progress under NEP was also held by many Soviet economists in the 1920s, including Al'bert Vainshtein. In contrast, the recent Soviet writers I have cited all accepted without question the present-day official statistics about the economic recovery during the 1920s, even though they were extremely critical of official statistics in most other respects!

Optimistic statistics were accompanied by an idealization of the social and economic conditions of NEP. Thus the playwright Viktor Rozov described how NEP transformed life in his provincial town when he was a schoolboy, so that 'everything began to glisten and laugh' (*Yunost'* 4, 1987, 6–11). Vladimir Dudintsev similarly recalled his boyhood observation of the full barns and general prosperity of the individual peasants (*Nedelya* 22, 1989). This theme was also very strongly emphasized by prominent economists, such as Academician Tikhonov, who advocated the return to individual peasant farming. Agriculture succeeded so well, Tikhonov insisted, because no one had the right to interfere in the economic activity of the peasant (*Literaturnaya gazeta*, 5 August 1988). Selyunin held that agriculture worked best in 1925, when legislation was adopted extending the rights of individual peasants to rent land and hire agricultural labour (Novyi i mir 5, 1988, 172–3).

In this idealized version of NEP, major economic problems hardly seem to exist. Chernichenko, a Secretary of the Union of Soviet Writers, simply declared that 'without compulsory agriculture and compulsory collections there would have been no food problem ever since 1928' (*Istoriya SSSR* 3, 1989, 53). Latsis praised the resolution on the five-year plan of the XV Party Congress in December 1927 for its judicious support for balanced growth, suggesting that this offered a crisis-free road to economic development within the framework of NEP. Some outstanding historians, who do not accept the rather naïve assessments of NEP which I have described, nevertheless share this enthusiasm for the XV Congress resolution. V.S. Lel'chuk, in an article written jointly with L.P. Kosheleva, declared that 'the XV Congress proposed a kind of optimum variant, from which we can learn even today . . . *How can one fail to enthuse about those who formulated such proposals, and voted for their realization*' (*Pravda*, 21 October 1988). Viktor Danilov praised the first five-year plan adopted in the spring of 1929 as a viable non-Bukharinist third alternative to the Stalinist course (*Gorizont* 5, 1988, 28–38).

While many western historians accept the view that the Bukharinist alternative provided viable policies for Soviet economic development within the framework of NEP, very few western historians would accept these judgements about the plans of the late 1920s. The XV Congress resolution was adopted in the midst of great battles about rival drafts of the five-year plan. But to the indignation of the Left Opposition, and of many of those on the side of the party majority, it failed to contain a single figure, or to offer a specific judgment on any of the major economic problems which were worrying the politicians and the planners. It was strong on noble principles, but avoided the difficult practical issues. And the 'optimum variant' of the five-year plan actually adopted in the spring of 1929, and even its more cautious 'initial variant', were both based on extremely optimistic proposals for increases in the productivity of labour and capital, and for the reduction of industrial costs. They also assumed a financial balance in the economy which had already been thoroughly disrupted at the time when these drafts of the five-year plan were drawn up and approved in the winter and spring of 1928–9.

This is by no means the whole story about recent Soviet assessments of NEP. Many other writers, particularly professional historians, present a more complex picture of the economy of the 1920s. Academician Koval'chenko complained that 'NEP is depicted almost as an era of general prosperity and well-being, although at that time the general level of economic development and the standard of living of the broad mass of the population was low, mass unemployment remained in the country, etc.' (*Kommunist* 2, 1989, 89). V. P. Dmitrenko criticized 'publicists, writers and economists' who presented a 'rainbow picture' of NEP, and failed to show that the economic successes of agriculture were accompanied by the 'economic weakness of the state', which proved unable to supply loans and industrial goods to peasants and private traders in adequate quantities (*Sotsialisticheskaya industriya* 27 September 1987).

On the state of agriculture during NEP, Danilov and N.A. Ivnitskii, in contrast to Academician Tikhonov, argued that:

> by the end of the 1920s the objective course of social-economic development, and particularly the development of the industrialization of the country, sharply posed the problem of the development of agricultural production and its reorganization . . . The low level of agricultural production was holding back the general economic development of the country, placed serious obstacles in the way of the industrialization which was beginning, and of the construction of socialism as a whole.
>
> (*Dokumenty svidetel'stvuyut*,
> Danilov and Ivnitskii (eds) (1989), 17–18)

They also held, against the strong and even bitter opposition of Chernichenko and Tikhonov, that during NEP a kulak stratum continued to exist as one section of the peasantry, and that 'the system of kulak exploitation was primitive, but also crude and without limits' (Danilov and Ivnitskii, 13; and see the 'round table' reported in *Istoriya SSSR* 3, 1989, 3–62).

Some recent Soviet literature has also shown that throughout the 1920s direct state management of industry, finance and prices was more important than it appears to be in the simple model of a market relation between the state sector and the rest of the economy. 'From the moment of the introduction of NEP', wrote G. Bordyugov and V. Kozlov, historians from the Institute of Marxism–Leninism, 'the party seriously limited the operation of the market in the relation between heavy and light industry'. They went on to argue that the great opportunity was missed in 1925, when the party should have begun to strengthen the co-operative elements in NEP, rather than embarking on the road of transferring resources from the peasantry to the needs of industry. (*Pravda*, 30 September 1988.) The historian Natan Eidel'man argued:

> The years 1921–1929 will remain in Soviet history as complicated and sometimes tormented attempts to create an optimum system in which socialist commanding heights in the economy would be combined with market spontaneity, and a strong centralized power would be combined with democracy and self-management.

Eidel'man, an historian of the pre-revolutionary period, added that the failure of the NEP alternative was due not only to the circumstances of the 1920s, but also to the 'long tradition over many centuries of super-centralization and "a non-commodity economy"' (*Nauka i zhizn'* 3, 1989, 107.)

Another viewpoint on NEP was at first only expressed by a small minority of writers, but more recently became much more influential. They argued, with increasing frankness, that the whole course of economic policy since October 1917 was doomed to failure; only a capitalist economy could have been successful. Grigorii Khanin diagnosed the economic difficulties of the mid-1920s as profound. According to Khanin, even by 1928 national income per head was 17 per cent below the 1913 level, while the stock of capital was 13 per cent above that level; a 'catastrophic decline' had taken place in the efficiency with which capital was used. These failures were due to the power of the bureaucracy, to the domination of industrial management by ex-workers with low qualifications, and to the elimination of efficient farmers. And the feasible level of capital investment within the framework of NEP was too low to avoid economic stagnation and military weakness. With extreme scepticism Khanin argued that 'the last chance for alternative solutions, it seems to me, was lost at the beginning of the 1920s; and even then it was small' (*Rodina* 7, 1989, 80–4). L. Piyasheva took a similar approach. An enthusiast for the free-market views of von Hayek, she rejected all schools of Bolshevik thought, and strongly advocated Kondratiev's and Yurovsky's strategy of eliminating price and other direct controls and strengthening the market (for example *Sotsialisticheskaya industriya*, 14 January 1988, and *Druzhba narodov* 7,

1988, 179–97). V. Evstigneev also claimed that the collapse of NEP was inevitable in view of the political and social environment in which it was established:

> In the conditions of a totalitarian social system even the more liberal, and especially market (or rather quasi-market) economic forms will inevitably, and sooner rather than later, 'grow into' the general totalitarian system and serve it, or will be eliminated as unacceptable.

> (*Voprosy ekonomiki* 3, 1990, 33;
> Evstigneev was a senior member of IMEMO,
> the Institute of World Economics and International Relations)

The rival assessments of NEP are highly relevant to the rival schemes for present-day economic reform. Should the Soviet Union move towards a free-market economy loosely controlled by the state, and including a substantial element of private capitalism in industry as well as agriculture?; this roughly corresponds to the alternative course under NEP supported by Kondratiev and Yurovsky in the 1920s, and by Tikhonov, Khanin and Piyasheva today. Or should it rather seek to develop genuine co-operatives, and the management of socialized industry by those who work in it, within the framework of a state-managed socialist market?; this roughly corresponds to the alternative course under NEP supported, for all their differences, by Chayanov and the Gosplan economists such as Groman and Bazarov in the 1920s, and by Danilov, Kozlov and Bordyugov at the present day.

The 'radical' pro-capitalist economists were for some time influential in Gorbachev's Presidential Council, predominant among Eltsin's advisers in the Supreme Soviet of the Russian Republic, and control the Soviets in Moscow, Leningrad and elsewhere. In their thinking these reformers have moved out of the framework of Soviet socialism. They now look back before the 1917 revolution for their historical precedents. Thus the influential economist, Nikolai Shmelev, declared about Stolypin, Prime Minister after the 1905 Revolution who attempted to establish peasant capitalist agriculture in Russia: 'I have an extremely positive attitude to Stolypin . . . Stolypin was the hope of the country and he began a very fruitful process. Today the situation is to some extent similar' (*Literaturnaya gazeta*, 26 July 1989). And Gavriil Popov, elected head of the Moscow Soviet following the election victory of the 'Democratic platform', has proclaimed that in agriculture 'we must do what was done by the unforgettable Stolypin; we must introduce *otrubs* and *khutors*', peasant family farms separated from the village commune (*Pozitsiya* (Tartu) 1, October 1989).

THE POLITICS OF ECONOMIC REFORM

In one major respect economic reform under Gorbachev differs fundamentally from the New Economic Policy. Gorbachev's reform, to the complete surprise of almost every western Soviet specialist, has been accompanied by and even preceded by attempts at far-reaching political reform.

In NEP Russia there was a considerable amount of intellectual freedom, and there were open conflicts and debates in decision-making – a kind of pluralism within a one-party system. But the introduction of NEP in 1921–2 was accompanied by eliminating other parties, by tightening up discipline within the Communist Party, and by the consolidation of the censorship. Throughout the first half of the 1920s, and during the period of 'high NEP' in 1925–7, the power of the party machine was greatly increasing, and the bounds of discussion were narrowing.

In the Soviet Union we are seeing a bold effort to bring about a change in people's psychology, and active participation in reform, through franker and more open discussion, and wide-ranging experiments in elections of foreman and managers, and of members of Soviets. The election of managers was replaced (with a few exceptions) by appointment as long ago as 1920, even before the introduction of NEP. In restricting appointment from above, the political reform temporarily returned, not to the spirit of NEP, or even of the end of the civil war, but to 1917, combined with something like the political economy of Adam Smith.

CONCLUSIONS

This paper has suggested that, in spite of the immense progress in the frank analysis of the Soviet economic system since 1985, Soviet interpretations of the past cannot be described as objective. In particular, many 'radical' economists seek to demonstrate on the basis of the Soviet past that there can be no such thing as a regulated market, or a combination of plan and market. This argument has understandable political motives: there are good reasons to fear that the conservatives who dominate the administration will seize on every opportunity to resist changes in the system. But as an economic historian I find this claim absurd.

Much of the practice of capitalist economies involves the regulation of the market; a substantial sector in many contemporary capitalist economies is administratively planned or managed. And in pre-revolutionary Russia as well as in the Soviet Union both the state and the market have played a major role in the economy. It is not an accident that the term reform is used to a much greater extent in Russian history than in the history of most other European countries. We have – in reverse chronological order – the post-revolutionary reforms or attempted reforms of 1987, 1965 and 1957 (and of 1921), and also the pre-revolutionary Stolypin reform, the serf reform and the great reforms of the 1860s, the Petrine reforms, and even the reforms of Ivan the Terrible. It was the state as a major economic and political actor that pushed all these reforms through.

Moreover, ever since the 1890s, both before and after the Bolshevik revolution, not only the state, but also its administrative economy, were of major economic significance. Before 1914 the state-managed railways and the military exercised a major influence on industrial development. In the 1920s the state directly managed and allocated resources to most industrial investment; state orders, as before the revolution, exercised a major influence on the shape of industry; and there was no period in the 1920s in which the state did not physically allocate at least a few major producer goods. On the other hand, though markets were in important senses extremely weak during the civil war and in the Stalin period, they played a significant role in the economy.

Stalinist and Brezhnevist ideologists underestimated the role of the market in these primarily administrative economies, and so also, for entirely different ideological reasons, have many of the present-day economic reformers; and this has hindered understanding of the Soviet economic system and the paths to reform.

This is not to deny the obvious point that the transition from a predominantly administrative economy to a predominately market economy is an extraordinarily difficult task, and would have been difficult to accomplish even with perfect understanding of the Soviet-type economic system. This point is reinforced, not only by the experience of both the Soviet Union and of the whole of Eastern Europe in the thirty-eight years since 1953, but also by the experience of NEP.

A serious weakness of this paper so far is that it has not discussed Soviet economic reform in the context of the economic development of the world as a whole. The struggle to introduce market economies in Communist countries has been taking place at a time when the thinking of western economists and politicians and, to a lesser extent, western government policy, has been dominated by enthusiasm for the unrestrained free market. There is no doubt that the contemporary technological revolution requires a major adaptation of all economic institutions throughout the world. The old state monopolies and the old state controls no longer work in the west.

But I would suggest that this very strong emphasis on the free market is a temporary phase in western development. The international financial markets, with their take-overs for short-term profit, and the multinational corporations, are failing to cope satisfactorily with the economic and human needs of the world in transformation. And several further major factors will impinge on western capitalism in the coming decades:

- The population of the newly-industrialized countries will no longer be prepared to tolerate the conditions in which they normally work.
- Much of the Third World, with its huge populations, is already in social and economic crisis; the non-industrialized areas of the world urgently require new international policies to manage this crisis.
- The growing dangers to the environment will also require the enforcement of international decisions – of some kind of supra-national economic planning or administration.

All this will mean that a new relation between international institutions and society will emerge. Planning and the market, or, if you like, the administrative economy and the market economy, will still be in tension and co-operation, this time on a world scale.

The history of the Soviet economy will eventually look quite different from this new vantage-point.

11 Reform economics and bureaucracy

Tadeusz Kowalik

INTRODUCTORY REMARKS

In what follows, I will write as a historian rather than an economist. But this is not the only reason for which I subscribe to Fernand Braudel's view that economists are prisoners of the present in the strict sense, for they are in the habit of permanently offering their services to governments (Braudel 1971). Indeed, I think economists are liable to yet another weakness, namely, an almost deliberate isolation from related social sciences, such as sociology, law or political science. That is why I was so happy to hear that our project 'would focus on a virtually non-existent field of economics, the history of political economy of existing socialism'. The project thus furnishes an opportunity to look back on the vicissitudes of economics through the eyes of a historian and to discuss matters I have been studying for a long time now with specialists from other countries. While our project is not likely to cause a revolution, it is at least going to serve as something like a confessional, after leaving which we may go on committing the same sins, but perhaps with less self-assurance than before.

One more circumstance makes me enthusiastic about this project. As I see it, economics is being 'socialized', that is, linked up with interdisciplinary research, in the west to a wider extent than in the east. Comparative economic studies and evolutionary economics are perhaps the best cases in point. In countries in which Marxism is an official ideology, these matters were – paradoxically – hardly being studied at all, probably out of fear of censorship, and also because economists were afraid of emulating the previous style of eulogizing economics. Studies in economics were given a broader historical scope, and economic research became more aware of other social sciences, when the economists moved from the east to the west. This is the case of Ota Šik, for example, or of Włodzimierz Brus, whose first 'institutional' book called *Socialist Ownership and Political Systems* (1975) was written while he still lived in Poland, but only after he had been forced into something like internal banishment.

Initially, I wanted to consider the relationship between economics and politics in reference to economic reforms of really existing socialism. What I have written here was meant to be just an introduction to the proper topic. However, the topic I had chosen proved to be comprehensive enough (Osiatynski's and Comisso's chapters are, as a matter of fact, on reform economics and polity).

In what follows, I am going to look at some implications of Lange's classical model and at views of 'pioneer reformers' in Poland. In particular, I am going to touch upon the issue of bureaucracy and its role in socialist economy, which was raised recently by Kornai (1986) and Nuti (1986).

SMILING AS A HISTORIAN'S PROBLEM

Historians and critics of modern economics alike take it for granted that economists wrote what they believed was true. Let me begin with economists who were not directly subject to Soviet-style preventive censorship.

The first case concerns the gap between what Lange wrote and thought when writing his *On the Economic Theory of Socialism* (1938) and the presentation of his model in the literature.

Setting out to see how the Hungarian reform stands in relation to Lange's Model, Kornai promises that his study 'does not discuss Lange's thinking in the thirties, but the so-called Lange model as perceived by the profession'. Yet Kornai soon forgets his promise and makes a lot of remarks concerning Lange's thinking. Here is one example of that inconsistency – 'The people at his (Lange's – TK) Central Planning Board are reincarnations of Plato's philosophers, embodiment of unity, unselfishness, and wisdom'. Kornai goes much too far when he says: 'The Lange of the thirties, although a convinced socialist, lived in the sterile world of Walrasian pure theory and did not consider the socio-political underpinning of his basic assumption'.

First of all, Lange did consider the basic social assumptions of his model, especially that of bureaucracy. He did that in his other studies too, not only in his classical work. Here is what he wrote in the second part of that study:

> It seems to us, indeed, that *the real danger of socialism is that of bureaucratization of economic life*, and not the impossibility of coping with the problem of allocation of resources. Unfortunately, we do not see how the same, or even greater, danger can be averted under monopolistic capitalism. Officials subject to democratic control seem preferable to private corporation executives who practically are responsible to nobody.
>
> (Lange and Taylor 1938/1964)

Lange can, of course, be said to have exaggerated when he asserted that managers are responsible to no one, or to have been overly confident about public functionaries being effectively controlled by a system of democratic checks and balances. He can also be blamed for having regarded the bureaucratization of public life and rational resource allocation as two different things, or, lastly, for having recognized the issue of the dangers inherent in bureaucratization as belonging to 'the field of sociology rather than of economic theory and must therefore be dispensed with here'. But no one can reasonably accuse him of having idealized bureaucrats, or having ignored the potential dangers of bureaucratization.

Indeed, in the 1930s Lange was among those few who acknowledged that danger, not only in regard to the Soviet-type economy, but also in reference to decentralized and market-type socialism. Market forces were supposed to have a smoothing rather than a neutralizing effect on that danger. Nor did Lange overestimate the importance of proper organizational structure of government offices as a way to ward off that danger. Here is what he said in 1939:

> The chief consideration in determining the form of organization of the socialist society must be, however, not so much economic efficiency, which is rather easy to attain, as the safeguard of individual freedom. For this purpose, a far-going division of powers is of foremost importance. Above all, the administration of the economic system cannot be in the same hands as the political organization (police, justice, etc.), and worker's self-government must be extended into every branch of economic life. But no institutional safeguards, however important, can substitute democratic vigilance. A socialist society can thrive only as a worker's democracy, vigilant and militant in defending its freedom . . . Only a militant working-class democracy (. . .) jealously preserving the right of control over its leaders, can create the great democratic ethos out of which a classless society is born.
>
> (Lange 1939)

In this, as in many other observations of his, we see that Lange was far from idealizing those 'public functionaries'. In fact, Lange seemed to share the fear of Dickinson – another proponent of the idea of market socialism – that this system was apt to bring with it 'the greatest tyranny the world has ever seen'. But both Dickinson and Lange thought that this tyranny was merely one among many possibilities, and that those militant and vigilant workers, whom they envisaged to be like those heroes of the Revolution extolled by Sorel, were perfectly able to avoid the danger.

If Lange was so closely aware of the dangers of socialism, then how could he arrive at the extremely abstract if not Utopian model he put forward? Despite being a disciple of Marx and Schumpeter, two of the most 'institutionalist' thinkers, Lange produced an economic model purged almost entirely of any historical references, a model relying on extremely unrealistic assumptions.

I think this apparent contradiction can be explained in this way: Marx and Schumpeter, in his eyes, represented economic sociology, a disciple for which Lange saw no room in his own economic theory. His theoretical model of socialist economy was symmetrical to, and in fact a variety of, the model of perfect competition.

To be true, Lange was skeptical of perfect competition already at that time. Yet he put much effort and time into the design of analytical tools to study it. For many years, general equilibrium theory was his chief topic of study. It was only in 'price flexibility and employment', initially an article which, to Lange's own astonishment, swelled to the size of a full-scale book, that he carried out a systematic comparison of that theory with the reality. Only years afterwards did Lange resort to the metaphor about the monkey to point out that probability calculus did not authorize anyone to preclude that the monkey is going to write the *Encyclopedia Britannica* one day, but, he asked, what sense did it make to busy oneself with studying as unlikely a possibility at all?

There is a lot to show that Lange took a similar view of his model. One of his friends and best disciples during the Chicago period told me recently that Lange often used to say that authentic free competition could only exist in socialism, because under capitalism monopolies put down all kind of true competition. But, the interlocutor (Leonid Hurwicz) remarked, 'whenever Lange said that, he used to smile, so I often wondered how seriously he treated his own model'.

I think Lange's smile will become less puzzling if you reflect on the feasibility of the idea of perfect competition. Any economist propounding that theory should be able to conjure up a self-ironical smile on his face. However, this explanation stops just there, and anything beyond that is difficult to explain. Still, I think the following tentative interpretation can perhaps hold water: the theory of perfect competition is more likely to hold under socialism than under capitalism, for the latter is based on various kinds of inequality, large fortunes, and so on. But to answer the question about the feasibility of a socialism based on free competition, we would have first to consider possible socio-economic consequences of socializing the means of production. We cannot say for sure that such a study would take us to conclusions which would be at odds with that vision. Or perhaps Lange's perplexing smile indicated his belief that all considerations of the future were wrapped in an enigma which modern scholars could not possibly make out? In fact, the smile would mean little more than his belief that free competition was just one of the things socialism was going to produce, maybe not even the most likely one.

There is perhaps evidence in support of that elsewhere in Lange's studies. Lange was an avid student of democratization processes. He used to say that democracy was a very sensitive flower which would bloom only in exceptionally favourable conditions.

I would like to refer to the case of Maurice Dobb, who is regarded as one of the most ardent theorists of central planning. Asked why he was often evasive about his vision of socialism, he surprisingly said:

I convinced myself that Socialism when it came would have probably a lot of features that I should personally dislike, but that my personal dislike would be irrelevant. So I wrote very little, if anything I am afraid, about my 'vision' of Socialism, apart from arguing for the advantages and feasibility of planning.

(Dobb 1973)

Like Lange's smile, this statement has also remained a puzzle. Dobb unfortunately did not say just why he was reluctant to articulate the features of socialism he thought he would find distasteful. He left no clue about where those features were likely to emerge. We can only guess they concerned not so much economic matters as socio-political or cultural ones. Nor did Dobb say exactly in what sense his dislikes would be irrelevant – would they be irrelevant in the sense that history was going to continue anyway, whatever Dobb's idiosyncrasies? Or maybe he preferred to keep silent about them as they were typical 'bourgeois' feelings of little avail for the oppressed and the miserable? Or maybe he was plagued by bad thoughts that the disciplined party member he was had to suppress?

Dobb wrote extensively about planning, and planning theory was absolutely his most important contribution to the political economy of socialism. Yet when we consider his views of socialism as socialist economics, then even some marginal remarks should not go unnoticed. For he had far-reaching doubts about the viability of socialist economy in the future.

They are contained in his first book *Capitalist Enterprise and Social Progress* (1925) of which not only the title alone but also the substance are closer to Schumpeter than to Marx. Dobb began his economist's career as an adherent of the idea of market socialism, which was close to the idea of guild socialism. Many passages in the chapter 'The Problem of Economic Control' of his 1925 book can be considered indirect criticisms of all kind of rationing and administrative socialism. But what is particularly interesting is that he had serious doubts even about a decentralized version of socialism. Regretting (once again in the style of Schumpeter) the progressing decline of the private entrepreneur in favour of an impersonal corporation, Dobb wrote:

How far on the other hand, either a collectivist or a Communist society would be likely to be creative is still more difficult to decide. Both would certainly lack much of the easy fluidity of individualism. The administrators would run the bureaucratic danger of becoming routinebound and unimaginative. They might be shy of facing uncertainties through timidity of opposition to the results of change and of the contumely which they risked should the dice fall for them on the wrong side. Democratic requirements might fetter them to the 'average daring of the community', instead of permitting those above this average to experiment on their own. Whether in conquest of these difficulties a Communist society might give birth to a creative will and spirit of progress to match the adventures of the undertakers' proudest hour is a secret as locked and barred against us as were the possibilities of capitalist enterprise to the mediaeval schoolmen.

(Dobb 1926)

BUREAUCRACY VERSUS SELF-MANAGEMENT

Let us see how the relationship between economy and bureaucracy was viewed by leading Polish reformers with ties to the Economic Council (1957–63). I have especially in mind the three outstanding figures and most powerful minds, Oskar Lange, Michael Kalecki and Włodzimierz Brus.

In order to recall their reform proposals at the time of the so-called Polish October, I am going to challenge Mario Nuti on what he says in his study about Kalecki as a planning theorist and adviser (Nuti 1986). Nuti is quite at home in the Polish economic scene so I was all the more surprised to see his article containing some erroneous propositions.

According to Nuti, Kalecki presented a 'comprehensive and coherent picture of the organization model of the socialist economy as an alternative to the Soviet-type model different from the "market socialism" of Lange and other reformers'.

At first glance, this general remark does sound convincing, for even non-professional readers know that Lange is regarded as the architect of the 'market socialism' concept, and that in the past and now, there have been other reformers who went along the same road. But Nuti says explicitly that even after the war, namely in 1956–8, Lange clung to his classical model, putting it forward as one element of Poland's road towards socialism, and that this effort was shared by other reformers. That is certainly untrue. Lange and Kalecki have never differed on the subject of the general reform framework. It is a paradox that the document Nuti refers to actually proves my point, not his (Nuti quotes from Kalecki's well-known article called 'Workers' Councils and Central Planning 1956):

> Kalecki envisaged in his model – in place of economic decentralization – general political decentralization under the guise of Worker's Councils which, in every enterprise oppose excessive bureaucratization and centralization, tendencies which appear when the enterprise director answer's only to central powers, and exercise initiative under the stimulus of material incentives.

Nuti continues: 'at the time, Oskar Lange regarded enterprise autonomy extending to prices and investment as a precondition of workers' self-management.'

To support his argument, Nuti quotes from Lange's (1956a) contribution called 'The new model must be based on the dynamics of the working

class and the socialist intelligentsia'. Here is, however, what Lange has
to say about prices:

> Price-setting must be used as a principal regulator to apply in the
> management of national economy. Accordingly, it cannot be turned
> over to individual enterprises but should basically remain in the hands
> of the state, that is, the central or local authorities, depending on the
> nature or importance of the given product to the national economy at
> large. Only in exceptional cases (. . .) should prices be allowed to be
> determined freely by the market; yet even then the government should
> exercise some or other kind of control.
>
> (Lange 1956a)

And this is what he says about planning of production and investment:

> National economic planning must embrace the basic sectors and
> sub-branches of national economy, that is, the production of producer
> goods, consumer goods production, industrial production, agricultural
> production, etc., and must set the mutual proportions between those
> sectors and sub-branches (. . .) Lastly, planning (. . .) must embrace
> employment of labour and its distribution among the basic sectors of
> national economy.

But as Lange is not talking here explicitly on investment, let me quote
from another article of his, which was published in the same month:

> Investment should be subject to central planning. Primary investment
> must be planned directly by the centre; subsidiary investment, of less
> significance to the whole economy, could be planned by departments,
> national councils and enterprises, within the framework of general
> allocations and directives laid down by the central plan.
>
> (Lange 1956b)

These quotations show that in 1956 Lange was as far away from the idea
of 'market socialism' as Kalecki was at the time; and that they did not differ
about the question of price-setting and investment. An almost identical
position was taken by Brus as well, and many other reformers working
for the Economic Council. Stefan Kurowski, Jozef Popkiewicz and Aleksy
Wakar, who were not members of the Council, stood in complete isolation
with their views which were closer to Lange's old classical model.

Generally, the following three articles of faith, which were heatedly
discussed at the time, were shared by Lange, Kalecki, Brus and many
others: (1) prices and investments as an inalienable attribute of central
planning; (2) full employment as an inalienable feature of socialism; and
(3) the system of workers councils as the countervailing power towards
bureaucracy. Their views about these questions furnished a basis for the
Economic Council's fundamental paper, the 'Theses on some directions
of change of the economic model'. Kalecki's six-volume 'Works' contain

many documents which indicate that he regarded the 'Theses' as the joint product of the entire Council and he defended them in talks with party and government officials.

Needless to say, the three principal authors of the 'Theses' did differ to some extent in their views. Even more conspicuous were the differences between their personal concerns and what they regarded as possible perils. Brus, for example, was less impressed by new instruments of planning (what came to be called Computopia) than the other two, whereas Lange was positively fascinated by that. But on matters of principle they did not differ.

Speaking about Kalecki's article called 'Let us not overrate the importance of models' (1957), Nuti pits Kalecki against other reformers of the period, apparently defying the circumstance that Kalecki was among the architects of the Polish reform of that time. And Nuti is certainly speaking against Kalecki's intention when he interprets the title as 'a message which should be repeated *ad nauseam* for the benefit of all East European reformers and counter-reformers alike'. Kalecki did not address his article in a daily newspaper to the reform economists, but to the general public, especially to journalists, who had flaunted the model as nothing short of a fetish. Which of the economists would not have agreed with Kalecki's main remark?: 'Just as the model cannot be blamed for all economic problems that have emerged recently, a change of the model cannot be a panacea for the national economy's ailings'.

The all-decisive point, however, is that in that article Kalecki was referring, not so much to a future economic model which was to emerge out of the Economic Council's proposals, as to the provisional, short-lived and very incoherent model which appeared as a result of the law on workers' councils and two other acts, namely, a law on factory fund and on powers of enterprise directors.

> The changes in economic management which found expression in legal acts expanding powers of enterprises and those concerning workers' councils and Factory Funds have led to the emergence of a new economic model. This model, briefly, entrusts the management of enterprises to workers' councils which operate within the framework of central planning in the strict sense of the word.
>
> (Kalecki 1957)

Kalecki tried to caution the general public not to overrate just that kind of model. But that was something that Lange and Brus had no need to be told at all. Indeed, it was strange that Kalecki himself did use the term 'new model' to describe such modest changes. But he soon made good that mistake so that later he used that term solely in reference to the postulated 'model', the one that was to appear as the Economic Council's brainchild. Naturally, today we are wiser by the years which have passed and we know that even that model, half-hearted and tentative as it was, must not be overrated.

Let us return to the question asked at the outset: how did the Polish reformers imagine the market could co-exist with the bureaucracy? Kornai is right in saying that the pioneer reformers of that time were naïve because they believed it would be possible to draw the precise line between planning and market; they believed that market, despite being treated as an instrument in the hands of the state bureaucracy, could nevertheless survive. But the Polish reformers certainly cannot be attributed the optimistic philosophy of seeing an almost perfect harmony between bureaucracy and market, as Kornai contends. I am positive that they were perfectly aware of the standing clash between those two institutions.

Kalecki wrote, for example, in a 1956 article:

We concluded above that a synthesis of central planning and workers' councils is desirable. This of course does not mean that such a system is necessarily viable, but in any case, it does create the basis for efforts to secure its viability.

One should not be deluded into thinking that such arrangements are free from inconsistencies and easy to operate. Undoubtedly, there will always be a tendency in them to reduce the prerogative of the workers' councils in favour of greater centralization, as well as a tendency for workers' councils to weaken the central plan. On the other hand, there will exist the danger of weakening the position of the workers' councils and bureaucratizing the whole system of management. On the other hand, pressure from the workers' councils may lead to a situation in which it will be necessary to slow the pace of economic development or become dependent on economic aid. Alternatively, after a period of chaos, 'order' will be restored with a return to a system of bureaucratic centralism.

(Kalecki 1956/1986)

Kalecki and other reformers, accordingly, can be said to have preached, not simply a 'harmony' between planning and market, but made a plea for an institutionalization of two elements – the autonomous enterprise led by workers council as a prerequisite of the market, and the plan in the form of a (transformed) central planning agency. I think they were convinced that without that kind of institutionalization the market was not going to survive the central and local administrations' assaults on it. The Polish pioneer reformers distinguished themselves by yet another remarkable feature.

But first let Kornai speak:

The pioneer reformers wanted to reassure all members of the bureaucracy that there would be ample scope for their activity. Their intention is understandable. The reform is a movement from 'above', a voluntary change of behaviour on the side of the controllers and not an uprising from 'below' on the side of those who are controlled. There is, therefore, a stubborn inner contradiction in the whole reform process: how to get the active participation of the very people who will lose a part of their power if the process is successful.

Now it is easy to show that this charge does not apply to the leading reformers in Poland, albeit I can easily see how this charge came about. Włodzimierz Brus's *Market in a Socialist Economy* (1961 in Polish) is, not without reason, regarded as the best summary of the Polish economic revisionism and reforms of the first wave. But in that book, written after the first wave of reform movement subsided, Brus deliberately side-stepped socio-political issues. Thus he wrote, for example:

The emergence of specific interest groups on account of the public ownership of the means of production, on the basis of a very close – almost symbiotic – linkage of political power and economic management is, given the inevitable hierarchization of the administration, undoubtedly one of the most important problems in the study of the mechanisms applied to resolve contradictions in the socialist system.

Yet he promptly remarked: 'This problem can only be hinted at here especially as it belongs in many social sciences and not economics alone' (Brus 1961).

Ignoring these 'interest groups' was particularly annoying when Brus proceeded to discuss the general framework of economic reform, for his approach could give the impression that the choice of the system of organization is of purely praxeological nature.

Incidentally, some Polish revisionists lashed out at Brus for having ignored socio-political factors (Hagemejer 1962). The situation, however, at the time the first Polish 'socialist renewal' bid peaked, was radically different. Many reformers, Lange and Brus particularly, argued in favour of self-management, seeing in it no less than a leverage society could use to curtail the administration's powers and thus also to force it to introduce reforms. In 1956–8, Poland was a scene, not only of a 'movement from above', but also an 'uprising from below'. The difficulty was how to reconcile these two movements in such a way that it would promote institutional changes, and not perform a clash of the two fundamentalisms. (Brus's pragmatic book had not preceded, unfortunately, the reformist movement but only recapitulated it.)

This brings us to the key question about why previous attempts at economic reforms failed, and what chance of success stands for the future. If reform is, to use once again Kornai's words, 'a voluntary change of behaviour', a movement from above only, then it inevitably develops into counter-reformation, or just a bogus kind of reform. Only in that way is it possible for 'the bureaucracy to reform itself'. If we are facing 'an uprising from below on the side of those who are controlled' alone, without the reformers being able to win over at least some sections of the administration, the reformist movement develops into a revolution, which tends to paralyse the government structures rather than forcing them to launch coherent reforms.

An 'uprising from below' alone, of course, is no solution at all, because revolutionary fervour as a rule does not last as long as it takes to enact and consolidate any radical package of reforms. This brings us to the question of institutionalizing public pressure. The Polish pioneer reformers trusted that the system of workers' self-management on the one hand, and the ruling party transmogrified into something like the Revolutionary Institutional Party of Mexico on the other, were a solution.

It was not that particular belief that brought them to their fall. Today I think that they clung to a vision of revolutionary workers' democracy, neglecting social and economic pluralism, the freedom of articulation and organization of interests. I do not think, however, that the demand for a restoration of fully-fledged political pluralism in the style of western parliamentarism was the only feasible alternative. As I see it, there was the unacknowledged, or perhaps underrated and never tried, possibility of introducing a kind of social (non-party) pluralism. In that light, even the bureaucracy itself would no longer appear as a united and uniform force, marked by the same features and faults, but as composed of different groups performing different functions inside the administration, that is, groups that are capable of changing into one another. The tradition by revisionists and first reformers of treating the bureaucracy as a monolith is, unfortunately, continued to these days.

PRE-WEBERIAN BUREAUCRACY

Let me once more refer to Kornai's study of Hungarian reform. As he puts it, overregulation is a rather predictable and self-evident result of the very existence of a powerful and huge bureaucracy, for: 'Power creates an irresistible temptation to make use of it. A bureaucrat must be interventionist because that is his role in society; it is dictated by his situation.'

Is interventionism indeed an intrinsic quality of all bureaucrats?

As Kornai himself refers to Weber in using the term 'bureaucratic' simply as 'a value-free denomination of a particular form of co-ordination', perhaps it should be recalled at this place that Weber used the term to denote a rational and impersonal procedure along systematic rules.

Let me quote Weber following Robert Solo, who thinks that just these words best express the Weberian idea of bureaucratic authority:

distributed in a stable way, delineated by rules . . . creating a firmly ordered system of super and subordination . . . which offers the governed the possibility of appealing the decision of the low office to a higher authority in a definitely regulated manner . . . with its management based upon written documents (the files) . . . where the executive office is separated from the household, business from private correspondence, and business assets from private fortunes . . . where management presupposes thorough and expert training . . . demanding the full working capacity of the officials . . . following general rules, which are more or less stable, more or less exhaustive, and which can be learned . . . where office holding is a 'vocation'. This shown, first, in the requirement of a firmly prescibed course of training, which demands the entire capacity for work for a long period of time and in the generally prescribed and special examinations which are prerequisites of employment.

(Solo 1982; Weber 1968).

This model of bureaucracy has nothing in common with the *Nomenklatura*, even though it is open for debate whether even as half-hearted reforms as the Hungarian one, lead to a reinforcement of the rule of law or to certain compromises between the *Nomenklatura* and the rule of law.

Maybe the East German economy was run by a bureaucracy closer to the ideal type of Max Weber. But the Hungarian, Polish, still more Bulgarian and Romanian bureaucracies do not fit in the Weberian Concept. I think they deserve to be called 'pre-Weberian' (the trade mark is of Jane Curry).

The political scientist and constitutionalist, Marek Sobolewski points out that the *Nomenklatura* makes Communist systems similar to feudal states rather than modern western nations. Whereas a king or a feudal lord ruled through his lieutenants and vicars, modern systems are based upon impersonal bodies of law which is put into practice by civil servants. The law:

became a better tool to run social processes and to control them, and the rule of law was more efficient and more effective, than governing through one's own men (. . .) The Communist system has yet to come to learn this truth. Despite all kinds of declarations (. . .) about the dictatorship of the proletariat being put into practice through socialist law, in actual fact that dictatorship is being put into practice through the *Nomenklatura*. This is happening despite the fact that for decades now that system has not been working effectively (. . .), that it does not guarantee the pursuit of a uniform official policy; that it does not prevent the emergence of various arrogant local chieftains; that it breeds what is an enormous corruption, etc.

(Sobolewski 1982)

Whether the *Nomenklatura* is the insurpassable boundary of reformability, as Sobolewski tends to believe, or whether it is doomed as the system gradually evolves from something like a *Polizeistaat* to a *Rechtsstaat*, remains a question. Indeed, I am sure it is the economy which is likely to be the first major sector of public life to be submitted to the rule of law. But this largely depends on whether or not modern reformers are going to become aware of this issue and whip up the general public's interest in liberating the economy – at least at the level of the individual business enterprise – from the *Nomenklatura's* tight grip. The safest way towards that is *via* the development of all kinds of self-government bodies, unions and associations.

BIBLIOGRAPHY

Braudel, Fernand (1971), *Historia i trwanie*, Warsaw.
Brus, Włodzimierz (1961/1972) *The Market in a Socialist Economy* (quoted from Polish and translated by Z.Nierada), London, Routledge & Kegan Paul.
Brus, Włodzimierz (1975) *Socialist Ownership and Political Systems*, London, Routledge & Kegan Paul.
Dickinson, H.D. (1939) *Economics of socialism*, London, Oxford University Press.
Dobb, Maurice H. (1926) *Capitalist Enterprise and Social Progress*, 2nd edn, 1981 London, Hyperion Press.
Dobb, Maurice H. (1973) 'A letter to Tadeusz Kowalik', 27 July.
Hagemejer, Helena (1962) Review article of Brus's 1961 book, *Kultura i Społeczeństwo*,
Kalecki, Michał (1956) 'Rady Robotnicze a Centralne Planowanie' ('Workers' Councils and Central Planning'), *Nowe Drogi* 11–12 in *Selected Essays on Economic Planning*, 6 vols, Cambridge and London, 1986.
Kalecki, Michał (1957) 'Nie przeceniac roli modelu' ('Let us not overrate the importance of models'), *Trybuna Ludu* (in M. Kalecki, *Dzieła (Selected Works)* 3, 1982).
Kornai, János (1986), 'The Hungarian reform process: visions, hopes, and reality', *Journal of Economic Literature* 24(4), 1687–737.
Lange, Oskar and Taylor, Fred M. (1938/1964) *On the Economic Theory of Socialism*, New York, Toronto and London (1938-University of Minnesota Press).
Lange, Oskar (1939) *An Economic Structure of a Socialist Society*, 'Controversy' 7, London.
Lange, Oskar (1956a) 'Budowa Nowego Modelu Gospodarczego Musi Sie Oprzeć na Dynamice Klasy Robotniczej i Socjalistycznej Inteligencji' ('The new model must be based on the dynamics of the working class and the Socialist intelligentsia') *Nowe Drogi*, 11–12 (*Dzieła* 2).
Lange, Oskar (1956b), 'Jak Sobie Wyobrażam Polski Model Gospodarczy' ('How I conceive the Polish Economic Model'), *Trybuna Ludu* (*Dzieła* 2).
Nuti, Mario Domenico (1986) 'Michal Kalecki's contribution to the theory and practice of socialist planning', *Cambridge Journal of Economics* 10.
Sobolewski, Marek (1982) *Granice Reformowalności Systemu Komunistycznego* (*Limits of the Reformability of the Communist System*), Krakow (mimeographed).
Solo, Robert A. (1982) *The Positive State*, Cincinnati-West Chicago.
Weber, Max (1968) *On Charisma and Institution Building – Selected Papers*, Chicago.

12 Reformability of the 'objective economic laws' of socialism

Pekka Sutela

I

To reform any object, one needs among other things to know its present state, an outline of its desired state, as well as an appropriate transition strategy. One determinant of pre-1989 Soviet policies was the ability of Soviet social scientists to offer relevant policy advice. The post-Brezhnev Soviet leadership repeatedly called for the active advisory role of the economists. And in fact, not only have economists like Abalkin, Aganbegyan, Latsis and Popov been among the prominent spokesmen of the reform, but the leadership has repeatedly relied upon academic expertise to a degree never seen in the USSR before.[1]

Even now only little is known of the exact degree to which expertise is being used, and this ignorance gives rise to complaints in the Soviet press,[2] but still Leonid Abalkin confidently said recently that 'today many decisions are being made on the basis of the recommendations of economic science'.[3] Evgenij Yasin saw this more as a challenge than an achievement. Referring to the doctrinal roots of many of the present policies, he emphasized that the reform should also be seen as a test of the, traditionally, most important variety of Soviet reform economics, its mathematical branch.[4]

But, indeed, were the economists able to deliver the goods? This has been much debated in the Soviet Union. The high-level disillusionment with Brezhnevite social science surfaced in 1983 and was followed by institutional reorganizations and high level appointments.[5] After the 27th Party Congress the issue gained new topicality. When *Kommunist*, the party journal, asked four prominent academic economists in early 1987 whether economic science was in the position to support effectively the new policies, two of them (L.I. Abalkin of the Academy Institute of Economics and P.G. Bunich of the Moscow Institute of Management) answered mainly in the positive, one (A.G. Granberg of the Novosibirsk Institute of Industrial Economics) chose to avoid the question and the fourth, A.I. Anchishkin, then the head of the Academy Institute for the

Economics and Forecasting of Scientific and Technical Progress, gave an unhesitatingly negative answer.[6] Other economists, especially those in administratively-responsible positions, provided other answers. In their view, in spite of all the acknowledged handicaps, the economists did have the capability of supplying more and better advice than the politicians were willing or able to use. N. Fedorenko claimed this for the Brezhnev years[7] and A. Aganbegyan for the *perestroika* period.[8]

There is abundant experience to show that most reform attempts in the world have suffered both from technocratic incompetence and bureaucratic footdragging. The recent Soviet reforms are certainly no exception. Soviet economists were for decades prevented from studying the state of Soviet society. They had no common understanding concerning the future state of society, too. Finally, the crucial problems of the transition have emerged as a complete surprise, not only to the decision-makers but also to the economists. This paper does not address any concrete problems of Soviet reform economics. Rather, it takes a look at some of the world-view aspects of Soviet political economy. The argument, however, is not about 'ideological constraints' to reforming; it is about the way in which Soviet economists conceived of the socialist economy before 1989, and about the possible influence which this might have on their recommendations. Ideological constraints, as usually understood, are something external to the economists. Here we are interested in the conceptual apparatus that has passed as Soviet economic theory for the last five or more decades.

An example may clarify the distinction. One way to interpret the experience of the 1965 Kosygin reform is that when it first met with such consequences of its own contradictions as rising unplanned investment and profit inflation, it could only withdraw, given its weak political support and the perseverance of a paternalistic ideology submitting to the axiom of the absolute primacy of the planners' preferences. (In PES, the Marxist–Leninist Political Economy of Socialism, this is called the Law of the Planned Development of the National Economy.) This, it should be emphasized, is a crucial question of any reform. If increased enterprise independence, one of the eternal goals of all the reforms, is to have real contents, it must mean the admission of conflicting interests in the economy and the ability to act against the planners' preferences, naturally within some political limits.[9]

It is in this sense that Abalkin was firmly within the confines of an 'old type of economic thinking' when he theorised about the unity of interests as an objective economic law of socialism in a 1987 book.[10] The argument in this paper is not that such conceptual issues would be a binding constraint in reforming. The argument is that such issues existed and, therefore, they were of some limited interest in the USSR and in certain countries of Eastern and Central Europe. Whatever the scientific qualities of the political economy of socialism (PES) may be, even the recent

Soviet political leadership – notwithstanding its eagerness to transmit a non-ideological and *delovoi* ('business-like') image – seemed to regard the question of reformability of PES a legitimate, even an important, one. I have discussed the historical ramifications of the question elsewhere.[11] To give just one example of anxieties, in February 1988 Gorbachev complained that 'the political economy of socialism has remained fixed on many conceptions. The practice is already outdistancing political economy. We are progressing by the method of trial and error'.[12] Obviously, he regarded this as a problem.

The same anxiety concerning the potentials of PES was shared by many in the Soviet economic discussion before 1989. L.F. Shevtsova noted recently that East European reforms were often late because of ideological constraints.[13] The lesson was obviously thought to be valid for the Soviet case, too. In another journal O. Ananin criticized the outline of the new political economy textbook by Medvedev, Abalkin and others for relatively neglecting PES proper, the study of production relations.[14] Finally, the shared understanding of many of the economists interviewed for an *Ekonomika i matematicheskie metody* round-table seemed to be that the reform policies were risking the fate of the Kosygin reforms due to their poor conceptual foundations.[15] To recapitulate, any intelligent reform (that is, one whose only claim for success is not mere good luck) presupposes a theory of the object to be reformed. In the USSR, in distinction from many centrally-managed states of Eastern and Central Europe, such a theory was long expected in a form at least commensurate with PES. The question of this chapter is whether PES itself and especially its specific conception of the objective economic laws of socialism is reformable to a sufficient degree to achieve this end or whether it necessarily remains an apology of the centrally-managed system.[16] As the present author is not a proponent of PES, the answer to the question is sought in recent Soviet discussions.

PES is a typical pseudo-science,[17] and as such one would like to see it abandoned. As ideologically, culturally and politically, this has not been probable until recently, its reformability was a crucial problem in the Soviet-type systems. Reforming PES would not imply turning it into a science, but would bring about some relevant (even if badly-defined) progress within its contours as a pseudo-science.

II

The centrality which was claimed above for the concept of 'objective economic laws' relies upon three arguments. First, this objectivity is a centrepiece of the 'materialist' philosophical foundations of PES, and as such is perhaps its most important building block. Second, as is to be seen below, objectivity is not a natural consequence of a realist (in the philosophy-of-science sense) understanding of science but a peculiar conception tendentially identifying traditional Soviet socialism with real socialism, the good society of the socialist movement(s). In this capacity, it has habitually been used as the measuring rod to condemn deviations and revisionisms. And finally, Soviet PES has a relevant tradition of disputes on the objectivity issue. This is of interest as such traditions are important in the internal logic of the discourse.

The full bearing of the issue of objectivity can only be understood against the background provided by the birth of PES.[18] This is a somewhat complicated story. Soviet histories of PES claim that the existence of a future PES was denied in classical Marxism because of counterposing capitalism with its anarchic markets, and causally-determined action against socialism/communism with conscious planning and teleological action. In this interpretation causal action is supposed to have been subsumed to objective laws while teleological action is supposed to have been free from them. This standard Soviet interpretation is false.

The death of theoretical social science was actually prophesied on the basis of contrasting reified capitalist and transparent Socialist/Communist social relations of production. In the former case a specific theoretical social science was necessary, Marx assured, while in the latter case only some general sociological laws, assumedly of little inherent interest, remained. Classical Marxism took it to be one of the defining characteristics of the good society that a descriptive study of organization, together with economic geography, would suffice to make the structure and functioning of the coming society clear and comprehensible to all.[19] Given what really-existing socialism proved to be, one should not be all too surprised by the fact that this fundamental point of classical Marxism was seemingly never openly confronted in the USSR.

Furthermore, given the peculiar Marxist heritage, either the Marxist conception of science or the idea of the Soviet Union as Marxist socialism had to be abandoned.[20] The first one was, but silently. It was substituted by the issue of existing or non-existing economic laws. This issue only became really central in the 1930s. The debates of the 1920s, notwithstanding their relative freedom and incomparably higher standards, usually addressed a somewhat different issue: how did the economic laws, rising from the still predominant presocialist forms of economic activity, coexist with the already perceptible embryos of the future? The Marxists largely agreed upon the wide outlines of the future, but strongly disagreed among themselves upon the dialectics of the transition. The awkward questions about the inherited image of the future only became central when the coming of the future was beginning to be officially claimed.

Contrary to what standard Soviet accounts claim, many of the classical Marxists admitted the existence of economic laws in socialism. In the USSR, such existence was only fleetingly denied by some enthusiasts during the Stalinist revolution when any talk of law-determined development could be taken as a programme of capitalist restoration. But within a few years a new orthodoxy propounded by people like L. Gatovskij and N. Voznesenskij became dominant. According to this new orthodoxy, economic laws did exist in the Soviet economy, but far from being objective in the epistemological sense, they were consciously created by the party/state. They could, thus, not act as constraints upon economic policies. On the contrary, such economic laws only existed as policies. On these foundations people who adhered to the existence of economic laws could well criticize those who did not for being too pessimistic about the possibilities of party/state policies. From the crude apologetic point of view, this pre-1941 truth of Socialist economic laws was, therefore, optimal. It is a different matter that as a propagandistic device its untenability should be obvious.

This orthodoxy only changed in 1941 when the existence of objective economic laws in the Soviet economy was decreed by Stalin.[21] On one level the new truth was a natural and even necessary extension of the just-created official Soviet understanding of historical and dialectical materialism. If the materialist interpretation presupposed the existence of matter or being as an 'objective reality' outside and independently of the human mind, how could the economic laws of socialism not be objective? If Marxism–Leninism was to cover and explain everything under and beyond the sun, how could it not be valid for socialism, too? Certainly, to argue otherwise would be to become a victim of idealism, perhaps the greatest of sins.

Thus, given the black and white either-or world of historical and dialectical materialism, the objective economic laws of socialism simply had to exist. This does not, however, explain their centrality in Soviet ideology. It is only made understandable by another determinant. As propounded in the 1940s by K.V. Ostrovityanov and others, even the doctrine of objective laws boiled down to a crude axiomatic apology. There were two fundamental classes of laws in PES, the guardians of Stalinist ideology in political economy explained. Certain laws were somehow derived from the officially-accepted definition of socialism: this is the background of a law like 'The Planned Character of Development' (*planomernost'*). Others were simply specific policies 'proven correct by history': collectivization (of all things!) was the example of the second class of laws often used.

There are at least three interesting things about the laws of PES as traditionally understood. First of all, as A. Pashkov already implied in 1936,[22] their invention was reserved for high authority. This still seems to be the case,[23] though the post-Stalinist depersonification of such authority has somewhat paradoxically made matters more complicated. It is impossible to say who can now decree a new law of PES. In this sense, and as compared with the adequate equilibrium of the Stalinist decades, the present situation is somewhat anarchic.[24] Second, there has simply never been an accepted way of corroborating or falsifying these laws.[25] And finally, declaring the laws objective opened a real Pandora's box of interpretation problems.

Saying that economic laws were objective meant, for example, that *planomernost'*, not specific plans themselves, was the economic law. This obviously implied an opening of a window for assessing plans as to their correspondence with or divergence from the economic laws. To close the window it was assured that Socialist economic laws are – under proper leadership and given a well-functioning bureaucracy – always cognized and implemented in practice. In this way, the old identification of state activities and economic laws was reinstated, and even the new doctrine boiled down to saying that what existed in the USSR or was made by the party/state was perfectly law-determined, not a result of possibly questionable political decisions. Thus, even according to the post-1941 interpretation of economic laws, Stalinism is not an arbitrary dictatorship but applied science. In fact, the state is portrayed as an almost powerless agent of the iron laws of history. It does not create, it is itself created by history.

This is the fundamental message of PES, and also the reason why the 'objective laws' doctrine was strongly criticised in the 'People's Democracies' as soon as it became politically possible. It was a way of opposing the copying of Soviet institutions and mores. At the same time, the message also makes evident why the 'objective laws' doctrine is by no means contradicted by the infamous Great Wall erected by Stalin between PES and economic policies in his economic *magnum opus*, the 1952 booklet. Objective laws, after all, were what the state was doing, not what the scholars may have been thinking.

III

The doctrine of 'objective laws' was thus open to different interpretations. It could be applauded because of the potential critical window it seemed to provide for. This was presumably the reason why Oskar Lange applauded the late Stalinist emphasis on the objectivity of economic laws.[26] On the other hand, the specific interpretation given to objectivity, at least tendentially equating reality and rationality, served as an apology of the Stalinist regime. The fundamental criticism raised against the official Soviet textbook of political economy in 1954, in the immediate post-Stalin atmosphere, therefore, concentrated on the very topic of objectivity. Writing in 1956, a noted Hungarian economist said that:

> the textbook creates the impression that the economic laws of socialism determine the development of socialist society in all details, and that a procedure in accordance with the laws is ensured, because the laws could be discovered and known and also because the harmful consequences of not proceeding in harmony with these laws are indicated.[27]

At the same time, it was plain that the so-called laws were of such a generality that they could offer no assistance in policy formation. In the Soviet Union, the impotence of PES was quite dramatically exposed by the so-called Grand Law-of-Value Discussion of the late 1950s. Together with the prevalent Khrushchevian science policy criterion of practical usefulness, this barrenness helped to breed new approaches in economics. Though both Lysenkoism and mathematical economics benefited from the call for practicable science, de-Stalinization was characteristically half-baked in economics, too. L.F. Ilichev, Khrushchev's ideologue, answered a call for reconsidering the theoretical ballast of the Stalinist decades in no uncertain terms: there would be no questioning of the main body of PES (as well as of Soviet socialism).[28]

Given the circumstances, in addition to pursuing orthodox PES, three alternatives remained for an economist. The first was simply to neglect political economy or at least to relegate it in forewords and postscripts, with the necessary citations of the current Secretary General or Party Congress often helpfully supplied by the publisher. This was the majority reaction, as evidenced among other things by the fact that even the Academy Institute of Economics tried to reorient its work towards applied questions.[29] Any interest that there might have been in PES subsided.

This was largely because the second alternative, gradual change within the existing PES framework, proved supremely difficult. There were some examples of attempts at reformulating and using the traditional laws of PES for slightly reformist goals: discussions around the so-called Basic Law are a case in point.[30] However, a perusal of the relevant literature, certainly an exhausting task, shows the diminishing returns in such exercises. The inertia of PES has also been demonstrated by the slowness with which concepts like scarcity or utility have been able to penetrate it. In the 1970s it was the Party Academy of Social Sciences' economists like Medvedev and Abalkin who campaigned ultimately successfully for such marginal change within PES.

Another example of the slowness of possible change within PES has been provided by the decade-long debates on the law of value under socialism. The idea itself, decreed by Stalin in 1941, could be and was interpreted in several ways. One particular interpretation, equating markets with the law of value, was later to serve reformist goals in various centrally-managed states. As the law of value existed objectively, developing markets was obviously the proper policy line, it was argued. At the same time, however, the idea of law of value in socialism ties its proponents to the labour theory of value. Within its framework progress towards a more rational price theory may be possible as the Novozhilov–Petrakov–Morishima interpretation shows, but it certainly is a tortuous path to follow.

The third alternative, finally, was an attempt at substituting PES by something new. This attempt was launched by the Marxism-inspired interpretations by V. Nemchinov and V. Novozhilov of the scarcity-and-choice logic, as popularized in the USSR by L. Kantorovich, but was only formulated in the late 1960s as SOFE, The System of Optimally Functioning Socialist Economy, by various scholars around the Academy Central Economic–Mathematical Institute, TsEMI.[31] If PES can be justly characterized as being normative-apologetic, SOFE is axiomatic-normative. The former basically claims that Soviet socialism is what it is supposed to be, the latter claims that Soviet socialism may not yet be, but at least can be made, optimal. Both share the fundamental normativeness of Marxism: history is moving towards an optimal regime. Furthermore, they both also assert that Soviet socialism is a progressive phase on that path. The primary difference is in whether the 'good society' has already come true or not. To a degree, the definition of the 'good society' also differs. For SOFE, it is efficiency writ large.

The Sofeists criticized PES of *a priori*sm, of living in a make-believe land of invented laws without any connection with empirical reality and without any means of proof or disproof.[32] For them, 'the task of a theoretical economist does not consist of calling one or another economic process a law'.[33] The political economists, on the other hand, tried to turn the table by asking from where the axioms of SOFE came.[34] The fact that both sides tried to prove the other guilty of an *a priori* methodology reflects the deeply-rooted realist attitude of Soviet scholars: in some sense, theories should be traceable to 'reality'. In the same way, laws should be objective. But given this common ground, some of the possible diversity of interpretations was made clear in an exchange between Nikolai Petrakov, a leading Sofeist, and Konstantin Valtukh, a conservative Novosibirsk economist, in the middle of the 1970s.

In various publications, Valtukh put forward a crude correspondence theory of truth. Economic models, he argued, should correspond to reality. He even denied the existence of theoretical concepts without an empirical counterpart. Petrakov and others argued in a 1974 review that in socialism such an approach might just prove a correspondence between a model and an economic policy earlier adopted.[35] What exists has been formed by previous policies. What is objective in Valtukh's sense, thus, may just be a consequence of earlier, totally-mistaken decisions. Following the logic of SOFE, Petrakov called for an interpretation of truth in the spirit of Marx's famous thesis on Feuerbach: the point is to change the world (that is, the Soviet Union). This leaves two questions unanswered: first, in which sense is such change 'objective'; and, second, what is the reason for believing that any (desired) change is possible?

IV

In a formal sense at least, the first post-1985 criticisms of PES repeated the 1983 accusations of scholasticism, abstractness and uselessness. A turn of social science towards practice was exhorted. With the deepening of the condemnation of the Stalinist past, together with a growing awareness of the necessary requirements of a successful economic reform, political decision-makers started to demand a reconsideration of Soviet past, present and future from the economists.

Naturally, attitudes towards PES differed. One political economist claimed in Pravda that the Soviet stagnation was not due to any deficiencies of PES but to a neglect of its correct findings.[36] A retired party *apparatchik* accused the economists of having kept silent for decades. Now they only offer such advice as implies the abandonment of the cherished achievements of socialism.[37] The overwhelming majority of published opinion, however, criticized both the economists and the decision-makers. Even if advice had been forthcoming it would not have been heeded, seems to be the majority interpretation of the Brezhnev years.

By 1988, the reform was running into the first problems, and the deficiencies in its 1987 conceptualization started to be acknowledged. The Soviet economists did not go as far as a leading western analyst of the reforms, who commented in the summer of 1988: 'If there is a crisis in the Soviet Union, it is a crisis in theory. These guys haven't thought through what they are about. And the result is enormous chaos.'[38] But at the Party Conference of June 1988, academician Abalkin seized the opportunity of lecturing Secretary General Gorbachev in public on the need for qualified statesmanship: 'You cannot really count on success if you are violating the objective logic of life, if you are not taking into account its laws.'[39] Any leadership that ignores the laws of political economy will bankrupt the nation, he said. (A year later Abalkin as a vice-premier was in a much better position to tell about the laws of political economy to the leadership.)

In PES the developments were contradictory. In early 1987, Gorbachev, as if echoing Petrakov, condemned PES for having elevated empirical features of the Soviet society into the status of theoretical dogmas. He called for an objective analysis.[40] In October 1988, Vadim Medvedev, the first economist member of the Politbureau since Voznesenskij, addressed an international conference on contemporary socialism calling for a reconsideration of the concept of socialism.[41] Medvedev argued that Lenin's ideas (and thus the correct Marxist–Leninist interpretation) of socialism had changed deeply during the first few years of the New Economic Policy (NEP): it is just the Lenin of NEP who gave the correct characterization of socialism.

Medvedev's speech reconfirmed that the USSR was still in the ideological phase of its development. Politics still needed Leninist sanctioning, and Medvedev condemned allegedly anti-Leninist and anti-Socialist ideas. At the same time, however, he also disputed several long-held dogmas, like the primacy of state ownership or the use of Soviet institutions as a yardstick for measuring and condemning those functioning in other Socialist countries. For Medvedev revisionism was in this sense richness of experience.

The deepest reconsideration of PES in Soviet literature was more implicit than explicit before 1989. The analysis of historical alternatives to Stalinism made it very difficult to claim that Soviet history was law-determined. The fundamental apologetic use of the idea of objective economic laws has also been repudiated in the condemnation of the Brezhnev decades. If planning and management consisted of central decision-making and what the centre did was objective[42] how was the stagnation possible? If *planomernost'* is an objective law, how is the present state of the Soviet economy possible?[43] Raising such questions is important also for showing once more the hollowness of PES, but so far the questions have not been answered in any convincing way. If Soviet past and present have not been law-determined, how did they come about? Soviet scholars still have quite a way to go before supplying consistent alternative answers.

There has been but little discussion on the fundamentals of PES. Obviously, different from writers or film-makers, Soviet economists did not have their masterpieces behind locks or shelved.[44] Before 1989, the leading Soviet economists were mostly Russian, middle-aged and male, hardly fluent in foreign languages and usually ignorant of western economics. Samuelson's textbook was cited as *the* western economics. Their formative experiences were in the 1950s and 1960s. Reading the latest authoritative volumes, Abalkin's textbook and its shadow by TsEMI,[45] one is disappointed by the proportion of what is new and what is old. But the real *déjà vu* comes when one realizes that the volume by Abalkin and others really had Medvedev as the nominal main contributor and Abalkin publicly opposed any freedom of others to write their own textbooks. That might give the opponents of *perestroika* the possibility of propagandizing their views among the students, he argued.[46]

One approach that has been consistently proposed by Yakov Pevzner is to emphasize the similarities between capitalism and socialism. As mentioned above, Marxism always thought there are some economic laws common to different modes of production, but they were regarded as few and of little intrinsic interest. Pevzner argued that in fact the similarities between capitalism and socialism are much greater than usually thought.[47] If accepted widely, such a methodological approach would make both the use of market institutions and the borrowing of western economics much easier. Naturally, Pevzner's approach proved controversial. While some economists proposed forgetting about any talk of 'bourgeois pseudo-economics', others stressed that capitalism and socialism remain different things.[48] According to a contemporary Slavophile view, the peculiarities of the Russian soul make the application of western rationalism in general impossible.[49]

Liberals, westerners, Marxists and Slavophiles, the Shmelevs, Pevzners, Rakitskijs and Antonovs are thus all active and public again. Lenin may now be criticized as a precursor of Stalin,[50] the Socialist nature of Soviet Union may be denied[51] and the views of Engels and Marx on the future may be deplored.[52]

The fact, however, remains that a reconceptualization of Soviet socialism is still a matter of the future. It has already been proposed in the Soviet press that a relative neglect of theoretical consideration – reformist pragmatism – is not only deleterious to the cause of reform but also makes its reversal easier.[53] At the same time, leading economists claimed that they were discriminated against in reform preparation,[54] accused one another of deficient judgement[55] or performed dramatic aboutfaces[56] in a way which can hardly help to build the public's trust in the economists, however well-founded such turnabouts may be.

V

Finally, let us return to the question asked in the beginning: were the objective economic laws of PES reformable? The position argued in this paper is not that PES was a binding form of ideology and as such an obstacle of reform. Marxism–Leninism has always been able to accommodate itself to any policy change. If a political economic argument for the orthodoxy of private property, capital income and wage labour under socialism is needed, it will be forthcoming. The argument of this chapter is a different and perhaps more subtle one. PES was the frame of reference within which Soviet economists, at least an overwhelming majority of them, learned to cognize the world and argue their proposals. Therefore, it simply had to have an effect on the way in which ideas were formed. This is why one may have some limited interest in PES, though it certainly does not make it the crucial topic in reform economics.

In fact one may well discern three paths of reforming the economic laws of PES. First of all, some alleged laws have already been forgotten. Not surprisingly, in recent years one heard little of such orthodox laws as 'collectivization' or 'primacy of state property'. *Planomernost'* was the next law to be forgotten. At the margin such developments would leave nothing of old PES. The major drawback of this strategy is its inability to explain why such characteristics of Soviet policies came to be regarded laws and why they no longer are such. For any satisfactory outcome, a discussion of the roots of PES is needed.

The second strategy is to acknowledge the laws of PES as what they were, apologetic generalizations of Soviet idiosyncracies. This, by and large, seems to be the path the recent Soviet leadership was taking by emphasizing the element of active choice in history. The USSR is no longer portrayed as showing the glorious future of mankind, but as one, possibly even deplorable outcome of historical processes and forces, the study of which admittedly still remains in its infancy.

The third and least satisfactory strategy is to argue for piecemeal change within PES by reinterpreting laws earlier admitted. The earlier discussions of the law of value were the obvious example. The labour theory of value remains a clumsy price theory, but at least its most glaring traditional handicaps can be dispensed with.

The answer, then, can only be yes: PES was reformable. This does not change the fact that it remained a pseudo-science and its main thrust was conservative. Neither does it change the fact that PES remained silent over most of the crucial issues to be faced in any serious reforming.

NOTES

At the time of writing the first draft of this chapter, the author was Visiting Research Fellow at the Centre for Russian and East European Studies, University of Birmingham. Financial assistance of the Yrjo Jahnsson Foundation is gratefully acknowledged.

1 Anders Aslund (1987) 'Gorbachev's economic advisors', *Soviet Economy* 3, 246–69.
2 See L. Plyasheva (1988) '"Tyazhelaya kolesnitsa istorii proekhala no nashemu pokoleniyu . . ."'('The heavy wheels of history went through our generation'), *Druzhba narodov* 7, 179–97, for the contrast between the openness of the debates of the 1920s and the still prevailing secretiveness. The example used by Plyasheva is the law on enterprise: there were different proposals for it, she complains, but nobody seems to be able to tell how and by whom they were debated.
3 L.I. Abalkin (1988) in 'Vybory v Akademii Nauk SSSR' ('Elections to the Soviet Academy of Sciences'), *Voprosy Ekonomiki* 3, 61–73 (cited on p. 61).
4 E. Yasin (1984) 'Administrativnaya systema tsen ili ekonomicheskij mekhanizm' ('Administrative system of prices or economic mechanism') *Ekonomika i matematicheskie metody* 2, 205–20. For an analysis on SOFE, the school in question, see Pekka Sutela (1984) *Socialism, Planning and Optimality*, Helsinki, Finnish Society of Sciences.
5 Anders Aslund, op. cit. (note 1) and Hans-Hermann Höhmann (1984), 'Hoffnung auf die Produktivkraft Wirtschaftswissenschaft', *Osteuropa* 7, 500–10.
6 'Ekonomicheskaya teoriya i praktika perestroiki' ('Economic theory and the practice of perestroika'), *Kommunist* 5 (1987) 30–9 and 6 (1987) 10–19.
7 See Fedorenko, 'TsEMI – 25 let' ('TsEMI is 25 years old'), *Ekonomika i matematicheskie metody* 5 (1988) 946–53.
8 A.G. Aganbegyan (1989) 'Reshitelnee vesti perestroiki ekonomicheskoy nauki i praktiki' ('The perestroika of economic science and practice must be performed more resolutely'), *Ekonomika i matematicheskie metody* 2, 197–201.
9 The great illusion of past Soviet reform theories (see Pekka Sutela, op. cit., note 4) has been the idea of the implementability of an optimal regime where 'global' and 'local' interests would coincide. In fact, this idea simply reproduces the classical Socialist Utopia in another economic language.
10 L.I. Abalkin, (1987) *Novyi tip ekonomicheskogo myshleniya* (*A New Type of Economic Thought*), Moskva, Ekonomika, especially p. 77.
11 Pekka Sutela, 'Ideology as a means of economic debate, or, the strange case of objective economic laws of socialism', to appear in *Jahrbuch der Wirtschaft Osteuropas* vol.13, no.1, 1989, pp. 198–220.
12 M.S. Gorbachev, *Pravda*, 22 February 1988.

13 L.F. Shevtsova (1988) 'Neizbezhnost obnovleniya sotsializma' ('The inevitability of renewing socialism'), *Rabochij klass i sovremennyi mir* 3, 3–14.

14 O. Ananin (1988) 'Politicheskaya ekonomiya sotsializma: stereotipy i tochki rosta'('Political economy of socialism: stereotypes and aspects of evolution'), *Voprosy ekonomiki* 5, 69–80. Compare with *Politicheskaya ekonomiya, uchebnik dlya vysshikh uchebnikh zavedenii* (*Political Economy Textbook for Institutions of Higher Education*), Moskva, Politizdat, 1988.

15 'Perestroika upravleniya ekonomikoi: problemy, perspektivy' ('Perestroika of economic management: problems and prospects', *Ekonomika i matematicheskie metody* 4 (1988) 709–45; 5 (1988), 890–924.

16 The argument is therefore not that PES would be a scientific theory of socialism or that its contents would be the most important question of reforming. It is only argued that an assumption giving it some importance in Soviet society does not seem too far-fetched.

17 For a definition of pseudo-science see Mario Bunge (1982) 'Demarcating science from pseudo-science', *Fundamenta Scientiae* III, 369–88. PES is often likened to another pseudo-science, theology, but in a sense PES is 'worse' than it. Nobody expects things like empirical falsifiability or exactness from a discourse dealing with personal experiences, while economics should in principle have some empirical contents.

18 For references and details, see Pekka Sutela, 'Ideology . . .' op. cit. (note 11).

19 That such fundamentals of Marxism can still be forgotten in Soviet literature bears evidence of the fact that, for good or bad, Soviet economists are surprisingly ignorant about and uninterested in Marx.

20 That the Marxian concept of science is indefensible is not a relevant issue here.

21 For a recent discussion see Dmitrij Valovoj (1988) *Ekonomika v chelovecheskom izmerenii*, (*Economy in Human Measure*), Moskva, Politizdat, 55–7.

22 A. Pashkov (1936) 'K voprosu politicheskoi ekonomii sotsializma v shirokom smysle slova' ('On the political economy of socialism in its broad sense'), *Pod znamenem marksizma* 1, and also reprinted in A. Pashkov (1973) *Voprosy ekonomicheskoi nauki* (*Issues of Economic Science*), Moskva, 473–511.

23 See Ananin, op. cit. (note 14).

24 In the dual sense in which the word is used in 'Soviet' language.

25 On this see, for instance, S. Shatalin (1970) 'Nekotorye problemy teorii optimalnogo funktsionirovaniya sotsialisticheskoi ekonomii'('Problems of the theory of optimal functioning of the Socialist economy'), *Ekonomika i matematicheskie metody* 5, 835–48.

26 Oskar Lange (1954) 'The economic laws of socialism in the light of Joseph Stalin's last work', *International Economic Papers* 4, 145–80. Lange selected to gloss over Stalin's Great Wall between policies and economics.

27 T. Nagy, reprinted in Nicolas Spulber (1979) *Organizational Alternatives in Soviet-type Economies*, Cambridge, 139.

28 L. Ilichev (1962) 'XXII sezd KPSS i zadachi ideologicheskoj raboty' ('The XXII Congress of the Communist Party of the Soviet Union and the tasks of ideological work') in *XXII sezd KPSS i voprosy ideologicheskoj raboty*, Moskva, 7–87.

29 Pekka Sutela, *Socialism, Planning* . . ., op. cit. (note 4), p. 152.

30 Ibid., 155–75.

31 There is a thorough discussion of SOFE in Sutela, ibid.

32 See, for example, N. Ya. Petrakov (1974) *Kiberneticheskie problemy upravleniya* (*Cybernetic Problems of Management*), Moskva, 91–3.

33 Petrakov, ibid., 93.

34 See, for example, Ya. Kronrod (1968) 'Ekonomicheskii optimum i nekotorye voprosy metodologii optimizatsii narodnokhozyaistvennykh planov' ('Economic optimum and some methodological questions of the optimization of plans of national economy'), *Voprosy ekonomiki* 11, 50–62.

35 N. Ya. Petrakov, *et al.* (1974) Review in *Ekonomika i matematicheskie metody* 5, 1038–44.

36 E. Pletnev, *Pravda*, 18 December 1987, p. 2.

37 V.I. Konotop (1988) 'Pochta "Oktyabrya"', *Oktyabr* 1, 179–86. Konotop was until 1985 the first secretary of the CPSU Moscow *oblast* committee.

38 Ed Hewett (1988) 'The 19th Conference of the CPSU: a Soviet economy roundtable', *Soviet Economy* 2, 103–36, cited on p. 121.

39 L.I. Abalkin, *Pravda*, 30 June 1988, p. 3.

40 See *Materialy Plenuma Tsentralnogo Komiteta KPSS 27–28 Yanvarya 1987 qoda*, Moskva, 1987, 8.

41 See 'Sovremennaya kontseptsiya sotsializma' ('A modern concept of socialism'), *Pravda* 5 October 1988, p. 4.

42 See the comments on the subjectification of the objective and objectivization of the subjective in V. May and I. Starodubrovskaya (1988) 'Planovoi fetishizm: neobkhodima politiko-ekonomicheskaya otsenka' ('Planning fetishism: a politico-economic evaluation is needed'), *Ekonomicheskie nauki* 4, 104–8.

43 O.T. Bogomolov (1988) *Ekonomika i matematicheskie metody* 2, 371.

44 Even the one manuscript we know of, Voznesenskij's *magnum opus*, is still said to have been destroyed.

45 See *Politicheskaya ekonomiya*, op. cit. (note 14), and Fedorenko (1988) *Ocherki politicheskov ekonomii sotsializma* (*Issues of the Political Economy of Socialism*) Pod red. N.P., Moskva.

46 See 'Obsuzhdenie v Otdelenii Ekonomiki AN SSR' ('Discussion in the Economic Department of the Academy of Sciences of the Soviet Union'), *Voprosy Ekonomiki* 7 (1988) 14–61, especially p. 61.

47 Ya. Pevzner (1987) 'Radikalnaya ekonomicheskaya reforma i voprosy politicheskoy ekonomii' ('Radical economic reform and the problems of political economy'), *Kommunist* 11, 50–8; 'Novoe myshlenie i neobkhodimost novykh podkhodov v politicheskoy ekonomii' ('New thinking and the need for new approaches in political economy'), *Mirovaya ekonomika i mezhdunarodnye otnosheniya* 6 (1988) 5–22.

48 See, for instance, the discussion in 'Ekonomicheskaya teoriya i praktika perestroiki' ('Economic theory and the practice of perestroika') *Kommunist* 3 (1988), 72–6.

49 Mikhail Antonov (1986) 'Uskorenie: vozmozhnosti i pregrady' ('Acceleration, possibilities and limits') *Nash sovremennik* (1988) 7, ('Origins'), 3–20.

50 Vasilij Selyunin (1988) 'Istoki' ('Origins'), *Novyi mir* 5, 162–89. This was probably one of the articles Medvedev criticized in his October 1988 speech.

51 One example would be Nikolai Petrakov (1988) 'Tovar i rynok' ('Commodity and the market'), *Ogonek* 34, 6–8, 22–4, who writes of a 'feudal command system'; others would include Yuri Afanasyev and Boris Rakitskij.

52 The first ones were Evgenij Yasin and Gavriil Popov (1988) 'K 110-letiyu "Anti-Dyuringa" F. Engelsa' ('The 110th anniversary of Engels' 'Anti-Dühring''), *Voprosy ekonomiki* 10, 86–108.

53 I. Semenov (1988) 'K diskussii o preodolenii dogmatizma v politicheskoi ekonomii sotsializma' ('About overcoming dogmatism in the political economy of socialism'), *Ekonomicheskie nauki* 10, 106–13.

54 See Nikolai Petrakov (1988) op. cit. (note 51).

55 N. Rabkina and N. Rimashevskaya, *Literaturnaya Gazeta*, 5 October 1988, p. 10.
56 S. Shatalin, *Sotsialisticheskaya industriya*, 30 October 1988, p. 2, begs the readers' pardon for having earlier advocated higher consumer goods prices.

Part III

Between reform
and transformation –
à la recherche

Introduction to Part III

Reform economics is often regarded as a normative theory of transition from planned to market economies. It is considered a liberalization (deregulation) programme that has to comprise simultaneous scenarios of economic and political transformation. Transition: from where to where? Through which stages? In a preconceived way or by a trial-and-error procedure? Which are the indispensable components of the transformation programmes? How can the processes of marketization and privatization be matched with political democratization (in particular, during deep economic crises)? What kind of political, cultural, psychological, etc. obstacles are likely to appear in the course of the transition? The papers included in this chapter address these timely problems of the transformation.

The authors try to distinguish between the concepts of reformation and transformation; in other words, to separate those programmes which observe the final limits of Soviet-type economies from those which break the tacit compromises of reformism. The *punctum saliens* of transformation is property rights – this is the premise from which most of the papers start. Marketization processes can be easily distorted and reversed if they are not accompanied by profound changes in the ownership structure. Denationalization: should it proceed through self-management, through the various forms of privatization or both?

Bajt and Tardos agree that privatization must be given precedence in the transition programmes. Bajt – contrary to the conventional interpretation – calls for the privatization of entrepreneurship and management instead of making proposals for a far-reaching deregulation of the capital market. In his view, a truly radical reform has to crown the marketization processes by introducing markets within the walls of the enterprises and in the 'non-productive' spheres, and, at the same time, embark upon the privatization of 'intangible' capital. As regards this last point, Tardos goes much further. While being also sceptical about the economic merits of self-management, and not idealizing the mixed economies of the west, he recommends the radical privatization of 'tangible' state property. However – writes Tardos – the method of changing property rights by direct reprivatization cannot apply in societies with large-scale nationalization, big monopolies, weak private capital, and egalitarian traditions. Besides privatization, clever schemes of 'plural ownership' must be found (for example, by establishing new holding companies) in the course of transformation, which work against eventual re-etatization even in the absence of real private proprietors.

In Comisso's perception, it is likely that competitive markets cannot operate properly in the absence of private ownership. Privatization, however, does not necessarily lead to democratization: 'the preconditions required for the creation of self-regulating markets in socialism are not so much "democratic" as they are "liberal".' Comparing the Yugoslav and the Hungarian reforms from the point of view of property rights, Comisso applies the concept of communal ownership to describe the non-public-yet-non-private property rights in Soviet-type societies. In her opinion, the reformist requirement of 'lodging property rights in the hand of economic actors' is not tantamount to privatization. The critical condition of transformation is not private property but the establishment of a boundary line between the proprietory and communal spheres of social life by replacing one-party rule with the rule of law.

Osiatynski, Podkaminer and Zhou examine the social factors which impede the implementation of the transformation programmes. Osiatynski provides a detailed list of the various types of opposition against privatization, economic decentralization and political pluralization proposed by the reform economists. He finds marketization and democratization partly incompatible, still he excludes the possibility of transformation in the form of 'reform-dictatorship'. Unlike the 'Newly-Industrialized Countries' – Osiatynski writes about Poland before 1989 – here the supporters of liberal reforms did not trust the ruling elite; and conversely, those who trusted them were opposed to marketization.

Podkaminer contends that the transformation programmes have to include sophisticated techniques of economic policy, otherwise radical institutional changes will continue to be accompanied by soaring inflation, growing shortages and falling living standards. He pleads for some price controls and more generous wage policies. Macro-policies must not be eliminated in the reform process – says Podkaminer – their institutional background, however, has to be altered to rule out the possibility of discretionary decisions. While in his case the traditional mistrust felt by the reform economists toward the state is the subject of misgivings, Zhou criticizes the arbitrary experimentation with macro-policies in China. He depicts the state apparatus as inclined to launch large-scale expansion drives which overheat the economy, relying on the advice of so-called 'new model inventors' who have a fragmentary education in economics, and following the slogan of 'crossing the river by groping after stones'. This kind of pragmatism – says Zhou – must, however, be distinguished from that of a genuine market theory which ought to govern the transformation process.

13 The theoretical and psychological obstacles to market-oriented reform in China

Xiaochuan Zhou

China achieved amazing success and progress in the initial reforms of its economic system, especially during the period from 1979 to 1984. However, the process of China's economic reform, in particular, the reform of industrial and commercial systems, has not got rid of the common problems of reforming the Soviet-type economies. In fact, the so-called urban economic reform, that is, reform of industrial and commercial systems, had no significant achievement between 1985 and 1989.

A TYPOLOGY OF CHINESE REFORM ECONOMISTS

There were three economic and reform cycles during the last ten years of economic reform – before 1982, between 1982 and 1985, and after 1985 (Zhou and Feng 1987). In 1986, almost the whole year was spent in preparing a so-called integrated reform, which included price, taxation, treasury, banking and trade reforms. But the reform efforts were abandoned at the end of 1986 as a result of political disturbances. Meanwhile, a new reform concept was developed. This tried to avoid price reform, introducing the enterprise contractual responsibility system, and developing administrative decentralization.

By mid-1988 economists were differing widely in their evaluations of the enterprise reform. Many analyses show that this experiment did not mean essential progress. Since the end of 1986 inflation has gradually speeded up and got out of control. The rate of inflation exceeded 20 per cent in 1988.

Some results have been made since 1985, such as the establishing of horizontal linkages among the enterprises, and the implementation of the manager/director responsibility system, but none of these could be considered as significant progress. If we look at the reform experiences of Yugoslavia, Hungary, Poland and other Soviet-type economies, and compare them with China's reform process, a number of similarities can be noted:

1 The reform lacks a clear goal model and guiding theory. Knowledge and theories are gradually picked up and summarized by a trial-and-error procedure.
2 Either because of political events, or because of the economic situation, the reform process is cyclical. In China, for example, when time is favourable for reform, the government may eagerly pursue economic expansion instead, but when the situation changes, it is willing to accelerate reform. By then it usually becomes too difficult to implement the reform measures because of the overall worsening of the situation.
3 Reforms of Soviet-type economies are often unable to overcome the transitional difficulties and are bogged down in a muddle characterized by out-of-control inflation, debt crises, stagflation or, sometimes, a combination of all these.
4 Due to frequent changes of economic policies and their related theoretical explanations, it is difficult to infuse the public with confidence in, and enthusiasm for, the reform.

There are many questions to be raised: Why are the market-oriented reforms in the Soviet-type economies so difficult? Why have the market-oriented reforms of the centralized command economies in some developing countries, such as in newly-industrializing countries (NICs), and of war-time command economies in capitalist countries, such as in Germany and Japan, succeeded?

Some economists have come out with the argument that these successes presupposed large-scale private ownership. A direct implication is that a market-oriented reform in a Soviet-type economy would be much smoother if large-scale privatization were promptly introduced. However, I do not share this opinion. I suggest that there might be a simpler solution, which will be discussed later in this chapter. In the reform or *perestroika* of Soviet-type economies there are a great many mistakes made by both governments and economists, which are not directly related to the ownership issues. Many mistakes were made in China as well, concerning the goal model, the sequence arrangement, inflation, debt policies, methodology and theoretical fundamentals, and so on. Although the restructuring of ownership, the clarification of state ownership and the establishment of related legal systems are major parts of the reform of Soviet-type economies, the main obstacles to the current reform process in China, as well as in some other Soviet-type economies, are not only related to the ownership problem, but also to some more fundamental mistakes resulting from the theoretical patterns and thinking modes which hamper the reform designers and decision-makers so frequently. They opt for carrying through a market-oriented reform, but refuse to accept the basic theory of a market economy and the empirical knowledge of related international experiences. They make the reform linger between rational and irrational activities.

Apparently there are two remarkable factors which determine the success of a market-oriented reform, especially in NICs. First, there is a politically-stable and powerful government which is capable of taking risks and has enough authority, possibly even a dictatorial one. Second, the leading reform economists apply market theory instead of a centrally-planned economy (CPE) theory. In NICs, for example, most leading economists graduated in the west.

In China the circumstances are different. After the tragedy of the Cultural Revolution and the new slogan initiated by Deng Xiaoping that 'practice is the only standard for testing the truth', people were impelled to rethink their old views. Comparative studies showed the relatively bad performance of CPE and suggested the necessity of economic reform. Due to political stability and a resolute reform-push of Chinese top leaders, initial reforms were quite successful. The economic potentials suppressed over several decades were rapidly released, but the guiding theories and the goal models of reform were very vague and even confusing. In the initial stage of reform there was no team of economists in China to act as reform designers and analysers. During that period, only the simple intuition of politicians and lower-level officials was utilized for remedying the illness of the Soviet-type economic system. At that time they focused on how the CPE could be supplemented with 'useful elements of a market regulation'. Along with the deepening of reform, the goal models became clearer. The reform gradually became more market-oriented. But the basic theoretical framework of market mechanism, and its related policy simulation and empirical analysis, were still not accepted. The negative feeling about capitalist economics remained.

In other words, the reform officials still believed that a generalized theory of dialectical and historical materialism was sufficient to solve any problems that occurred in the reform process. This led to interesting disputes among economists. I suggest that prior to 1989 Chinese economists could be classified into three schools according to their theoretical attitudes, although there are more schools of thought regarding practical strategy and policy issues:

(a) **Plan improvers** (represented by Wu Shuqing, Liu Hong and Wang Mengkui) (Wu Shuqing 1988; Wu Shuqing *et al.* 1988; Liu Hong *et al.* 1988). They are traditional economists who still favour the CPE. When serious macroeconomic malfunctions are caused by the reform, their opinions attract the attention of the government.

(b) **Market-oriented reformers** (represented by Wu Jinglian, Liu Guog-uang, Zhou Xiaochuan and Zhang Zhuoyuan) (Wu Jinglian and Zhou 1988; Liu Guoguang 1986; Zhang Zhouyuan 1987). They are radical reform economists applying basic market theory, although with differing interpretation of the degree of market mechanism. They do not refuse to seek a new approach for some specific economic problems of China, but they believe that the market-oriented reform needs a guiding theory of market economics (Wu Jinglian 1988). Unfortunately, they are often criticized for 'the divorce of theory from practice', 'idealism' and 'book worship'.

(c) **New model inventors** (represented by Wang Xiaoqiang, Li Yining, Chen Yizi and Hua Sheng) (Li 1988; Chen 1988; Wang 1988; Hua 1985). They are invention-oriented economists not believing that there is any available theory which would be able to solve the reform problem in China. They are constantly trying to develop and create new theories. They sometimes dominate the mainstream in designing reform policies. They reject the old system and favour radical reform. They do not want (or have no opportunity) to study the market theory systematically. In China, there are constantly emerging new theories and concepts with mixed features, in which one could find some educational background of socialist political economics, a fragmentary knowledge of market mechanism and a response to the short-run performance of the current reform. They prefer new theory, new concepts and even a new style of language which are above comprehension, not only for foreign economists, but also for the Chinese experts. Since some leading officials have a similar way of thinking, there is plenty of room for these economist-inventors to manoeuvre.

This tendency brought an inevitable dependence on trial-and-error procedures in China's reform process. The method is called 'crossing the river by groping after stones'. However, given the complexity of economic interrelationships and the time-lag of policy responses, not every policy decision can receive immediate and clear feedback from practice. Some policies are good in the short run but harmful in the long run. The reform cycle is also connected with economic thoughts and policy tendencies. When difficulties occur in the economy, the views of the plan improvers are often more respected; while if mandatory planning and administrative measures do not manage to improve the economy, the market theory or certain theoretical inventions may be accepted to push the reform. Regardless of whether or not the market theory is accepted, these inventions will play a role. They may be out of control when the economy goes forward smoothly. There are two connected phenomena in Chinese reforms: (a) the eagerness for success and short-term growth in the absence of appropriate macroeconomic management leads to an 'expansion drive'; (b) this, in the absence of a guiding theory of reform, results in an 'invention drive' in reform-making. If these drives go out of control, they will bring the economy to an imbalance, and this would result in another reform cycle (Zhou and Feng 1987).

Reform not only needs a theoretical guide and an extensive study of past experience, but also innovation, especially in some fields where there is neither ample theory nor practical experience to address specific problems. In the reform of the Soviet-type economy, there is a need for innovation as regards the future of the existing enormous state-owned enterprises. There is no simple way of privatizing them, but an unmanageably large number of state-owned enterprises cannot be maintained either. The models involving worker self-management and full worker ownership have left a lot of problems unsolved. But I consider it unnecessary for socialist reformers to make experiments in fields where clear theoretical explanations and historical experiences are available. For example, there is no need to try the result of an inflationary monetary policy or of unequal competition, and so on. If some unnecessary and unsuitable inventions are stubbornly applied, while the real key problems are ignored, the reforms are bound to suffer a setback.

UNCLEAR REFORM OBJECTIVES

At the initial stage of the reform, it was considered unnecessary to have a clear, stable goal model of reform in which the elements are logically consistent, co-ordinated and integrated. In China it was believed that the reform would gradually gain success and the economic system will become better and better if efforts are constantly made to discover and overcome the current shortcomings. However, it was gradually discovered that the absence of a clear goal model leads to unforeseeable controversies over the choice of reform strategy and policy alternatives. In addition, it results in a cyclical repetition of reform policies. Another major mistake at the initial stage of the reform was the blind confidence in the possibility that the CPE and the market economy could be arbitrarily pieced together, and the advantages of both systems could be combined while their disadvantages ignored.

At the end of the 1970s, the government's reform goal was the 'combination of planned economy and market regulation'. This brought many results but was coupled with a sectoral imbalance in resource allocation. In early 1982 some high-ranking party leaders responded to this phenomenon. They said that the model of reform was 'to rely mainly on the planned economy while taking market regulation as a supplementary measure'. Thereafter, a delegation of three important officials was sent to the Soviet Union to study how to strengthen and scientifically improve the planning system. In 1984 this course was officially revised in the Report of the Third Plenary Session of the Twelfth Central Committee. A more market-oriented reform was decided upon, the goal of which was defined as a 'planned socialist commodity economy'. In 1985 the new theoretical concept of the integrated reform was advanced by the Proposal of the Communist Party for the Seventh Five-year Plan in three major fields, that is, co-ordinated enterprise reform, marketization and changing the macroeconomic regulation from a direct to an indirect one. This programme, however, was not implemented.

A clearer goal model of the reform was presented at the 1987 Party Congress, according to which 'the state will regulate the market, and the market will guide the enterprises'. The function of the market mechanism was more strongly emphasized than ever, and the inconsistent two-piece-framework of 'plan' and 'market' was abandoned. However, there still remained plenty of room for different interpretations about how the state regulates the market.

The school of the market-oriented reformers holds that a correct and clear goal model would be 'a market economy with effective macroeconomic management'. This could be explained as an equivalent to the slogan that 'the state will regulate market and the market will guide enterprises'.

EXCESSIVE ENTHUSIASM FOR INVENTIONS AND EXPERIMENTS

Some Chinese officials (and economists) who have a narrow economic educational background (that is, political economy of socialism) do not really understand the basic discipline of market mechanism. The political economy of socialism does not teach how to analyse policy impacts, nor does it teach how to gain experience from practice by empirical analysis. In China there are people who are interested in spreading the fallacy that economics lacks any basic discipline; that economists can endlessly argue about everything; that ten economists always have eleven opinions which are far from reality, and that only silly people care about what they are talking.

A likely most grievous defeat of the theoretical rebellion against western economics in recent years is connected to inflation in China. The 'inventive' economists should particularly learn from it. As soon as the party and the government decided to undertake a more comprehensive reform programme, and the Communiqué of the Third Plenary Session of the Twelfth Committee was issued, in the autumn of 1984, someone invented the theory of 'increasing money supply in the phase of economic take-off'. This caused rapid money creation at the end of 1984 and in the first half of 1985. In 1985 the inflation rate reached 15 per cent while the foreign exchange reserve was rapidly exhausted (which greatly helped to alleviate price inflation). In the summer of 1985 the expansion of aggregate demand began to be controlled so strictly that the price index started to stabilize by 1986. Some inventors were unwilling to acknowledge the defeat of the 'increasing money supply' theory, and tried to solve this problem by a new inventive approach, for example, by resorting to 'using poison as an antidote to poison'. They stated: 'There is no excess aggregate demand. On the contrary, there is a remarkably insufficient aggregate demand in both investment and consumption, which has caused recession.' Then, credit creation was increased on a large scale in the spring of 1986. This led to price inflation several months later. In the autumn of 1986 some moderate price reform measures were implemented. The government permitted a moderate price fluctuation for a small group of products in terms of varying qualities, seasons and other conditions. In late 1986 price inflation was 6 per cent on a yearly basis.

Some economists blamed this on the permissive monetary policy at the beginning of that year. But the inventors had a brand-new explanation. According to them, the year 1986 demonstrated the 'very special characteristics and particular conditions of China, under which price inflation is not necessarily related to money supply, but depends on the starting signals of price adjustment given by the government'. This meant that the governmental policy allowing for price-differences had caused price inflation. In early 1987 the expansion of aggregate demand obviously dominated the economic policy. In fact, the tight policy of aggregate demand implemented in the summer of 1985 had already been stopped in early 1986. In the summer of 1987, given the pressure of increasing inflation, some leaders of the government proposed tighter monetary and fiscal policies and tried to implement it. This evoked strong resistance (Cheng 1988). As a result, the tighter policies were rejected by the end of 1987.

It was necessary to give an explanation to the public as to why price inflation still existed in 1987 without central price adjustment. At that time a new explanation was given: within the 7.3 per cent inflation in 1987 (actually it was around 12 per cent according to western statistics), a share of 4.7 per cent was caused by a price rise of agricultural goods and food. This was due to structural changes and land constraints and had nothing to do with monetary policy and fiscal deficits. This explanation prevailed from late 1987 to early 1988. Some inventors even advanced the theory about 'the advantages of moderate inflation' which strongly criticized the tight policies proposed in the summer of 1987. In early 1988 some economists (Liu Guoguang 1988) criticized the inflationary policy of the government and gave a serious warning. But these opinions were ignored. The money supply increased by more than 30 per cent in the first half of 1988 and the inflation rate reached 15 per cent. Industrial consumer goods were the main target of inflation. In many cities a purchasing panic broke out with a rush of deposit withdrawals from banks during the summer. The state council had to change its policy and stabilize the economy.

Inflation not only affects the interests of wage-earning households, but also leads to a significant decrease in the public confidence in both the government and the reform. It harms political stability and leads to a strong critique of social injustice (because some people are making a lot of money by rent-seeking). Moreover, an indirect consequence of inflation is the postponement or abolishment of essential reform programmes for fear of rising inflation. This is why price reform has been crippled and has made little progress in the past few years. The 'inventions' in inflation theory were punished by reality.

A typical statement of this invention-oriented way of thinking is: 'China's economy is very particular and exclusive from any explanation by any theory of our predecessors. Chinese reform is unprecedented, thus no theories and experiences are available for reference.' Now we have to wait and see whether the recent lessons of inflation can be carefully summed up, or on the contrary, some new and untested experiments, which are against the common sense of economics, will be made.

Let us examine now decentralization as a principle of reform. There are controversies in China concerning the patterns of decentralization. The central government has chosen the pattern of transferring decision-making rights to local governments of various levels. This is called 'administrative decentralization' or 'bureaucracy-oriented decentralization' rather than 'economic decentralization' (that is, decentralization of decision-making to enterprises). This choice is justified by the great dimensions of the country. Since each Chinese province is as large as other medium-sized countries, it would be quite natural to let them govern themselves as countries. A real problem is to find a decentralization pattern of decision-making without a mechanism of price and/or market co-ordination. China wants neither to run the risk of a price reform nor to postpone the major steps of decentralization. In fact, the macroeconomic management functions and responsibilities, such as fiscal policy, money-supply control and balance of foreign exchange, have already been decentralized to each provincial government. These governments are thus largely empowered to regulate the local economy (Wong 1985). Some provinces have even further decentralized these functions and responsibilities to smaller regions.

Local governments are competing with each other for greater money supply. Provincial officials often exercise protectionist acts against each other; thus, the market is segmented into smaller pieces. Investments tend to go to inefficient, small-scale factories; the possibility of local monopolies has increased significantly, and so on. In fact, some economists opposed administrative decentralization both from a theoretical point of view and from international and historical experience. They warned that local governments are professionally unqualified and are not responsible for macroeconomic balances, so they will probably contribute to inflation. These economists believe that decentralization of this kind will decrease economic efficiency. They have also illustrated the dangers using the examples of national decentralization in Yugoslavia and farming tax in some European countries in the last century (Lou 1988).

However, the psychological tendency to a skeptical attitude against theoretical analysis and international experience, as well as the fetishization of inventions have finally resulted in carrying on administrative decentralization. Now, more and more officials have become aware that out-of-control inflation is likely correlated to this kind of decentralization.

EXCESSIVE DEPENDENCE ON THE METHOD OF TRIAL AND ERROR

When reformers are facing unknown and disputed reform proposals, the approach of trial and error seems always to be both available and preferable. Moreover, it also conforms to the principle of 'practice is the only criterion for testing the truth'.

However, experiments in a social-economic environment must be prudently and scientifically designed. Such experiments face the difficulty of whether or not the conditions could be repeated, and whether or not the conclusion or evidence could be independently determined and then statistically tested. There are some other interrelated problems:

1 In many cases the result of a social-economic experiment cannot be reproduced. The external conditions are often complicated, and once an experiment begins, internal results and external conditions interact with each other.
2 Many experiments are not well designed. Often they enjoy preferential policies and/or fiscal concessions which would be unaffordable on the national scale. As a result, it is not clear what type of result and impact a trial experiment will have.
3 Experiments supported by leaders may be successful because of various explicit or implicit assistance, or of exaggeration by potential flatterers. Facts contradicting this success cannot be found unless the experiments are carried out everywhere.
4 The design of experiments, including conditions, facilities, measures and assessments, can be mistaken in the absence of theoretical analysis. A partial experiment may shift the resulting burden to others or may effect the balance of macroeconomic variables. This may not be significant due to the small scale of the experiment, therefore it can be thoroughly exposed in the popularization of the experiment. For example, a rise of enthusiasm may be observed in an experiment of linking up wages with the profit of a particular factory, but its impact on inflation in the whole country may not be noticed.
5 Even if some experiments failed, it would not be easy to discontinue the preferential policies because of considerations of political stability and external creditability. This promotes competition for experiments among local governments.
6 If an experiment leads to unfair resource allocation, (which, in fact, often occurs in China), there are two difficult factors to be measured: first, how much do those involved in the experiment benefit from it at the detriment of the outsiders? and second, how much is lost in terms of inefficiency of overall resource allocation?

This chapter does not advocate that experiments should not be practiced at all, but it is necessary, at least, to understand the difficulties and to have an appropriate theoretical guide of designing an experiment and seeing the significant differences between social-economic systems and those of natural sciences. The trial-and-error approach is not the only way for the reform, and it is far from being a substitution for theoretical analysis and the study of international experience.

The experiments with the Special Economic Zones (SEZ), for example, did not clarify their objectives: were these experiments designed for creating an export processing zone or free harbour, or for establishing a market-oriented reform model as a demonstration for the nation-wide reform? Attention was not paid to whether the experiment conditions and external effects were confined so that the result could be easily observed. There was neither a well-defined nor a widely-accepted measurement of indicators that could evaluate the results of the SEZ experiments. Thus it is unclear whether these models could be popularized, nor is it clear in what situation they could be popularized. It is also unclear how to evaluate their negative effects, how these effects have been generated, and whether we should allow preferential policies and destroying fair competition or not.

The experiments in the provinces of Guangdong and Fujian, especially in Guangdong, have drawn much attention. In the recent years a great number of local delegations, organized by other regional governments, have visited Guangdong in an effort to learn the experiences of the reform experiments. There are many good experiences indeed, but some unfair advantages were also often taken as positive results: for example, the advantage of high prices and wages to attract resources from the neighbours and shift inflation burdens on to them; the flexible modification of central government policies to provide new preferential treatments.

As far as the experiment of the enterprise contractual responsibility system is concerned, it has failed to comprehensively evaluate the micro- and macroeconomic variables. Even if its microeconomic achievements were great (Pong *et al.* 1988), its large-scale popularization after only half a year of experimentation was somehow too hurried. It is not clear whether the contractual system contributes more to enlarging production or to demand expansion caused by concessive incentives or by the indexation of wages. A large number of enterprises is bargaining with the governments to gain some easy contracts. As a result, the contractual system may be a major source of the expansion of aggregate demand and inflation.

THE LACK OF MARKET THEORY AND THE SURVIVAL OF THE CPE THEORY

Many people imagine that the economic reform has already defeated the old system, that the CPE theory is gone forever, that the reform process is irreversible and that nobody can bring back the old theory, although the new model has not yet been attained. However, that is not the case. As long as there is no convincing new theory in economic analysis, the obsolete CPE theory could be referred to at any time.

China's price-policy analyses are almost monopolized by the state price administration and its subordinate institutions. Their analytics is very doubtful. They use mainly the theory of labour value and Marx's theory of production price, but they never mention the assumptions they rely on. The artificial price-vector equation in the input–output model they use illustrates that the prices of products should be determined by the sum of input costs, depending upon a fixed input structure, plus a certain average profit. This approach entirely rejects the role of the demand side. It neither includes the aggregate demand, nor the existence of any demand elasticity for any given price. The input composition is also completely without any substitution elasticity. Import and export, as well as international specialization in world market, are left out of the account. Thus, they do not improve resource allocation at all.

This means that the model is irrelevant to the Chinese economy, which has already halfway transited to a market-oriented economy. Policy analyses have all been made by this or similar models for many years, and they have almost never been correct. The analytical conclusions of this approach are always against price reform. According to them, the price reform is useless, causes inflation or needs a new round of budget subsidies. Nevertheless, the government tends to carry out the price reform. This is a ridiculous matter. A possible explanation might be that the government does not care about theory but relies upon the price bureau because it is used to doing so.

Actually the analytical model was originally a so-called 'artificial theoretical price-model' for designing the goal vector of price reform. After having been widely criticized, this model was used as an analytical tool for price-related policies. When inflation problems occur in terms of the general price level, the reasons of inflation must be determined so as to prevent them in the future. If there is no correct theory available for guiding the analysis, Chinese officials will probably resume the old policy of administratively controlling prices and adjusting supply and demand through the state regulation of inventory level.

This method comes from the 1950s and has been used in recent years. It has two consequences. First, if price inflation is caused by a loose monetary policy, administrative control is of no use even if the state inventory is exhausted, for then the trade enterprises may even ask for more money to support larger inventory reserves. Second, the state-owned retail stores are commanded to control the price level, but are not allowed to compete fairly with privately-owned retailers. Thus, the state-owned retailers will decline day by day. It is well known that the service, attitude and responsibility of the state-owned department stores are bad. It is not only because of state ownership, but also because they have too many non-economic objectives to serve and are outside the competitive environment. Privately-owned, individual and some small collective retailers have profit maximization as a clear objective. When inflation is out of control, the authorities do not consider whether or not the old CPE concepts went wrong, but emphasize the necessity of building an even larger fund for market risk and inventory reserves.

The traditional CPE theory overestimates physical production while underestimating, or even depreciating, all the service sectors. When talking about economic efficiency, traditional CPE-oriented officials pay attention to the output of material production while attaching little importance to the process of information exchange and the efficiency of resource allocation (Barry 1985). The reform frequently faces the contradiction between reform progress and economic growth. Sometimes they require different macroeconomic policies: the short-run growth needs a budget deficit while the reform needs a tight money policy to end inflation. If the decision-makers ask for both of them, they may find a simple solution in raising economic efficiency as a result of increasing supply. Thus, the reform will be concentrated on those fields where there seems to be the highest potential for production efficiency. But since the CPE concept of efficiency is biased towards physical production, the (industrial) enterprise reform is always taken as the central task of economic policy. Thus, the price reform, and other reforms promoting the service sector and information industry, are always of second or even lower priority (Fang Jue 1988).

Nevertheless, the enterprise reform, and the expected enhancement of efficiency, are far from satisfactory. In case of economic difficulties, especially when there is inflation, some state officials complain that the difficulties are generated in the commercial sector – a typical conclusion in the framework of the CPE theory. They hold that there are too many trade companies ('too many buddhist monks with too little porridge') and each one raises its prices. As a result, transactions and prices are more strictly controlled. The bias towards physical production efficiency has remained for the entire ten-year reform period (Fei and Reynolds 1987).

CONCLUSIONS

As mentioned above, many problems in China's economic reform do not seem to be very difficult ones in terms of economics. Neither do they seem to be in close connection with the socialist system of public ownership. The difficulties come from the prevailing theory and way of thinking. The probability of making so many mistakes as in China by other non-socialist countries in their transitions from a command economy to a market-oriented economy seems much smaller. Some of them have already passed the transitional period. If we in China can overcome the theoretical and psychological obstacles, the reform of Soviet-type economies might not be so difficult.

The obvious shortcomings in the theory of reform have many causes:

1 The disadvantages of the old system are not sufficiently understood and a series of CPE concepts are not appropriately criticized. Therefore, the old theories are often used for seeking solutions for the reform problems.
2 The Soviet-type model of economy is being abolished, but the mistakes in the CPE theory, the background of the Soviet-type model, have not yet been sufficiently learned.
3 Although the principle that 'the practice is the only criterion for testing the truth' is well accepted, the theory of market economy is still being treated as an axiomatic system fabricated by abstract scholars rather than a summarized practical experience of our predecessors.
4 Socialists tend to believe that their economy is extra-special. This makes them refuse to note the experiences which have been summed up in western economies and in developing countries with market economies. Thus, only their own – Chinese – experiences seem to be useful. This leads to a tendency to apply the trial-and-error method.
5 The revolutionary leaders, especially those of large Soviet-type economies, have a feeling of pride and heroism. After having admitted the inefficiency of CPE, they might be psychologically unwilling to borrow the model of others. This facilitates a bias towards reform inventions. The reform motto in China is 'to establish a socialist commodity economy with Chinese characteristics'. The Chinese characteristics are often overstressed (Zhang Yongjiang *et al.* 1988). This has left much room for inventors to manoeuvre and caused great costs to the reform.

Now, Chinese reformers begin to think about the above-mentioned phenomena, particularly, after the recent surge of inflation. I strongly believe that the reformers will find a correct way to establish the new economic system. There is no doubt that we will still have some obstacles to overcome, but our goal is to try to find a less costly and less painful way of doing so.

BIBLIOGRAPHY

Barry, N. (1985) 'False starts and second wind: financial reforms in China's industrial system', in E. I. Perry (ed.) *The Political Economy of Reform in Post-Mao China*, Cambridge, Mass., Harvard University Press.
Chen Yizi (1988) 'Deepening reform, innovating theory', in *China: Development and Reform*, The Research Institute of China's Economic Reform, 6.
Cheng Wanquan (1988) 'The reasons of inflation and countermeasures', *People's Daily* 8 April.
Fang Jue (1988) 'The correct choice of the priority sequence of economic reform', *Economics Weekly*, 28 August.
Fei, John and Reynolds, Bruce L. (1987) 'A tentative for the rational sequencing

of overall reform in China's economic system', *Journal of Comparative Economics* 11(3), 490–502.

Hua Sheng (1985) 'The way of price reform with Chinese characteristics', *Economic Research* 2.

Li Yining (1988) *Clue for China's Economic Reform*, Beijing, Prospect Press.

Liu Guoguang (1986) *Collected Works of Liu Guogang*, Shansi People's Press.

Liu Guoguang (1988) 'Facing inflation carefully', *Economic Daily*, 5 April.

Liu Hong, *et al.* (1988) 'The basic idea of economic reform in the forthcoming eight years', in *The Great Ideas of China's Reform*, Beijing, Shengyang Press.

Lou Jiwei (1988) 'Leave the road of the current locality-oriented decentralization', in Wu Jinglian and Zhou Xiaochuan (eds) *The Integrated Design of China's Economic Reform*, Beijing, Prospect Press.

Pong Zhaoping, *et al.* (1988) 'The contract responsibility system may become a chance to activate urban economic vigour', *Economic Daily* 2 February.

Wang Xiaoqiang (1988) 'Go beyond the logic of private ownership: separating management from ownership, contractual responsibility system and asset of legal entity', in *China: Development and Reform*, The Research Institute of China's Economic Reform, 4.

Wong Christine (1985) 'Material allocation and decentralization: impact of the local sector on industrial reform', in E. I. Perry (ed.) *The Political Economy of Reform in Post-Mao China*, Cambridge, Mass., Harvard University Press.

Wu Jinglian (1988) 'Considerations about the strategic choice of the reform', *Comparative Study of Socio-Economic System* 4.

Wu Jinglian and Zhou Xiaochuan (eds) (1988) *The Integrated Design of China's Economic Reform*, Beijing, Prospect Press.

Wu Jinglian, *et al.* (1988) 'The situation and choice of China's economic reform: the integrated reform', in Wu Jinglian and Zhou Xiaochuan (eds) *The Integrated Design of China's Economic Reform*, Beijing, Prospect Press.

Wu Shuqing (1988) *Model, Operation and Regulation*, Beijing, People's University Press.

Wu Shuqing, *et al.* (1988) 'Program for China's economic reform during 1988 and 1995', in *The Great Ideas of China's Reform*, Beijing, Shengyang Press.

Zhang Yongjiang, *et al.* (1988) 'Rebuilding public-owned large enterprises with Chinese characteristics', *Beijing Daily*, 4 April.

Zhang Zhouyuan (1987) *Socialist Price Theory and Price Reform*, Beijing, China Social Science Press.

Zhou Xiaochuan and Feng Ailing (1987) 'Seeking essential progress and getting rid of the reform cycle', *Economic Research* 5.

14 The scope of economic reforms in socialist countries

Aleksander Bajt

REFORMS AND 'REFORMS'

This paper is conceived as a discussion on the logic of economic reforms in socialist countries. By socialist we mean not only the economies of the Soviet Union and Eastern Europe but those of China and Yugoslavia as well. Our question is this: Are the economic reforms that are being designed and/or have already been implemented in former socialist countries able to achieve the desired goals? Are they likely to be successful? What are the conditions for their success?

In what follows we shall first identify two types of deficiencies in economic systems and, on the basis of this, draw a line between reforms and 'reforms'. Confining our interest to the former we shall then evaluate the processes of marketization as one direction of reforms. The third section is to identify how marketization may become capable of achieving the reform goals. A second direction in reforming socialist economies – privatization – will be dealt with in the fourth section. The final section discusses how managers–entrepreneurs could make privatization economically efficient.

The two types of deficiencies will be defined by making a distinction between the economic system and the mechanisms used in its operation. By economic system we understand the decision-making, that is, essentially, the motivation and incentive structures of the economy. Centrally-planned economies and free enterprise systems are examples of economic systems as understood here. While operation of the former is based, down to the micro-level, on state decisions, it is characteristic of the latter that all processes result from the individual units' decisions.

No economic system operates in a fully satisfactory way. Imperfect markets leading to monopolies, unemployment, and economic fluctuations appear to be the main deficiencies of the free enterprise system. While the centrally-planned system was designed to do away with them, it succeeded only partially. The capitalist business cycles were replaced by investment cycles (Bajt 1971), unemployment by shortages in markets (Kornai 1979), imperfect markets by impotent planners, and so on. So it can be said that the operation of all economic systems, and their mechanisms, are deficient, and that this lowers their performance below the potential levels.

Unfortunately, deficient mechanisms are not the only source of economic inefficiency. To a much greater degree, this is determined by the decision-making structures of the economic systems themselves. As predicted by economists such as Mises and Hayek, systems without independent, privately-owned economic units, exhibit much lower efficiency than the free enterprise systems. That is, while inefficiency stemming from deficient mechanisms is known to all economic systems, inefficiency deriving from the centralized decision-making structure is specific to socialist systems.

Research on the comparative efficiency of economic systems is still to be done. One of the reasons for the lack of such studies is the high rate of growth of material, particularly industrial, production in the first decades of socialist growth. Some newer results, taking account of costs of fast growth, however, point at an about 30 per cent lower net productivity of labour (Bergson 1987) and also efficiency of investment (Bajt 1987), compared with capitalist economies. More specifically, it is not so much the level of technology than its utilization that presents the real handicap of socialist economies (Nishimizu and Page 1982). With net productivity of labour and efficiency of investment lagging that much behind, the actual material gross product of socialist economies must be considerably below the potential product. My estimates for Yugoslavia show that already in 1980, the actual gross material product amounted to only one-half of the potential product.

In socialist countries, inefficiency has been experienced everywhere, poor utilization of resources in particular. The resulting low real earnings and living standards, exhausted agricultural labour force surplus, inability to generate new technology, all leading to declining rates of growth, bordering to stagnation in many cases, and high and increasing foreign debt, forced the politicians to face the problem and search for ways to overcome it.

Many measures undertaken to improve the efficiency of socialist economies apply to their mechanisms. Yet, however successful these may be, being system-neutral they do not touch the basic decision-making structure, or they touch it only marginally. Yugoslavia is a case in point. Although through replacing central planning by markets in product price formation, she successfully mastered shortage – the most characteristic deficiency of socialist economies according to Kornai – her economy remained by and large as inefficient as those of other socialist countries.

In this chapter we are not interested in 'reforms' purporting to improve the operating mechanisms. Rather, our subject is reforms in the decision-making, that is, motivation and incentive, structures of socialist economies. As such, these are not system-preserving but rather system-transforming reforms. Their goal is catching up with the efficiency of the free enterprise system. To achieve this, they reinstitutionalize some fundamentals of the latter. So reforms are retroversion rather than convergence processes.

MARKETIZATION PROCESSES

If catching-up with capitalist efficiency is defined as the goal of socialist economic reforms, the question arises: why are the capitalist results not aimed at simply by resorting to the free enterprise and private-property-based economic system? The answer is obvious. It is the mono-party system that prevents it. Since social or state property is the material basis of its power position, this is regarded as the *minimum minimorum* of socialism. Thus, in designing economic reforms, economists in socialist countries have been facing a serious constraint, the 'social property constraint'. On the other hand, it is exactly this constraint that provides room for reform thinking. The free enterprise system need not be invented. It is ready to be applied. Only a political decision is needed.

In our view, retroversion processes develop along two distinct although not independent tracks. The first is the introduction of markets to centrally-planned economies, their allocation and distribution processes, hitherto exclusively dependent on state or planners' preferences. Let us call it marketization. The second consists of the introduction of privately-owned factors of production, both domestic and foreign, to socialist economies. It will be labelled privatization. While in the first years of the Russian revolution (re)marketization and (re)privatization were mainly parallel processes (NEP), the period after the Second World War is characterized by marketization (retained and reallowed private farms in Poland and Yugoslavia are not overlooked). Only recently, marketization has been joined by privatization, taking probably the lead in socialist (post-socialist) economic reforms.

A most likely reaction to the above distinction would be that in the last analysis, that is, when the economy gets fully marketized, this will automatically imply privatization. And *vice versa*. We shall explicitly agree on this later on. An additional response would be that markets presuppose independent enterprises. In fact, if enterprises were independent, markets would be created automatically. Unfortunately, in socialist countries the early marketization processes meant central simulation of market prices without much independence of enterprises.

The following appear to be the most distinctive phases in the marketization processes, listed by and large in order of historical appearance:

1 Raising consumer goods prices to drain surplus demand from the consumer goods markets. Frequently, higher prices are introduced only for one part of total supply of one and the same goods, thus leading to the so-called dual price system.
2 Bringing producer goods prices up to the level corresponding to the 'market' determined consumer goods prices. In many instances this also leads to dual prices.

Our contention that early marketization amounted to the imposition of market-simulated prices is illustrated by the extensive discussions on 'normal prices'. Reforms around 1968 were particularly strongly preoccupied with 'normalization' of prices (see, for example, Hejl, Kyn and Sekerka 1967; Belkin 1963; Ganczer 1966).

Steps (1) and (2) did not appreciably affect efficiency; they at best prevented it from sinking even lower. This is understandable since the non-market generation of prices degraded these reforms to 'reforms'. As for the 'normal price' discussion, it proved rather sterile. Price formation was conceived as a normative process, based on uniform factor prices for the whole economy, and on the average cost principle. It wholly ignored the marginal-productivity-based allocation of resources.

3 A shift from simulated (normative) to market-type product prices. Typically, this process starts with the consumer goods sectors, and subsequently extends to the producer goods sectors. This implies the independence of enterprises in production and sales decisions, which to some degree spreads to decision-making in general.

This step was most resolutely taken in Yugoslavia in the 1960s, implementing decisions of the 1958 Party Congress. Even one part of capital allocation was handed over to enterprises, not to speak of income distribution (wage formation). As a result, efficiency improved, in particular, labour and total factor productivity increased. Yet, significant as they were, these improvements could not change the generally low level of efficiency, characteristic of the whole post-war period (Bajt 1985).

4 Introduction of factor, that is, capital, foreign exchange and labour markets by abstaining from state intervention. Attainment of high allocative efficiency is the goal of this step.

The present reform efforts in practically all (post-)socialist countries aim at achieving (4), although degrees in radicalism differ already in design and still more in implementation. It appears that (4) necessarily implies (3), and logically this is certainly so. The logic breaks down, however, when factor prices are simulated. In this case, (3) comes after (4).

With a view to assess how relevant (4) is for efficiency, let us assume that all markets, product and factor alike, are introduced and operate well; they produce equilibrium prices expressing relative scarcities that all economic agents are obliged to pay for the use of factors, and are able to obtain by selling their products. In this way net product incomes, total proceeds minus total costs, are unequivocally determined. Indeed, some problems such as externalities (Coase 1960) and monopolies still remain unsolved, but at this level of discussion we may disregard them. By unequivocally ascertained product incomes, redistribution between enterprises, a rule in case of disequilibrium prices (for instance, zero or negative real interest rates, not to speak of administrative product prices), is made impossible. Product incomes of individual enterprises are their *own* product incomes, produced by their own employees, not by employees of other enterprises. If, in addition, enterprises are allowed to decide on allocation, product incomes are their own incomes also in the allocational sense.

Allocation and distribution based on market prices of products and factors ('integral markets') improves the efficiency of economy. It creates a hard-budget-constraint situation (Kornai, 1986a), with appropriation without production being impossible. In this way property rights, the main concern of Pejovich and Furubotn (1970), get well defined. The crucial question that arises now is: is such a hard budget state of affairs likely to provide for the efficiency catch-up, defined here as the goal of economic reforms? At least implicitly, Kornai's answer is affirmative. I say 'implicitly', since he finds shortage, one of the deficiencies in the operation of the system, rather than inefficiency to be the main difference between capitalism and socialism. So hard budgets are explicitly believed to eliminate shortage. When commenting on ideas of the radical Hungarian reformers (Kornai 1986b), he does not spell out any criticism that could serve as an indication that (3) and (4) are regarded as unable to do the job.

TWO MISSING STEPS IN MARKETIZATION

In my view, steps (3) and (4), while no doubt necessary, are not sufficient for catching up with capitalist efficiency. Two more steps are needed. These are:

5 Marketization of the internal structure of enterprises, that is, introduction of the so-called 'inside market', as opposed to the 'outside market' surrounding the enterprises and providing them with parameters in decision-making.
6 Marketization of the whole 'non-productive' sphere, most importantly, of the whole population, each and every individual as supplier and generator of productive factors such as labour skills (human capital) and savings (financial capital).

In arguing for the above view we could draw on the Yugoslav experience. It is true that, due to administrative intervention, factor markets have never led to equilibrium rates, at least so far. Interest rates were typically negative in real terms and wage rates for equal work highly differentiated across firms (which resulted from the 'income price' ideology that the whole income derives and therefore belongs to labour). Thus improvements in allocative efficiency expected from (4) never materialized. In my view, however, these could only be marginal compared with the improvements stemming from (5) and (6). Theoretically, and as far as labour is concerned, this is trivially clear. Without high labour inputs (high X-efficiency) there can be no allocative inefficiency, at least in the Ward (1958) sense (Bajt 1988). Yugoslav practice seems to confirm this. With (4) missing, the improved efficiency in the 1960s (Bajt 1985) could have only come from (3) and, as it strengthened the position of managers, from penetration of the outside market logic into the internal exchange processes (Bajt 1986), that is, from (5). Of course, with (4) included and encompassing wages, improvements in efficiency could have been still larger than experienced. None the less, both in the Yugoslav 1960s and in general, without a full institutionalization of (5) efficiency remains far behind the comparative capitalist efficiency.

Due to many factors acting in conflicting directions, which even in an econometric work do not lend themselves to reliable quantification, the Yugoslav experience may not be too convincing. We therefore turn to theory. From the modern literature on team production, for example, from its game-theoretic variant, we know that a co-operative behaviour of workers regarding their labour inputs is not easily secured. Free riders try to maximize utility by lowering labour inputs below the contractual ones, resulting in Nash equilibrium below the Pareto optimum. This is possible because not all dimensions of labour input are observable and measurable, that is, because of the informational asymmetry, and because, even when measurable, their measurement may be prohibitively costly. This is so even in capitalist firms where managerial function not only exists but is in general performed satisfactorily. For this reason the property-rights school insists on treating firms as inside markets with owners of inputs as sellers and the 'central agent', that is, the manager (managers and shareholders, respectively, in the case of managerial inputs) as the buyer. They start a bargaining process in which the 'metering' of output (marginal product) with large margins for discretionary decisions (such as evaluation of the non-measured dimensions, termination of labour contracts) by the principal (manager in the case of workers, shareholders in the case of managers) replaces outside markets where easily-measurable goods are being exchanged (Alchian and Demsetz 1972). In enterprises with managerial function inexistent or poorly performed, which appears to be the case in socialist enterprises, not only of the self-management brand, sliding of Nash equilibrium to low levels of efficiency is practically unavoidable. Arguments pointing to 'collective will', 'solidarity in productivity' and the like that would transform socialist enterprises into well-co-operating and efficient units neither appear persuasive on *a priori* grounds nor are corroborated by practice.

For these reasons, firms' product incomes necessarily get depressed to low levels, and so get real wages. This is a typical X-inefficiency situation (Leibenstein 1966). Well-operating managers, and more generally, entrepreneurs, are badly needed to overcome it.

Suppose now reformers accept (5). Where would the managers-entrepreneurs come from? Where would all the other labour inputs come from, both in the quantitative and qualitative sense? The lagging of the actual social product behind the potential one, typical of socialist countries, amounts, by definition, to the lagging of managerial and labour inputs behind the efficient ones. The first explanation would be that, with soft budget constraints, these inputs are not really needed. There exist a good many ways for the survival of 'chronic loss-maker' enterprises (Kornai 1986b). With budgets hardened these inputs would appear, just as they do in profit-making enterprises. In our view, however, it is the profit-making majority of enterprises that highlight the soft-budget problem: real wages accommodate throughout the economy down to the Nash-equilibrium levels to make firms profitable. It is this 'inner' softness of budgets, not subsidies and the like, which makes survival of socialist economies possible. The causes (low managerial and labour skills) would persist even if, by the introduction of (4), firms' budgets were rigourously hardened.

Labour skills derive from specific processes whose products get accumulated in human capital. If they are not needed, if products are appropriated by people who are not their producers, they not only are not supplied; they get generated on a narrower scale. There are two alternative explanations for this. First, similarly to budgets of enterprises, budgets of individuals are not hard either. Some people are able to appropriate incomes that do not derive from their work. Unfortunately, this is merely a description of the situation. A deeper analysis would start from the fact that within a market system, that is, on the basis of equilibrium prices of labour and managerial inputs, appropriation of other people's product incomes would simply be impossible. Since appropriation of other people's product incomes is an essential characteristic of socialist systems, there obviously must exist institutional mechanisms that interfere with the market evaluation of individuals' product incomes. These are administrative distribution (wages and salaries) schemes together with non-economic (political) promotion mechanisms. With such schemes and mechanisms existing, securing income rather than productivity becomes the first priority. As this is done on a large scale and persists over long periods, low overall efficiency of the economy is expected in the future. Therefore, improvements stemming from (5) and (6) are not likely to become substantial overnight. Structural adjustments, identified as shifts in people's utility functions, more explicitly, substitution of labour for leisure, usually require much time, frequently whole generations.

While administrative distribution schemes are eradicated by (4), a full implementation of (6) requires elimination of the non-economic promotion criteria for all individuals as well. Just like enterprises, individuals also have to become independent, their product incomes being exclusively dependent on their own labour inputs and their market evaluation. In some sense they must become their own entrepreneurs. They have to be put in a market environment virtually from their birth onwards. Every decision on the allocation of time available to them should be made in the function of maximization of their future income streams. This constitutes sufficient motivation for generating new labour and entrepreneurial abilities. It is here, in this 'non-productive' sphere, where efficiency of productive processes is being decided upon, where technological progress is being not only generated but applied to production of goods and services, both material and intellectual.

The independence of enterprises, and more so of individuals, is the core of (5) and (6). Indeed, if interpreted rigorously, the independence of enterprises unavoidably leads to (5) and (6). Steps (5) and (6) and even (4) are listed as separate in the process of marketization only because in (3) the independence of enterprises was defined as a rather limited one. Certainly, this interpretation is quite realistic. Note, for instance, that under (3), even in Yugoslavia not all investment decisions belong to the 'self-managed' enterprises and that their managers are appointed by the political organizations and not by workers.

PRIVATIZATION OF FACTORS

As conceived by the reformers, privatization relates to bunches of factors, to whole enterprises, and most typically, to their tangible parts. Therefore, just as nationalization abolished private ownership of the means of production (land and capital equipment, or simply capital), privatization would amount to the reinstitutionalization of private ownership of the means of production.

Of course, for private ownership of capital not to be void, the legal owner must enjoy all property rights, that is, he must have the right freely to decide on all product income flows generated by his factors. This is not always the case. Private owners are frequently prevented from enjoying some or all of the property rights, that is, they cannot utilize (consume and/or invest) product incomes of 'their' factors. Most typically, this is done by means of administrative intervention in the price structure. By lowering the price of one's product below its market-equilibrium level, the corresponding part of his factor gets nationalized.

This is particularly relevant in the case of intangible factors, such as labour, entrepreneurship and innovation. Their very nature makes nationalization in the usual sense, as applied to tangible capital, impossible.

It is therefore implemented in an indirect way, by administrative intervention in the distribution process, most typically, into the wage (personal
incomes) structure. In this specific case, therefore, re-establishment of the
property rights is secured by deregulation, for instance, by suppressing the
administratively-imposed wage schemes. The imposition, and suppression,
of *uravnilovka* (levelling-off of incomes), a well-known characteristic of
socialist payment systems, is a case in point.

The above distinction between private ownership of tangible factors and
the property rights of product income flows, puts us in a favourable position
in studying the logic of privatization efforts. As the former may be void – a
pure legal form, or 'juridical illusion' (Marx) – the privatization of tangible
capital does not necessarily involve appropriation of its product incomes by
the owner, or involves this only partly. Thus it also may be void. If this is
the case, the incentive structure will not change considerably, and efficiency
will not improve. As under socialism this is predetermined by the social
property constraint, a more promising strategy of reducing inefficiency
appears to be by means of the property rights directly. Complementary to
this approach is focusing our attention on intangible factors, thus bypassing
the ideological *noli me tangere*.

Let us start with the introduction of private capital, domestic and foreign,
in the socialist sector. It derives from an erroneous assumption that capital
is the main limiting factor of the development of socialist economies. Yet,
in no time period, and in no socialist country, capital has been a limiting
factor. Domestic savings have traditionally been very high, probably too
high, and quasi-voluntary (*ex ante*), not resulting in inflation. In Yugoslavia
where wages were a priority for labour-managed firms, quasi-voluntary
savings were promptly replaced by forced saving, brought about by the
creation of new money. Demand for foreign capital, a low percentage
of total capital formation anyhow, even in the 1970s, was mainly based
on primitive financial structures which, in conditions of decentralized
decision-making, were not able to concentrate the existing savings, and, in
the 1970s, on the negative real interest rates in the world capital markets.

The really relevant point against the introduction of private capital in the
socialist sector, however, is that private investors would be at the mercy of
low socialist efficiency. Even if they had some control over management,
this would be more formal than real. Even in capitalist corporations,
separation of management from ownership reduces control of the latter
over the former (Berle and Means 1932). The theory of the managerial
firm (Marris 1963) originates exactly from realizing that the contribution
of ownership to efficiency tends to become less important. Therefore, if
pure lenders and preferred stock holders are guaranteed a fixed rate of
return, its payment will directly press wages in the low efficiency socialist
sector to even lower levels.

Consider now the logic of private firms. Two developments appear
to be most promising: (a) establishment of small firms with entirely or

predominantly domestic capital; (b) direct investment of foreign capital into large, capital-intensive high-technology firms, with foreign management as the decisive factor. Since there is no doubt that entrepreneurship–management is the limiting factor in socialist development, this sounds reasonable. Efficient control in small socially-owned firms is too costly. So they simply do not exist. Especially, private farms would contribute to efficiency. As they produce for competitive markets, their adverse effects on the socialist sector would be minimum. The point here is not the absence of monopoly profits, but that without competitive markets these can be obtained artificially, by using personal contacts to solicit favourable contracts. This, together with a skill drain, hurts the socialist sector. As for the efficiency of the private sector itself, the social property constraint makes its behaviour myopic, thus predetermining a lower efficiency than that of similar firms in the capitalist set-up. In other words, the 'socialist' private sector will be private more in form than in efficiency. As long as social property is the basis of the system, private property cannot be really private.

As far as foreign firms are concerned, they are confined to low shares in total production and are therefore unable to change the order of magnitude of its overall efficiency. To a large degree, their own efficiency is predetermined by the low standards of the socialist sector, and is further impaired by their myopic behaviour. Yet, the slip in the logic of foreign firms is the following. If foreign firms are invited to socialist countries for the sake of the entrepreneurship–management they provide, then why is the development of domestic entrepreneurial–managerial skills not allowed, why does the system adhere to inefficient administrative, central planning and management methods, or, in the case of Yugoslavia, why is it assumed that each and every worker possesses the necessary entrepreneurial–managerial skills? In other words, why do the reformers stubbornly resist steps (5) and (6) in marketization, particularly (6), that involves a re-establishment of the entrepreneurial–managerial property rights?

Importing foreign entrepreneurship–management with a view to improving economic efficiency only makes sense if it is to be spread over a predominant part of the economy. In principle, since entrepreneurship-management may be imported independently of capital, the social property constraint does not contradict this. Property may still remain social or state property. However, such development would reduce domestic population, with the exception of the ruling political elite together with her suite – the whole establishment (social services, administration, defence, and so on) – to sheer labour force. They may be perhaps better protected than by trade unions in capitalist countries, but they will be certainly unable to acquire entrepreneurial–managerial skills, and therefore to climb up the social control ladder outside its establishment crosspieces. This would very much resemble the Ottoman system where management and state administration were performed by foreigners.

The above discussion enables us to propose the following conclusion. Neither investment of private capital into the socialist sector nor establishment of private firms, both domestic and foreign, promise any improvement in the present low level of socialist efficiency. The main exception seems to be production for competitive markets, above all in agriculture. Our pessimism springs from the social property constraint. Without this, both forms of privatization would present beginnings of a general privatization process, leading to the welfare state type of socialism. While the social property constraint is a handicap, it need not be fatal. As in the case of modern capitalist corporations, efficiency increasingly depends on management, why wouldn't the efficiency strategy of socialist countries also be based on a revolution of their management methods? Independent enterprises, that is steps (5) and (6) in the marketization process, together with the implied privatization of management, as opposed to reprivatization of enterprises (capital), appear to be all that is needed.

PRIVATIZATION OF CAPITAL VIA MANAGERS

Here, we could continue with discussing privatization of labour and innovation. We shall skip this for two reasons. All that is relevant is implied in steps (5) and (6) of marketization. As for innovation, quite a large part of it is covered by privatization of management. Discussion of the other – 'inventive' – part of it can be postponed; for many years to come improvements in efficiency should be based on proper utilization of the existing technology.

Instead, we shall point to two possible inconsistencies in our own interpretation. Step (6) in marketization obviously implies political pluralism. Does it not negate the social property constraint? The second inconsistency is related to management. Does not its privatization involve the privatization of capital, the restitution of private ownership of the means of production? Here, we will only discuss the second problem.

Speaking technically, increases in product, brought about by the managers' entrepreneurial-managerial activity, is theirs. No doubt, once the product is increased on the national scale, the main part of the increment is transferred, via competition, to wages. Still, with labour markets operating well, that is, with wages essentially independent of profits of the respective enterprises (systems like efficiency wages, 'gift exchange', inclusive of profit-sharing as understood in the west, do not contradict this), the managers would be left with high residuals. Normally, these are earmarked for investment, both direct and financial, making thus growth and expansion, inclusive of take-overs of less efficient firms, possible.

With all control by the shareholders and generosity in rewarding managers, these not only shirk but appropriate both income and capital beyond the contractual levels, thus becoming owners both in economic (income) and legal (capital shares) sense. Could independent socialist enterprises thus be prevented? The general egalitarian mentality that depresses managerial salaries stimulates rather than hinders the non-contractual appropriation. How could this problem be overcome?

Let us start with control. Substitution of state control for owners' control of managers is obviously ruled out by (5). Any direct control necessarily leads to state interference with the firms' decisions and blurs responsibility. This also applies to para-statal institutions, representing social property, as discussed in Hungary (Tardos 1982). As guardians of the constitutional order, both the administrative and judiciary branch exert only indirect control over the most general 'rules of the game', without interfering with decision-making in the firms. Thus, with independent enterprises, direct control over managers can only be vested with workers. Pejovich and Furubotn (1970), believe that workers are able to exert quite an efficient control over their managers. In any case, within independent socially-owned enterprises, managers are the only agents who could do the job. Many economists, Kornai (1986b) included, dismiss self-management on grounds of its past performance. Fortunately, since enterprises in Yugoslavia never enjoyed independence from the state and the political elites, records of Yugoslav 'self-management' are not too conclusive.

As for managerial rewards, there is a general agreement among observers that they have to be high enough for eliciting the required managerial inputs (Bergson 1978; Murrell 1984). Authorities such as J.S. Mill and A. Marshall regarded low managerial rewards in collective enterprises as a cause of their low profitability. As is well known, utility functions of managers include, beside material rewards, arguments such as growth, expansion and take-overs, based on 'animal spirits' (J. Robinson), but also social status and respect, and not least social control. In the degree a society succeeds in substituting the latter for the former, the same entrepreneurial inputs are secured by substantially lower material rewards.

None the less, even in cases of successful substitution of social and psychological for material rewards, managerial pay will necessarily be very high and even with no illegal appropriation it may lead to the accumulation of big fortunes. Even in this optimistic case, managers' savings may become an extremely important source of privately-owned capital. While savings of the major part of the population could for quite a time to come be channelled into housing, in the managerial sphere reinvestement of incomes appears to be unavoidable. If so – why should we not start privatization of capital and enterprises right away?

On the basis of the aforesaid, the answer should be clear. For ideological reasons (the social property constraint) straightforward privatization is not likely. Limited privatization does not lead to efficiency. Compared with this, the managerial type of reform not only promises efficiency but it promises it for the near future in which the threats of privatization cannot yet be felt. From the politicians' point of view this should be a decisive advantage.

The real problem with this perspective is that politicians may be frightened more by risks of losing their control over managers, than over private owners investing in the socialist sector and establishing small private firms. While the former jeopardize the core of the social sector, the latter penetrate only its periphery. Privatization of management, if tried at all, may thus be halted long before it can evolve into privatization of social property. The post-1965 development in Yugoslavia serves as a good example. For the first time in history, a socialist country headed for creating independent enterprises and a managerial class (Bajt 1974). Much before any indications of managerial appropriation of social property could be visible, the reform had been violently stopped and many of the most able managers dismissed for allegedly 'usurping the self-management rights of the workers'. Only, it was the politicians rather than the workers who decided.

BIBLIOGRAPHY

Alchian, A. and Demsetz, H. (1972) 'Production, information costs and economic organization', *American Economic Review* 62, 777–95.

Bajt, A. (1971) 'Investment cycles in European socialist countries: a review article', *Journal of Economic Literature* 9, 53–63.

Bajt, A. (1974) 'Management in Yugoslavia', in M. Bornstein (ed.) *Comparative Economic Systems*, Homewood, Ill., R.D. Irwin, Inc., 193–200.

Bajt, A. (1985) 'Efikasnost samoupravnog privredjivanja' ('Efficacy of the self-managed economy'), *Privredna kretanja Jugoslavije* 147, 29–49.

Bajt, A. (1986) '"Economic growth and factor substitution: what happened to the Yugoslav miracle?": some comments', *Economic Journal* 96, 1084–8.

Bajt, A. (1987) 'Stvarni i potencijalni proizvod u 1980' ('Real and potential product in 1980'), *Privredna kretanja Jugoslavije* 171, 42–52. Published also in A. Bajt (1988) *Samoupravni oblik društvene svojine* (*The Self-management Form of Social Property*), Zagreb, Globus. In this book some of the ideas discussed in this paper are elaborated in more detail.

Bajt, A. (1988) 'The firm in Illyria thirty years later: why is it allocationally overefficient?' (manuscript).

Belkin, V.D. (1963) *Tseny edinogo urovnia i ekonomicheskie izmereniia na ikh osnove* (*Uniform Price Levels and Economic Measurement*), Moscow.

Bergson, A. (1967) 'Market socialism revisited', *Journal of Political Economy* 5, 655–73.

Bergson, A. (1978) 'Managerial risks and rewards in public enterprises', *Journal of Comparative Economics* 2, 211–25.

Bergson, A. (1987) 'Comparative productivity: the USSR, Eastern Europe, and the West', *American Economic Review* 77, 342–57.

Berle, A.A. and Means, G.C. (1932) *The Modern Corporation and Private Property*, New York, Macmillan.

Coase R.H. (1960) 'The problem of social cost', *Journal of Law and Economics* 3, 1–44.

Ganczer, S. (1966) 'Price calculation and the analysis of proportions within the national economy', *Acta Oeconomica* 1, 55–68.

Hejl, L., Kyn, O. and Sekerka, B. (1967) 'Price calculations', *Czechoslovak Economic Papers* 8, 61–81.

Kornai, J. (1979) 'Resource-constrained versus demand-constrained systems', *Econometrica* 47, 801–19.

Kornai, J. (1986a) 'The soft budget constraint', *Kyklos* 39, 3–30.

Kornai, J. (1986b) 'The Hungarian reform process: visions, hopes, and reality', *Journal of Economic Literature* 24, 1687–737.

Leibenstein, H. (1966) 'Allocative efficiency *versus* X-efficiency, *American Economic Review* 56, 392–415.

Marris, R. (1963) 'A model of the "managerial" enterprise', *Quarterly Journal of Economics* 77, 185–206.

Murrell, P. (1984) 'Incentives and income under market socialism', *Journal of Comparative Economics* 8, 261–76.

Nishimizu, N. and Page, J.N. (1982) 'Total factor productivity growth, technological progress and technical efficiency change: dimensions of productivity change in Yugoslavia, 1965–78', *Economic Journal* 92, 920–26.

Pejovich, S. and Furubotn, E.G. (1970) 'Property rights and the behavior of the firm in a socialist state: the example of Yugoslavia', *Zeitschrift für Nationalökonomie* 30, 431–54.

Tardos, M. (1982) 'Development program for economic control and organization in Hungary', *Acta Oeconomica* 28, 295–315.

Ward, B. (1958) 'The firm in Illyria: market socialism', *American Economic Review* 48, 566–89.

15 The political conditions of economic reform in socialism

Ellen Comisso

While the introduction of democracy in Eastern Europe and the Soviet Union is highly desirable for many reasons, it is unfortunately unclear if enacting a major economic reform or transformation is one of them. On the contrary, it would seem that the basic preconditions required for the creation of self-regulating markets in the economy are not so much 'democratic' as they are 'liberal'.[1] That is, the political requirements of economic reform do not lie so much in the creation of institutions for popular control of the state, but in the establishment of mechanisms that would limit the use of political authority in the economy regardless of who exercises it. As such, the use of markets as the basic regulator of economic transactions appears much more closely related to the creation of limited sovereignty than to the introduction of popular sovereignty, desirable as the latter may be.

Three conditions appear to be particularly important for the efficient operation of a market economy: (1) property rights must be lodged in the hands of actors with purely economic responsibilities; (2) a neutral third party must enforce them; and (3) policy-making authority – including the authority to specify property rights – must be placed in the hands of institutions that themselves neither exercise nor enforce them. While Yugoslavia came fairly close to satisfying the third condition, no former socialist state satisfied the first two, largely because doing so would require subjecting the Communist Party itself to laws, thereby depriving it of its 'leading role' in their implementation.

Taken together, these three conditions describe a degree of differentiation between the state and the economy that appears to be a fundamental requirement for economic actors to partake of the benefits of international specialization in an international political order of sovereign nation-states. In this regard, it is perhaps best to begin with a discussion of what is entailed in the notion of property rights and why they are important for economizing.

Property rights do not refer to relations among men and things, but rather *to the sanctioned behavioral relations among men that arise from the existence of things and pertain to their use.* Property assignments specify the norms of behavior with respect to things that each person must observe in his interactions with other persons, or bear the cost for non-observance.[2]

Property rights can be broken down in a variety of ways, but typically they include 'the right to use, to derive income from the use of, to exclude others from, and the right to exchange the goods (or services) in one's possession'.[3] As such, 'property rights specify how persons may be benefited and harmed and, therefore, who must pay whom to modify the actions taken by persons'.[4]

All actions have harmful and/or beneficial effects that are suffered or enjoyed by someone:

> What converts a harmful or beneficial effect into an externality is that the cost of bringing that effect to bear on the decisions of one or more of the interacting parties is too high to make it worthwhile . . . 'Internalizing' such effects refers to a process, usually a change in property rights, that enables these effects to bear (in greater degree) on all interacting persons. [Consequently] a primary function of property rights is that of guiding incentives to achieve a greater internalization of externalities.[5]

Understood in this way, property rights are not simply a license to act with respect to goods and services; they also imply that the consequences of acting, be they negative or positive, are borne by the agent.

Several points should be noted in this connection. First of all, the notion of property rights is a plural one, in the sense that it describes a number of rights which may or may not be simultaneously possessed by the same subject. For example, the individual who rents commercial premises and derives an income through his/her use of those premises that may be a different person from the individual who owns those premises; in that case, the right to use the property is divorced from the right to exchange it. Thus, property rights are not necessarily indivisible; nevertheless, the value of any one property right will clearly be affected by the cost of acquiring other property rights over the same object.

Second, just as property rights are not indivisible, they are not unrestricted either:

> To 'own land' usually means to have the right to till (or not to till) the soil, to mine the soil, to *offer* those rights for sale, etc., but not the right to throw soil at a passerby, to use it to change the course of a stream, or to force someone to buy it. What are owned are *socially recognized rights of action.*[6]

Again, the kind and degree of restrictions characterizing any single property right will affect its value. In this regard, it is important to note that while we ordinarily assume that a restricted property right is of less value than a non-restricted one, this is not necessarily the case in a non-Robinson Crusoe world with positive transaction costs. Taxation to provide public goods (parks, schools), the provision of which increases the value of adjacent property to a level whereby owners are more than compensated for the taxes they pay is a case in point. The 'gated community' is another example: here, homeowners purchase homes within a development with numerous restrictions attached to usage (rights to remodel are severely limited; often even the colour of the house cannot be altered without community approval), and far from the restrictions lowering the value of the property, their uniform enforcement is a prime factor explaining the premium prices such residences command.

Third, whether property rights are divisible or indivisible, circumscribed or unrestricted, simply specifying what they are (that is, which actions with respect to goods and services are permitted) is far from equivalent to declaring to whom they belong (that is, who may carry on such activities). Hence, while it is tempting to equate the exclusive right to use, to derive income from the use of, and to transfer or 'alienate' ownership with private property,[7] this is only the case if private individuals exercise/are assigned these rights. In fact, the rights can be assigned to other agents and often are in the real world. For example, an urban government may purchase buses, derive income from charging a fee to individuals wishing to travel on them, and sell them to a junk dealer (or another municipality) when they are ready for retirement. Moreover, granting a given bundle of property rights to one agent does not necessarily mean all agents with access to property rights have a claim to identical bundles. Certain rights (for example, eminent domain) may be reserved for agents with specific qualifications. In fact, examples of municipal owners exxercising more (or less) restricted property rights than private owners possessed of similar assets or of monopolists enjoying more limited rights than owners of goods sold under competitive conditions are frequent.

Property rights systems are traditionally differentiated from each other with reference to the subject of property rights, that is, who may exercise them. The options here are considerable, and numerous classificatory schemas exist. Broadly speaking, in capitalism, property rights are lodged in the hands of private individuals who exercise them for self-regarding purposes. Those purposes may be wealth maximization, but need not be. In contrast, a socialist property rights system is one in which property rights are lodged in the hands of a public agency or agencies, who exercise them for public purposes. Again, such purposes may be wealth-maximization, but need not be.

In either case, the ownership system should be at least in principle differentiated from the allocation system; the latter will have a critical impact on how property rights are used. Thus, the argument for the economic superiority of capitalism turns out to be much more an argument for the superiority of competitive markets as a mechanism for allocating resources and an assertion that competitive markets cannot operate properly in the absence of private ownership.[8] While there is a great deal of empirical evidence supporting this proposition, its theoretical status remains contested,[9] in part because state ownership has tended to appear only in contexts in which market competition has been intentionally eliminated ('socialist transformation') or where it has been costly or difficult to create (for example, natural monopolies). In contrast, in the occasional cases in which publicly-owned firms have been subjected to competitive conditions similar to those facing private sector counterparts, their performance has not necessarily been inferior.[10]

Meanwhile, varieties of both private and public property rights systems should be distinguished from a third alternative, namely communal ownership. Here, individuals and groups have the right to freely use property as they wish, and no one is excluded from doing so; indeed, 'this nonexclusion principle is the most important feature of communal property'.[11] As is well known, communally – 'owned' resources tend to be overexploited, and individual (or corporate) users have little incentive to improve or even maintain it since any benefits from doing so cannot be appropriated. In short, to use Demsetz's terms, 'externalities' cannot be 'internalized' where communal property is concerned. In political theory, communal ownership is a key characteristic of both the social contract theorists' state of nature and of Marx's Communist society. In both cases, communal ownership prevails due to the absence of law and institutionalized mechanisms for its enforcement. One result is that

> simply setting the entitlement [as communal] does not avoid the problem of 'might makes right'; a minimum of state intervention is always necessary . . . If large Marshall has grown some communal cabbages and chooses to deny them to small Taney, it will take some state action to enforce Taney's entitlement to the communal cabbages.[12]

This brings us to the final aspect of property rights relevant to our inquiry, namely, the fact that property rights are first and foremost legal rights. Significantly, the original Greco-Roman notion of law was that of a boundary between the household and the public domain.[13] While that legal separation traditionally has been viewed as the basis of the private/public dichotomy, for our purposes it is best described as the distinction between proprietary and communal space, between the economic and political. It follows that in the absence of enforceable and enforced laws (or their equivalent) specifying proprietary rights, there can be no genuine economic actors and/or that to the degree such rules are attenuated, property relations take on communal aspects. By 'attenuation' here I mean not that property rights are restricted by legal means, but that property rights over a given asset are either undefined and/or cannot be exercised due to the action of non-legal and non-economic forces.

Here, it would appear. Lay the root of the problem in 'actually existing' socialism, where the 'leading role' of the party continually caused an erosion in the boundary between the proprietary and communal sphere. As a consequence of this role, even the state lacked clear title to its assets, as party officials could, and often had, to intervene in the actions it took to dispose of them. This was no less the case in Yugoslavia, where self-managed enterprises could and did make decisions 'as if' they had claims on the income streams generated by the assets they 'managed', but in practice found they required the support and protection of political leaders to exercise their rights. Because laws in general were subordinated to political priorities, property rights defined in laws necessarily suffered the same fate, regardless of who held them.[14] As a result, the 'norms of behavior with respect to things' in practice corresponded neither to the state, 'social'/self-managed, co-operative, or private ownership system but rather came to resemble the communal ownership arrangement.

Here, a comparison of Hungarian and Yugoslav experiences with economic reform reveals certain striking similarities along precisely these lines, similarities that seem particularly marked once one takes into account the very significant differences separating the two states and economies: their degrees of national homogeneity, their natural resource endowments, their position in the international political order, the level of centralization in government, the mode of industrial management, the pre-socialist level of development, and so on.[15] Such differences did indeed make the 'content' of the reform story different: in Hungary, recentralization was the *bête noire* of reform; in Yugoslavia fragmentation within non-competitive markets was the basic obstacle. Yet underlying this difference in content was a striking similarity in 'form': in both cases economic transactions reflected and followed political lines. In a real sense, then, the major cause of the differences in the Yugoslav and Hungarian reform processes was simply the fact that ownership rights were lodged at different points in the political structure: in the Yugoslav case they fell into the hands of regional elites, and in the Hungarian one they were held by the centre. In neither case were they exercised by actors with purely economic responsibilities, since without a legally binding articulation of property rights *bona fide* economic actors could not arise. In effect, 'socialism' was as much an intervention system as an ownership system.

The consequences were predictable in light of our earlier remarks about communal ownership. First, the 'norms of behaviour with respect to things' articulated by laws defining property rights could not and did not apply uniformly to 'each and every person' when those obligated to observe certain norms of behaviour could themselves specify the norms. Instead, the 'costs for non-observance' varied in inverse proportion to the political influence of the individual violating them or, alternatively, the 'norms of behaviour' were simply altered to reflect the political priorities of the day. As noted above, in the absence of state enforced norms, communal ownership by itself does not solve the 'might makes right' problem, and the subordination of government authority to party priorities meant the 'small Taneys' typically had scant recourse, even when they were large enterprises. Indeed, it was precisely this inapplicability of state-enforced norms to party actions that led many observers to conclude (in this author's opinion, erroneously) that a 'new ruling class' existed.

Further, communalizing state and/or socialist property also predictably led to the 'overexploitation' of assets by the individuals and groups (that is, the ruling party and its officials) with a right to freely use them. The 'forced growth' pattern achieved via the political maintenance of extremely high investment rates is symptomatic in this regard. In Hungary, high growth rates were typically accompanied by the aggravation of shortage tensions and balance-of-payments problems; the result was invariably increased central intervention and the politicization of economic transactions (whether it be in the form of maintaining 'supply obligations' or export campaigns). In Yugoslavia, too, high investment rates by no means implied an efficient allocation of capital; on the contrary, it reflected the tendency of regional politicians to construct economic monuments and the need to fund enterprise losses through inflationary expansions of the monetary supply. In both cases, high investment rates provided selective benefits (from increased opportunities for patronage to greater influence on non-economic questions) to the political elites who participated in capital allocation at the same time that the communal character of investment resources created disincentives for them to be used efficiently.

Finally, the communal character of assets made it impossible to 'internalize' many of the costs of economic transactions. More precisely, in both Yugoslavia and Hungary, the political impacts of economic transactions (that is, their effects on central or provincial political elites) were internalized to a much greater degree than were their economic costs and benefits. This followed from the fact that once property rights were shared by political actors, the 'cost' of bringing political effects to bear tended to be much lower than the cost of bringing economic consequences to bear. The logic here is quite similar to that underlying Kornai's discussion of 'soft' budget constraints: producers are relatively insensitive to costs and thus relatively open to pursuing goals justified on political grounds. The result was that those who could affect the income flow deriving from the state or society's assets did not bear the economic costs (or benefits, for that matter) of their actions.

The foregoing suggests that a critical condition of successful economic reform in or after socialism is establishing a boundary line between the proprietary and communal spheres of social life. This means, as noted earlier, specifying ownership rights in laws and lodging them in the hands of economic actors as a first step. Significantly, this does not mean creating unrestricted property rights nor does it mean that all economic actors need have the same property rights. It does, however, mean devising laws that apply to classes of economic actors (as opposed to the *ad hoc* case-by-case assignment of property rights that are the mark of communalization) and enforcing them uniformly.

Moreover, 'lodging property rights in the hands of economic actors' does not necessarily mean lodging them in the hands of private individuals exclusively, although clearly this is one way in which this condition could be satisfied. Self-managed enterprises, institutional investors, pension funds, wage-earner funds, enterprises in which the national government possesses a dominant share, can all be economic actors, provided their rights over the assets they control are specified through a suitable legal framework. As I have tried to show above, the problem in 'actually existing' socialism was communal ownership, not 'state' or 'social' ownership in and of themselves.

At the same time, legally specifying property rights in laws that apply to classes of economic actors will mean little if adequate provision is not made for their enforcement. In a modern economy, this means establishing a neutral third party to adjudicate disputes arising out of transactions between economic actors with legally specified property rights, typically an independent judiciary. 'Independence' in this context

> is conceived not in terms of a tripartite constitution with checks and balances but simply in terms of a professional judiciary sufficiently insulated from other governmental influences to operate within its own sphere under the rule of law. The courts of Great Britain and czarist Russia would show the range of this sort of independence. It may be found all the way from liberal constitutional systems . . . to pure autocracies.[16]

Thus, 'independence' does not mean judges are independent of the sovereign (since all judges derive their legal authority from it) or that judges have the power to invalidate statutory enactments (an idiosyncratic feature of the American judiciary), but it does mean that a judge can rule against the sovereign in particular cases. It does not mean that judges are immune from political influence (again, in all western legal systems, opportunities for appointment promotion are normally controlled by the government in power) but it does mean the absence of direct outside interference in the outcome of particular cases. It does not imply that all cases are decided purely on the basis of pre-existing rules (again, in all societies, judges invariably engage in law-making) but it does mean that if a pre-existing rule exists, it should be applied. It does not necessarily mean that the sovereign is a popular one, but it does mean that the sovereign is a law-abiding one. As a result, 'the courts are totally dependent on the sovereign for their legal authority, independent of him for the decision in particular cases but dependent in general in the sense of applying the law he has provided'.[17]

In short, if one thinks of the specification of property rights as a system of public rules, that is, a description of legally – sanctioned behaviour with respect to things, judges enforcing those rules should treat similar cases similarly, with the relevant similarities and differences being those identified by the rules themselves.[18] As such, the role of courts is to preserve the legal boundary between the communal and the proprietary spheres, with the rules governing the relationships within each being laid down by political authorities.

This brings us to the third condition necessary to establish non-communal ownership in or after socialism: that the power to specify property rights must be lodged in institutions (for example, a legislature) which themselves neither exercise nor enforce them. That is, the specification of property rights is a collective/political act par excellence, in so far as property rights involve a recognition by others of what individuals holding them may do. Because of this 'two-sided' aspect of any given property rights system (that is, for a right to be exercised, it must be recognized by those who do not have it as well as those who do) those who exercise rights cannot unilaterally specify what the rights are. On the contrary, an authority 'above' economic transactions must specify the conditions under which they can take place and be bound by its own rules should it engage in them.

Significantly, specifying property rights is not a 'once and for all' act; on the contrary, to the degree a given specification of rights proves to have costly social consequences, it may prove desirable to modify it. Yet if the same institution that exercises property rights also specifies them, modifications will reflect the immediate exigencies of the possessor, rather than their general effects. In effect, if the essence of an efficient property rights system is one in which the costs and benefits of transactions fall for the most part on the agents who engage in them, one cannot put the agents in a position in which they can simply shift the costs on to others by modifying the structure of property rights when the need arises.

In short, if one condition of economic reform is to establish genuine economic actors, its corollary is establishing a genuine political authority. To some degree this was done in Yugoslavia; there, if ownership rights were not lodged in actors with purely economic responsibilities, self-management meant they were at least lodged outside the national government itself. Thus, there was at least the possibility of using policy measures to guide the economy since an authority without ownership rights of its own existed to formulate them. Yet in so far as the Communist Party (or more precisely, its regional incarnations) remained the *éminence grise* behind both the government and the enterprises, the government's ability to make binding policy decisions remained weak.

Satisfying these three conditions would have clearly entailed a major modification in the status of the Communist Party in socialist systems. It would not have, however, necessarily implied an end to socialism as an ownership system; indeed, the above analysis suggests that it is only by subjecting the party to laws that ownership can be lodged in the hands of public actors with an economic orientation. It is equally important to note that while establishing a non-communal ownership system is a necessary condition for a market to exist, it is also not necessary and sufficient. As noted earlier, what economic actors possessed of property rights will do with them depends heavily on the allocation system within which they exercise those rights. The question then is, if we assume a reform of the ownership system along the lines suggested above, will a self-regulating market arise as a consequence?

Here, while it is clear that both the facility with which political actors could manipulate economic decisions for political ends as well as many of the incentives for them to do so would be eliminated with an end to communal ownership arrangements, it is also worth recognizing that the causes of the political intervention that proved to be the Achilles heel of reform efforts in Hungary and Yugoslavia were not solely the determination of political leaders and/or the Communist Party to hold on to power at all costs. In many cases, it was the inability of the market itself to deliver either socially or economically optimal results that led to intervention. Moreover, not all intervention took the form of directly interfering in the exercise of property rights; in many cases, it involved the perfectly 'legal' form of acting on property rights, a power that all governments retain and which a 'reformed' political authority operating under a 'rule of law' would also presumably possess.

In this regard, it is important to remember that 'market failures' are a prime (and economically justifiable) cause of government intervention in capitalist economies.[19] Accordingly, it is to be expected that they would be an equally important and justifiable cause of government intervention in a socialist economy. More to the point, the absence of (or limits to) private ownership in the means of production which presumably accompany any version of socialism (centrally-planned or market) makes the economy more vulnerable to market failures than a capitalist counterpart would be. Moreover, those vulnerabilities are especially pronounced in economies whose previous development was based on central planning.

As I have elaborated these economic problems elsewhere, I will merely comment on two of the causes of the socialist equivalent of market failures here for illustrative purposes.[20] My point here is to suggest that in addition to an ownership reform, establishing a market mechanism for the allocation of resources in an economy in which some form of public ownership is to be the dominant form of property-holding calls for special institutional mechanisms and policy measures for which there are no real precedents in the capitalist experience. At the same time, if market forces do not govern economic transactions, even the fact that property rights are lodged in economic actors is no guarantee that they will be used efficiently.

The first problem any 'actually existing' socialist economy committed to economic reform faces is that of monopolies. For various reasons, all socialist economies (including Yugoslavia and even the Soviet Union, despite its size) are/were highly concentrated, and simply emancipating enterprises to make their own decisions in such circumstances will not necessarily lead to a better allocation of resources, even (indeed especially!) if firms are subject to 'hard' budget constraints.

While the private sector could be the source of new entrants, if the dominant mode of ownership is to be a public one, the size of the private sector will necessarily be limited. More precisely, while the number of private businesses need not be limited at all, the amount of assets in the hands of any single private business would presumably be restricted in order to insure that personal income is, for the most part, a return on labour, not property. Such restrictions need not take the relatively arbitrary form they usually assumed (limits to the number of employees, discriminatory taxation, political harassment) but could be contained within laws specifying property rights; if legal recognition is not given to the forms of private ownership (limited liability in particular) that allow for great accumulations of private capital, private enterprise will simply not arise on a very large scale.

The same strictures would presumably apply to direct foreign investment: after all, it is unclear why foreigners should be permitted to exploit opportunities for accumulating unearned income a country's own citizens are barred from enjoying. Alternatively, one could simply relax restrictions on all forms of private accumulation and ownership, as was the thrust of the last new Hungarian enterprise law before 1989, with the intention of creating a 'mixed' economy in which the private and socialist sectors would compete with each other. The problem, however, is that if all new entrants come from the (foreign or domestic) private sector, the result will be a gradual (and perhaps even rapid) privatization of the economy. The 'creation of competition' problem may thus be 'solved', but not within the framework of anything corresponding to socialism.[21]

The Yugoslav reforms of 1965 sought to resolve the difficulty by providing avenues for existing socialist firms to found new ventures. The assumption that they would do so, however, proved erroneous, and not simply because of the insecurity of property rights we have already described. Even capitalist firms rarely found entirely new ventures; on the contrary, they acquire shares in or take over existing firms or diversify their own divisional structures.[22]

Pursuing vigorous antitrust measures that would break up socialist giants may also be of but limited utility, especially in Eastern Europe. That is, East European states are small countries, and small countries are always characterized by high concentration rates. This is particularly the case if they are export-oriented, since economies of scale are critical for making products cost-competitive on international markets. Japanese firms, for example, have often overcharged domestic consumers in order to make their products more attractively priced abroad. An antitrust strategy might thus have the consequence of creating more domestic competition at the expense of being able to compete internationally.

In the long run, import competition is probably the best solution to monopoly abuses. It is in the short run ('the transition') that the problems arise. The first problem, of course, is the balance-of-payments constraint: how much can small countries already saddled with large debts afford to import? Over the long run, the amount would presumably rise as export capacities grow, but in the short run, demand for imports can be expected to be well above the desired level of supply. Bringing the two into equilibrium could be accomplished by allowing the currency to float, but this would presumably have the same dramatic inflationary consequences in the short run it has had elsewhere (for example, Mexico). Even if we discount for the moment the political tensions rapid inflation usually produces, its economic consequences alone would be extremely deleterious: labour discipline would drop, investment flows would be distorted, and so on. Meanwhile, avoiding inflation could be accomplished by a strict contraction in the monetary supply, an action which is likely to be equally costly in both social and economic terms. Consequently, the immediate impact of an import competition strategy might well be to wipe out in the short run the very recuperative capacities it needs to stimulate for the long term.

To make a long story short, then, the lack of competition on the socialist market-place is an extremely serious problem; it is a prime cause of the administrative regulation and intervention that everywhere impeded reform efforts. Moreover, the presence of monopolies and widespread collusion on the market-place is also a major factor making worker support of reform efforts lukewarm.

That is, 'distribution according to work' is normally a popular slogan among workers, whom one suspects would welcome measures to allocate labour rationally and improve labour productivity *if* the results showed up in their pay-packets. Likewise, both Western and Eastern European experience suggests that even blue-collar workers are not universally in favour of levelling, but are quick to protest income inequalities that appear economically unjustified.[23]

It is in this context that the lack of competition among enterprises has its pernicious effect. Not only can employees of monopolistic firms receive high wages without correspondingly high productivity, violating the principle of equal work for equal pay, but individual earnings come to reflect the firm's market position more than individual job performance, blunting the effects of incentives as well. As Flakierski notes in the Yugoslav case, 'The level of wages for a particular job depends more in what region, branch, or firm you work than on your qualifications, skills, or responsibilities, and there is little or no relation to the principle of distribution according to work'.[24]

Likewise, one can imagine independent trade unions having economically beneficial effects in a competitive economy: by regulating the industry-wide price of labour, unions would give the management of individual firms an incentive to cut costs through technological innovation since it cannot simply drive down wages. But in an economy permeated by monopolies, the effect of union wage demands will merely be to create inflation and/or shift unemployment to the non-unionized population.

Finally, the apparent unwillingness of political elites to apply bankruptcy laws to firms operating at perennial losses is also closely related to the monopoly problem. Here, it would seem that a major cause for the reluctance to allow 'exit' from the market is the lack of institutional mechanisms for entrance to the market: if a local enterprise closes down, there is literally nothing to take its place. In this regard, the economic causes of monopoly and 'soft' budget constraints are one and the same: namely, the need to find a way for new ventures to come into existence once the state and/or the party is no longer in the business of directly managing fixed assets. This is not a problem for capitalist economies, where individuals risk their own capital, and – perhaps ironically – it is not even a problem in classical state socialism, where the state founds new ventures. And while bankruptcy requires merely the presence of political will (or the enforcement of laws), mechanisms for the founding of new firms in the state sector have yet to be devised. Significantly, an ownership reform alone will not solve this problem either: while it would allow existing firms to form new ventures, the incentives for doing so would remain weak.

This brings us to the second economic obstacle to the establishment of market under late socialism: the lack of capital market. Here, there is a real question as to whether or not a genuine capital market can exist when (a) a single entity (call it the 'state' or 'society') owns virtually all assets by definition; and (b) personal incomes are a return to labour.

One solution is to let independent profit-based state-owned commercial/investment banks handle investment decisions. This was essentially the option selected by Yugoslavia in 1965, and the model underlying the last Hungarian banking reform before 1989. In practice, both schemes proved to have serious flaws, some of which are in principle correctible (for example, the fact that Yugoslav banks ran up against a ceiling on interest rates and so were lending money at a negative rate could be corrected by allowing interest rates to rise to equilibrium levels and forcing the liquidation of firms who suffer prolonged losses; in Hungary, extremely high budget deficits due to enterprise losses essentially wiped out the independent crediting capacities of the new commercial banks in the first year of the reform), but others of which may be fatal.

In the short run, there is a serious problem of adverse selection, that is, how to determine the good risks from the bad in a situation in which the latter may be willing to bid for capital at any price.[25] In the long run, there is a real question as to how state-owned banks will solve the key economic question: balancing risk/the possibility of loss against the possibility of gain. Socialist banks may choose to maximize the possibility of gain, minimize the possibility of loss, or pursue yet other strategies. In a market with numerous suppliers of capital with a wide variety of financial instruments, one can assume a wide variety of strategies on the part of lenders. But in a small country with a limited number of banks with a limited number of instruments, the lending strategy of any one of them will have a major impact on the overall distribution of investment. Hence, the rules banks adopt to govern lending decisions will be critical, raising the question of who should make them. If it is the government, credit allocation will necessarily be politicized, and the problems of communal ownership will reassert themselves; but if it is the bank management, 'private' motives and goals will play a heavy – and not really legitimate – role. Considered in this light, the controversy that broke out in the early 1970s in Yugoslavia about 'centres of financial power', and which had such ill-fated results, was not the simple political struggle it appeared to be at first glance.

Finally, it is unclear what relationship will emerge between the debt capital circulated through the banks and the equity embodied in the firms. If projected rates of return on investments are the main criteria banks employ to evaluate projects, managers in the enterprises may have strong incentives to run down the assets. Conceivably, arrangements could be made for banks to convert debt into equity, particularly where high risk ventures are concerned. But should a small number of banks acquire ownership shares in a large number of enterprises, the banks' concerns about the enterprises they own are likely to figure heavily (and rationally) in their future lending decisions, presumably at the cost of new competitors.

The 'socialist' stock market alternative, in contrast, appears to be a possible solution. Essentially, it seeks to 'pluralize' the public owner both by allowing enterprises to issue and purchase equity shares and by granting a number of public institutions (pension funds, universities, research institutes, and so on) the equivalent of 'endowments' consisting of shares in state firms. Such institutions would 'manage their portfolios' in a way that they would seek to protect the value of their assets while maximizing the returns from them. The income streams thereby generated would then go, not directly into the pockets of individuals, but into the various funds spent by the institutions for the purposes under which they were established and/or to make additional investments.

Such a scheme, it would seem, has considerable potential. Most versions of it would also allow private individuals to purchase shares, an aspect that would probably make it more practicable, but less socialistic. Nevertheless, it too has some drawbacks. First of all, institutional investors of the type described above are notoriously cautious, and rightly so: after all, universities and pension funds are public trusts, and as such unsuitable for high risk ventures. Hence, this type of capital market would not serve the needs of venture capital, although conceivably this might be an area in which banks could play a major role.

Second, many of these institutional investors will have 'fixed' endowments such that the only way new capital will be brought into the system is through the use of dividends to purchase it. But assuming that our institutional investors are relying on their dividends to cover some significant portion of their operating costs, it is unclear why they would reinvest them. For example, the endowments of universities like Yale or the University of California, Berkeley, have grown because private donors (typically, alumna) give them new money, not because they have reinvested their dividends from the existing endowment. Indeed, in so far as a university is a non-profit operation (as is a pension fund, we might add), it would tend to derive far more utility from using its dividends to fund student scholarships, say, than to play the stock market, even if the latter offered sure financial gains. Hence, although the 'stock market' solution has the great virtue of creating 'real' owners that retain a 'socialist' character, it still has the problem of creating owners with a peculiar set of risk preferences and financial motives.

Creating competitive product and capital markets are far from the only difficulties a viable economic reform or transformation must overcome; I merely use them as illustrations. For the moment, the point is simply to suggest that if an ownership reform is a necessary condition of a viable economic reform, it is far from necessary and sufficient. Appropriate policy measures would also have to be devised to take account of the peculiar characteristics socialist ownership is likely to involve.

The central thrust of the ownership reform described above is to place limits on the political control of economic actors via constitutional provisions binding on all actors and which are costly to change. While clearly such a change does not exclude placing what is left of political authority in the hands of popularly and competitively elected representatives, neither does it require widening opportunities for popular control of (a limited) sovereign. While efficient markets cannot operate when the costs and benefits of transactions are not internalized to a substantial degree by the agents engaging in them, they certainly can function in the presence of authoritarian or elite-based political systems.

'Democracy' (or even its weaker form, 'democratization') is thus not a requirement of economic reform in any logical or institutional sense, and one suspects that the connection between the two in recent socialist discourse was more of product of the way political debate was constructed in the socialist states (that is, if the establishment has accepted the desirability of economic reform, one could advocate democratization as a means to achieving it where one could not advance arguments for democratization as a good in itself) than of any organic tie between them. At the same time, the process of economic reform in socialism itself had an extraordinarily divisive impact on Marxist–Leninist parties, such that leaders within it themselves began casting about for wider constituencies to support their own programmes. As a result, broad groups previously excluded from political life suddenly found themselves acquiring real strategic value. Thus, even if there was no 'necessary' link between economic reform and democracy in socialism, the 'conjunctural' tie between them was undeniable.

Be this as it may, in the modern world, representative democracy – by which I mean majority rule, minority rights, universal suffrage and electoral competition – is in any case a highly desirable attribute of political systems. The question confronting the socialist (and post-socialist) world, then, is given the need for economic reform and the desirability of a democratic political order, is the latter likely to facilitate the former? Here, the rapidity of political change in Eastern Europe and the Soviet Union suggests this question is likely to be answered much more quickly in practice than in theory. Nevertheless, since such possibilities have never prevented intellectuals from speculating before, I will invoke the authority of tradition and proceed with this analysis now.

There was a fairly large number of proposals for democratic reform recently floating around in the socialist world prior to the winter of 1989.[26] Most of these early proposals continued to grant the Communist Party a privileged status in the political system, if only in recognition of existing geopolitical realities. Nevertheless, it either would have lost its monopoly of the means of collective action or have been converted from a top-down 'cadre' type party to a 'bottom-up' mass organization like, say, the Italian or the Finnish Communist Party. Even in Poland and Hungary, even the privileged status of the party was granted largely to guarantee its commitment to the design of an alternative political order.

The common denominator of all such proposals was giving 'society' greater control to order its own affairs. As they related to economic reform, the line of reasoning appeared to be the following. 'Society' would, for the most part, benefit from economic reform and supports it. The chief source of political opposition to reform, however, is the current political leadership, whose power and privileges would be threatened. Consequently, the theory ran, if 'society' is 'emancipated' to organize itself, it will be able to block political initiatives not in its 'interest', making economic reform not only possible but necessary; moreover, in so far as reforms would then have a broad social – and not merely narrow – political base of support, they would become 'irreversible' as well.

Moreover, the argument continued, the prolonged economic crisis of the past decade is but an indication of why democratization is necessary, for unless the population has confidence in political leaders, it will be unwilling to make the sacrifices a successful economic adjustment requires. Accordingly, 'austerity' can only be managed on the basis of genuine popular consent and making 'society' a genuine political actor in its own right. In effect, a real 'social compact' is in order: the population will sacrifice its standard of living only if leaders sacrifice the right to exercise arbitrary power.

The reform experience before 1989 did indeed suggest this line of reasoning was far from unfounded. In Hungary, political support for economic reform in the 1960s and 1970s was far more extensive outside the Hungarian Socialist Workers' Party (HSWP) than within it, and had reformers been able to mobilize it, the outcomes of the political battles of the 1970s might well have been different. In Yugoslavia, too, had the political structure and the interests of political elites not made it impossible for interests to aggregate on a non-geographical basis, the political barriers to the creation of a unified national market might have been considerably reduced. And as for the ability of the former political leadership to manage the economic crisis, it was not only the population that lacked confidence in it, but the political elite itself (indeed, had the latter not occurred, there would hardly have been any discussion of democratic reform to start with). Thus, in Poland, the Polish United Workers' Party (PUWP) would clearly not have made concessions to Solidarity had it been able to revitalize the economy alone.

This much said, there is still some cause for skepticism as to whether or not people participating in the sacrifices that affect them is likely to lead to an exit from the current economic crisis, much less a viable economic reform and the introduction of 'self-regulating' markets. Let us thus look at the economic obstacles that would remain, and the political consequences that could result.

On the economic front, let us assume that the first consequence (or accompaniment) of democratization would be the ownership reforms outlined above. Nevertheless, as we have seen, if the communalization of ownership was a major force 'pushing' political intervention into the economy, what we have described as market failures were key factors pulling them in as well. In this regard, it is difficult to understand why different leaders facing the same economic circumstances would not act the same way; simply making leaders accountable to 'social forces' will not in itself create competition on product markets or create a capital market. Moreover, to the degree democratic reform entails introducing organized political competition, it suggests that any institutional solution that does emerge to the economic problems described above is likely to have a partisan cast to it, particularly in so far as it will entail highly-differentiated distributionary consequences. Here, even when measures may appear to be in 'society's' broad interest, there is no guarantee they will be in the interests of the political coalitions that aggregate societal interests. The view, surprisingly widespread among former reformists, that large industrial 'lobbies' carry political clout merely because they are tied to Communist Party leaders, and that such enterprises will simply be left to suffer the fate allotted them by 'impersonal' market forces following a competitive election, seems oddly oblivious to the fact that such enterprises employ thousands of people, all of whom will be voting in democratic elections.

In addition, Communist politicians are hardly unique in their desire to remain in power; all politicians like to stay in office and use what the access to the state incumbency gives them for this purpose: the extensive patronage networks that riddle the Italian state sector are a case in point, and studies of the American Congress suggest that familiarity with the classics of Marxism–Leninism is quite irrelevant to the desire to see large public projects constructed in one's district. Ironically, the closer leaders are tied to their individual constituencies, the more legislation is likely to embody inconsistencies, effectively recreating a field for administrative intervention under new auspices. Significantly, the states that have played a major role in managing the economy successfully (from France to the East Asian NICs) have done so by insulating economic policy-makers from popular pressures to a substantial degree; in effect, it has been the state, not 'society', that has been emancipated to pursue its own interests, and especially so where the international market-place supplies the main competitors to domestic firms.[27]

The second economic obstacle democratically elected leaders are to confront is the debt crisis. While it is clear enough that the former political leadership did not succeed in managing the crisis – not to mention the fact that it bore the onus for creating the crisis to begin with – the ability of an elected and/or responsive leadership to perform significantly better is open to some question. In this regard, debt relief is probably a necessary condition for an improvement in the economic situation regardless of who is in power. While changes in the domestic political structure of East European debtors may make relief more probable, it is important to note that similar changes in Latin America brought forth no such outcome in the 1980s; the 'lost decade' was clearly not a Communist monopoly.

The argument that the population will be willing to make sacrifices for a leadership it has confidence in appears valid to only a limited degree. That is, its validity rests heavily on the degree to which sacrifices are shared equally and on the availability of opportunities for individuals to avoid making them altogether. Wartime is the prime example of when the hypothesis holds best: then, there is no alternative to sacrifice since a state's territorial integrity is under attack, and measures like conscription and extensive rationing act to equalize distributionary consequences. But even during wartime mobilizations, black markets (and the fortunes that are made on them) tend to flourish. Economic reform under severe austerity represents a rather different situation: the state now gives up its power to redistribute income in the interests of efficiency and – especially if democratic norms are adhered to – opportunities to avoid making sacrifices are plentiful but unequally distributed. In this regard, it is difficult to believe that individuals will be willing to lose their jobs and/or find their individual standard of living eroding merely for the collective right to cast one vote out of several million once every few years. For a democratic reform to produce economic reform, it would appear that public/collective benefits must be supplied in addition to individual/private ones and not as a replacement for them. Put another way, maintaining a coalition that collectively enjoys the benefits of democracy requires furnishing its members with selective benefits/side-payments as well. Participation (the right to demonstrate in the streets, organize trade unions, and so on) is one such selective benefit and its importance should not be minimized, but presumably people participate not only for its own sake, but also to satisfy the demands they make on public authorities through participation. Nevertheless, the essence of economic reform is precisely to deprive the state of many of the means it currently uses to make such side-payments.

It is conceivable that some of the distributional consequences of economic reform could be mitigated by increased economic integration with Western Europe. Such an integration would presumably involve not simply a greater exchange of goods and services, but direct foreign investment within Eastern Europe as well. Should this occur, it would accelerate privatization and also limit governmental space for manoeuvre in the economic policy sphere. For example, if an 'open borders' policy implies capital would be free to flow into Eastern Europe, it also means that capital would be free to flow *out* of Eastern Europe as well.

Opening the borders also implies freer labour migration. Here, Yugoslavia's experience suggests that exporting workers can relieve unemployment, but the political consequences of doing so can be extremely serious. Within Yugoslavia, nationalist movements have been closely correlated with the demographic composition of the 'seventh republic' (that is, Yugoslav workers employed abroad),[28] and the underlying cause seems not to be simply economic tensions, but the fact that political elites in the respective republics most seriously affected by worker emigration felt themselves competing with western countries for the loyalty of their own citizens.

As far as this author is aware, an austerity and restructuring of the kind that appears to be required in Eastern Europe has never been imposed through 'popular consent' in any case. The Latin American experience of the past few decades is instructive in this regard, and here the main question confronting Eastern Europe and possibly even the Soviet Union is simply whether the relevant analogy to be drawn is with Latin America of the 1960s and 1970s, with its bureaucratic-authoritarian outcome or Latin America of the 1980s, with its democratization combined with economic stagnation – and in some cases, near collapse.

While there are some extraordinary parallels between the events in Poland prior to the declaration of martial law and Latin America in the 1960s and 1970s,[29] somewhat to this author's surprise, the evolution of the political situation in both Poland and Hungary at present appears quite analogous to the situation of the 1980s. What has made the difference is not that 'society' is organized; if there is one lesson to be learned from the Poland of 1980–1, it is that the simple existence of organized social groups making demands on political authorities is neither equivalent to, nor even a prelude to, even a relatively stable competitive political order. On the contrary, what is most promising at the present stage is the coming-into-existence of genuine political parties, that is, parties which are not 'social movements' but parties in the standard sense of the term: organizations that present candidates to an electorate with the hope of controlling the government on the basis of the votes they amass.

It is well beyond the scope of this analysis to elaborate the conditions under which competitive political orders have replaced authoritarian regimes, but it is worth noting that the events of the past two years in Poland and Hungary are more or less consistent with the flow of events elsewhere.[30] While the outcome of these processes remains indeterminate, and a distinctly repressive result entirely possible, what we know about similar processes elsewhere none the less gives grounds for at least envisioning an outcome that seemed utterly ridiculous some time ago.

Yet even assuming a competitive political order results, what political leaders within such an order will do in the realm of economic policy is a very open question. The bases for a 'societal corporatist' solution do not seem to be present due to the absence of a concentrated and domestically-controlled private business sector. That is, where societal corporatism has been used for purposes of macroeconomic regulation, it has typically involved pitting (domestic) business against labour. Such an arrangement is feasible because business will sit down with labour when it is faced with the possibility of heavier sanctions from the government, and labour will negotiate with business because it is well aware that private entrepreneurs have means of disciplining labour that can be exerted independently of the government. When there is no 'private' ownership interest, however, one cannot have 'societal' corporatism: organized labour simply confronts the state-as-owner. But once the state is no longer the 'neutral' representative of the 'public interest', the fundamental condition of neo-corporatism is lacking.

Likewise, if power is shared among partners in a coalition government, there is a strong temptation for members to blame each other for the undesirable consequences of actions the government takes, with a political stalemate the consequence. Alternatively, if all the members of a governing coalition agree to share responsibility for actions that entail negative consequences for large sectors of society, the likelihood is that political entrepreneurs outside the coalition will mobilize the discontent, encouraging defection from the base, so to speak. Here, the fact that voters are encapsulated within one or another party in an election at time t_1 is no guarantee that they will retain their party loyalty for the next election, particularly in a polity with relatively weak allegiances to any political party.

Thus, to return to the theme advanced above, while the tie between economic reform and an ownership reform appears close and necessary, the tie between economic reform and democratization is highly conjunctural. In effect, two separate streams – the creation of markets and the desire for competitive politics – have converged in the current historical period, due to a peculiar combination of international and domestic circumstances. Should those circumstances change, the streams may very well diverge again.

NOTES

1 On this distinction, see Giovanni Sartori (1971) *Democratic Theory*, New York, Praeger; Robert Dahl (1971) *Polyarchy: Participation and Opposition*, New Haven, Yale University Press.

2 Erik Furubotn and Svetozar Pejovich (1972) 'Property rights and economic theory: a survey of recent literature', *Journal of Economic Literature* 10, 1138.

3 Douglass North, 'A transaction cost theory of exchange', unpublished manuscript, September 1987. Other formulations of the activities included under 'property rights' appear in Deborah Milenkovitch (1971) *Plan and Market in Yugoslav Economic Thought*, New Haven, Yale University Press, 94–5; Stephen Cheung (1978) *The Myth of Social Cost*, London, Institute of Economic Affairs, 51–2; Richard Carson (1975) 'Property rights', in Carmelo Mesa-Lago and Carl Beck (eds) *Comparative Socialist Systems: Essays on Politics and Economics*, Pittsburgh, University Center for International Studies, 317–47; and Leszek Balcerowicz (1989) 'Remarks on the concept of ownership', *Oeconomica Polona* 1, 75–95.

4 Harold Demsetz (1967) 'Toward a theory of property rights', *American Economic Review* 57, 350.

5 Ibid. 367.

6 Armen Alchian and Harold Demsetz (1973) 'The property rights paradigm', *Journal of Economic History* 33, 17.

7 As Cheung does in *Social Cost*, op.cit., 51–2.

8 The most eloquent case to this effect is made by Ludwig von Mises (1974) in 'Economic calculation in socialism', in M. Bornstein (ed.) *Comparative Economic Systems,* 3rd edn, Homewood, Ill., Irwin, 120–7.

9 See, for example, Branko Horvat (1982) *The Political Economy of Socialism*, Armonk, M.E. Sharpe.

10 See Raymond Vernon and Yair Aharoni (eds) (1981) *State-Owned Enterprise in the Western Economies*, New York, St. Martin's Press; Raymond Vernon (ed.) (1987) *The Promise of Privatization*, New York, Council on Foreign Relations.

11 Carson, 'Property rights', op.cit., 318.

12 Guido Calabresi and A. Douglas Melamed (1983) 'Property rules, liability rules, and inalienability: one view of the cathedral', in Mark Kuperberg and Charles Beitz (eds) *Law, Economics and Philosophy*, Totowa, NJ, Rowman & Allanheld, 42–3.

13 See Hannah Arendt (1958) *The Human Condition*, Chicago, University of Chicago Press, 58–63; Balcerowicz, 'Remarks', op.cit., 67.

14 It is important to note here that even when private individuals are nominally the subjects of property rights, they cannot exercise them when recognition of those rights depends on the whims of a ruler. The Philippines under Marcos was apparently such a case. See Stephen Haggard's discussion of 'crony companies' in 'The Philippines: picking up after Marcos', in Vernon, *Privatization*, op.cit., 90–121.

15 The similarities and differences between the two experiences are explored at length in the unabridged version of this manuscript (see Ellen Comisso (1988). The political conditions of economic reform', unpub. manuscript (mimeo)). The political contradictions of economic reform in Hungary, along with additional sources, are explored in Ellen Comisso and Paul Marer (1988) 'The politics and economics of reform in Hungary', *International Organization* 41, 421–53; less general but more graphic accounts of the political exercise of property rights in Hungary appear in Mihály Laki (1983) *Vállalatok megszünése és összevonása* (*Liquidation and Merger of Enterprises*), Közgazdasági és Jogi Könyvkiadó, Budapest; Éva Voszka (1988) *Reform és átszervezés a nyolcvanas években* (*Reform and Reorganization in the 1980s*), Közgazdasági és Jogi Könyvkiadó, Budapest; Mária Csanádi (1984) 'Függöség, konszenzus és szelekció' ('Dependence, consensus and selection'), Pénzügykutatási Intézet kiadványai. On Yugoslavia, see Janez Jerovsek, Veljko Rus, and Josip Zupanov (1986) *Kriza, Blokada i Perspektive* (*Crisis, Blockade and the Prospects*) Zagreb, Globus; Harold Lydall (1989) *Yugoslavia in Crisis*, Oxford, Clarendon Press.

16 Martin Shapiro (1981) *Courts*, Chicago, University of Chicago Press, 32.

17 Ibid., 67.

18 See John Rawls, (1971) *A Theory of Justice*, Cambridge, Mass., Harvard University Press, 59, 236.

19 Readers should be advised that I use a rather broad notion of 'market failures' here that includes, but is not limited to, the presence of 'externalities' as defined by conventional economic theory. My use of the term is roughly similar to the one proposed by Dennis Young and Albert Hirschman: it describes 'situations where exit does not do a good job of stirring up management and of restoring efficiency' (Albert Hirschman, 1981, *Essays in Trespassing: Economics to Politics and Beyond*, Cambridge, Cambridge University Press, 237).

20 See Ellen Comisso (1988) 'Market failures and market socialism: economic problems of the transition', *East European Politics and Societies* 2, 433–65.

21 One cannot help but suspect that this was precisely an appealing route to follow for many in socialist states some time ago.

22 My impression–possibly erroneous–is that the preference for employing the totally-owned subsidiary as a means of diversifying into new products or markets applies to foreign investment as well. The 'joint venture' format is usually used only in contexts where risk is greatly reduced by having a partner from the host country share in equity; thus, it is used most widely in less-developed countries in which the government is itself a major market actor. Political risks to the venture in these cases can be significantly reduced if, say, the government itself has a stake in equity.

23 See David Stark (1986) 'The dynamics of organizational innovation and the politics of reform in Hungary' paper prepared for the Conference on the Social Consequences of Market Reforms in China and Eastern Europe, Santa Barbara, May (mimeo); Jan Adam (1989) 'Work teams: a new phenomenon in income distribution in Hungary', *Comparative Economic Studies* 31, 46–67; Ellen Comisso (1979) *Workers' Control Under Plan and Market*, New Haven, Yale University Press. An analysis suggesting that many of the demands for and against wage differentiation in western economies arise as much from the

exigencies of union leaderships as from workers' inherent preferences appears
in Peter Swenson (1989) *Fair Shares: Unions, Pay, and Politics in Sweden and
West Germany*, Ithaca, Cornell University Press.

24 H. Flakierski (1989) 'Economic reform and income distribution in Yugoslavia',
Comparative Economic Studies 31, 102.

25 See Egon Neuberger (1959) 'The Yugoslav investment auctions', *Quarterly
Journal of Economics* 72, 88–115.

26 Most proposals fall into three somewhat overlapping groups: (1) proposals
to introduce limited electoral competition (usually through a National Front,
but possibly by allowing alternative political parties to organize as well;
(2) proposals to establish 'societal' corporatism by reforming the mass
organizations; and (3) proposals to democratize the Communist Party itself.
   An example of proposal (1) was elaborated in János Kis (1986) 'Társadalmi
Szerződés', samizdat ms. (mimeo). The programme endorsed by *Mladina* in
Slovenia would appear to fit here, as would the design of the (1989) Polish
electoral system (see *New York Times*, 4 June 1989, p. 10 for a snapshot
description) (see also László Urbán (1988) The necessity of a political
institutional reform from the point of view of the economic reform in Hungary',
unpub. ms). Proposal (2) is described in David Ost (1988) 'Towards a corporatist
solution in Eastern Europe: the case of Poland', *Eastern European Politics and
Societies* 3, 152074. For proposal (3), see Werner Hahn (1987) *Democracy in
a Communist Party*, New York, Columbia University Press and Mihály Bihari
(1987) Reform és Demokrácia', *Medvetánc* 2, 165–227. Increasing electoral
competition within the Communist Party of the Soviet Union (CPSU) was also
an aspect of Soviet political reforms.

27 See John Zysman (1985) *Government, Markets, and Growth: Financial Systems
and the Politics of Industrial Change*, Ithaca, Cornell University Press; James
Alt and K. Alec Chrystal (1983) *Political Economics*, Berkeley, University of
California Press: Chalmers Johnson (1986) 'The East Asian NICs', *International
Organization* 41.

28 See William Zimmerman (1987) *Open Borders, Nonalignment, and the Political
Evolution of Yugoslavia*, Princeton, Princeton University Press.

29 See Guillermo O'Donnell (1979) *Modernization and Bureaucratic-Author-
itarianism*, Berkeley, Institute of International Studies; Samuel Huntington,
(1968) *Political Order in Changing Societies*, New Haven, Yale University Press;
Ellen Comisso (1986) 'Introduction: state structures, political processes, and
collective choice in CMEA states', *International Organization* 41, 195–238.

30 See G. O'Donnell, P. Schmitter and L. Whitehead (eds) (1986) *Transitions to
Democracy* 4 vols, Baltimore, Johns Hopkins University Press.

16 Opposition against market-type reforms in centrally-planned economies*

Jerzy Osiatynski

INTRODUCTION

The opposition against market-type reforms in centrally-planned economies (hereafter CPEs) attracted the attention of sociologists and political scientists rather than of economists. The latter often devised projects of market reforms, disregarding the former's findings. Yet an important contribution of empirical sociology has been that it helped abandon the economists' comfortable world of either micro- or macro-economic analysis, in which whatever is intended is being achieved, and introduced group interests, political premises and consequences of economic reforms, and a distinction between projected reforms and the actual social and economic change. As will be seen, my intellectual debt to the Polish school of empirical sociology goes well beyond the references provided below. The main purpose of this chapter is to bring together the economists' and sociologists' trends of thought on economic reforms and opposition to them.[1]

Our starting point will be Włodzimierz Brus's seminal distinction between the three fundamental features of a traditional CPE (TCPE). If they are set against those of a fully-fledged market economy, the implications of a market-type reform of the TCPE may be exposed.

1 The first fundamental feature is the monopoly of ownership of the means of production;
2 The second is the centralistic system of organization and management of the 'socialized sector' of the economy;
3 And at the heart of the system there is the 'institutional' role of the Communist Party and the dominance of polity over the economy. The essence of this third feature is the supreme role of the party in managing the economy, and 'the double subordination system whereby the party apparatus, particularly at its centre, [has] the incontestable right of

supervision and interference at every level of the economic structure'
(Brus 1986:100).

At the enterprise level the party's interference is exercised through
its executive organs both outside and inside the enterprise. One of the
supporting pillars of this role of the Communist Party is the *nomenklatura*
system of appointments to and dismissals from specified posts.[2] The
institutional role of the party is based on the Communist control over all
organized forms of public life (with some exceptions such as the Catholic
Church in Poland). Moreover, since this control is outside any explicit legal
framework, it does not imply formal public accountability.

As far as the system of economic planning and management of the sector
of socialist enterprises is concerned, five spheres of economic decision-
making are usually distinguished in economic practice and theorizing: A –
current ('routine', in János Kornai's parlance) operations; B – investments;
C – pricing; D – foreign trade; E – money and banking. This distinction
enables one to expose the differences between the TCPE on the one hand
(A, B, C, D, E decisions all centralized except for working regulations and
the like, of the A domain, which are left for the enterprise management),
and, say, the Hungarian New Economic Mechanism of 1968 (A – wholly; B
– hardly; C, D, E – partly decentralized down to the enterprise level), or the
Yugoslav system (A – all, B, D, E – mostly, C – partly made at the enterprise
level), on the other hand. Furthermore, this typology offers a convenient
framework for examining the nature of projected economic reforms.

Before examining the sources of opposition to market reforms, a
systematization of the types of economic reforms is suggested below.

MAIN TYPES OF ECONOMIC REFORMS IN THE TCPEs

The following typology is one of many possible classification schemes. Its
watershed is the change (or changes) which a given type of reform introduces
into the fundamental features enumerated above, and the relation of the
projected new system of economic planning and management to the market
economy. Four main types of economic reforms will be distinguished.

1   A 'non-reform' reform

It represents no institutional changes in the system of economic planning and
management but merely a reorientation of economic policy. Its essence is
the mastering of economic and socio-political troubles within the old system,
and its philosophy is that 'though the system is perfect, the people are not'.
Since mistakes were made in economic policy, policy changes are a necessary
and sufficient remedy.

This type of 'reform' usually consists in restoring a more balanced
development through (i) deceleration of economic growth, (ii) reduction

of the relative share of investment in national income, (iii) reallocation of investment from the capital goods to the consumer goods sector and from industry to agriculture, (iv) restructuring the existing capacities (in particular, partially converting the armament industry), (v) relaxation of forced collectivization and tough procurement measures, and also encouraging private agricultural production, and (vi) less discrimination against the private non-agricultural sector.

Examples of such 'reforms' are many. As a rule, they represent the first reaction of the Communist authorities against social and political unrest or open revolts. They dominated the 'New Course' policies in Eastern Europe in 1953–5, as well as the deferred counter-reaction to economic reforms of type (2) which were attempted in the USSR in 1955 and 1965, in the German Democratic Republic in 1963, in Poland in 1964, and in Bulgaria, Albania and Romania in 1965 (see Brus 1986, Chapters 24 and 25). They are usually accompanied by a short-lived political liberalization. If reserves of easy access exist, such 'reforms' can indeed bring tangible improvements in the standards of living, and bring them quickly, too (as in Poland in 1956–7). However, if one abstracts from internal reserves (which, as a rule, are used up before the crisis starts), conditions which favour armament reductions, contracting foreign debts and so on, do not necessarily coincide with domestic economic troubles, and even when they do, such policies, needless to say, merely buy time unless genuine systemic reforms are undertaken.

2 'Improving' (or 'perfecting') the system

This type of reform leaves the fundamental features one and three intact and, in feature two, spheres B, C, D, and E of decision-making are also unaffected. With respect to current operations, more autonomy is granted to enterprises (often, in fact, to their immediate supervisory agencies instead), the number of obligatory targets is slightly reduced, gross output plan targets are substituted for net ones, and some forms of management and workers' profit-sharing are introduced. The essence of such reforms is a limited shift from direct, mandatory planning of output of individual enterprises in physical terms to individualized planning in financial terms. However, the central planner, not the market, continues to decide what, how, where and when to produce (sell, buy, and so on); he implements his plans largely by old, quantitative instruments, but partly also by new, quasi-price ones.

In practice such reforms soon fall back to the traditional system of economic management (see Bauer 1986) with an important difference. Namely, mass political terror, coercive allocation of labour and outright abuse of work and pay conditions are replaced by financial incentives for the work-force and enterprise management.

3 'Central planning with a built-in market mechanism'

The term was invented by Brus as was, by and large, the underlying theoretical model (see Brus 1972). Its essence is that the system of planning, whereby obligatory targets are imposed by superiors over subordinates, is abandoned. Hence allocation of inputs in physical terms is abandoned, too. Annual plans are still drawn up, but are not binding on any hierarchical subordinate (however, firms must conform to specific output targets which relate to COMECON deliveries and government contracts). While the decision-making concerning sphere A is decentralized down to the enterprise, the central planner continues to assume responsibility for investment decisions (though the investment powers of firms are also somewhat increased).

This system is also called 'central planning with regulated markets'. 'Regulation' is effected by the central planner through a system of financial incentives which provide the link between the micro- and the macroeconomic interests (via profit-sharing schemes), through parameters which affect financial results of the enterprise (and hence financial rewards for its work-force and management) such as taxes, subsidies, interest rates, foreign exchange rates, and, of course, prices. The Hungarian New Economic Mechanism (NEM) is a practical approximation to this theoretical construct, as is the 1981 Polish reform.

Next to the above-mentioned changes in the second fundamental feature, there are also some minor changes in the fundamental features one and three. The co-operative sector enjoys a greater autonomy and, perhaps even more importantly, there is some increase in the share of private business outside agriculture. (Due to methodological difficulties, the data is not wholly reliable, but this share seems to have increased in Hungary and Poland by a few percentage points.)[3] With respect to the role of the party, some observers of the Hungarian scene point out that under the NEM the importance of technocratic expertise increased at the expense of the party's interference with routine business.

There is no need to discuss here the achievements and shortcomings of the Hungarian NEM (see, for example, Kornai 1986, and Laky 1980). Some problem areas must be noted, however. One may refer to pricing, which – while balancing supply and demand – serves as an instrument of government policy options, and is constrained by public protests against price rises of basic consumer goods and services. Another area is *ad hoc* tax exemptions (subsidies, and so on), and *ad hoc* changes in foreign exchange regulations (aimed at export promotion). Yet another problem follows from high concentration rates and the monopolistic rather than competitive behaviour of firms in the market.

In consequence, it is sometimes argued that the NEM represents merely a shift from an individualized physical planning base to an individualized financial planning base (Granick 1975, 309), and that it did not significantly alter the behaviour of enterprises (c.f., e.g. Kornai 1986, and Márton Tardos's chapter in this book). While the failures of the NEM had been attributed mainly to its inconsistent introduction, recently its very concept was found incapable of generating a viable market. As in reform type (2) (see p. 249), the central planner continues to determine what, how, when and where to produce (and so on), but financial 'persuasion' is used in preference to administrative coercion. Market mechanism is supposed to follow not the market signals, but the planner's visions and options. However, the scope of the central planner's interference is limited.

4 A 'market break-through' reform

The concept descends from that of 'crucial reform'. The latter comes from Kalecki and Kowalik (1971) who used it with reference to reforms introduced in the aftermath of the 1929–33 world crisis. They considered them crucial because they contributed to the further dynamic development of the capitalist system, yet did not undermine its fundamental features; indeed, they *stabilized* it. Later the concept of 'crucial reform' was referred to a socialist economy (see Kowalik 1986). It postulated that market-type relations should replace fundamental features one and two of the CPEs. With respect to fundamental feature three, it required that the *nomenklatura* system is limited (eliminated at the enterprise level), and various forms of pluralism are introduced; none the less, the mono-party system was to be retained. Thus, the crucial reform would have stabilized the 'leading' position of the Communist Party. Would this be equivalent to stabilizing the essence of a socialist economy in any sense similar to that in which the crucial reform stabilized the essence of the capitalist system? And, more importantly, is a fully-fledged market reform at all compatible with the retaining of the 'leading' position of the Communist Party? Any answer to such questions must by nature be highly speculative, especially after 1989.

A 'market break-through' reform is 'crucial' in a more simplistic sense, in so far as it aims at replacing *all* fundamental features of the CPE and thereby at *destabilizing* the essence of the Communist economic system, and substituting it for a 'market socialist' system. Its aim would be (a) to establish a truly pluralistic structure of the ownership of the means of production, with the private sector being large enough to influence the pattern of microeconomic behaviour of the other sectors; (b) to substitute the vertical links between the economic units for horizontal ones (and to deconcentrate and demonopolize the economy, to provide freedom of entry and exit); and last but not least by far, (c) to eliminate the institutional role of the Communist Party (or of any other political party, though not of the government) in the economy.

In the new system there would probably exist a large non-private sector in which most state enterprises would be subject to workers' self-management, the share of co-operative sector would be higher than in a typical market economy, there would be many forms of 'mixed' property firms, and there would be workers' participation in the management of private firms. Clearly, the socialist character of such a system could not be sought at the level of its microeconomic operation, or in the above-mentioned property structure of capital assets, but rather at the level of macroeconomic policies with respect to national income distribution, personal incomes differentiation, regulations concerning conditions of work, the system of wage bargaining, measures preventing other than frictional unemployment (especially among the youth), social security systems, and so on. While this concept of a socialist economy is an 'open-ended' one, it differs from the blueprints of the social-democratic parties with respect to the multi-sectoral pattern of ownership, as well as to the role of workers' self-management, various forms of labour participation in organization of production and distribution, and to the large powers given to local councils.

For a long time, most economic reforms in the CPEs were limited to changes in some elements of fundamental feature two and no 'market break-through' reform were started. In three instances, however, some revisions of the other two fundamental features were also attempted. An expansion of the private sector and a genuine autonomy of the co-operative sector were explicitly postulated in the projects of the Czechoslovak reform drafted in 1966–8 (see Brus 1986,211 ff.), as well as in those of the Polish reform of 1981, where under the pressure of 'Solidarity' an equal treatment of the private, co-operative and state sectors was proclaimed (see *Kierunki* 1981, thesis 16). With respect to the monopolist role of the party, this was point-blank rejected in Czechoslovakia after January 1968, when Dubček came to power; in the Polish 1956 and 1981 reforms, this role was meant to be curbed by workers' self-management; moreover, this was also the essence of the struggle 'Solidarity' fought and lost in 1981 over the *nomenklatura* system.

All these attempts were quickly countered by police rather than political measures, as in Czechoslovakia in 1968, and Poland in 1981, or soon degenerated into a combination of reform type (2) and (3) (see above), as in Poland in 1956. The failures seem to show evidence that unless a 'market break-through' reform is undertaken, the other types of reforms must sooner or later return to the traditional system of economic planing and management.

OPPOSITION AGAINST MARKET-CLEARING PRICES

Another characteristic trait of the CPEs is repressed inflation. Periodically, it must give vent to price rises if the consumer goods (and services) are allocated through the market rather than through administrative rationing. Any such restoring of market-clearing prices is by no means tantamount to introducing the market mechanism, which would require that supply is also made price-elastic, but it is a necessary condition for market-type reforms. Market-clearing prices invariably meet with opposition which often undermines the economic sense of the price rises. What are the sources of this opposition?

For the public at large, repressed inflation implies that consumer goods are allocated, not through prices alone, but also through time lost in queues, favouritism and corruption, and by supplementary payments in kind (coal allotments for miners, meat allotments for employees of slaughterhouses and meat processing plants, and so on). If the supply of consumer goods and changes in stocks are given, their total consumption in physical terms is given too, and a rise in consumer goods' prices to market-clearing levels cannot change it. If involuntary savings (which may be treated here as the money equivalent of repressed inflation) represent, say, 10 per cent of households' incomes, the value of market supplies plus households' voluntary savings being short of these incomes by as much, a rise in prices that would absorb this gap could not affect total consumption, even if households' real incomes fell by 10 per cent. From this premise it is sometimes concluded that opposition of the public against such price rises is unfounded and based on a 'socialist money illusion'.

This conclusion is not entirely correct, however. Introducing market-clearing prices implies changes in the distribution of consumer goods from households where time rather than money is abundant (households of three generations, retired people, women on maternity leave, and so on), to households with high employment participation rates. Therefore the consumption of large sections of the society will be affected. Moreover, as the above example shows, the 'money illusion' refers here to every one out of ten monetary units spent. Thus, in practice, it rather resembles a game of 'musical chairs', with high probability of success for all participants, if not in this round then in the next.

Opposition of the public against price rises undermines the foundations of 'commodity production' and pushes economic relations back to pre-capitalist modes of production. Moreover, this opposition, which is given relatively little attention both in the theory of economic reforms and in their practical implementation, has already been in the past and may well continue to be in the future a very important obstacle to market reforms in the CPEs.[4] It cannot be effectively alleviated without winning over the public to such reforms, which in turn requires the political democratization of the system and some institutional forms of participation of the public in political life, that is, a 'market break-through' reform. An integral part of this is a social revolution: the establishment of institutional foundations for parliamentary democracy. Will that be enough to alleviate the opposition against price rises? At any rate, the process of reaching this end proves long and politically painful.

Repressed inflation implies also preferential rationing of consumer goods through privileged access (special shops and delivery systems), special entitlements to purchase cars, residential and recreational lots, and other consumer durables (also additional supplies of rationed goods), all below market-clearing prices. Opposition of the beneficiaries of these privileges against them is often pointed out, but its actual importance is uncertain. It is clear, however, that the narrower the social and political base of the power system, the more elaborate must be the system of formal and informal privileges which find reflection not merely in wage rates, conditions of work, retirement age, health care, holiday facilities and various 'fringe benefits', but also in such preferential rationing (see Staniszkis 1972 and, especially, Narojek 1986).[5]

OPPOSITION AGAINST 'NON-REFORM REFORMS'

This is possibly the weakest opposition of all, since by nature such reforms do not infringe upon any fundamental feature of the TCPEs. None the less, any reallocation of inputs and restructuring of capacities is at the expense of some and to the benefit of others. Thus, such reforms are opposed by sectoral and industrial interests which have to foot the bill of such policy reorientations, mainly heavy industry, metallurgy, machine building, armaments productions, non-residential construction, and so on (see Kozek 1986). Opposition is the stronger, the more permanent the new policy options appear to be. It is forthcoming from the affected segments of economic administration, from the bottom to the top of the organizational structure of the economy.

Because of strong personal ties between this administration and the government and party apparatus, the former is quite influential and capable of dressing up its particular interests into ideological form, saying, for instance, that the 'principles of socialist reproduction' are violated and a revision of the 'Law of Faster Development of Department I' is attempted. The termination of forced collectivization and the diminishing discrimination against the private sector in general, is heralded as a reintroduction of capitalism, and the better terms for private farmers and non-agricultural business is proclaimed as undermining the leading political position of the working class.

Similar opposition is forthcoming from the work-force of enterprises whose privileges are endangered (and from local public opinion in the areas where new investment projects are expected to be abandoned, and thus new employment opportunities and infrastructural investments would be lost). This latter opposition appears whenever sectoral and/or industrial wage and income differentials are to change. It was particularly clear in the early phase of the Hungarian 1968 NEM reform, when in order to mitigate rising income differentials between state industry on the one hand and the co-operative and private sectors on the other, the former were granted a large tax-free preferential increase in wages in 1973.

Similar conflicting interests are bound to occur, and are not easy to solve under the parliamentary democratic system either. Under the mono-party system of the CPEs, however, they require exceedingly high political determination and the 'iron fist' of the top political authorities, and the final results are still uncertain (as evidenced, for instance, by the recent 'urban economic reform' in China – see Zhou's paper in this book).

OPPOSITION AGAINST REVISING 'FUNDAMENTAL FEATURE ONE'

Without much harm to the argument we may now turn to the opposition against a 'market break-through' reform, as it also embraces opposition against reforms of type (2) and (3) (see above). The factors opposed to such reforms can conveniently be grouped under three headings which correspond to the three fundamental features of the TCPE.

Changing the property structure of a TCPE is clearly a formidable task, not only due to involved vested interests but also for 'technical reasons' (these are discussed by Berg 1987, whose main points are summarized below). The government sector is much too large and the domestic private market much too small (and operating in a restrictive legal framework) to permit a fast reprivatization that would otherwise appear sensible.[6] As in many less developed countries, the government is willing to dispense with those state-owned enterprises which are economically non-viable rather than with the profitable ones. Divestiture may then mean simply closing the least viable firms and their wasting away. Moreover, since CPEs are usually small countries, transforming a public sector monopoly into a private sector monopoly is not very attractive. For all these reasons (and the ideological ones) domestic political constituency for such measures is usually small.

Another option is the leasing of a part of state-owned capacities, or of some state-run economic activities to the co-operative and private sectors. Where rigid price controls are likely to continue, more important than privatization of the state monopoly may be a change in the legal framework of its operation and the introduction of private competition.[7] Another preferred measure may be the contracting out of some services of the public sector (such as waste collection or street cleaning). Yet another may be the partition of large state enterprises and monopolies (so that co-operation between their individual plants, factories, and so on, would result from their commercial ties rather than from administrative orders). Clearly, all measures aimed at increasing the competitiveness of the economy are opposed by the beneficiaries of the old system: the work-force and the management of inefficient state enterprises alike (see Rychard 1988). They are also opposed by enthusiasts of an instantaneous and all-embracing privatization of the whole economy.

Changing the property structure means that while the public sector is reduced, the private sector is reintroduced or expanded. This is easier said than done. The reaction to the new rules which, since May 1987, permitted some private activities in the Soviet economy outside agriculture, was particularly striking in this context. They were met with distrust and lack of interest. The guarantees for the stability of new legislation and of a change in political attitude towards private entrepreneurship were missing. In other countries (for example, Poland and Hungary), on top of this, the accompanying tax regulations were unclear and often formed on an *ad hoc* and *ex post* basis. The system of granting concessions to private economic activity invited corruption, as did the system of input supplies for the private sector. All this makes the legal position of a private business extremely shaky. (All the same, expansion of the private sector into 'no man's land' is usually easier than privatization of the state-owned enterprises.)[8]

In CPEs there is also opposition, partly genuine and partly engineered by the official propaganda, against increasing income differentials for the benefit of the private sector, as well as by the populist egalitarian demagogy directed against 'privatizers' and 'commercialization' of social life. Polish empirical studies show, however, that egalitarian values are accepted less often by workers than officially claimed, and that when egalitarian views are indeed advanced they often express merely opposition against such income differentiation and privileges which the workers find unjust (see, for example, Kolarska 1985). In the light of these findings it is argued that the 'egalitarian preference of the public' argument is misused, mainly in order to legitimate the existing power structures and the traditional economic system with its sectoral and other preferences (ibid.,52).

All this undermines the stability and economic viability of the private sector in CPEs. It also partly explains why it shares many negative features of the state sector (waste of inputs, low quality, insufficient innovation, and so on).

The above argument applies partly to the co-operative sector, too. It was treated by central authorities with distrust, as 'incompletely socialist', even after it had been wholly controlled and subordinated to central planning. Granting the co-operatives a genuine autonomy is opposed by those who favour all-embracing central planning and fear the 'anarchy of the market'. It is opposed by the co-operatives' supervisory agencies whose existence would no longer be justified (see next section). It is opposed by the management and members of those co-operatives which hitherto have enjoyed preferential treatment in supplies of rationed inputs. Finally, it is also opposed by the co-operatives' management and the local administration in places where a genuine autonomy of co-operatives would no longer permit misuse of their resources for satisfying private needs in exchange for patronage, and so on (this refers also to some state enterprises, for example, in construction, food processing, durable consumer goods' manufacturing and garage services).

The importance of this opposition does not appear very significant as it can be dealt with by changing the regulatory environment and by a greater transparency of the co-operatives'. This implies political changes, however.

OPPOSITION AGAINST REVISING 'FUNDAMENTAL FEATURE TWO'

As I have dealt with the sources of this type of opposition elsewhere (see Osiatynski *et al.* 1985), I shall only reiterate here the main conclusions with respect to individual, social and occupational groups opposed to such revisions.

First and foremost they are opposed by the intermediate level of economic administration and the agencies carrying out the allocation of raw material and other inputs for state enterprises and co-operatives. Clearly, as a result of such changes they would be deprived of power if not wholly eliminated. Since there are strong personal links between this apparatus and the middle level party apparatus, this opposition is capable of effectively blocking those measures which undermine their social and political position unless they are accompanied by appropriate changes in the political system.

Also ill-disposed to such revisions is part of the central economic administration, for example, branch ministries, as well as the central and regional government and party administration, whose powers would then be changed to the benefit of autonomous enterprises. A thorough change in methods, scope and instruments of central economic planning, necessitated by such revisions, requires not only new attitudes and habits on the part of central and regional planning boards but, more importantly, new professional qualifications, perhaps even a new generation of planners.[9]

Such revisions are also opposed by the less active and venturesome enterprise managers whose attitudes, motives of action and decision-making criteria were completely moulded in the 'command economic system'. Furthermore, such changes are often blocked by the political apparatus at the enterprise level and higher up, not only because it partially expresses the interests of the aforementioned social groups whose party membership is relatively high, but also because in the traditional system of economic management the enterprise is both an economic and a political institution. Since this opposition partly overlaps with that against revising the 'fundamental feature three', we shall discuss it in the next section.

OPPOSITION AGAINST REVISING 'FUNDAMENTAL FEATURE THREE'

The politization of the CPE is deeply rooted in its ideological and political doctrine, and the underlying fear of the 'anarchy of the market' and of the resulting cyclical fluctuations in employment, prices and incomes.[10] It requires that the government administration, guided by directives of the party's executive agencies, approves the plans formulated by the economic units (or simply imposes plans on them), creates conditions favourable for their implementation, and controls them.

Paradoxically, this politization of the economy 'from above' is reinforced by a similar trend 'from below': when there are no other forms of articulating the interests of employees, they use enterprises for this purpose. Consequently, the enterprise becomes a battle-ground for economic as well as political, social and other interests (see Morawski 1986). This, in turn, leads to a double interdependence between the rulers and the ruled in exercising a 'negative authority': 'not only the governed depend on the ruling elite . . . but there is also an equally strong opposite dependence, often leading to an "incapacitation" and paralysis of the rulers' (Adamski 1985,37).

Moreover, the question arises whether the higher-up tiers of the system of economic administration are at all capable of controlling the lower tiers. Even in the early phases of the CPEs, when the powers of supervisory agencies against their subordinates were much greater than now, it could be legitimately asked who ultimately controlled whom (see Staniszkis 1980, who claims that control 'from above' is not possible, and Rychard 1987, who shows that it leaves the would-be controllers at the mercy of the controlled). Thus, the struggle for distributive shares in the allocation of inputs, retaining of profits, wages and social benefits, and so on, pervades the system which becomes increasingly incapable of reconciling the interests (see Zienkowski 1986).

The ideological and political doctrine requiring a total subordination of economic decision-making to the political apparatus is an important factor operating against market reforms in the CPEs, certainly more important than the material and other interests of the party and government administration. However, depolitization of the economy, especially at the level of state-owned enterprises, becomes a political question *par excellence*. The same applies to the setting up of lucid and controllable rules for co-ordinating various branch, regional and other interests (in place of informal and backstage deals that in practice render any economic calculation impossible).

CONCLUSIONS

It is sometimes argued that microeconomic efficiency does not need to be necessarily combined with parliamentary democracy, and that an autocratic rule may be equally effective in achieving dynamic improvement in the standards of living, provided that the economy is left to the market. Examples of some Newly-Industrialized Countries are quoted in support of this proposition.

Be it as it may, the question the CPEs are facing is entirely different. As observed in a report of the Polish Sociological Association some years ago, a specific characteristic of the Polish drama was the following: on the one hand, those social groups which were likely to support the reform programmes put forward by the Communist leadership neither trust it, nor enjoy its confidence, and, on the other hand, those who trust the political leadership and enjoy its confidence are on the whole opposed to reforms (see Executive Committee 1987,61–2). This was unlikely to change without a 'market break-through' reform and the implied far-reaching democratic changes.[11]

It remains an open question, though, how such reform can be initiated and accomplished. I tend to agree that it must be both inspired and partly engineered 'from above', and partly engineered and supported – within the newly-created institutional framework – 'from below' (see Morawski 1986; Kowalik 1986). Unless such reforms are implemented (whereby the 'crucial reform' could be treated as a 'half-way house'), the CPEs would face a prolonged stagnation and relative decline.

Maybe the Polish experience of the 'Solidarity' and 'Post-Solidarity' period could be of some relevance in this context. First of all it shows a strong preference of the adherents of reforms for a 'peaceful revolution'. Second, it shows that a determined mass pressure may induce some expansion of market relations and some forms of licensed pluralism; no doubt, Poland of the late 1980s – with genuinely independent economic associations promoting private entrepreneurship, an association of workers' self-management organizers, political discussion clubs, two regional student organizations, with the Communist coalition partners gaining increasing independence from the PUWP, with attempts to establish a social Counter-Crisis Pact, and with the (December 1988) Plenum of the Central Committee of the PUWP pledging to drastically reduce the *nomenklatura* system – was certainly a different country than a decade before.

In Poland and Hungary we have seen that the old political and economic system disintegrated rapidly under the pressure 'from below', showing somewhat different attitudes of the respective ruling elites. In Hungary the social pressure was lower, or at least less vocal than in Poland, while (because ?) the Hungarian ruling elite appeared to be more reform-minded and co-operative. The Polish ruling elite was deeply divided about the nature and need of any radical reform, as well as about their political survival, while the pressure 'from below', mainly of the 'Solidarity' members and sympathizers, was stronger. The intense political struggle in these two countries has clearly shown that the opposition to any market break-through reform discussed in this chapter can be overcome in the CPEs only if accompanied by political democratization of the system.

While any discussion of conditions under which communist rule ends goes beyond the scope of this paper, the experience of the Central and East European countries after 1989 clearly indicates a strong positive correlation between the public conviction that the Great Transformation is tantamount to an end of the communist system on the one hand, and to the public support for the 'break-through reform', including the readiness of the population to accept even large short-run losses in standards of living, on the other hand. This banal truth explains why, for example, the first post-communist government in Poland could get away with about 30 per cent reduction in real wages after the reform was started, in January 1990, while its communist predecessor had not been allowed a reduction of about 8 per cent only a year earlier. (Cf. Osiatynski 1991.)

NOTES

*I am grateful to J. Kofman, T. Kowalik and A. Rychard for their helpful comments on an earlier draft of this chapter.

1 Our findings are meant to apply to the six CPEs of Eastern Europe and the USSR; the sources of opposition to market reforms in Yugoslavia and in the non-European CPEs may well require a separate investigation.

2 Exact data on the scope of the *nomenklatura* system in the economy of any CPE (for example, on the ratios of positions covered by this system to total numbers of managerial positions in the state and co-operative sectors of the economy) is not available. (For lists of posts, in the economy and elsewhere, falling under the *nomenklatura* of the Polish United Workers' Party's Central Committee, regional committees, and district committees, dating from 1972, see D. MacShane 1981: Appendix 5. For a list of posts falling under the *nomemklatura* of the PUWP's Central Committee, its Politbureau and its Secretariat, dating from August 1986, see 'List' 1987.) Interestingly, in spite of strong pressures in Poland in the early 1980s to limit the scope of this system, it continued to include even the position of a foreman. The *nomenklatura* system in the economy was seen by a senior Polish sociologist as a means of surplus appropriation due to monopoly in the ownership of the means of production (see Szczepanski 1987).

3 For doctrinal reasons, the output and employment of the genuinely private enterprise, for example, in some supply and purchase contracts or subcontracting business, is often included in the co-operative sector's official statistics, and thereby in those of the 'socialized sector' of the CPEs. Also, for other reasons (for example, tax evasion), the shares of the private sector in total output and employment are underestimated. This holds probably more for the Hungarian economy before the 1968 reform than ever since. In 1986, the relative shares of active earners in the Hungarian private and co-operative sectors outside agriculture and forestry were 6.3 per cent and 11.2 per cent respectively (see Hungarian Central Statistical Office, 1988, Table 4.4, 68–9).

4 This was particularly well demonstrated by the November 1987 Polish Referendum in the course of which the more ambitious plans for introducing market-clearing prices were vehemently rejected. It might be mentioned in passing, that the public at large, devoid of everyday personal experience with the market economy, often does not clearly perceive the link between market-clearing prices and the introduction of market mechanisms, but the reformers did not seem to take much notice of this.

5 While similar phenomena exist elsewhere, too (for example, with respect to the police, army, or fire brigades), they are kept in check by a system of a genuine public control over government spending.

6 Participation of foreign companies in privatization must be limited lest the economic sovereignty of the country is lost.

7 Berg (1987,11) argues, for instance, for allowing private competition for passenger traffic with the public transport monopoly, instead of a change of ownership, if the rates structure remains unchanged.

8 Iván Szelényi rightly notes that a political coalition of the state and party elite on the one hand, and of some other social groups (the retired, disabled, and non-working poor), which have little or no private income, on the other hand, could form a political force capable of preventing such changes; none the less, he observes, the Hungarian Communist Party favoured 'the expansion of private

business, rather than the transformation of government-owned firms into joint stock companies' (see Szelényi 1989).

9 For a more detailed analysis of the tasks of central planners under the system of market determination of output and capital expansion, see C. Jòzefiak (1988).

10 As long as the market system, unrestricted or controlled, is unable to cope with unemployment, the fear is justified. While other than frictional unemployment appears to me a social pathology, it is, I believe, largely a value judgement whether unemployment outside factory gates is to be preferred to unemployment inside factory gates, and what the trade-off is between the micro-economic inefficiency of a CPE and the economic and social welfare it secures, as compared with the macroeconomic inefficiency due to unemployment, and the economic and social welfare of a market economy. I shall not go any further into this matter since the subject of this chapter is not to argue for market reforms (which in themselves may or may not be a sensible idea), but merely to show factors opposing them once they are tried.

11 Therefore, I find any contraposition of 'democratic socialism' and 'market socialism' (see Nuti 1986) rather misleading in the context of economic reforms in the CPEs.

BIBLIOGRAPHY

Adamski, W. (1985) 'Aspirations – interests – conflicts' (in Polish), *Studia Socjologiczne* 2.

Bauer, T. (1986) 'Reforming or perfecting the economic mechanism in Eastern Europe', *EUI Working Papers* 86, Florence.

Berg, E. (1987) 'Privatization: developing a pragmatic approach', *Economic Impact* 1.

Brus, W. (1972) *The Market in a Socialist Economy*, London, Routledge & Kegan Paul.

Brus, W. (1986) 'Institutional change within a planned economy', in M. Kaser (ed.) *The Economic History of Eastern Europe, 1919–1975*, vol. 3, Oxford, Clarendon Press, Chs 23–6.

Executive Committee of the Polish Sociological Association (1987) '*Report on the Polish Society in the second half of 1980s*' (in Polish), *Dwadziescia Jeden* 4.

Granick, D. (1975) *Enterprise Guidance in Eastern Europe: A Comparison of Four Socialist Economies*, New York, Princeton.

Hungarian Central Statistical Office (1988) *Statistical Yearbook 1986*, HCSO, Budapest.

Jòzefiak, C. (1988) 'Factors blocking economic self-regulation', in *Tendencies for Systemic Changes in the Second Phase of the Polish Economic Reform*, Wroclaw, Polskie Towarzystvo Economiczne (Polish Economic Association).

Kalecki, M. and Kowalik, T. (1971) 'Osservazioni sulla "riforma cruciale" ('Thoughts about the "crucial reform"',) *Politica ed Economia* 2–3; for an English edition, see 'Observations on the "Crucial Reform"', in M. Kalecki, *Collected Works*, vol.ii, Oxford 1991, Clarendon Press.

Kierunki reformy gospodarczej (1981) ('Directions of economic reform', in Polish), Warszawa, Komisja do spraw Reformy Gospodarczej.

Kolarska, L. (1985) 'Social interests, egalitarian values, and changes in the economic order' (in Polish), *Studia Socjologiczne* 2.

Kornai, J. (1986) 'The Hungarian reform process: visions, hopes, and reality', *Journal of Economic Literature* 24 (4), 1687–744.

Kowalik, T. (1986) 'On crucial reform of real socialism', Research Report no. 122, The Vienna Institute for Comparative Economic Studies.

Kozek, W. (1986) 'Reasons for breakdown of Polish economic reforms' (in Polish), *Studia Socjologiczne* 3.

Laky, T. (1980) 'The hidden mechanism of recentralization in Hungary', *Acta Oeconomica* 24 (1–2).

'List of posts which require consultation, recommendation and approval by the Central Committee, the Politbureau, and the Secretariat of the Polish United Workers' Party's Central Committee' (in Polish) (1987) *Dwadziescia Jeden*, 4.

MacShane, D. (1981) *Solidarity: Poland's Independent Trade Union*, Nottingham, Spokesman.

Morawski, W. (1986) 'Economic and political reforms as counter-crisis measures', in J. J. Wiatr (ed.) *Satisfying the Needs under Crisis* (in Polish), Instytut Socjologii, Uniwersytet Warszawski.

Narojek, W. (1986) *Prospects of Pluralism in Etatist Society* (in Polish), Londyn, Aneks.

Nuti, D.M. (1986) 'Michał Kalecki's contribution to the theory and practice of socialist planning', *Cambridge Journal of Economics* 10 (4).

Osiatynski, J., Pankòw, W. and Federowicz, M. (1985) *Self-Management in the Polish Economy, 1981–1985*, Bologna, Biblioteca Walter Bigiavi.

Osiatynski, J. (1991) 'Opposition against market breakthrough reforms revisited', paper presented to the conference "Positive Legacy. Obstacles to the Transformation in Eastern Europe', Vienna, IWM

Rychard, A. (1987) *Power and Interests in the Polish Economy in the early 1980s* (in Polish), Uniwersytet, Warszawski.

Rychard, A. (1988) 'Social and political preconditions for and consequences of economic reforms in Poland', Research Report no. 14, The Vienna Institute for Comparative Economic Studies.

Staniszkis, J. (1972) *Pathologies of Organization* (in Polish), Warszawa, Ossolineum.

Staniszkis, J. (1980) 'Systemic conditioning of the functioning of an industrial enterprise' (in Polish), *Przegled Socjologiczny* 30.

Szczepanski, J. (1987) 'Economic values' (in Polish), *Zycie Gospodarcze* 10.

Szelényi, I. (1989) 'Eastern Europe in an epoch of transition: toward a socialist mixed economy?' in V. Nee and D. Stark (eds) *Remaking the Economic Institutions of Socialism*, Stanford, Stanford University Press, 208–32.

Zienkowski, L. (1986) *Struggle for distribution of incomes* (in Polish), Warszawa, Glòwny Urzed Statystyczny.

17 Macroeconomic policy for the transitional reforms in the centrally-planned economies

Leon Podkaminer

> Equilibration of the economy necessitates a restructuring of prices and incomes . . . Prices of goods must be made to correctly reflect the demand-supply conditions while the monetary incomes have to be linked, in a fair manner, to the effects of the workers' performance.
>
> (From 'The Governmental Program of the Second Stage of Economic Reform', Warsaw, 1987:4)

INTRODUCTION

If there is a shortage of sausage, it is respectable in economics to advocate its higher price. It is equally respectable not to advocate higher wages, and instead, to invoke moralistic concepts ('fairness') even if there is a shortage of labour. This asymmetry in the economists' attitudes towards formally indistinguishable economic parameters seems to have been with the profession since the days of Adam Smith. Nowadays it survives in the political and economic debates in the west. Clearly, it has also been always present in the prevailing views on the proper macroeconomic policy of the centrally-planned economies (CPEs). It is particularly interesting that in this respect the reform economists do not really differ from the veteran hardliners of the command system.

The asymmetric treatment of prices and wages in the CPEs is not a mere intellectual or academic curiosity. It transforms into the actual mode of operation of various social and economic institutions and, most directly, into specific macroeconomic policies affecting the markets for goods and labour. The consequences of instinctive management of wages and prices may be dismal.

The subject is of critical importance, especially as we try to establish some hypothetical visions (or 'theories') of the reform processes in the CPEs. This is because, while there is some understanding of the initial conditions from which the reforms start and of the terminal conditions to which they should lead, the transition proper seems to have been an underdeveloped subject. Yet clumsy or mistaken macro-policy during the transition, and in particular, the policies having a direct bearing on the economy's equilibrium, inflation, income distribution, living standards will determine the fate of the systemic changes.

We want to advance three specific propositions in this paper. First, there is the issue of the general role of macroeconomic policies in maintaining conditions conducive to the fulfilment of the major goals of the reform process. We would argue that 'no macroeconomic policy' will, given the prevailing instincts, tend to become a rather bad macro-policy. Second, unlike many 'reform radicals' we would defend a view that some price controls, even if contrary to the new dogmas, may constitute a valuable part of a useful macro-policy consistent with the ultimate goals of the systemic reforms. Third, there is a very broad set of issues related to the labour problems which includes closely-connected phenomena: labour market disequilibrium, real wages, living standards, pay systems. Although we do not intend to develop here any definitive treatise on 'labour and reform', we shall suggest that a key macro-guideline for the successful transitional reform may well turn out to stipulate for a sustained rise in real wages.

The general role of macroeconomic policies during the transitional reforms

The distrust or negligence of any more active macro-management, detectable among the reform economists, has a definite 'conservative' flavour. In this respect they resemble typical western conservatives who also distrust institutional arrangements giving some effective power to a central bureaucracy. (There are other similarities too, over attitudes to social services, subsidies, unemployment, income inequality. Often the welfare state ideals of the western social democrats seem less preferable to the reformers than Social Darwinism lurking behind the ideals of the western Right. A clinical test of their social attitudes is provided by their easy acceptance of 'austerity measures' – as far as wages are concerned – and enthusiasm for 'adequate incentives' – when it comes to private enterprise and initiative.)

Yet the history of economic development of the market economies supports the view that some degree of interventionism through macro-policies may be a necessity quite regardless of the 'systemic properties' of the economies in question.[1]

The task of successful macro-policy is difficult because it has to respond to the signals emitted by the economy. And these signals tend to be 'coded' and sometimes convey misleading messages. Disequilibria in particular are bound to entail great interpretative difficulties.[2] The correct 'decoding' of the confusing evidence arising under disequilibrium requires, first of all, a much better understanding of the intricacies of contemporary western economics – but also of the true complication of a macro-policy even if conducted in an unreformed CPE. It should no longer be acceptable to restrict the macro-analysis and policy for the CPEs as fully conforming to a crude monetarism (as proposed by Portes). Equally refutable seems the 'theory' endowing the central decision-makers in the CPEs with various super-human virtues: complete command of modern (and perfectly adequate) macroeconomics, perfect knowledge of all relevant macro-parameters and good intentions (That is, fixation on maximization of the social welfare function.)[3]

There is also a diametrically different image of the 'central planners' (be they classical bureaucrats busying themselves with sending production directives, or inventing rules and regulations on wages and prices). The image emerging from the writings of the leading Polish and Hungarian economists is one of the sluggish, incompetent, careless and selfish imbeciles following or extending ('perfecting') some absurd routines. In neither vision do the central planners learn by doing. In the former they already know everything worth knowing. In the latter they have no incentive to learn – presumably because things are too difficult to be understood anyway.

Between the two polar images there is, in all probability, a place for bureaucracies capable of and striving for improvements in their own performance. Without such an 'ideal' bureaucracy, capable of learning by doing, which will probably only emerge under special conditions, any hope for a successful transitional reform seems unrealistic.[4]

While having little else to say about other ('moral' and 'social') conditions conducive to a successful macroeconomics of the transition, we believe we can contribute a bit to the purely 'technocratic' qualities of the potential policy-makers. To do so we now have to start a much more technical discussion of specific economic issues.

Macroeconomic management of prices

Western authors writing about centrally-planned economies have always emphasized the existence of disequilibria in the consumer goods markets. To them it has been a quite natural consequence of the rigidities of central planning and fixed prices (especially the relative ones). In absence of fairly unregulated and competitive markets with sufficiently flexible prices and under the supply-side's notorious irresponsiveness to the market signals, imbalances between the demand for and supply of various goods are to be expected. In contrast to the market economies where there are forces constantly at work to eliminate visible (and even invisible) excess supply and excess demand for any commodity, no such forces have been so far operating on any appreciable scale in the CPEs. (Certainly, the 'market forces' of competition do operate on the black markets and in the underground economies of the CPEs. Also, some legalized private sectors are permitted in some CPEs.)

The disequilibria in the CPEs tend to be extensive, persistent and one-sided (that is, characterized by prevalences of excess demand). In contrast, in the market economies the disequilibria tend to be rather 'shallow', short-lived and 'one-sided' (that is, characterized by alteration of periods of excess demand and excess supply, with more visible signs of persistent excess supply.

Interestingly, for a long period of time the East European economists did not show much interest in the subject of disequilibrium in the consumer market. Much more important to them was the disequilibrium between the supply of and the demand for material production inputs – as leading to their rationing, inefficient allocation among productive uses and to the loss of potential output. Disequilibria in the consumer markets were primarily viewed as harmful because of their effect on the producers who are relieved from competitive pressures arising under equilibrium or excess supply. The fact that consumers might not like the imbalances was regarded as something relatively unimportant – both in economic and socio-political terms. As long as the volume of consumption grew quite fast and the shortages did not intensify beyond 'reasonable' or 'normal' levels, the situation was, in effect, rather inconsequential. There were many doubts among the East European economists about seriousness of theoretical or empirical enquiry focusing on the 'consumer'. This is a lasting legacy of Marxist refutation of 'bourgeois' approach to economics, overstressing the role of 'individual' and 'ahistorical' and not 'mass' and 'historical' forces.

This helped to preclude serious study of the consumer needs. Planning of the supplies of consumer goods – and also the regulation of the demand for them – was left to the bureaucrats and decision-makers on the assumption that this is a practical problem which is best resolved by experienced practitioners. It is only relatively recently that the East European economists have started to pay much more attention to the subject. Kornai's (1979), (1980) and (1982) path-breaking contributions are still relatively fresh. It is therefore natural that they contain many elements and implications yet to be critically appraised. In particular, Kornai's reasoning implies a fairly static model of the centrally-planned economies. Shortages or disequilibra are not seen as experiencing significant or characteristic movements over time. Also, their connection with the investment's fluctuations is, despite references to earlier literature on the subject, rather weak. Of course, Kornai correctly stresses the overwhelming presence and importance of the shortages. Yet, persistent shortages are hypothesized to be an inherent feature of the CPEs, necessarily following their systemic properties. One implication of Kornai's vision is that, before some form of fundamental reform is successfully carried through, the tendency of the shortages to conform to some 'normal' pattern must prevail.

Now we come to the most crucial and yet very delicate problem. Should the reform stipulate, together with other radical systemic changes, for the removal of all constraints on price-setting (and thus, hopefully, unleash the long-absent equilibrating forces) or, rather, at least during the transition, should it accept some forms of bureaucratic controls and supervision over pricing? The answer to this dilemma, as far as we can see, has tended to affirm an indispensability of free pricing. Yet there are some grounds to favour the alternative option.

First, it is quite essential that we better understand and define the concept of equilibrium and of equilibrating processes in the market economies.

It is misleading to identify the real life of market economies with equilibrium. It is only in the elementary textbook microeconomics that the general equilibrium and the competitive free market system are identical. In practice free and competitive markets (and even more so the imperfectly competitive ones) have a tendency towards elimination of revealed imbalances. This does not lead necessarily to a general equilibrium. Protracted imbalances under the market system (for example, on the labour market) indicate that, unlike in the Walrasian model, it can fail to produce equilibrium. This important fact is often overlooked by the reform economists who identify the reform with strict equilibrium.[5] Importantly, the policy-makers in the CPEs often use a similar argument. The economic reform must await equilibrium. This is not correct. Some rationing and price controls do not preclude competition and a fairly efficient profit-oriented decentralized system. Then, it is often and quite incorrectly assumed that price flexibility is a universally good thing. This is not necessarily so. Price rigidity is, under sufficient supply and demand flexibility, equally conducive to efficiency, without exposing the economy to inflationary or deflationary risks. Let us go back now to practical lessons folllowing the attempts at price liberalization conducted, at various times, in various CPEs. One universal lesson is that these attempts resulted in intensified inflation without inducing any perceivable equilibration of the markets. One interpretation of this phenomenon should perhaps point out to the fact that abandonment of the policy of price stability, or acceleration in inflation may generate inflationary expectations on the part of the consumers who may be motivated to mobilize their voluntary savings and attempt to convert them into consumer goods (particularly the durables) sooner rather than later. Paradoxically, higher prices may also – at least in the short run – mean higher demand. On the same principle, a reduction in prices, even in face of falling supply, or deceleration of open inflation in favour of the repressed one, may stimulate deflationary expectations resulting in lower current demand and higher voluntary savings. The policy of frozen prices may be very well justified just as a rational tool of temporary stabilization policy. Certainly, it must be clearly understood that the policy of stimulating expectations probably never can go on indefinitely. There are some time horizons, and usually (dimly) perceived thresholds, when the consumers may, after all, want to enjoy the fruits of their thrift. If then their money appears to be unable to buy goods in the market, a disaster is likely to follow.[6]

Besides, even if we rule out 'perversive' expectational aspects of the changes in prices and incomes so that the voluntary savings decisions of the consumers are no longer affected by these speculative considerations, there is yet another, and possibly crucial, element. Namely, even if falling real wages (or real purchasing power of the consumers' monetary assets) assure, in purely arithmetical sense, the reduction in total demand, there may be some side-effects of this policy. The discussion of these feedbacks is reserved for the next chapter. Presently it may suffice to say that falling real wages may – under conceivable circumstances – affect the 'normal' shortage of labour (and the quality thereof) in such a way as to additionally upset the 'normal' operation of the economy. Hence the cure applied to heal one unwelcome consequence of expanding investment (that is, expanding aggregate excess demand for consumer goods) may be worse than the illness itself. For, it may unfavourably affect, via falling supply of labour, the supply of consumer goods. It follows from the preceding reasoning that the maintenance of 'normal' aggregate excess demand for consumer goods through the manipulation of the overall real wage bill and overall price index – and hence of the aggregate nominal price and wage movements – is a quite risky task, unlikely to be realized without some knowledge of mass psychology (that is, expectations) and intricate determinants of the supply of labour. The questions related to the advisable manipulation of relative prices of various consumer goods, in accordance with changing relative scarcities of the supplies, may seem much simpler. According to Engel Law, with growing incomes the demand for food stagnates while the demand for other goods accelerates. This tendency underlies observed structural changes in the world economy – and, of course, observed decline of the necessities' sector. This tendency is absent from the CPEs. As a matter of fact, food tends to become rather more expensive in all East European countries secularly, irrespectively of the timing of their remarkable investment cycles. Apparently, Kornai's 'normal' path of relative prices' developments stipulates for making food still more expensive – while in the market economies it tends to become relatively cheaper and cheaper (and this despite the protectionist polices with respect to agriculture).

There are several reasons why pricing of the consumer goods does not conform to the theoretically-justifiable expectations. First, in pricing of the consumer goods the authorities tend to follow the proportions once introduced and apparently 'working'. This is the 'normal' inertia of risk averse behaviour in hierarchies.

Second, when the changes are made, there are often some specific reasons given to rationalize the otherwise 'normal' outcomes of decision-making. One such reason, often referred to when prices are changed, is that food prices are heavily subsidized, while various non-food commodity prices contain huge turnover tax or profits. This is considered to be unacceptable, upsetting the whole operation of the national economy. Yet this is not a valid case because the prices used in the evaluation of the costs (and hence of the eventual 'subsidies' and 'profits') related to various commodities represent fictitious entities. Under alternative pricing of inputs, the commodities that seem to have caused deficits may turn out to be highly profitable – and vice versa. In the specific case of foodstuffs, regarded as responsible for the losses of the state budgets in all East European countries, the major factor responsible for the apparently high costs may have been the mistaken doctrine of the parity of incomes of rural and urban population. If the rural-urban income differentials had been allowed to be shaped by relative productivities then rural incomes would have been much lower than the urban ones. Third, the authorities may have vested interests in supporting distorted relative prices. Fast rising prices of many 'luxuries' such as cars, housing, access to elitist services of high quality would deprive their nominal monetary incomes, of much of their real (yet hidden) purchasing power. The welfare loss would not be even approximately offset by lower relative prices of foodstuffs whose weight in the total expenditure of higher income groups tends to be low (Engel Law). Certainly, keeping the prices of 'luxuries' administratively depressed creates their shortages. Yet the authorities themselves, and their clientele need not worry much about that. Because they themselves supervise the distribution of these 'attractive' goods, they can be always assured of the satisfaction of their own needs – and at the artifically low prices, too.[7]

There is yet a fourth reason underlying incorrect relative price response under investment expansion. This is related to the sufficiently distorted relative prices of goods supplied to the market. Namely, 'normal' shortages of undersupplied (or underpriced) goods tend not only to increase the stocks of savings kept by the consumers (That is, add to their) 'inflationary overhang', or 'compulsory savings'), but also they tend to increase the demand for other, possibly unrelated, goods and services. This is the essence of the concept of 'forced substitution' or 'spillover effect' discussed extensively in Kornai (1980) or, with the application of the formal tools of the theory of neo-classical household behaviour under rationing, in Podkaminer (1982, 1988a).

The spillover story is the following: increasing excess demand for a group of goods (in the case of investment expansions these tend to be housing, durables and other industrially-produced consumer goods and services) increases observed demand for all other commodities – such as foodstuffs, alcohol, tobacco and apparel. As long as the observed or effective (that is, spillover-increased) demand for food (or alcohol, tobacco or any other good) is lower than their corresponding supplies, there may be little justification for the view that higher food prices are justified by their shortages. Because 'normally' there has been little place in the centrally-planned economies for the actual supplies of anything to be much higher than observed demand, the barrier of the availability of foodstuffs is usually approached quite quickly. In this situation, the impression would be that the shortage of foodstuffs (and also of alcohol, tobacco and apparel) grow. In a sense this is true: given all relevant parameters, the consumers would want to buy more food than available. This creates lines, hoarding, profiteering, black markets, and also may sanction official rationing of foodstuffs. In a sense, too, it is true that higher prices of food would cut the level of the observed demand for it and hence restore a more acceptable partial equilibrium on the food market. Yet, at the same time, a more general analysis indicates that equilibrium achievable simultaneously on the foodstuffs and 'luxuries' markets would require counter-intuitive policies. Namely, it would require that prices of the 'luxuries' be raised relative to those of the foodstuffs – thus making the latter relatively cheaper. Or, if the relative quantities are considered, it would require that the supplies of 'luxuries' be increased – even if this must mean cuts in the supplies of foodstuffs.

The appearance at some stage of economic development (often during the investment expansion and often during the attempted reforms) of intensive food shortages is then as inevitable, as it is misleading and likely to result in various decisions, which in the end, adversely affect the continuation of the investment plans and the reforms.

Unlike the shortages of many luxuries, which tend to go unnoticed and may evade any publicity, the evidence of shortages of foodstuffs, eventually evoking the image of famine, has always been of major social and political importance. Various centrally-planned economies have tried various methods for overcoming their serious, if transient food 'shortages'. A reflection on theses methods is important because they partly explain the appearance of inflationary tendencies. Moreover, they also partly explain the structural retardation of some CPEs, manifested by the high level of agricultural investment and employment.

The first subject to comment on is the propensity of the Polish, Hungarian and Yugoslav (recently also by the Chinese and the Soviet) authorities to eradicate 'excessive' demand for food by means of raising food prices. In itself, while this policy cannot bring about equilibrium in the markets for undersupplied luxuries, it can, given sufficient determination of the authorities, result in reducing the spillover-induced demand for food to the level of available supply. However, there are usually some other side-effects of this approach defeating the original purpose of the scheme. With growing food prices, too many low-income groups come under the pressure of intolerably high costs of basic necessities. This easily translates into a politically explosive potential.

The food price increases inevitably result in higher monetary incomes, minimum wages and family allowances intended to sustain the (low) living standards of a large part of the population. This has some further consequences. Rising monetary incomes of the poorest social strata upsets the income differentials throughout the society. Hence, this directly affects the effort levels and productivity of the income groups whose incomes were not increased. With some delay – and at the cost of foregone output – this must be corrected by extending the income increases to the higher-income groups. In an arithmetical sense there is, therefore, no actual gain in increasing the food prices. The compensation paid out to the consumers tend to be, in the end, much higher. Hence, eventually, the 'price reforms' do not make much of economic sense even if aimed solely at the reduction of the demand for food. Certainly, under equilibrium, the demand for any good is unlikely to be affected by simultaneous increase in income and the goods prices. Under disequilibrium, the food price increases make the undersupplied (that is, underpriced) non-food goods even cheaper. Thus they incite even greater excess demand for these goods – and, consequently, even greater spillover-induced demand for food. Clearly, the food price 'reforms' are self-defeating. Moreover, they are responsible for the bursts of accelerating and otherwise superfluous and avoidable open inflation.

By way of conclusion, it may be stated that the absence of consciously-designed price policies is likely to result in inflationary processes without easing the market disequilibrium. The price controls have so far been unsuccessful, not because they always have to be detrimental. Their failures stem from misunderstanding of the character of disequilibrium.

Macroeconomic policies and the labour issues

Typical disequilibria on the consumer goods market have an important impact on the quality and quantity of labour supplied by the consumers. Our analysis so far has suggested that as shortages intensify, one should expect falling quality and quantity of work supplied by the consumers. A sufficiently high level of shortage of consumer goods should therefore be accompanied by growing labour problems: falling productivity, mounting shortages of workers, increased absenteeism, abnormally high turnover, declining quality of work performed, and so on.

The consumers' reluctance to work more or less 'normally' in an abnormally deteriorating market situation may thus precipitate an avalanche of delays, unforeseen costs, foregone output, and so on.

There are numerous opinions about the state of the labour markets in the CPEs and about the policies to be resorted to. While some experts deny the existence of persistent labour shortages (Portes and his followers) some others (Kornai) hold the opposite view. A basic, almost linguistical error in the interpretation of the facts is often made by the commentators calling what they observe in Eastern Europe 'hidden unemployment', or 'unemployment of the employed'. Often such definitions are used in connection with comments on the 'policy of full employment adopted by the socialist countries'. However, if involuntary unemployment is to denote the presence of statistically significant numbers of persons unsuccessfully seeking employment at (or even below) the going wage rates, then quite obviously the East European (ex-) socialist countries have never suffered from it. Although some genuine unemployment might occur regionally and affect some groups of population (for example, the women), the vacancies have always tended to exceed, many-fold, the aggregate numbers of persons looking for jobs. And both of these numbers have always been minor fractions of the labour turnover. 'Hidden unemployment' is a useful term to describe the falsification of statistics meant to conceal the genuine level of involuntary unemployment. It does not make, however, any sense to describe a situation characterized by poor utilization of persons actually employed. It may be true that, with lower total employment, the productivity of the employees would probably be much higher, or even that the total output would be higher. Still, we do not see it proper to describe such a situation as 'unemployment of the employed'. For, it would suggest that if, by some order or administrative decree, the total level of employment were reduced, the output and productivity would rise generally (partly because of the revealed or restored open involuntary unemployment).

The suggestion that an across-the-board, administratively-enacted, reduction in the level of employment would have a salutary effect on productivity and inflation can be encountered in 'reform' proposals. Of course, this does not make much sense because any general and indiscriminate reduction in employment would victimize the enterprises where labour is utilized efficiently while not affecting the ones where it is actually redundant. Output in the economy subject to indiscriminate reduction of employment would be reduced. The positive effects of involuntary unemployment (if any) might well be smaller than the losses of foregone output. Moreover, the bulk of the laid-off workers would probably consist of 'trouble-makers' – That is, innovative, efficient and socially-minded employees usually disliked by the bureaucratic management of the state-owned enterprises. A selective reduction of employment, combined with the closing of obsolete and inefficient plants, or a retreat from structurally-backward and unpromising sectors such as agriculture, shipbuilding and mining could have truly beneficial effects. Certainly, if the centre should be expected to help distinguish between promising and unpromising sectors, there is no instrument other than the market competition to eliminate inefficient enterprises employing too much labour in particular sectors.

Similarly, we do not see it proper to ascribe to the East European countries any consciously adopted priority for full employment. True, the authorities often locate the new investments in the regions where surpluses of labour can be detected. However, this may be caused by a concern about labour shortages prevailing in other locations, and not necessarily about the situation of the population of the relatively underdeveloped areas.

The centrally-fixed levels of total employment tend to be universally lower than actually realized. This would corroborate the notion that the actual employment levels reflect some mix of macroeconomic policies and systemic features not necessarily corresponding to the alleged preference for full employment. There may be no intention to keep full employment. To talk about full employment as an achievement of the East European countries is to make a virtue out of possibly unintended, or even regretted, coincidence.[8]

There is a relatively uncontroversial issue of the 'systemic' causes of high demand for labour observed in the CPEs. It is generally accepted that the labour shortages are endemic because the enterprises' demand for labour (not unlike for any other inputs) does not tend to be curbed by considerations of eventual costs and profits. Given the fact that the factory managers may get penalized for the unfulfilment of the production tasks, it is natural to expect 'insatiable' demand for all inputs.

As long as the motivation system is more output-oriented than efficiency- (or cost-) oriented, the unreliability of the supplies of material inputs may be countered by means of labour buffer stocks. An adequate size of the permanently employed labour force becomes essential. Although this behaviour, called 'labour hoarding', is often viewed as harmful, it is not unambiguously such. The total output of the economy where the firms did not hoard labour would not necessarily be higher.

The 'insatiable' demand for labour, and hence the permanent labour shortages, do create conditions conducive to a deterioration of work ethics, productivity, effort and quality and induce abnormally high levels of labour turnover, having clearly devastating effects. Also, it is quite obvious how this contributes to increased waste of material inputs, energy and careless utilization of the machinery and equipment. There is some imprecision, yet, in the implication that the labour shortages can, after all, be blamed on the 'lack of discipline' or the 'permissiveness' of socialist managers. A further implication of this interpretation is that it would be possible to eradicate the low productivity – and hence labour shortage – with a sufficiently determined political or administrative campaign restoring 'order and discipline'. Symptomatic is the view that

> the socialist countries are confronted with a known cure which, however, cannot be effectively applied for various reasons. To cure the tight [labour] market effectively would require. . . . the tightening of labour discipline in all respects. Tightening labour discipline beyond a certain point is almost impossible in socialist countries. Workers need some vent for their frustration . . . To deprive them of that privilege would be dangerous.
>
> (Adam 1987: xv–xvi)

We do not think that this train of thought properly reflects the actual causation. For one thing, the lack of strong and committed trade unions capable of protecting the workers against arbitrary decisions of the managers and the comparatively rather harsh provisions of the labour laws, effectively minimizing the employees' rights *vis-à-vis* those of the managers, permit and often encourage quite outrageous behaviour towards the employees, especially towards the blue-collar workers. If this behaviour tends to be somehow contained, it is chiefly because its ferocity has been blunted by labour shortages. The managers consider it wiser to accept some 'normal' misconduct of the employees for fear of their plants being deserted. And the workers, especially in big urban areas where there are many state-owned firms competing for labour, have been learning the limits of their relative immunity.[9]

An interesting alternative view of the labour situation is provided in a recent contribution by Rosefielde (1988), developing some earlier ideas about the state of the socialist labour market proposed by Birman. Basically, the core of this contribution seems to me very convincing. Yet its verbal presentation is likely to cause immense confusion. Rosefielde and Birman correctly notice that in the Soviet Union work is often extracted from the population by administrative means, and not on the basis of contracts accepted voluntarily by the employees. This, however, does not seem to justify the notion that labour supply is excessive at the going real wage rate:

> Labour demand [that is, the demand for labour], like non-labour demand [that is, the demand for other production factors], is derived from desired levels of product supply, but wages are not set above reservation levels . . . As a consequence, with supply [of labour] established by obligatory work laws and wages, labour is normally not in a state of shortage. The labour participation rate exceeds the competitive norm because of shortage. The labour participation rate exceeds the competitive norm because more people are compelled to work than would voluntarily offer services at the going wage.
>
> (Rosefielde 1988,230)

Now, even if obligatory work laws and other regulations[10] serving to secure a desirable level of total labour supply (matching the total demand for labour fixed in the central plan) are believed to be succesfully manipulated by the central authorities, at the micro-level the enterprises may – and often do – try to employ more workers (or to require longer working hours) than visualized by the centre. Hence actual demand for labour may exceed the (involuntarily extracted) 'supply' of it. The sum total of the actual demands for labour may be much greater than the available total supply of it – even if the central authorities successfully nationalized the population's entire free-time resources. Again, it is a mistake to equate high labour participation rate with the absence of labour shortage.

Besides, the work laws may possibly look very restrictive. Yet, it may be legitimately questioned whether they always determine the actual labour supply. It is not implausible to assume that their abolition would not make any visible difference. Moreover, the very existence of obligatory work laws may suggest that there is a general labour shortage (or, otherwise, that the authorities believe it to be).

Consideration of the factors contributing to the supply of labour is now in order. Certainly, there are many ways in which the formation of the labour supply may be approached. A highly stylized economic model that disregards many important psychological, sociological, organizational and other aspects of the problem (akin to Malinvaud's 1977 model of quantity-constrained households' behaviour in the market economies) suggests the following qualifications.

In presence of simultaneous involuntary employment of labour and rationing of consumer goods, the restoration of equilibrium in both labour and goods' markets may require a *rise* in real wages – that is, in nominal wages (rising faster than nominal prices). The visible manifestations of disequilibrium, usually observed in the CPEs, do not provide any obvious and generally valid basis for the policy of *falling* real wages that are universally suggested by the economists during the reforms.

An example of the difficulties in prescribing correct policies is provided by Rosefielde (1988,231, 241–3) who believes that it follows from the neo-classical analysis that 'involuntary excess supply of labour' (that is, rationing of leisure) is intensified by both diminution of real wages and curtailments in the supply of consumer goods. As far as the variable component of 'involuntary excess supply of labour' is identified with supply of labour (that is, when we assume that the level of demand for labour is given, and so is the upper bound on leisure), this need not be true. In particular, under normality of leisure and consumption of goods the correct result is the following. If higher supply of consumer goods induces higher supply of labour then lower real wage rate induces higher labour supply (and vice versa). In other words, if labour supply happens to be actively constrained by shortages of goods (and hence by diminishing marginal utility of earnings) then making goods even cheaper (through rising real wages) results in further accumulation of involuntary savings, and hence cannot in any way induce the households to voluntarily supply more labour.

Certainly, it would be utterly unrealistic to suppose that the macro-economic price-and-wage policies in the CPEs have been derived from a clear-cut and rigorous analysis of the sort suggested above. Yet, in a sense, the basic macro-policy followed quite universally in East European countries can be identified as the policy of minimizing real wages. Hence it is perhaps acceptable to view the authorities in the CPEs as primarily aiming at reduction of the dangers of too big an excess demand for the consumer goods.

Whether or not justifiable on macroeconomic grounds, the persistent policy of minimizing the real wages – in times goods and bad, and irrespectively of the given phase of the investment cycle – may have had profound negative effects, which were rarely, if ever, clearly perceived by the economists usually sharing the economic decision-makers' anxieties about the 'wage inflation' problem.

The first effect relates to the depressed labour costs at least partly responsible for the size, severity and the overall consequences of the labour shortages. The labour shortages prevailing in the CPEs cannot be blamed on too low a supply of labour. Rather, as rightly pointed out by many authors, they should be seen as related to the abnormally high demand for labour formed by the state-owned enterprises. Certainly, the standard explanation for the labour-demand formation in the CPEs has invoked a 'systemic' insensitivity of the public employers to any costs and profits. Yet, it is perhaps important to acknowledge that the demand for especially cheap inputs – such as labour – could be inflated even if costs and profits mattered. Quite possibly, the 'insatiable' demand-for-inputs syndrome described by Kornai has stricken roots and persisted only because the inputs in question are so grossly undervalued relative to the output prices.

Certainly, if the enterprises are allowed to increase their prices mechanically (for example, by constant mark-ups on their costs) or they can always expect to be bailed out by subsidies when not being able to repay the debts incurred, there may be little use to advocate higher nominal wages. Ultimately, on the macroeconomic level this policy would only amount to open or repressed inflation. However, the policy of rising real wages ultimately implies nominal wages rising faster than nominal prices. This implies that stricter controls are being imposed on prices than on wages.

This policy may be expected to have some salutary, equilibrating effects with respect to the labour markets. Basically, the effects would appear because the firms would at last have an economic incentive for rationalization of employment. Equally important is that technologically obsolete firms, and sectors employing too much labour per unit of output, could not continue to rely on the administrative allocation of cheap labour. Outcompeted from the labour market, the wasteful producers would have to cease their operations. Under sufficiently strong rise in real wages, lower employment could be expected to produce higher output. Whether or not the total wage bill would, in the short run, rise faster than the total output (and in particular the total supply of consumer goods) is a separate question. The most important effect would be the absence of labour shortages. This would start an absolutely new phase in the developments of the labour relationships in the CPEs.

In macroeconomic analysis labour supply and demand are treated in purely quantitative terms, as amounts of working time. The issue of the quality of work performed is, however, probably as important. Yet, it is also much more intricate. Its consideration has been conspicuously avoided by most economists interested in the CPEs.

Ultimately, work quality is related to the quality of goods and services. The absence of shortages of both consumer goods and labour are important prerequisites of the improved quality of work. With the disappearance of labour shortages, some discipline of the labour force (constraining work shirking, absenteeism, abnormally high and destructive levels of labour turnover, and so on) may start to develop. The motivational role of some unemployment may not be especially strong unless the wages earned by the employed are substantially higher than the incomes and benefits to which the unemployed are entitled. Keeping the wages of the employed at relatively low levels will therefore defeat the purpose of 'motivational' unemployment.[11]

There are also some other qualitative implications of the levels of real wages (and living standards). First, too low real wages, while possibly inducing maximum supply of the quantity of labour, imply low levels of leisure enjoyed by average households. Leisure, however, may be deemed a 'superfluous luxury' only beyond some thresholds. Some relaxation, like adequate nutrition, humane housing and transportation, proper education and health services have important productive consequences. They endow the work-force with necessary physical and mental abilities indispensable for quantitatively and qualitatively valuable performance. Too low wages inducing the households to cut excessively on the consumption of the inputs responsible for the work potential (including leisure) are counterproductive even from a narrowly-technocratic point of view. Not infrequently, the inefficiencies of the CPEs, and especially their labour problems, are blamed on the excessive levels of supplies of free goods provided by the state-owned health, education, transportation, and so on, services. According to the former Polish official propaganda, this welfare-state approach is responsible for the weakening motivation for hard work, and so incompatible with the 'economic reform'. In view of the comparatively meagre quantity (and very poor quality) of the social services provided free-of-charge in most CPEs, the opposite view seems to be correct. Commercialization or reprivatization of these services is likely to further diminish the quality of life and hence also contribute to deteriorating work quality.

Second, too low real wages – like their stagnation – tend to narrow the wage differentials, which otherwise could play a positive motivational role. Third, while too low real wages induce a very large quantity of labour supplied by the households, they will quite automatically depress its average quality. The reason for this is very simple. At a high level of employment, labour of intrinsically lower quality (for example, supplied by persons mentally or physically handicapped) is employed along with intrinsically more valuable labour. Under these circumstances, the performance standards may tend to be adjusted to the levels of the least efficient persons. (Hence, high real wages discouraging both excessive supply of labour and excessive demand for it, are essential.)

Of course, it may be argued that under the pay systems linking individual employees' earnings to their individual performance the wages may, in general, remain low without causing significant deterioration of the performance standards or the income differentials. However, this argument implicitly assumes that individual performances are being constantly monitored and quantitatively rated – as in the well-known piece-rate systems. Yet, monitoring is neither costless nor neutral with respect to many qualitative aspects of the work performance. Any pay system relying on excessively individualized rewards has many drawbacks often overlooked by economists insisting on 'linking rewards to performance'. The progressive disappearance of the piece-rate systems in the advanced market economies may be in part attributed to the fact that these systems are useful mainly in promoting maximum quantitative output, under fairly static technological conditions.

The dominant role of the piece-rate systems in the CPEs (and especially in the USSR) can probably be explained by the preference given to maximization of the quantities produced of various, otherwise pretty homogeneous, goods. Of course, to some extent the reliance on these systems is explained by the state of the labour markets and the levels of real wages. Because it is difficult to develop and cultivate, under excessively high labour turnover, long-run loyalties and goodwill between the employees and the employers, the piece-rate systems appear to be of immediate practical avail.[12] Certainly, there is some negative feedback here. Once implemented, the piece-rate systems tend to hinder co-operation, and hence provide for the self-perpetuation of casual relationships between the managers and the managed.

The correct strategy for the elimination of the low productivity syndrome in the CPEs differs from the usual prescriptions advocated by other authors. Equilibrium of the markets for consumer goods and labour is seen as a very important element. The usual policy of falling real wages may lead to counter-productive outcomes. A constructive policy stipulates rather for rising real wages. Of course, correct macro-policy may also fail to bear fruit. Unless supplemented by various 'reform' measures effectively restoring not only the market institutions, but first of all, the refined institutions of contemporary capitalism, the policy of high real wages may soon bring about hyperinflation and the collapse of any economic order. The policy of rising real wages should also be supplemented by an extensive modernization of the pay systems and income policies, often heading into counter-intuitive directions. Apparently, economy-oriented, unduly individualized pay systems should be substituted with those stipulating for wise egalitarianism in earnings policies, emphasizing the role of seniority, rewarding such apparently elusive characteristics as 'loyalty' and 'dedication'. The missing component of labour quality will not only require high wages and the absence of persistent labour shortages, but also the development of 'goodwill' or 'co-operative moods'. Without these elements the innovative behaviour – and ultimately higher profits associated with outstanding quality – are unlikely.[13]

CONCLUDING REMARKS: REFORMS, MACROECONOMIC POLICIES AND INSTITUTIONS

The task of correct macroeconomic manipulation of the instruments to which the labour supply and the demand for consumer goods respond is very difficult. Under shortages of consumer goods and labour prevailing in the CPEs, the observable disequilibrium symptoms are likely to be misleading. They may prompt policy actions ultimately defeating their declared purposes.

The emphasis on 'correct' real wages, meant as an indisputable wisdom of the policy of repressed real wages, probably constitutes the most essential fallacy. That this policy is ultimately responsible for the unsatisfactory developments in the CPEs – including their propensity to fluctuate, or, more recently, to decline – may only now become a subject of serious debate.

The recognition of the importance of correctly elaborated, and not instinctive macroeconomic management of the reforms in the CPEs is necessary, though an unregulated decentralized economy may also display destructive fluctuations whose avoidance requires competent macroeconomic policies and competent macroeconomic theorizing.[14] An economic reform accompanied by soaring inflation, intensifying shortages, falling living standards and growing income differentials is unlikely to survive. This is well evidenced by the history of the past 'reform cycles'.

Of course, a successful macroeconomic policy cannot be conservative in the sense of relying only on monetary or even fiscal tools. It must have some say on wider issues. In particular, it cannot give up some responsibility for conscious controls with respect to prices and incomes. The fears about the role of bureaucracy given wide powers on such sensitive matters as prices and wages are, quite understandably, very real as the omnipotence of the governments had been typical in the pre-reform CPEs.

The misuse of the potentially-useful tools cannot yet be a justification for an absolute ban on them. Macroeconomic policies relying on controls and regulations have to be retained in the reformed CPEs. Yet the institutional environment of decision-making must also be altered to rule out discretionary macroeconomic policies. Labour, through its trade unions, has to be given a role in co-determining the policies. And the public at large has to become, through the normal course of democratic processes, ultimately the superior of the policy-makers.

NOTES

The hospitality of The Vienna Institute for Comparative Economic Studies where the final version of this text was prepared is gratefully acknowledged.

1 There is a tendency to restrict macro-policies to a manipulation of monetary or, at best, fiscal instruments. The effectiveness of both has been historically proven to be very limited. Narrowly-defined macro-tools cannot protect against inflation, unemployment, instabilities, recessions and slow growth. It is difficult to see why a narrowly-defined macro-policy should be sufficient for the CPEs during the transition (and after).

2 This holds true also for the market economies where the distinction between classical and Keynesian unemployment may be quite difficult and the policy actions counterproductive (see Malinvaud 1977).

3 This is the theory invented by R. Portes (1979) and underlying numerous 'disequilibrium econometrics' studies for the CPEs.

4 These include the development of authentic national elites taking responsibility for their societies, restoration of parliamentary democracy and a (possibly very slow) evolution from the current social disintegration towards a structured social integration respecting both human individuality and associative needs.

5 The modern understanding of the market processes, stressing the crucial role of the informational aspects of decision-making (for example, as in the rational expectation theories) does not support the simplistic ideas about static equilibrium (see Frydman 1982, Fisher 1983 and Hahn 1985). Among the few authors working on the CPEs who perceive the problem is Dietz (see his paper in this book).

6 For a number of years the Gierek government in Poland successfully gambled on the expectations of the population by increasing monetary incomes and containing the growth of consumer prices. As long as the supplies grew at an appreciable pace, this strategy worked even if the incomes much outpaced the nominal value of the supply of consumer goods. Problems started when supplies fell. The government tried to pre-empt possible market collapse with increased prices – precipitating (or possibly even causing) the collapse.

7 In Podkaminer (1988b) it is demonstrated that the distorted relative prices in Poland were contributing to much higher income inequality than implied by the official face-value data. White-collar workers benefited from the situation much more than other social groups. Importantly, the gains from price distortions are highly correlated with rising nominal expenditure or income, which means regressive income taxation.

8 Early theoreticians of the CPEs (for example, Kalecki) modelled them as consciously pursuing the goal of full employment. Whether that reflected purely theoretical considerations or was a rationalization of the labour shortages that had been as painful in the early 1950s as they were recently, is unclear. Interestingly, neither Kalecki nor the Kaleckians have asked any questions about the determinants of labour supply. That seemed to them to be determined exogeneously – presumably by demographical and other non-economic factors.

9 Filtzer (1988) presents a convincing analysis of labour relationships in the USSR during the first years of forced industrialization. His interpretation of the linkages between labour shortages, labour productivity, work discipline, pay systems, labour turnover and real wages seems applicable to all European CPEs.

10 Apart from the 'anti-parasitism' laws which explicitly aim at constraining, administratively, the amount of leisure taken by population, there are also some quasi-economic mechanisms safeguarding extraction of working time from the

population. First, some rationed goods and services are only available to persons with sufficiently long record of employment (in the socialist sector). Second, most occupations stipulate for some minimum quantities of working time to be supplied by the employees. In practice an individuals' voluntarily-decided working time may equal, say five hours a day. Yet he may have to stick to the eight-hour shift – or get fired.

11 This statement is consistent with the theory of 'efficiency' wages, as reviewed in Stiglitz (1987). The theory suggests that it is rational for the firms to set the wages at levels higher than dictated by the postulate of quantitative balance between labour demand and supply. Basically, the effort (or quality) of the employed labour is shown to be maximizing the firms' profits just with wages not clearing the markets. (Hence the rationale for the term 'efficiency' wages.) Stiglitz's paper is worth reading also because it offers valuable comment on other issues such as the properties of various pay systems, relevant for our following discussion.

12 In a sense the merits of the piece-rate systems as securing desirable quantitative output are often exaggerated. The managers tend to 'manipulate' the performance norms and the earnings of the workers so as to offset the effects of work stoppages caused by irregular deliveries of raw materials or their poor quality. Once the norms are demonstrated to be susceptible to manipulation, they tend to be subject to a constant pressure for 'adjustments'. Under sufficiently strong influence of labour shortage the pressures may turn out to be successful.

13 There are many concurring mechanisms shaping the 'Socialist' features of the internal pay systems that are often characteristic of the dynamic and profitable firms in the contemporary market economies. Egalitarian tendencies may discourage excessive labour turnover due to the frustration of the less successful workers (see Frank 1984). Reliance on seniority serves to facilitate the development of firm-specific skills (see Aoki 1986). In general, the social-democratic and trade-unionist approach to the matters of wage, income and consumption policies may have initiated and greatly assisted the evolution of the pay and income systems of the west (see Lundberg 1985 on the 'Swedish approach' or Freeman and Medoff 1984 on the role of the trade unions). And these systems have turned out to be the vehicles of modern quality and innovation-oriented growth, still absent in the East European CPEs.

14 This point was raised recently by Brus and Laski (1988).

BIBLIOGRAPHY

Adam, J. (1987) *Employment Policies in the Soviet Union and Eastern Europe*, 2nd edn, London, Macmillan.
Aoki, M. (1986) 'Horizontal versus vertical information structure of the firm' *American Economic Review* 6.
Brus, W. and Laski, K. (1988) 'Capital market and full employment', *European Economic Review* 33(2–3), 439–47.
Collier, I. J. (1986) 'Effective purchasing power in quantity constrained economy: an estimate for the German Democratic Republic', *View of Economics and Statistics* 1.
Filtzer, M. (1988) 'Labour and the contradictions of Soviet planning under Stalin' *Critique* 20/21.
Fisher, F. M. (1983) *Disequilibrium Foundations of Equilibrium Economics*, Cambridge, Cambridge University Press.
Frank, R. H. (1984) 'Are workers paid their marginal products?', *American*

Economic Review 4.

Freeman, R. B. and Medoff, J. L. (1984) *What Do the Unions Do?* New York, Basic Books.

Frydman, R. (1982) 'Towards an understanding of market process: individual expectations, learning and convergence to rational expectation equilibria', *American Economic Review* 4.

Hahn, F. H. (1985) *Money, Growth, and Stability*, MIT Press.

Kornai, J. (1979) 'Resource-constrained versus demand-constrained systems', *Econometrica* 47, 801–19.

Kornai, J. (1980) *Economics of Shortage*, Amsterdam, North Holland.

Kornai, J. (1982) *Growth, Shortage and Efficiency*, Oxford, Basil Blackwell.

Lundberg, E. (1985) 'The rise and fall of the Swedish model', *Journal of Economic Literature* 1.

Malinvaud, E. (1977) 'The theory of unemployment reconsidered', London, Basil Blackwell.

Podkaminer, L. (1982) 'Estimates of disequilibria in Poland's consumer markets, 1965–1978', *Review of Economics and Statistics* 3.

Podkaminer, L. (1988a) 'Disequilibrium in Poland's consumer markets, further evidence or inter-market spillovers', *Journal of Comparative Economics* 12(1), 43–60.

Podkaminer, L. (1988b) 'Income effects of disequilibrium in Poland's consumer markets. Evidence from households' budgets', Research Report no. 146, The Vienna Institute for Comparative Economic Studies.

Podkaminer, L. (1989) 'Macroeconomic disequilibrium in centrally planned economies: identifiability of econometric models based on theory of households' behaviour under quantity constraints', *Journal of Comparative Economics*, 13(4), 580–2.

Portes, R. (1979) 'Internal and external balance in a centrally planned economy', *Journal of Comparative Economics* 3(4), 325–45.

Rosefielde, S. (1988) 'The Soviet economy in crisis: Birman's cumulative disequilibrium hypothesis', *Soviet Studies* 2.

Stiglitz, J. E. (1987) 'The causes and consequences of the dependence of quality on price', *Journal of Economic Literature*, 1st edn.

18 The property rights in Hungary

Márton Tardos

The issue of restructuring the system of ownership has been put on the agenda by a policy that determined post-war economic development in Hungary, or at least the mainstream of that development. Until quite recently, Hungarian citizens were told that '. . . the economic system of socialist society is based on the public ownership of the means of production. Under public ownership of the means of production, goods are produced for the welfare of the whole society and not of certain members or groups of the society . . .'; '. . . personal ownership of the productive assets shall be prohibited . . .'; 'the inequality resulting from the system of private ownership will cease'.[1] During the last years of Communist dictatorship, people – not without astonishment – read about an attempt to organize a Stock Exchange in Budapest, an institution that typically reflects the conditions of a capitalist economy. The confusing situation was a consequence of the inefficiency of Traditional Central Planning (TCP). This had been recognized very soon after nationalization, even by most of the partisans of the socialist system, which led to its step by step modification.

However, those who unswervingly pursued nationalization after 1945 resisted any reform measure of the system for a long time. Moreover, no comprehensive reform was made until the New Economic Mechanism (NEM) was introduced in 1966–8. Then, too, the change was focused on the management of state and co-operative enterprises which were, in practice, very similar. Substantial freedom was offered to these enterprises, but the so-called 'market-like' regulation remained under the bureaucratic state hierarchy dominated by party bodies. Although the private sector was encouraged by the reform, the NEM constrained the increase of its share, and limited its activity to small-scale production and the service sector.

According to the general opinion of that time, if companies are freed from the constraints of target planning, the introduction of a semi-market system which can be called Modified Central Planning (MCP) would be capable of meeting the efficiency requirements of the market while retaining the promised advantages of socialist ownership.

To explain the weakness of the MCP in Hungary, and the fact that this weakness triggered renewed central interference, we use a simple model of the market (see Figure 18.1).[2] Here the argument is not based on the ideal of free competition that is so often cited. On the contrary, the imperfections of the markets in contemporary capitalist mixed economies, caused by the considerable influence of the state and of large oligopolistic companies, were taken into account. In my searching for the causes of the self-regulating features of the market I emphasize only that a fully-fledged market system must meet effective demand, which is not the case in MCP.

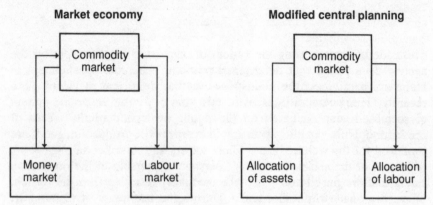

Figure 18.1   Commodity and factor markets

Normally, in a market economy different types of markets (such as the markets of goods and services, labour, capital, money and land) are interacting. These markets mutually influence each other without encountering spatial and temporal barriers: a change in the commodity markets is accompanied by changes in, for example, the capital, the labour and the money markets. The entrepreneur, in making a decision to use his savings or to mobilize new funds, takes into account the expected market prices of labour and capital. When an investment is unlikely to yield returns on the input costs of wage, capital and other expenses, the entrepreneur gives up the idea of attracting external savings.

For companies operating at reduced profitability or making a temporary loss, links to the capital and labour market facilitate corrections. They are not automatically weakened by inadequate growth or a decline of profit in their adjustment to the labour market. Wage raises are not penalized by taxation. Likewise, under deteriorating business circumstances companies do not lose contact with the money and capital markets. They may feel sure about getting the necessary funds provided that their partners are convinced about the profitability of a given project. Business failure is a threat; however they can resort to a broad range of actions to avoid it without any support from the government administration. In such conditions bankruptcy is an extreme solution. As a regular method for solving problems it would be too expensive.

As has been seen above, in the Hungarian MCP of 1966–8, self-regulation was given the green light only in the product markets, and within the boundaries of central price regulation. This restriction asserted itself, not only in the markets of products with centrally-set prices, but also in the area of free prices where business agents were influenced by state guidelines, and therefore prices were not clearing the markets. The margin of self-regulation was even narrower in the capital and labour markets. Before 1980, the profit formed in the commodity market determined the sum available for wage rises, and – separately – for investment purposes. Since 1980, companies have been free to decide about the utilization of net profit for investment as well as for wage increase. Essentially, however, the logic and routine of the system have remained unchanged. Any one forint of net profit could and should be used by companies regardless of its returns. These peculiarities have offered a good cause for state intervention to correct the consequent anomalies. In turn, state intervention reduced the effect of the reform, and the market pressure on the firms became weaker.

Thus, during the last twenty years TCP was replaced by MCP in Hungary but a fully-fledged market system did not emerge because the influence of property owners was absent and employee representation was weak. The functioning of commodity markets was constrained by state intervention and in reality there was no capital and labour market operating. The missing items were substituted by indirect regulation from the centre.[3] The financial status of the companies was determined by firm negotiations. Under such conditions neither target planning nor the regulating power of market and money was effective. Tamás Bauer used the phrase 'no plan, no market' to describe this way of regulation.[4]

The power structure was nevertheless changed by the emergence of indirect forms of control. The system of centralized state hierarchy was weakened and the financial levers did take over a considerable part of the role of state administration. It was the leverage of large companies that increased first of all.[5,6] However, this did not mean the full elimination of the centralized hierarchy. The state companies, as part of the centralized hierarchy, fought a desperate struggle both with one another and with the central authorities for the allocation of resources. The justification for their claims was based on their 'social mission' assigned to them by the centre, and not on profit motives.

Hungarian sociologists agreed that this inconsistent state of affairs was rooted in the conflict between the traditional political and ownership structures and the imposition of market reforms. Therefore the compromise formulated in 1968 and repeatedly amended afterwards was not really promising. The enterprises freed from the pressure of target planning continued to adapt themselves to the objectives of the centre. Their excessive demand for resources was not moderated, and they did not develop real sensitivity to costs or prices. The attempts of the centre to impose upon them the pressure of the market was ineffective and had only negligible effects. The economic administration was still believed to be responsible for the smooth operation of the entire economy in all its detail, among others for the survival of the companies. Instead of physical planning, the state administration used financial levers to enforce its objectives on the enterprises which acted in harmony with these 'social expectations', and were sometimes forgetful about the return on capital which ultimately resulted in the external debt crisis.

At this point opinions diverged. One – small – group of analysts expressed strong anti-capitalist views and a correspondingly intense aversion to the market.[7] They rejected the market in general and even more from the point of view of relatively backward countries. They were emphasizing that in the framework of socialist ownership the reform could not achieve more than it did. According to their view the restructuring of the Stalinist model of economic control continues to require powerful central planning, and the systemic reforms are to blame for the debt crisis.

The reform economists on the other side agreed about the need for profound change in the old system of economic control. They also agreed in tracing back most of the problems to the system of directive planning, asserting that the aggravation of the economic difficulties was a consequence of the ambiguities of the reform and of the mistaken economic policy of obstructing the reform.

This group differed mainly over the scope for further development of the reform concept. Some authors assumed that the model developed in 1966–8 essentially never sought to achieve more than was in fact achieved. In their opinion the central policy-makers had no intention of increasing enterprise autonomy and the influence of the market too much because they did not want to reduce their own power.[8] Others attributed most of the difficulties to the emergence of an opposition to the reform in 1969 that reached its climax in 1972. They defined the compromises and withdrawals of the reform as predominant causes of the economic and social crisis in Hungary.[9]

Radical reformers, including myself, agreed on the following: the changes of 1968 would not have been sufficient for establishing an efficient market system even if there had been no powerful opposition to the reforms.

There was no reasonable ground to anticipate success unless a new programme extending the 1968 objectives was drawn up after launching the reform, with a view to radically restructuring ownership, evolving capital and labour markets, enhancing the role of the private sector and profoundly changing the political institutions.

THE CONTENTS OF THE REFORM OF OWNERSHIP

I should once again like to focus on the reasons why the former socialist societies failed in their attempts at enhancing the market incentive and the role of profit in the framework of economic reforms.

The experience of the East European economies, including the Hungarian economy, shows convincingly the absence of an independent business subject, namely, an individual committed to increase the value of assets at his disposal or in his ownership. Efficient markets cannot exist without a big number of business subjects, who have no other measure but the expected profit to evaluate the efficiency of the management of real or financial assets. The assumption is in agreement with standard economic theory asserting that the value of assets is equal to the net present value of expected profits. This concept adopts the theory of F.A. Hayek about the function of a free price system.[10]

It follows that the former socialist countries, hoping to create markets, must find the lacking business agents who are able to mobilize the globally 'scattered fragments of inconsistent knowledge'. This task can only be undertaken by individual owners with sufficient information about the opportunities of resource utilization and who have a direct and explicit stake in resource utilization. Furthermore, the business agents need a legal environment which sets the conditions for their economic activities.

The above requirements exceed the model of the MCP and the suggested ideas of W. Brus and the framework of the New Economic Mechanism of Hungary.[11] They are more far-reaching than the practical reform processes were in Yugoslavia, Hungary and the other socialist countries (China, Poland). They imply a fundamental change towards private property rights and restructuring the political order to provide for a multicentric representation of political interests.

WHAT MUST NOT BE INCLUDED IN SUCH A PROGRAMME

Whatever radical rupture with the earlier ideas and practice of socialist planned economy is implied, the required changes do not mean a direct imitation of the existing economic institutions of the advanced western industrial countries in their idealized form. We have no reason to believe that the situation is perfect in these mixed economies where markets and plural ownership freely assert themselves. Countless economic problems remain unsolved, ranging from unemployment, inflation, unequal opportunities for the sexes and for various strata, and so on.

There is even less reason to suppose that a market economy would be an absolute and automatic answer to the justifiable demands of society in a moderately developed or underdeveloped country where the actual objective is to provide an 'acceptable' standard of living for the members of society or to try to come closer to the performance of the advanced countries.

Here is a list of issues that will be left open even after a fundamental change of property rights:[12]

- Areas of the economy where a centrally-controlled public service system must be given priority over market.
- The extent and method of use of fiscal and monetary tools to regulate aggregate demand in order to fully utilize the factors of production and avoid inflation.
- The extent of state preferences to which it is necessary to encourage or discourage certain business activities in order to ensure that the resulting benefits will exceed the damage inevitably caused by the resulting disruption of market conditions.
- The method and acceptable degree of using welfare programmes to neutralize social tensions caused by the intrinsic conflicts of a market economy and the injustice caused by the inequality of the starting conditions.

In countries like Hungary, which are lagging behind the advanced countries, and in which solutions are yet to be found to develop technical culture, to improve the education of the people and to prompt the participation of citizens in contemporary division of labour, the problems noted above will become more extensive and specific.

Countries where nationalization was practically total, and which have adopted the system of planned economy, face additional challenges. The difficulties to be reckoned with besides the resistance of centralized hierarchies are the following: the task of a business-oriented restructuring of property held by the state and by large co-operatives is extremely complicated and has nowhere been accomplished successfully yet and, on the other hand, the standards of social conduct of the people and the companies have been undermined by the financial manipulation needed to fulfil the poorly-funded plan and mandatory targets.

IS THERE A 'THIRD WAY'?

The need to eliminate both central planning and the intrinsic shortcomings of the capitalist market economy have encouraged some authors to study the changes of a 'third way' developed in the 1930s.[13] This alternative actually combines indicative planning and an economy where small-scale private firms and self-managed or co-operative companies dominate.

Historically, the programme is based on the co-operative movement staged 150 years ago. Co-operative and self-managed business operates successfully in the environment of the capitalist market economy. Such business forms are able to adjust to competition prevailing in market economies while adopting several socialist principles, the most important being the equal participation of members in management and the assertion of the employment interests of members. These co-operatives and self-managed companies are successful even if they give high priority to the income of the members, probably because the struggle for survival prevents the payment of extravagant wages and salaries.

Compared to state enterprises, co-operatives and self-managed business units have been relatively successful in the East European countries, too. However, even the advocates of the co-operative movement are aware of how insignificant is the difference between the efficiency of state and co-operative companies. It is also admitted that the management of East European co-operative and self-managed companies is different from the historical traditions of the co-operative movement in the west. As already noted, the rights of the members are severely limited by substantial state intervention, and co-operative business management is often far from transparent to members because most of the co-operatives are of exceptional size to alleviate state control.[14] The co-operative and self-management enterprises are nevertheless a practicable alternative in Eastern Europe. However, those forms of them which were introduced in Hungary in 1984 should not be expected to succeed unless the excessively large organizations are split up, and the resulting devolution of authority is not restricted via informal political pressure any longer. Another contribution to the development of co-operatives and self-managed firms could be an increase in the scope of equity shares and bonds, that is, a reduction of the undistributable assets. This could enhance the interest of the work-force in increasing the value of assets.

However, a programme for developing co-operatives and self-managed firms cannot provide the main solution for abolishing state ownership. The teams of workers in co-operatives or in self-managed companies are not competent owners of enterprise assets. Despite ideological illusions, people employed in co-operatives, just as in state companies, have retained the characteristics of hired workers without representing any real proprietary interests.

Workers and co-operative members, who had no substantial assets of their own, had no alternative but to sell their labour to an institution offering a job. This lesson, learned from their daily experience, determined their wage-earner status in real socialism. Several decades after the nationalization of industries, there was no real reason behind the frequently-quoted arguments that this status was only a legacy of the past, a product of petty-bourgeois ideological inheritance. So it is clear that the transformation of property rights in Eastern Europe should not offer a prominent role to the co-operatives or self-managed firms. At the same time, there is no reason to require that the existing co-operative and self-managed firms should be dismantled by administrative measures – it is reasonable to give them a chance to survive in the emerging economic competition. It is very likely that small co-operatives and small self-managed firms may have a bright future. Such organizations are transparent to their staff, therefore holding a share in the business and having the right to participate directly in decision-making offers real advantages to the members.

THE ROLE OF PRIVATE OWNERSHIP

It is widely assumed that the shift to the market in East European societies will be directly followed by the spread of private property. This opinion is based both on the success of private firms in western market economies and on the achievements made by private business in Hungary and other countries of the former Eastern bloc.

As far as the present situation of private ownership in the Hungarian economy is concerned, the share of the private sector in the gross domestic product increased significantly from the rockbottom level of the mid-1960s. Private wealth has shown a still more remarkable increase. According to some estimates, at present the latter amounts to 30 per cent of the national wealth.

There have been numerous positive consequences of the relative growth of private business in the Hungarian economy albeit its ambiguous position. First, it stabilized the supply of some essential products (fruit, vegetables and meat) and increased the range of industrial production and services. Second, the private sector offered more and more jobs year after year.

Notwithstanding these positive factors, the results of private business are still not satisfactory. The macroeconomic efficiency of the private sector has remained moderate because of the limited use of capital which was due to the fact that private investors had no confidence in the future political and economic development. The lending activity of banks has remained constrained. Because of all of that, even the labour costs of private business are too high.

Waste manifests itself in the excessive use of the unpaid family work-force in the household. In trade and services waste is represented by the remuneration of the work-force at rates that would not be justified by the demand and supply of labour if the workers had a free choice between jobs offered by the state, co-operative and private sectors, or if the private sector did not offer good opportunities for tax evasion.

So two kinds of vicious circles have developed in the private economy hampering the development of the national economy but supporting the undisturbed business of the state and co-operative companies. One of the vicious circles is in agriculture. This circle ties down an easily substitutable, that is, redundant, work-force to rural life through the extra incomes of household and auxiliary farms. At the same time, this waste meets the interests of the large-scale agricultural plants that could not survive without this labour under the present conditions.

The second vicious circle is in industry, trade and services. The private entrepreneurs functioning here, and the groups of elite workers legally or illegally employed by them, are interested in finding work for the limited number of contractors in non-competitive areas. Most of the substantial incomes earned in this manner are kept from the sight of the tax authorities and spent for consumption. The investments of private business are negligible. The situation is not without advantages for most private entrepreneurs because they usually do not face any difficulty in selling their goods and services produced without large capital inputs but with high labour expenses. At the same time, the private firms do not drive the state and co-operative companies into bankruptcy: on the contrary, the supply of semi-finished products by private business tends to stabilize the state sector.

This 'clever' division of labour between the so-called 'socialist' companies and private firms has another harmful consequence, too. Because of the extremely high wages of private entrepreneurs, state and co-operative companies have only limited opportunities to be too exacting about the performance of their employees. That is to say, as long as the 'private' entrepreneurs and the workers employed by them do not and cannot consider themselves free in their choice of jobs and investments, that is, as long as they have continuously to reckon with both economic and political risks, the economic leverage of private operations will remain limited.

PLURAL OWNERSHIP

The aforesaid can be summarized in the following:

- In the Hungarian economy, which has pursued a policy of reform for more than 20 years, the autonomy and the business orientation of companies have not been established despite the elimination of mandatory planning.
- The poor business performance of companies may not be attributed solely to the mistaken methods of fiscal regulation. As long as the activities of companies are not evaluated by business criteria, that is, by profits and by the growth of the value of assets, and the aims of state and co-operative enterprises are derived from the objectives of the centre or the welfare of employees, there cannot exist real competitive markets and companies cannot be expected to rationalize their resource utilization, a fact that triggers intervention by the state.
- Bearing their own interests in mind, the agents of the powerfully restricted private sector tend to adapt themselves to the wasteful management style of state and co-operative enterprises; moreover, they are forced to do so as long as the political security of private investment activities is not granted.

It follows that an economic reform kept within these boundaries holds little promise of a breakthrough and a different level of production efficiency. However, it is not easy to create the conditions of plural ownership required for an effective market. The lessons of countries facing this problem show that the inverse of Karl Marx's statement (namely, that there was no historical precedent for the 'scientific socialism' he dreamt of) is equally true. The new social order was consolidated as a result of radical 'revolutionary' steps made towards socialism after 1917 in the Soviet Union and after the Second World War in Eastern Europe. A return to the abandoned market path of development also requires profound and abrupt changes in the underlying conditions of property rights. This proposition is paradoxical because the need to reshape real socialism does not mean that the errors of capitalism will be avoided. It is also paradoxical because, if we accept that we have to return to the main path of the market economy after a long 'adventure', we have to realize as well that this return is obstructed, not only by the existing power structures, but also by the legacies of socialism.

The method of changing property rights by direct privatization and reprivatization does not offer a full solution. The privatization activities of western conservative governments may be revealing but cannot be imitated. Western privatization always finds support from private capital that continues to dominate the economy even after partial nationalization.

In the countries of real socialism, where nationalization and agricultural collectivization were carried out, the existing private sector does not have sufficient capacity to acquire the state companies. On the other hand, in the direct distribution of state assets to the citizens, what may appear as a rational programme can also be questioned. Tibor Liska is known to have a clever and ambitious solution to the problem. Essentially, he assumes that citizens are equally provided with coupons or vouchers by the state. Through this system enterprising citizens may make their bids for restricted property rights to desks organized for this purpose and authorized to administer the property of the state. However, this genuine approach seems to be unrealistic even if its naïve socialistic aspects postulating equal chances for all citizens, and the opposition of the existing power structure to this kind of distribution, are not considered. First, to put Liska's suggestion into operation is more difficult than the other possible solutions. Second, he assumes that in the society all citizens would become entrepreneurs. But most likely, not all citizens can turn into entrepreneurs, and the expected status of the new enterprising elite will prompt social resistance against the programme.[15]

The simplest of the practicable programmes for the creation of plural ownership is the continuous restructuring of companies, for example, in the framework of the company law issued by the Hungarian Parliament in 1988. According to this law existing companies and banks or their affiliate investment banks could invest their funds in floated or bankrupt companies or in new companies. The new companies can be, among others, limited liability or incorporated firms. This scheme would also allow the transforming, by administrative decree, of the state companies into limited liability, joint stock companies or the like.

More radical changes could be also made if the large self-managed companies would decide to dismantle themselves. This could be carried out in two stages: in stage 1, their internal facilities and locations could become limited liability or joint stock companies, while in stage 2 the corporate centre would become a holding company. Holding companies, limited liability and joint stock companies formed from internal plants could mutually become the owners of each other. A cross-holding could be developed while the corporate headquarters would be established if the state transferred the ownership rights from its hands to a large number of new owners – to public investors – in order to restructure state property. This could be implemented without issuing securities, as I proposed nearly twenty years ago. Companies would be distributed among a few holdings to operate the assets. At that time I gave these holdings the name of production and commercial banks.[16, 17] It is important to note that in my opinion of that time this alternative could work only if companies were distributed at random to holdings, that is, without applying any regional or sectoral guideline.

An alternative, more complex method of transfer, includes the issue of stocks. The state would provide cash – for the purpose of acquisition of capital – to such dependent institutions of the state budget which it wishes to decentralize and detach from the budget. Institutions like insurance and pension funds could be considered here because the business autonomy of such institutions must remain limited or at least uncertain as long as they do not own a substantial amount of capital. The second line of new holders could include organizations of county, city and village administration, public service units (theatres, schools, hospitals, and so on) as well. Providing such organizations with funds could be a means of making them independent of the state budget. These alternatives, together with the promotion of private investment in business and securities, seem to be suitable for establishing a plural ownership system in a country dissatisfied with nationalization.

The benefit of direct privatization and of the reorganization of state enterprises into limited and joint stock companies lies in the fact that they do not require new institutions. At the same time, both have their disadvantages. Genuine privatization is a very slow procedure in a country where private wealth is negligible. A continuous course of restructuring state ownership does not offer a way for genuine private ownership. Moreover, such a process would facilitate first of all the restructuring of bankrupt companies.

The various schemes based on the property rights of public investors are in my mind unavoidable.[18, 19] This approach was originally contrasted with the opinion that the state and party control could easily distort such a reasonable but administrative action. I also think that the scheme involving the flow of securities is more promising. The mere appearance of securities in business is an automatic drive towards a better return on capital because it requires the payment of dividends. Besides that, the trade of securities will start, too. The establishment of a stock exchange is also necessary. Consequently, this alternative would provide a framework, not only for the establishment of control over managers by the owners, but also for continuous monitoring of the value of capital assets. So it would create a capital market.

Naturally, there are also arguments against this method of transformation. Two superficial criticisms are as follows: (a) it needs sophisticated knowhow in the capital market which is not as yet available in the country; (b) it makes the economy more sensitive to market risk. The first argument may be rejected because investment in shares and broking are not forms of witchcraft, and the benefits gained by practising them are higher than the costs of learning them. As regards the second criticism it is true that the economic losses caused by speculation might be quite considerable ones; however, such problems can be also taken as a reflection of the actual intricacy of investment projects.

A more fundamental objection concerns the degree of passion that citizens represented by new investors (insurance companies, pension funds) should or could have in the returns on capital. This is a rather ambiguous issue. If new institutional investors are authorized to use the returns on capital only for the purpose of new investment, and are not allowed to apply it to their own activities, or when the losses or the gains do not affect the situation of the persons they represent, then such organizations will operate, not under economic pressure, but merely with a set task, that is, it would be just as easy to manipulate from the centre as in the case of holdings which I recommended before. If, however, current operations such as insurance are affected by the results of investment, then the behaviour of such organizations in the money market will be governed by the pressure exercised by their owners and not exclusively by their commitment to the original functions of the organizations. It follows, therefore, that it is advantageous in this respect to offer full freedom to the citizens to use the assets of the public investors. However, it entails other problems. Investors may be inclined to draw unreasonably large amounts of money from the market to assure better performance, for example, in their current insurance operations or in the activities of municipalities. So if this alternative is chosen, provisions have to be made to protect the insured, the retired, and so on, and the investment activities of the municipalities have to be restricted. None the less, all these complicated problems are manageable. The reform of the ownership structure of a post-Communist country is not only a difficult, but also an unprecedented, task. There is a pressing need for a good solution but there are no perfect alternatives to suggest.

NOTES

1 *The Political Economy of Socialism*, Budapest, Kossuth, 1967, 56–7. When the first draft of this chapter was written in 1988, the word 'privitization' was officially banned in my country (not to mention the term of 'rapid mass privatization' that is so popular in our days.)
2 Márton Tardos (1985) 'A szabályozott piac kialakításának feltételei' ('Conditions for the development of a regulated market'), *Közgazdasági Szemle* 11.
3 László Antal (1985) *Gazdaságirányítási és pénzügyi rendszerünk a reform útján (Economic Control and Financial System in Hungary in the Course of Reform)*, Budapest, Közgazdasági és Jogi Könyvkiadó.
4 Tamás Bauer (1982) 'A második gazdasági reform g és a tulajdonviszonyok' ('The secondary economy and ownership relations'), *Mozgó Világ* 10.
5 Mária Csanádi (1985) *'Függöség, konszenzus, szelekció'* (*Dependence, Consensus, Selection*), Pénzügykutató Intézet (Financial Research Institute), Budapest; M. Csanádi (1988) 'A párt és az állam kapcsolatrendszere' (System of relations between party and state), *HVG* 27 August.
6 Éva Voszka (1988) *Reform és átszervezés a nyolcvanas években (Reform and Restructuring in the '80s)*, Budapest, Közgazdasági és Jogi Könyvkiadó.
7 Andrea Szegö and György Wiener (1981) 'A nyereségképzôdés magyarországi törvényszerüségei' ('The rules of profit generation in Hungary'), *Pénzügyi Szemle* 7–8.
8 Iván Schweitzer (1981) 'A vállalati szervezet és a gazdasági mechanizmus néhány összefüggése' ('Enterprise organization and economic management'), *Közgazdasági Szemle* 7–8.
9 Gábor Révész (1988) 'A gazdasági reform eltorzulásának folyamata' ('The deformation process of economic reform'), *Közgazdasági Szemle* 6.
10 F.A. Hayek (1945) 'The price system as a mechanism for using knowledge', *American Economic Review* 35.
11 W.Brus (1972) 'The market in a socialist economy', London; MSZMP Határozatai és Dokumentumai' ('Guidelines of the Hungarian Socialist Workers' Party Central Committee on the Reform of the Economic Mechanism'), in *HSWP Resolutions and Documents 1963–1966*, Budapest, Kossuth.
12 A. Nove (1983) *The Economics of Feasible Socialism*, London, Allen & Unwin.
13 O.Šik (1972) *Der dritte Weg*, Hamburg, Hofmann & Campe.
14 Gyula Tellér (1984, 1985) 'Ó-mechanizmus, új mechanizmus, ipari szövetkezetek' ('Old mechanism, new mechanism, industrial co-operatives'), *Medvetánc* (1984), 5 (1985).
15 István Siklaky (ed.) 1985 'Koncepció és kritika' ('Concept and criticism'), Budapest, Magvetö.
16 Márton Tardos (1972) 'Gazdasági verseny hazánkban' ('Economic competition in Hungary'), *Közgazdasági Szemle* 7–8.
17 Similar concepts were proposed by Sándor Balázsy, Sándor Kopátsy, György Matolcsy and György Varga.
18 Márton Tardos (1988) 'Gazdasági szervezetek és a tulajdon' ('Business organizations and ownership'), *Gazdaság* 3.
19 Márton Tardos (1988) 'A tulajdon' ('Property rights'), *Közgazdasági Szemle* 12(3).

Epilogue

Compassionate doubts about reform economics (economic science, ideology, politics)*

János Mátyás Kovács

Most of us are more impatient to do good, and probably we are not sanguine about our ability to engage usefully in full time scientific work. Nor, perhaps, are we wholly satisfied with what Samuelson calls our own applause . . . I concede to Samuelson, nevertheless, that to a scientist educated hands make more melodious applause than ignorant hands, but too often the educated hands seem to be sat upon by educated asses.

G.J. Stigler

Reform economics – what is this supposed to mean? More exactly, what *was* it supposed to mean during the last thirty to forty years in Eastern Europe until the end of the 1980s?[1]

Let us depart from what the socialist economic reformers themselves used to say about the boundaries of their own discipline. As a rule, they placed the Stalinist political economy of socialism at one end of the spectrum, while at the other, there remained in the last analysis two taboos: large-scale private ownership and multi-party democracy. In an attempt to marketize the planned economies, the reformers tried to combine certain principles of collectivism and liberalism under real (Soviet-type) socialism. The reform concepts were based on what I will call below the '*plan-and-market discourse*'. In this discourse, the order in which the socialist reformers put the terms 'plan' and 'market', as well as the conjunction 'and' between them, have far-reaching effects on the scholarly features of the discipline.

What follows is a sketchy overview of this peculiar field of economic knowledge as seen by a student of the history of economic thought. In the first few pages I draw the main contours of the self-image of the reform economists; then some doubts are raised about the composition of this portrait; finally a rearrangement of the picture will be suggested.[2]

A SCHOOL THAT LEARNS BY DOING

Let us assume that reform economics did exist, that is, that in the 1980s, socialist reforms had a coherent scientific economic theory. Seemingly, this is not a risky assumption. In Hungary, Poland and Yugoslavia, but from time to time also in Bulgaria, China, Czechoslovakia and the Soviet Union, a great number of intellectuals declared themselves reform economists, reformers or reform makers during the past few decades. Official representatives of central economic policy, as well as quasi-independent academics, professed to be engaged in the development of reform concepts. They often designated their opponents as followers of the 'counter-reformation'. In the reformers' camp the only distinction that was usually made was between the moderates and the radicals. Thus, even some members of the political opposition could be somehow classified under the heading of proponents of reform economics. Since some of the Communist Parties in Eastern Europe have started referring to themselves as 'reform-parties', this language became so binding and the word 'reformer' so inflated that even the blatantly anti-reform moves had to be wrapped in pledges of allegiance to the cause of socialist reforms.[3]

'I am a reform economist' – one might proudly and publicly introduce himself as such, for instance, in the Hungary of the 1980s, be one a cabinet member, a fellow of a research institute or a manager of a firm. He could, of course, add: 'I am a socialist (Marxist)', but this confession was outmoded and not compulsory. It was not a case for criminal investigation. You did not say: 'I am a Marxist political economist and not (or not primarily) a reform economist'. Even those few hard-liners who quarrelled with radical reformers every now and then, rarely questioned the scholarly nature of the reform concepts as vehemently as in the debates beteween *tovarniki* and *beztovarniki* over the last seventy years in the Soviet Union, or at the end of the 1950s in Hungary. (To avoid misunderstandings, let it be said that until the last few years it has also been against the etiquette to proclaim aloud: 'I am a liberal reformer but no Marxist'.)[4]

By the 1980s, economics had a large – in many respects predominant – reference group in the reformist countries of Eastern Europe, which was distinguished by a kind of cohesion (scientific?, ideological?, political?). Since the members of this group were very productive at every level of activity deemed scholarly (from writing new textbooks on the political economy of socialism, all the way to elaborating the 'scientific principles' of actual reform programmes), with short breaks for more than thirty years, there was no reason to dispute their right to belong to the *school of reform economics*. At least there was none from the point of view of the sociology of science.

Economic reformism appeared to have tangible results: reform projects seemed to keep their promises even in the most exotic economies of real socialism when the dysfunctions of the planned economy called forth liberalization packages in order to prevent deep crises and accelerate modernization. Accordingly, reform economics as a *programmatic* doctrine looked justified in the international arena. If the patient was getting better, it was the reform that cured him; but if he had a relapse (as in Hungary, Poland and Yugoslavia in the last decade), it was definitely the under- and not the overdose of the 'reformed medicine' that led to the recurrent crisis – or so the reformers said.[5]

Beyond the normative roles (such as the selection and harmonization of economic objectives and means – *nota bene*, in the beginning reform economics called itself praxeology, too), reform economists also undertook other tasks of social science. They sometimes even considered the critique of Stalinist political economy, as well as the empirical description and the logical explanation of how a socialist economy worked, more important than the devising of new stabilization policies or means of deregulation.[6]

The emphasis on criticism was to underline the *innovative* capacity of reform concepts, distancing them from the mighty predecessor and rival, the Stalinist political economy: to praise cool-headed scientific analysis over romantic Utopias of communism, empirical realism over empty generalizations, such as the 'objective laws of socialism', logical verification over constant reference to sacrosanct authorities, and the understanding of the complexities of economic systems over the twists and turns of dialectical materialism. Reform concepts were assumed to represent reason rather than belief, to tell the truth instead of mixing glaring lies with a conspiracy of silence.

Hence, reform economics reckoned itself not only as a distinct theory imbued with moral superiority, but also as a branch of knowledge embodying a higher level of scholarly sophistication and enlightenment. The inevitable comparison with Stalinist political economy gave the impression that reform theories included so many new scholarly thoughts that one could rightly speak, and not merely in a sociological context, of the birth of a new school (programme, paradigm) of economic science. Consequently, both as the only doctrine criticizing Stalinist economics from inside (economic revisionism), and as a scenario prescribing the ways of transition to a market-type model of planned economy (economic reformism), reform economics seemed to deserve a special chapter in future textbooks on the history of economic thought.

The theorem of superiority over Stalinism was supplemented by the image of *growing sophistication* in economic science: the theory of reform was supposed to proceed towards deeper scientific cognition in a learning process of varying pace and structure but of fixed direction.[7] Originally, this pattern of evolution was not constructed for Soviet-type societies only. Frequently, it also included the 'cosmopolitan' values of progress and modernity. According to the original expectations of its disciples, reform economics would help the socialist economies join the mainstream of world economic development in a way that the experiments of deStalinization (democratization) in Eastern Europe – as if in remuneration for the techniques of marketization borrowed from the west – would serve as a remedy for the social maladies of the advanced industrial societies. Thus, providing patterns might raise reform economics to the highest levels of normative economic science in the world: by carefully composing the theory of 'socialist market economy', reform economists could refine the scholarly principles of 'social market economy' (or of any type of mixed economy).[8]

In fact, this was a new – softer – version of the old hypothesis of convergence. While in the 1960s there had been scholars in the west emphasizing the *actual* convergence of the 'first way' with the 'second way', that is, the increasing regulation of market economies with the deregulation of state economies, as of the early 1970s, there were some in Eastern Europe who only believed in the *theoretical* possibility of the 'third way'. This was supposed to attract those scholars, both in the East and the West, who would expectedly grow disillusioned with the neo-liberal fashion of the time.[9]

Surprisingly enough, many reform ideas remained within the framework of Marxism (and Leninism, cf. the analogy of the NEP) as far as the revealed intentions are concerned, but undoubtedly even much farther. In the 1960s, reformism – at least in its degree of anti-Stalinist fervour – was still inseparable from neo-Marxist tendencies (in Hungary from the Lukács school of the 'renaissance of Marxism', in Yugoslavia from the Praxis group, and so on). After all, one could until recently observe attempts at restoring this 'winning combination'. So the conspicuous 'secularization' of reformist thought in Eastern Europe during the 1970s and 1980s notwithstanding, it would be too much to characterize the reformers as *'closet capitalists'* – a phrase still appearing in western publications. It was mainly unreconstructed socialists or sober pragmatists – and not secret agents of capitalism – who were crouching in the reformist closet. Until the end of the 1980s they did their best to invent clever techniques of (simulated) marketization which did not blanketly call into question the primacy of state ownership and one-party rule.[10]

AUTHENTICITY, SCHOLARLY EVOLUTION, SYNTHESIS: THE IMPERFECTIONS

Unfortunately, until 1989, the gradual process of enlightenment in Eastern European economics did not bring with it a genuine discussion of liberalism, in which the reform economists would have been faced with liberal economic science in the west. Reformers were usually challenged by critics who combined neo-Stalinism with new-leftist ideology or welfarist social policy considerations.[11] Consequently, reform economists had to defend themselves against the charges (often quite primitive ones) of excessive rather than insufficient liberalism. This kind of accusation was not difficult to refute by referring to the fact that (1) the ominous closet capitalism of the reformers was intended to avert the 'worst', because it was to prevent collapsing Stalinist-type socialism from turning into full capitalism; and (2) reformism in itself did not create new 'anti-socialist' phenomena but rather made those of Stalinism visible.

So, scepticism in reformist circles concerning the scientific relevance of reform economics could only flow from two other sources: from the exhaustion of all major practical possibilities of reform-making under real socialism; and, in connection with this, from the emergence of a more radical doctrine aiming at the liberalization (privatization and democratization) of Soviet-type economies and polities.

As regards my doubts, let's follow this train of thought:

(a) First, some historical facts are collected to witness the *inhibited evolution* of reform economics as a science.
(b) Then I will ask whether it would have been at all logically possible to construct a scientific theory of 'socialist economic liberalism' (market socialism) as a new paradigm of economic thought. Or the reformers could not realistically expect to create more than a kind of '*borderline-case economics*' that examines phenomena atypical in 'normal' market economies.
(c) Finally, let us leave economic reasoning aside and consider reform economics as a mix of economic, ideological and political doctrines. In an attempt to find a political (sociological) interpretation, reform economics will be defined as a '*middle-of-the-road' theory of trans-formation*.

Without basic works

Dealing with reform concepts, one immediately comes across the problem of delimitation. This field of knowledge appears to refrain from any firm designation. The invention of the general and value-free term of 'reform economics' did not always consign to oblivion such old euphemisms as the 'theory of the economic mechanisms', the 'dialectics of plan and market' or the 'concept of regulated market'. At the other extreme, even such high-sounding phrases as 'revolutionary reform', 'self-managing market socialism' or 'third way' did not necessarily cover attempts at fundamental liberalization of the planned economy.[12] True, speaking modestly about decentralization, indirect control, self-management, and so on, instead of demanding private ownership and multi-party democracy, may have stemmed from intelligent caution. In such cases the historian is used to taking the basic texts of the school under survey to clear the underlying notions of the theory.

But where are these works to be found? As is known from the few case studies of early reform thinking in Eastern Europe, during the 1950s and 1960s, the economic doctrines of 'revisionism' did not converge into a well-identifiable school of economics embracing the whole region. Oskar Lange and his disciples in Poland, the 'optimal planners' (the so-called 'computopianists') in the Soviet Union, the first self-management theorists in Yugoslavia, the 'naïve mechanizers' in Hungary in the second half of the 1950s, and later, between 1964 and 1968, the architects of the simultaneous economic reforms in Moscow, Belgrade, Prague and Budapest, borrowed most of their theoretical munition from three thin books (Kornai's *Overcentralisation in Economic Administration* (1959), Brus's *The Market in a Socialist Economy* (1972), originally published in 1961, and Šik's *Plan and Market under Socialism* (1967)) as well as from a number of journal articles.

These books and their authors were influencing each other rather weakly (the translations were lacking or completed very slowly, the scholars did not have the chance to communicate with each other, and so on). As a result, the few cross references did not reflect real scholarly discussions. There was, for instance, virtually no opportunity for the Soviet mathemetical economists to be convinced say, by the market reformers of Poland or Hungary; the views of the proponents of the *Neues Ökonomisches System* in the GDR did not affect the ideology of self-management in Yugoslavia, and so on, not to mention the low level of domestic scientific debate in the individual countries, for example, between the followers of mathematical and verbal economics. Ironically, a kind of synthesis was more often reached by the 'official samizdat' publications, that is, by semi-confidential overall reform programmes compiled from the materials of dozens of expert commissions which were in charge of preparing reform packages for the politicians.[13]

If we search for the *magnum opus* (or *opera*) of reform economics in the 1970s and the first half of the 1980s, we find that the 'egalitarian' nature of reformist literature did not change. A vast amount of short papers criticizing the reversal of the economic reforms started in the 1960s and supporting new reform initiatives, a great advance of more empirical than abstract-analytical studies of how a pre-reform and a partially reformed economy work, but no bestsellers of synthetical (in other words, descriptive *and* normative, empirical and analytical) reform economics – this may be a brief inventory of the last two decades of economic thought in Eastern Europe.[14]

Furthermore, virtually no aid was rendered by western colleagues or accepted by socialist reform economists in this period. Astonishingly, Ota Šik's work on the *Third Way* (1972) or the series of essays published by Włodzimierz Brus about the theory of reform (all written in political emigration) had only limited effect upon economic thinking in Eastern Europe in the 1980s. Even the thought-provoking attempt made by Alec Nove at constructing *The Economics of Feasible Socialism* (1983) had almost no impact on the reform theorists. I think that much more than the old evil of provincialism was involved here. Reform economics was actually lacking the basic works even outside the sphere of Soviet-type socialism. There was hardly anything to import from western 'reformers': not only because the reform-minded émigrés coming from Eastern Europe were usually not able to display a much higher level of scholarly sophistication than what they had shown during the 1960s; but also because when they nevertheless logically progressed further, they went beyond the permissible ideological and political limits of reformism under real socialism in the question of pluralization of the property rights and the political structure.[15]

To avoid misunderstandings, I do not regret the absence of a *Das Sozial* (the socialist equivalent of Marx's *Das Kapital*), which so many Marxists expected to be written as soon as 'the socialist production relations mature'. I only would like to point to the apparent lack of synthetic works on the economics of reforming the Soviet-type systems. (Synthesis, of course, does not inevitably require the compilation of thick volumes.)

It was, perhaps, not quite accidental that János Kornai, a scholar who (a) had embarked upon a reformist critique of the planned economy in Hungary as early as in 1956; (b) has since then learnt what economic science means in the west; (c) was working in a country where reformism turned into a quasi-legitimate ideology, did not show much interest in formulating a coherent theory of reform based on the combined message of his 'overcentralization' and 'anti-equilibrium'. Instead of providing an ideal model of the future economic system and a critique of its alternative theories, rather he kept insisting in his *Economics of Shortage* (1980a) published nearly a quarter of a century after *Overcentralization*, on the study of how a socialist economy *was* constituted and not of how it should have been. In an attempt to describe and explain the Soviet-type economic system, he constructed valuable analytical instruments that could be used by the reform economists in formulating their proposals, but he hesitated to perform a thorough *empirical* analysis of the economy and – until the second half of the 1980s – to make comprehensive *normative* statements about the ways and means of radically changing it.[16]

Yet the very concept of the shortage economy presupposed the acknowledgement of the economic advantages of non-shortage ones. Thus, Kornai's work was, in principle, not devoid of normative models referring to western mixed economies, even if he did not idealize their market (in particular, private market) elements at that time. So why not simply assume that a non-shortage economy could not be conceived with scholarly rigour in the framework of even a radicalized version of reform economics? Why not assume that under the constraints of the prohibition of large-scale private ownership and multi-party democracy there was no room for making a synthesis in reform economics? Because – even if the reformers had been able to describe and analyse the actual state of the economy over the decades of real socialism – for the lack of specification of its future state (cf. the ambiguous concept of the *Third Way*), they would have been unable to postulate the ways of transition to that state.[17]

Speculative institutionalism

Coming back to the delimitation problem, in the absence of the 'prophets', the 'Bible' and the 'catechism', the Eastern European literature of reform economics looks in retrospect extremely *fragmented, unbalanced* and *eclectic* from the point of view of the different fields of economic theory and periods of time. The reform ideas were in most cases pigeon-holed into thematic subcategories (price policy, wage control, investment regulation, and so on); the description of the economic system to be reformed was frequently confused with normative statements about the reform process itself; and the numerous 'vice-prophets' came as often from academic circles as from the sphere of politics or business administration, not to mention the mass media and the *belles-lettres*.

The prophecies were uttered on very different levels of scholarly abstraction and quality. So it is doubtful whether, when building up the definition of reform economics, one could use the bricks of 'internal consensus' and 'dominant discourse' without the mortar of reformist rhetoric. Quite possibly, in the case of socialist reformism these terms of the sociology of knowledge first of all meant a generally-accepted minimum of ideological and political solidarity, while the common domain of economic scholarship was practically confined to a couple of golden rules (tacitly accepted on the basis of day-to-day experience) of how to deregulate the 'old mechanisms' (material incentives, enterprise autonomy, indirect financial control, and so on) within the limits of reform thinking.

No doubt about it, this common domain could be defended with a greater or lesser degree of persuasiveness (cf. Kornai's 'naïve' and 'radical' reformers); its boundaries, however, did not expand proportionately. The 'Hungarian school' of reformism, for example, was never united even in its critique of the Stalinist state (compare, for example, Tibor Liska's animosity with Márton Tardos's tolerant attitude towards nationalization – both economists belonged to the radical reformers' camp). Its disciples were probably even more divided when it came to designing the animators of the future plan-market models (cf. Liska's independent entrepreneurs, the managers of state holdings advocated by Tardos, or the self-management bodies envisioned by Tamás Bauer – again, all authors were regarded as radicals). The same applies to Aleksander Bajt and Branko Horvat in Yugoslavia, Gennadii Lisichkin and Nikolai Petrakov in the Soviet Union or Václav Klaus and Karel Kouba in Czechoslovakia to quote some names at random.[18] One could assume that consensus was strongest in examining the malfunctions of what was between the past and the future, that is, the economic system being reformed . . .

However, one does not have to be a German schoolmaster to expose the surprising imperfections even in what was called the 'theory of economic mechanisms', a broad field of reform economics which was claimed to be the most advanced, as opposed, for instance, to economic policy research. (As regards the latter, the reformers readily admitted that their general critique of forced industrialization and autarchy, a pioneering work started back in the 1950s, was not followed by subtle proposals for demand management, income distribution, structural policies, stabilization of economic growth, and so on.)

Examining the reformist theory of the mechanisms (a strange umbrella concept that included both planning and market institutions), one could always find large gaps in the survey of basic rules of the economic game in a Soviet-type society. There were big holes in the description and analysis, not only of the upper echelons of economic guidance (political interventionism, interdepartmental bargaining, relations with the Soviet-Union, and so on) where research was effectively hindered, but also of the mezzo- and microeconomic levels. Here, I am afraid, the accumulation of a huge amount of empirical information resulted in neither an appropriate *analytical* clarification of a series of basic categories used by reform economists (plan bargaining, campaign, administrative market, sectoral management, responsibility for supply, propensity for centralization, and so on), nor in the adjustment of these categories to the analytically more elaborated concepts of shortage, investment cycles or shadow economy. In this context it is perhaps an overstatement, quite often made by Soviet economists, that Kornai's *Economics of Shortage* (1980a) would provide a systematic macroeconomics of real socialism.[19]

Filling the gaps in the understanding of how the economic mechanisms work was not necessarily hampered by old socialist taboos such as bankruptcy, unemployment, capital market, import liberalization, and so on. The fact that you were not allowed to think about, for example, the economic advantages of unemployment, did not have to prevent you from analysing the roots of overemployment. In the field of comparative socialist systems, however, diplomatic caution did considerably inhibit scholarly research. The first comparative studies of the history of economic mechanisms in Soviet-type societies were only published in the 1980s, accurately reflecting the sluggish progress of scientific inquiry.[20]

Still, sluggishness in most other fields was rather due to the methodological approach taken by the reform economists. The examination of the economic mechanisms by the reformers, who had been organically rooted in a Marxist way of conceptualizing interests, organizations, power relations, and so on, began along the lines of *institutionalist* thinking. More exactly, it was a peculiar – let us say, a '*speculative*' – kind of institutionalism. Its means were often not empirical enough to comprehend economic behaviour, yet in many cases too empirical to make use of the abstract-analytical apparatus of modern economic science.

As a consequence, there emerged a large set of 'soft', pseudo-abstract categories such as plan, market, self-management, commodity-money relations, enterprise autonomy, economic mechanism, material incentives, centralization–decentralization, and so on, which governed reformist thought in interpreting and predicting the behaviour of economic actors. These categories were, on the one hand, often inoperational if not empty (cf. the never-ending reproaches of the legal experts to the reform economists); and on the other, subanalytical, should they be compared even with the first Lange model, the main concepts of which were at least mathematically compatible with one another.[21]

Certainly, in the first stage of reform thinking (anti-Stalinist revisionism) it was not useless to challenge, for instance, the 'law of planned and proportionate development' by means of the possibly less amorphous concept of 'commodity-money relations'. But after having left the field of this scholastic debate, a medical scalpel would have been better suited than a hatchet to properly dissect economic reality. To say 'market' instead of 'commodity-money relations' is only the first – linguistic – step in refining the instruments . . .

Reform economists had at one time pioneeringly declared the need to combine the planning and market institutions within the state sector. Also, they trusted in the logical possibility of making flawless, at least workable, combinations.[22] This did not, of course, exclude 'dialectical contradictions' between plan and market (remember the Marxist origins of the reformers). Nevertheless, these contradictions were not considered 'antagonistic': the relationship between plan and market was conceived as a subordination of the market to the plan rather than mutual adjustment (hence the term 'planned market' instead of 'marketized plan'). The concept of the economic mechanism was intended to express the 'leading role' of the plan. The analogy of the machine served as an example of the executive, mediating function of the market, which is basically governed by exogenous objectives. It was also assumed, optimistically, that in the course of their interaction, plan and market in the last analysis reinforce themselves, stimulating each other to reveal their advantages and suppress their drawbacks.

Thereby the reform economists distanced themselves from a war communism-type theory of extreme centralization and demonetization. But did they also display much community of ideas when, having accepted this combination thesis, they started to specify analytically the internal proportions and institutional patterns of the combination? In other words, was there a sufficiently large common domain of scholarly assertions on plan and market which could reasonably be labelled as reform economics, or was this domain, on the contrary, so extended in a speculative way that even a sort of 'sound Stalinism', also 'reforming' the model of war communism, might find a place in it? (Remember the hesitation of the early reformers in assessing Stalin's 1952 interpretation of commodity production under socialism.)

To speak about the consolidation of the scholarly position of the reformist school in Eastern Europe over the past decades may be misleading if reform economics could not be distinguished unambiguously from Stalinist political economy. Unfortunately, there were for a long time *striking similarities* in abstract economic discourse (objective laws of the economy, priority of state ownership, theory of labour value, macroeconomic (holistic) approach, and so on), as evidenced, for example, by the protracted debate over the '(in)evitability of the operation of the law of value in a socialist economy'. The ex-disciples of reform economics still owe the history of economic thought a systematic critique of Stalinism, say, by dissecting the notorious textbook on the political economy of socialism published in 1954 in the Soviet Union. Eclecticism does not nullify the intellectual debt. Examining the structure of even the most irreverent economics manuals published in the last ten years in Hungary, Poland or Yugoslavia we see a peculiar mixture of Marxian theory of labour value and mode of production; the 'basic law of socialist economy' as formulated by Stalin and wrapped in welfare economics; a portion of state interventionism á la Keynes; some theory of optimal planning; Kornai's shortage model; and a compendium of idealized rules of economic organization and policy in the given socialist country.[23]

Radicalization versus 'learning by learning'

As far as the intellectual shortcomings of reform economics are concerned, there were, of course, several excuses to be taken into account: the unavoidable naïvety of the newcomers, their being at best only tolerated, the practical tasks consuming the energy of the reform theorists, the lengthy period needed for any economic theory to unfold even in 'peace-time', and so on. Occasionally, it was also noted, rather cynically, that it would hardly have been possible to perform worse than the rival, the Stalinist political economy, did. According to the firm belief behind these justifications, time was on the side of the reformers, who succeeded in refining their scientific apparatus when they were allowed to do so. How long one can go on forgiving a theory's peccadilloes on the grounds of youthful 'wild oats' is debatable. Similarly, the out-competing of Stalinism must be considered in retrospect a *domestic quarrel* (what is more, a parochial and scholastic one). In any event, thirty to forty years of evolution (if disregarding another three decades of the prehistory of Soviet reform-economic thought, say, from Bukharin to Voznesenskii) should have appeared to be long enough to start the Eastern European economists meditating upon why reform economics – persecuted or tolerated – was not able to get beyond the adolescent stage.

Could it have done so at all? Or would growing up also have meant the end of reform concepts? Scholarly refinement was a central category of historiography of reforms in the 1980s. With the final state of the theory veiled in mist, the future was replaced by the process of approaching it. '*Seeking ways and means*' was the most popular phrase used to express the experimentalist ambitions of the reform economists who refused to offer

Utopian recipes for market socialism. Growing sophistication in a 'trial and error'-type learning process slowed down only by two troughs between the three waves (in the 1950s, 1960s and 1980s) of the reform – who would have argued with this assessment?[24]

Evidently, the reform theorists have intellectually matured as they left behind the positions of perfecting the planning targets in the 1950s and reforming the economic mechanisms in the 1960s and 1970s, flirting in the 1980s with the idea of the 'reform of the reform' (Hungary), with that of a 'crucial reform' (Poland) or of an 'urban reform' that would complement the rural one (China). These radical moves, they assumed, would have finally changed what had not been permitted before, without totally antagonizing those who did not permit these changes.

Reform economists covered a great distance on a dangerously winding road to gather enough strength by the end of the 1980s to present the iconoclastic programme of marching ahead to a non-socialist mixed economy. Socialism, the reformer-*routinier* of Eastern Europe said at that time, was a tiresome detour, which under the pretext of destroying the feudal relics of East European societies, did its best to reinforce them. Therefore the economic and political reforms must display anti-feudal features: they should create (not merely reconstruct) (a) a genuine workable market economy through privatization and dismantling most of the state controls; (b) a democratic polity by transforming the authoritarian and/or oligarchic nature of the party-state. In a word, the reforms are to give rise to (and not merely to revitalize) a 'civil society' in a *Rechtsstaat*.[25]

What did the Eastern European economists learn in the course of this tiresome detour? The main lesson was, I would say, that they taught themselves how one must *not* make reforms. That is to say, learning to their own cost, they revised nearly all their former conceptions about the improving workability of the market when it is under severe institutional constraints, as well as about its quasi-automatic self-liberation.

Experiencing the fallacies of partial reform moves, the disciples of reform economics could not help asking where the built-in limits of marketization were and what would happen if they were transgressed. So they made ground-breaking efforts to describe how extremely distorted markets work in Eastern Europe, but, at the same time, less ground-breaking ones to recollect what their western colleagues had said about the functioning of much less distorted markets. No doubt about it, this was really a kind of learning-by-doing, as the reformers said, even if the course of evolution was slightly irregular. For the reform economists did make rapid advances in comprehending the economic reality of Soviet-type systems and systematizing the ends and means to change it, whereby they tried to do their best as reform-makers. However, they were rather slow in '*learning by (and for) learning*', that is to say, in adopting and producing fine techniques of economic analysis.

By coining the term 'speculative institutionalism', I intended to reflect upon the manifold backwardness of the Eastern European economic profession. Many historians of western economic thought maintain that institutionalist considerations may support the critique of the abstract-deductive models of neo-classical economics, rather than lay the foundations for a new, independent theory. In the post-socialist economics of Eastern Europe, however, we equally need the logical exactitude and disciplining force of abstract-analytical studies as well as the realism of institutionalist inquiry. Moreover, institutionalism does not necessarily entail down-to-earth empiricism: the objections to its speculative nature in the case of reform economics do not preclude the possibility of making reasonable generalizations and conducting meaningful abstract-analytical research on the grounds of institutionalist premises.

To forestall misunderstandings again, I have nothing against empirical surveys.[26] What I would suggest is that (genuine) empirical and (genuine) abstract studies be simultaneously developed. The crux of the matter is, as ever, the selection of the underlying concepts of the theory. As long as we had in Eastern Europe a series of both empirically and analytically 'soft' concepts in reform economics, that exhibited only the disadvantages of the rival western schools of economics (general equilibrium theory and its critics), that is to say, these concepts could be neither empirically verified nor logically harmonized, explanation and prediction remained weak points of reformist economic science.

Learning by learning? It seems to me that the reform theorists tended to adopt a surprisingly uncooperative (I would not go as far as to say provincialist or hostile) attitude towards the economic profession in the west. *Indifference* is, perhaps, a better word. They – primarily the mathematical economists among them – usually did not reject the application of the scientific apparatus of western economic theories (in Hungary, for example, there were practically no ideological restrictions against 'bourgeois' economics over the last twenty years).

Nevertheless, reform economists did not make special efforts to explain why they systematically left out of consideration the scholarly achievements of whole new schools in economics; why they did not take the risk of 'Sovietizing' some of the central notions introduced by these schools. Should we assume that mainstream and 'out-of-the-mainstream' economics were unable to help refine substantially the scientific performance of reform economics?

The cracks in the neo-classical synthesis, as well as the appearance of those alternative research programmes which strived to fill them in, even at the risk of sacrificing main wings of the scientific edifice, simply escaped the attention of the majority of Eastern European economists over the last fifteen-to-twenty years.[27]

'Underground' economics

To maintain or raise the scholarly level of reform economics in the course of reform-making was a complicated task. Not only because tactical solidarity frequently prevented the reform economists from challenging each other on scientific matters . . . The need for new reforms was always so obvious, the costs of the changes for the reform economists, as well as the intellectual standard of the political counter-arguments were so low and the expertise of the economic authorities who were negotiating over the reform proposals was so sketchy that the architects of reform could often rely in their writings on rule of thumb and common sense.

In reformist circles metaphors such as *subterranean river* described the cumulative evolution of reform ideas as a stream of economic thought which, though repeatedly pushed underground, breaks out anew with ever greater force.[28] Some branches of this river, however, tended to be absorbed in the earth or, alternately, to re-emerge. Important ideas were forgotten, became blunted or distorted, then perhaps were reinvented; whole trains of thought run parallel with the mainstream but digressed from it at a certain point or got entangled (see, for example, the history of the concept of 'socialist entrepreneurship' from the Soviet *nepman*, through the theory of Liska in the Hungary of the 1960s, to the 'responsibility system' in China or to the intra-enterprise associations in Yugoslavia and Hungary during the 1970s and 1980s). Basic attitudes of reformation appeared by turns (political and economic reform, reform from below and from above, reform of the economic regulators and/or the organizations, and so on); and there was a never-ending faith in planning which recurrently affected most of the reform concepts even if it was not always as open as with 'computopia' or 'planometrics'.[29]

Consequently, the river was sometimes more 'polluted' when it came to the surface again than it had been when going underground (see, for example, Tardos's proposal for the liberalization of the capital market in Hungary, formulated in the early 1970s, revived at the beginning of the 1980s but soon replaced by a self-management scheme). Moreover, the growing violence of the outbursts might lead the observer astray: the systematization and gradual extension of reform thinking did not necessarily imply a simultaneous rise in scholarly invention. What was undoubtedly growing (in a cyclical way) was the ideological and political fervour of reform economics. This kind of *successive radicalization*,[30] however, made the original scientific problems of reform theories more explicit rather than solved them. In the beginning, the secularization of Stalinist political economy, of course, paved the way for scholarly research. None the less, after a while, scientific inquiry could prove counter-productive for dedicated reformers because it reinforced the need for going beyond the reformist political premises.

TOWARDS 'SOZIALE MARKTWIRTSCHAFT'?

Evolution inhibited – at first hearing this term endeared itself to a matter-of-fact reform economist. He said: If we had not been forced underground from time to time, we would have elucidated and diffused our knowledge in a regular way; sorry, reform theories developed through stormy party meetings and not through pleasant chats in university cafés. At the second hearing, however, when the internal (logical) factors of inhibition were also touched upon, the attraction surely evaporated.

When the combination of plan and market was generally accepted by the Eastern European reformers in the 1960s as the core of the new theory, the message of the never-ending debate on socialist economic calculation was interpreted one-sidedly as a call for the partial rehabilitation of the market under socialism. However, the warnings on the part of the liberal critics of state planning about the dangers of *only partially* curbing state power in the economy were neglected.[31]

The logical contradictions inherent in the relationship between plan and market (in particular, when it comes to real-socialist ways of planning and to marketization without privatization) were simply denied, eased by a rhetorical twist or treated as *external* political constraints on the reform. Hardly any reformer would have opposed this statement: if the meshing gears of plan and market squeak, it is not because they do not fit together theoretically, but because – to put it bluntly – somebody poured sand between them. Consequently, the 'enemy' became externalized from the very outset. It was not considered a component of a controversial theoretical complex, but an agent impeding the development of an otherwise potentially coherent theory from outside.

From the 'bad market' to 'building up a market economy'

The reformers originally conceived of the plan as a *sterile* (politically neutral) institution: they held not the plan as such, but the Communist hard-liners, who were not considered to be involved with the plan-market combination, responsible for blocking marketization.[32] The assumption, however, that even the most reform-minded, market-oriented planner disturbs – *ex officio* – the spontaneous order of the market process, sounded heretical even in the second half of the 1980s when in reform economics the desired scope of planning was already relatively narrow. For an Eastern European reformer to say plan *or* market instead of plan *and* market was a neo-Stalinist deviation, rather than a liberal critique of reformist thought at that time.

The market was also regarded by the early reformers as a *neutral* institution, which is indifferent to property rights. It was a widespread assertion that the market can be recreated within the state sector; if it still does not work there adequately, not the lack of private ownership but rather the intrinsic failure of the market is to be blamed.[33]

In the reformers' view, the grand concepts of plan and market were able to embrace everything in the economic history of socialism: on the one hand, from state dirigism to indicative planning, and on the other, from the abolition of forced procurements in agriculture to the stock market. On the level of economic theory these concepts were portrayed, at best, *symmetrically*. It is well known that in the beginning, the supremacy of planning, that is, a remarkable asymmetry in favour of the 'good' plan, could not be disputed in reformist circles. However, even later, when the 'bad' market succeeded in emancipating itself in reform thinking, the basic philosophy remained intact: the principle of 'give the market a (revocable) chance to help where the plan fails' was never definitively replaced by that of 'give the plan just a slight (revocable) chance where market fails'.

Instead, during the 1980s, the reformers started to entertain the view of a kind of abstract symmetry between the 'good plan' and the 'good market'. In the dominant discourse of reform economics there was no room for the idea that plan and market cannot be balanced in a speculative equation, for example, because the plan in Soviet-type economies is more 'contagious' than the market: a drop of planning is able to spoil a barrel of market. Then, plan and market can be within a hair's breadth of turning into plan *without* market.

Using the analogy of modern capitalism (as portrayed by Galbraith) to support the combination thesis, reform economists from time to time entertained hopes of creating a mixed economy 'with an Eastern appeal'; in other words, with the *differentia specifica* of the plan having a larger share in the mixture (larger than that of the market?; larger than that of the plan in the west?). The question of how large it should in fact be was usually answered in allusive terms, which suggested in an implicit way that all kinds of the combination were viabble from the point of view of economic rationality. The authenticity of reform economics was based on this assumption rather than on the perhaps more realistic one that plan and market are at least as capable of imparing each other's positive effects as they are of improving them.[34]

The first shock came in the late 1960s and the early 1970s when the reform economists in Belgrade, Budapest and Moscow (not to mention those in Prague) realized how quickly the non-reformed segments of the economy assimilated the partly-marketized ones. The survival of the shadow economy also surprised the reformers, who had expected that the marketized state economy would make both the 'old mechanisms' and the illegal/informal private entrepreneurship superfluous.

Since the invention of the convergence theorem, decades have passed, and the fact that it was much easier to liquidate or distort the market in the west than to establish it in Eastern Europe, became a common experience of the reform economists. At the end of the 1980s there were signs in the reformist literature of a switch from the pattern of modern capitalism to that of capitalism's early days, when it managed to get rid of the feudalistic restrictions on the market. According to the last slogan of the reformers, the market (not socialism) has to be built up. However, it has not been generally admitted until recently that even a *markedly smaller* proportion of the state than ever envisaged by the reform economists to cure the maladies of real socialism was capable of destabilizing the capitalist mixed economies (cf. the end of the Keynesian revolution).[35]

To sum up, the plan-and-market discourse could only serve as a framework for a *deformed* (distorted) version of liberal thought in Eastern European economics. The liberal aspirations of the radical reform economists were usually blocked by the inherent *statism* (élitism, interventionism) and *constructivism* of reformist thought. The typical reformer wanted to 'introduce' the market economy; he always had a positive reform programme, a master plan to experiment with, and found the idea of '*leben und leben lassen*' inadmissibly passive. Nevertheless, because he lacked a definite image of the future (where does the third way end?), these positive programmes tended to focus on the initial steps and the process of reformation rather than on its final stages. Consequently, if it makes sense at all to speak about liberalism in this context, reform economics embodied a sort of '*processual*' liberalism, rather than a liberal discipline derived from a definite – though abstract – ideal vision of the future or the past.

Even the more radical reform concepts did not rely on a profound philosophical (ethical) basis, on strong arguments about the intrinsic 'beauties' of the market and the virtues of private property, that is, on a radical liberal dream. Instead, the reformer saw the market in a *pragmatic-utilitarian* way as a device for 'repairing' the Soviet-type economy. In his view, the market does not embody justice in itself. It is, however, capable of working as a machine (cf. the term 'economic mechanism') which is geared, or even at times switched on and off, by the planners. This interpretation lent a *mechanical* (engineering) character to reformist liberalism.

No doubt about it, these deformations were considerably reduced in the course of the learning-by-doing process outlined above. None the less, liberalism in reform thinking remained *rootless* in a double sense. On one hand, the liberal tradition in economics in Eastern Europe was weak or broken, on the other, it was not reconstructed by importing or reinventing the basics of western liberalism. In the absence of a firm philosophical background, the trial-and-error procedures of reform-making could only lead to a pragmatic (profane) rediscovery of liberal thought. Liberal ideas resulted from practical choices, I would say, for want of a better solution, and were often against the moral conviction of the reform economists.

To be sure, the romantic anti-capitalist feelings inherited from Marxist teachings by the early reformers began to wane as the years passed.

Churchill's *bon mot* that democracy is the worst except for all other political systems, however, is still popular in Eastern Europe whenever economists discuss private property and the free market. Marketization *and* privatization tend to be considered musts, but they are regarded as necessary evils rather than 'the best of all possible worlds'. The latent animosity even the more liberal economists feel towards the 'inhuman' market is supported by traditional arguments that defend the principle of equal opportunity. *Egalitarian* considerations (whether they came directly from the Marxian Utopia of communism, western social-democratic thought, or from recent critiques of new classical liberalism) have not ceased to permeate reform and post-reform thinking until now.[36]

Waiting for the Grand Theory

From the very beginning, reform economics was inevitably confronted with the question (also well known for social-democratic ideologues): how can *Marxism and liberalism* be coupled? This question could be raised on every level of economic theory, beginning with the philosophical-methodological premises (how can the holistic and deterministic approach of Marxism be associated with the essential individualism and subjectivism sustaining liberal thought?), all the way to the actual proposals for mixing economic institutions in a Soviet-type society (how can the party-state be harmonized with medium- or large-scale private property and/or with autonomous forms of collective ownership?). That is to say, in addition to facing the problem of how to reconcile interpretations of liberty, equality, tolerance, virtue, rationality, common good, private initiative, and so on, between the two worlds of ideas, reform economics had to clarify analytically the underlying issue of whether the market could work in a modern economy without large-scale private ownership and political democracy at all.

We know from the experience of the 1960s that the Marxian paradigm permitted a partial reinterpretation of Communist values, based on anthropological principles. Even the notion of the 'entrepreneur' could somehow be squeezed into the official version of reformist ideology under the disguise of *homo faber*. But we also clearly remember how, in Hungary, Poland or Yugoslavia, committed neo-Marxists came into conflict with themselves when, during the 1970s, the vision of communism proved indefensible, either in terms of pure economics or in terms of the final goal of the transitional – market socialist – society. As the limits of market liberalization loosened up in many countries of Eastern Europe, the prospect of communism without commodity production, alienation, division of labour, and so on, grew ever gloomier.[37]

The transition became an end in itself instead of a means of approaching communism; what is more, its direction appeared to be reversed. When the old scenario of socialist transition written back in the Soviet 1920s, which was based on the theorem of the 'expanding islands' (whereby the islands of the state economy are gradually absorbing the sea of the private/market economy) proved to fail, the dedicated Marxists had to leave the scene of the reforms. As regards politics, there were, of course, strong factors at work which prolonged the silent symbiosis of neo-Marxist and reformist thought (common critique of Stalinism, reforms delaying the collapse of socialism, need for mutual legitimization, and so on).

Reform economics can be described, somewhat irreverently, as a game of *searching for surrogate capitalists*.[38] The reformers found these agents of marketizing the Soviet-type economy in the figure of a manager of a state enterprise or holding company, in a member of the board of self-managing firm or co-operative, not to mention a great number of mixed types. In experimenting with the various structures of property rights to find an adequate measure of 'enterprise autonomy', the Marxists had to definitely pull out of the game after the radical wing of reform economists started to shift from advocating decentralization, indirect control, self-management, and so on, to proposals for real (non-simulated) privatization. From that point on, reformism unambiguously meant a kind of capitalist ideology to them.

And the liberal theorist, when would *he* have pulled out of the game if he had entered it at all? For an uncompromising liberal the game was suspicious from the very beginning when the socialist reform economists started operating with limited, *partitioned* and *simulated* concepts of liberty, property rights, rationality, and so on. How can liberalism be merely economic, how can socialism not be collectivist? – he would justifiably ask. A nightwatch-state which is awake during the day, too? The invisible hand which is conspicuously held fast by a visible one? What is a *socialist* market? What is socialist democracy? Why plan and market? Why not market and, perhaps, some plan?

'Libermanism is not liberalism' – declared the western observer resignedly back in the 1960s.[39] Since then, there were analysts in the west who – instead of calling the reformers closet capitalists – described the ambiguous 'liberal-collectivist' concepts of reform as intellectual attempts at being only a little pregnant. This also reflected the substantial lack of interest on the part of the majority of liberal economic theorists in any development of reform economics as science. Considering it a kind of 'political geography', they usually relegated reform economics to the field of Sovietology or, at best, to that of comparative economic systems.[40]

Less steadfast liberals did not concern themselves with philosophical reservations. They simply asked: surrogate capitalists amidst fundamentally collectivist property rights; simulated market with a self-deregulating state; informal pluralism within a formally monolithic political system, and so on – are these unstable, amorphous combinations appropriate for providing a solid base for a new school of economic science?

Coming back to the game analogy, this question can be reformulated as follows: is there a phase at all in searching for the surrogate capitalists (somewhere between the liberalization of small- and medium-scale private property) where the Marxist has not yet quit while the liberal has already entered the game? Can this phase last long enough to be defined as an object of a new scientific paradigm? One can, of course, reverse the question: let us imagine a phase where the Marxist has already left the scene but the liberal has not yet entered it. We encounter a large theoretical gap, a gap which the reform economists of Eastern Europe were not unfamiliar with (cf. the concept of the 'third way').

To be sure, in the real world there do exist meeting points for certain derivatives of socialist and liberal theories in the field of social-democratic type mixed economies. One might think, therefore, that the leftist variants of the doctrine of *Soziale Marktwirtschaft* could have been a reasonable target when reform economists were searching for a coherent concept of market socialism. But evidently, the two reformisms were not the same. Reform economics would have certainly gained in scholarly coherence by accepting – like social democracy in the west – large-scale private ownership and political democracy. At the same time, this radical move would have undermined its basic ideological principle, namely, reformism under real socialism. In addition, it is by no means proved beyond a doubt that by crossing the border of the plan-and-market discourse one would really reach the realm of a new scientific paradigm of economic theory. At this juncture, I turn to my colleagues in Austria, Germany or Sweden: let them ask if 'social-democratic economics' is still possible after the neo-liberal wave of the last two decades.

The logical experiment of building up a Grand Theory of socialist economic reform, a theory that did not emerge from the historical zigzags of reforming real socialism, proved unsuccessful. Wisdom of hindsight shows that it was a vain effort to make virtue out of necessity: that is, to search for a new paradigm of economic science within the limits of the plan-and-market discourse. Why not admit in retrospect (speaking in, if you please, Kuhnian language) that (a) the consensus within the scientific community of reform economists was rooted in a minimalist definition of the plan-and-market discourse rather than in the maximal (or at least reasonable) amount of scholarly principles of economics; (b) the values represented by the reformers were ambiguous (cf. liberalism versus collectivism); (c) the concepts applied were shaky and the methodological apparatus of economic research was often eclectic and obsolete (cf. 'speculative institutionalism'). Furthermore, it was unlikely that a coherent synthesis of reform thinking could ever be provided; the adoption of intellectual traditions was disturbed (cf. 'deformed liberalism') and the revolutionary-innovative power of the new theory was doubtful.[41]

Nevertheless, reform economics was capable of providing an authentic *in vivo* analysis of economic disequilibrium (shortage), centralization (monopolies) and hierarchical bargaining, business cycles, state redistribution, non-monetary transactions, shadow economy, and so on, namely, of those phenomena of excessive market distortion which could otherwise only be examined in 'normal' market economies in small scale, almost *in vitro*. Therefore, one could justifiably regard this hybrid discipline as an attempt that aimed at the construction of a general economic theory of market socialism but finally resulted in a kind of '*borderline-case economics*'. In any event, if reform economists had stopped flirting with the half-solutions of socialist marketization, there might have been an opportunity to follow a great many lines of thought, started three or four decades ago, to their logical ends. When a reformer wanted to comprehend market behaviour within the state economy, he was probably quite original and stimulating in describing how it did *not* work there, but he was rather frustrating to read as he persisted in trying to design a way for it to do so.

A THEORY OF TRANSFORMATION?

I am convinced that the above qualifications do not imply a dismissive attitude towards a number of intellectual achievements of reform economics. And commonplace though it may be, there are times in history which do not particularly favour the advance of economic science. '*Inter arma silent musae*' – the reform economist said. Sometimes – as we have seen – '*extra arma*', too – I add hastily.

Let us see if reform economics could be described in a less ambitious way: instead of forcing the definition on to the level of pure economics, why not consider this branch of economic thought a subdiscipline of the theory of economic and political liberalization (deregulation) in Soviet-type societies? Why talk about 'carelessness' in scientific matters, if it is well known that economic reform thinking was organically permeated by ideology and politics? In fact, it *was* possible to implement a series of socialist economic reforms under the banner of some controversial guiding principles without a clear picture of the points of departure and destination of the changes desired (with some exaggeration, adopting the old reformist slogan 'the movement is everything, the final goal is nothing'). What is more, maybe there was no other way to implement them . . .

The structure of the mix: towards a political theory?

If the reform concepts are treated as a mix of economic, ideological and political statements, and interpreted in their sociological context, the scholarly deficiencies may turn into advantages. For incoherence, eclecticism, amorphousness, and so on, though pejorative terms in the vocabulary of the history of science, may serve as proof of the flexibility of a *pragmatic discourse* if we look upon reform economics in such a way.

Understanding the plan-and-market discourse as a 'clever' language[42] may lead to the evaluation of economic reformism according to its success at solving the old paradox of reform-making: how to transcend the *status quo* without upsetting it? As a result, the scholarly qualities will be replaced by a degree of political efficiency in manoeuvring between extremes such as war Communist planning and the free market.

In describing the non-economic components of reform economics, it seems a more plausible choice to separate first the ideological constituents. So, economic reformism can easily be depicted as a reflection of the political Utopia of democratic socialism. According to this interpretation, reform economics was by definition *political* economy, even if it sometimes appeared as a sort of economics, a seemingly neutral science of economic technicalities.[43] If we prefer the functional analysis of ideologies to mere *Ideologiekritik*, we can also disentangle in retrospect the programmatic, legitimating, modernizing, critical, and so on, roles assumed by reformist thought, and reconstruct the conflicting values, interests and power relations represented by the various groups of reformers.

Both kinds of analysis demonstrate that the evolution of reform economics over the last thirty to forty years in Eastern Europe meant radicalization, that is to say, the reinforcement of the theory's ideological and political pillars, rather than refinement in terms of economic science. Once a self-restraining world outlook revealed through economic arguments, socialist reformism gradually grew into a self-proclaimed political theory, too.[44] So, knowing that the reform concepts were not able to promise Eastern Europe a grand economic theory in the past, can reform economics be interpreted as a component of a grand *political* theory of socialist reforms?[45]

The majority of what we have regarded as obstacles to scholarly evolution in economics, however, also applies to political science. To put it simply, oscillating between the doctrines of 'maximal' and 'minimal state', public and private ownership, and so on, also damages a political theory if it claims to be coherent.[46] But should a reformist theory of politics claim to? Can't its adherents declare: it is exactly this oscillation that we want to understand and make perfect. Can't the absolutist requirements of the theory of science be more easily neglected here than in economics?

In the middle of the road

I use this metaphor in a triple sense, indicating not only the ideological and political ambiguities of the reform economists, and the compromises made on the level of economic scholarship, but also the very nature of the theory's subject. For reform economics did its best in terms of authentic scientific performance when working as a kind of deregulation theory, in which the problem of 'from where to where' was blurred but the *process* itself of dismantling controls remained discernible. I would not call it an evolution or transformation theory, although it was able to describe the way of transformation up to a certain point: it allowed you to step off the pavement and zigzag more or less safely among the cars in the middle of the road, but it could not show you what was on the other side of the street.

To extend the analogy, reform economics was really good at teaching its disciples how to break down the barriers separating the pavement from the road (or rather, how to sneak under them), but as a peculiar theory of transformation-without-end, it could represent at best the controversial concept of *'permanent reform* along the "third way"' that leaves the pavement of real socialism without arriving at any form of capitalism.[47]

In any event, although the reformers often remained uninformed about the state of things on this side of the street, too, the theory of reform, conceived as a *pilot programme* proved capable of clearing the way for a kind of more liberal post-reform (that is, transformation) economics that does not observe the limits of reform economics any more.[48]

Furthermore, few would challenge the view that, in principle, deregulation could be best studied using the example of Soviet-type state economies where the fabric of regulation was incomparably more comprehensive, intricate and durable than in most western war economies in contemporary history, and where government intervention became an organic (self-reproducing) part of the system. While economic deregulation in Soviet-type societies also means something similar to the transition from a war to a peace economy (therefore one could hardly expect from the reform economists radically new doctrines in this field), the specifically Chinese, Polish or Yugoslav techniques for dismantling the controls form an authentic part of the overall literature on economic liberalization.

Bargaining within paradoxes

Does portraying reform economics as a middle-of-the-road transformation theory really offer the historian new means of understanding reform concepts retrospectively?

In the past few decades, the political process of economic reform-making revealed a series of paradoxes responsible for the incoherence of reformist thought, which stemmed from its starting compromises. Reform – from below or from above? All at once or step by step? In economic life alone or also in the political system? In the economic institutions or in economic policies as well? In a slump or during an upswing? Well-known practical dilemmas[49] like these appeared on the theoretical level as paradoxes without proper logical solutions.

For often the same factors which allowed the launching of a reform process were also active in reversing it later on (cf. the survival of the core of the party-state that was ready to intervene on seeing the short-run destabilizing effects of market reforms). When the reform measures were portioned out from above cautiously, as a medicine for crisis prevention, they might not attain this aim, because the medicine was neutralized by the non-reformed parts of the system. At the same time, reform economics would have lost its genuinely reformist character if its representatives had opted for the radical solution of the paradoxes, and initiated a genuine reform movement from below, launching vigorous offensives simultaneously in broad segments of the economy and politics. This could have killed the reform project in its embryonic stage. Both were lost causes. Finally, as far as the third solution is concerned, that is, when the reformers tried to mix the moderate and radical solutions, it happened that either the recommended way was logically not viable (for example, a little bit of capital market did not function as a market), or it offered a complicated stratagem of 'guerilla warfare' to the reformers, which could not be incorporated into a coherent economic concept. (In the real world, of course, the reform economists could not avoid manoeuvring between the rocks of quasi-reforms and abortive reforms, seeking a way that was still acceptable to both below and above.)

Relying on these paradoxes, one can, probably, grasp the evolution of reform ideas better than by the simple model suggested by reform economists of 'we develop if we are permitted to'. Through the paradoxes, the starting political compromises between plan and market got built into the economic theory and the theorists themselves (for example, one could always recognize the 'eternal planner' in the reformer). So the analyst cannot make success without elaborate models of political interaction.

Abandoning the strictly hierarchical interpretation, according to which the fate of reform economics was almost totally dependent on the political authorities (an interpretation that might have been correct in the late 1950s in Hungary, after 1968 in Czechoslovakia, and so on), and, at the same time, doubting the rival thesis that intellectuals have taken 'class power,'[50] we can arrive at a *dynamic model of bargaining*. This model would include the factors of both co-operation and conflict between the representatives of reformist economic science and politics. A discussion of the bargaining process then reveals a host of varying strategies on the part of reform economists (offensive and defensive, radical and moderate, overplaying, delaying, evasive or bluffing, and so on). These may explain important motives for launching or keeping back certain reform ideas, and extending or contracting the scope and the 'clamourousness' of the reform proposals.

Also, the apparently *cyclical* elements of the evolution of reform economics can be more realistically studied in this way, since we do not have to attribute, for instance, the subsequent bursts of reform thinking, for want of a better explanation, exclusively to the decline of the economy, or to the internal development of reform economics.[51] Instead, we can trace the fine irregularities of change (storing, irradiation, synergism, simulation, mutation, substitution, and so on, of reform ideas) as well.

The bargaining approach also illuminates how reformist thought was 'straightened out' in China, Hungary, Poland and Yugoslavia after the dramatic ups and downs of its initial stage. It shows why reform economics often refrained from touching the final taboos even in times of its expansion, and why it did not necessarily have to go through a *catharsis* during the contraction phases. In order to understand this pattern of self-correction, we must study the sociological preconditions for the partial integration ('étatization') of reform economics in certain countries of Eastern Europe, as a result of which it became a semi-official ideology more or less protected by a reform-minded government administration. The gradual separation of reform economics from the university political economy department and the 'partnership' of the reformers with some members of high-level economic management that was mediating the reform proposals of the academics with the ultimate bargaining partner, the hardliners in the Communist Party leadership, were spectacular features not only of the long-lived Hungarian New Economic Mechanism.[52]

Reform economics was inconceivable without the political *métier* of economic theorists, that is, without the establishment of their role as experts, which gave them bargaining chips. It was often this kind of long-run professionalization and radicalization (that is, increasing utilization of the expert power) that many observers tended to mistake for scholarly refinement.

'Reform bargaining' was based on a varying degree of co-operation, the foundations of which had to be continually reinforced by updating the starting compromises to avoid its getting out of control.

And what if they cannot be reinforced any more? Are there still reserve models of reform economics before one exceeds the final limits of the plan-and-market discourse on the way to a social market economy? Will the disciples of a socialist market economy attempt (and survive) this illegal border crossing or, scared off by the risk, will they become instead agents of a stagnant or decaying reformist thought? Maybe reform economics will leave the scene of economic thought in both cases: either as a mutant subspecies of 'social market economy' or as a hybrid incapable of life – these are burning questions for the Eastern European economists of our time. When I put them I realize compassion made me forget most of my doubts.

This is how I finished my first paper written in the framework of our 'Plan and/or market' project in 1988. Since then entering the social-liberal discourse has become 'legal' for the former reform economists. Nevertheless, reformist thought has so far preserved some of its important features for posterity.

In the beginning, the majority of the project participants assumed that in the evolution of late socialist reform concepts, there were two directions left. We thought that reform economics might progress towards a theory of corporative state economy and even towards that of a political dictatorship with a *laissez-faire* economy. In essential points, both scenarios would remain within the limits of the compromises made by the socialist reformers. In the second half of the 1980s, some reform economists in Eastern Europe were inclined to accept these ideas when they lost their faith in the rapid disintegration of the Soviet-type party-state. Since then there have hardly been any predictions about the fate of real socialism that did not fail. These two possibilities of change in Eastern European economics, however would still be too early to exclude even if many of the states in the region have in the meantime been deprived of the bulk of their Soviet-type characteristics.

Sociologically, a great many radical reformers (from Balcerowicz in Poland, through Tardos in Hungary, all the way to Popov in the Soviet Union or Bajt in Yugoslavia) have proved capable of 'sliding' into a transformer position and becoming advisers to new democratic governments and parties. Theoretically, however, it has not been so easy to change. As a contrast to the bold expectations in the west, there is no neo-liberal (libertarian) breakthrough in economics under post-socialism. The strong legacy of what I called above 'deformed liberalism' of the reformers could not be entirely broken, first of all because the daily tasks of *engineering the transformation processes* in a deep economic crisis reinforce the statist-constructivist attitudes and social commitments of the ex-reform economists. The imaginary pendulum that was supposed to swing from the extreme of totalitarian collectivism to the other extreme of *laissez-faire* has already swung to the other direction but seems to stop not very far from the point of suspension. The reformist dream of halting the pendulum right in the middle proved to be a Utopia. The 'transformist' dream of moving it much closer to a liberal position may also become one . . .[53]

NOTES

*I wish to express my gratitude to Aladár Madarász and Márton Tardos, who offered valuable comments on the earlier drafts of this chapter, and to Cara Michelle Morris for reading the text.

1 This chapter has been written in the past tense to express – probably exaggerate – hopes in the end of the era of socialist reformism in Eastern Europe. In the 'unfinished revolutions' of the Soviet Union and China (not to mention some countries on the Balkans) there remained great reserves of reformist thought even after 1989.

In what follows, the last three to four decades in the life of the 'reform countries' of Eastern Europe will feature as the principal subject of analysis. The history of economic reform concepts under socialism, however, extends beyond these limits: it begins in 1921 with the introduction of the New Economic Policy in Moscow, and the frontiers of Eastern Europe stretch as far as Beijing. (The expressions 'reform concept', 'reform theory' and 'reform programme' will be used interchangeably in the chapter. In this context, theory does not necessarily mean scientific theory.)

2 This chapter is not the end-product of an exhaustive historical survey of reform concepts in Soviet-type economies. As it was said in the Prologue, the systematic comparison of socialist reform programmes by our research group was interrupted by the conversion of these programmes into scenarios for the post-socialist transition. In writing this paper I borrowed a great deal, despite all our disagreements (and my Hungarian biases), from the participants of our 'plan and/or market' project. I owe special thanks to them (see notes 3, 4, 5 in the Prologue).

3 Cf. Kornai's typology of Hungarian reformist thought (Kornai 1986). Admitting the elegance of his classification scheme, I must confess that I could hardly find a single economist in my country who would not have had reservations about its underlying principles. As regards Kornai's typology, I have doubts about the separation of Langeism from naïve reformism; the mixing of the characteristics of reform, reform evasion and anti-reform in the term 'Galbraithian socialism'; the inclusion of Liska's entrepreneurialism in the type of the radical reformers; and about the understatements used both when appreciating and criticizing the latter. For my critique of the existing comparative schemes, see Kovács (1990a) (see also Klaus and Jezek 1991).

4 Cf. Lengyel (1989), Szamuely (1986) and Kovács (1984, 1986). See also the answers of Hungarian economists to the questions of *Acta Oeconomica* about the concept of 'socialist market economy' (On Socialist . . . 1989).

5 For the logical problems of justifying reform moves, see Brus (1986) and Rychard (1988), as well as Bajt's, Osiatynski's and Zhou's papers in this book. See also the recent debate among Hungarian economists on reform and recentralization (Antal, Berend and Szamuely 1989).

6 Cf. Kornai (1980a), Lengyel (1989) and 'On Socialist . . .' (1989). In Hungary and Poland (and lately in the Soviet Union) the economists were generously assisted by sociologists in empirical research. See Aven's and Osiatynski's papers in this book. See also Rychard (1988) and Kovács (1991).

7 Here are a few quotations from the Hungarian literature of reform economics for illustration:

> The history of our subject (the critique of the economic mechanism) proceeds (along the lines of increasing generalization and objectivization . . . We see a clear picture of scholarly activities becoming more and more comprehensive and raising ever broader questions.
>
> (Bródy 1983)

> Our science – has it marked time or advanced? . . . Our science has covered a very great distance . . . The iteration between science and politics has had a fruitful effect on both. It is the overview of the history of the last four decades that may rightly convince us that the course of further development will follow this trend.
>
> (Hoch 1985)

> By the 1980s, there had taken shape a descriptive concept of the economic mechanism built on solid foundations both from the point of view of economics and of sociology. It is associated with normative economics, which vigorously demands the reform of the economic mechanism. This is the launch-pad from which the new generations take off in the debate on economic mechanism..
>
> (Lengyel 1984)

For recent sceptical interpretations, see 'On Socialist . . .' (1989).

8 Providing patterns was for a long time a strong priority of the ideology of the 'self-managed market economy' in Yugoslavia (cf. Horvat 1982). Until recently, Šik has also insisted on the idea of 'humane economic democracy' (Šik 1972, 1979, 1985, 1987). For the Polish versions of the concept of self-management, see Kowalik's and Osiatynski's chapters in this book. See also Kowalik (1986). Hungarian reformers usually showed moderation in recommending the 'export of humanization' to the west (see Kornai 1980b).

9 See Liska (1985, 1989), Šik (1972, 1979), Kowalik (1989) and also Brus's and Nove's chapters in this book.

10 Cf. Bauer (1979, 1984), Horvat (1982), Šik (1972). See also Brus's, Kowalik's and Sutela's chapters in this book. For a critical view of the relationship between Marxism and reformism, see Rakowski (1978) and Kolakowski (1978). See also the debate between Ernst Mandel and Alec Nove in *New Left Review* (Mandel 1986, 1988), Nove (1987) and 'On Socialist . . .' (1989).

11 Nina Andreeva's recent philippics are known too well. See also Szegö's and Latouche's rough attacks on the Hungarian reformers, in which conspiracy and social-Darwinism belong to the lighter accusations (Szegö 1983), Latouche (1985). For similar criticisms in China and the Soviet Union, see Zhou's and Sutela's chapters in this book.

My sceptical attitude towards socialist reformism has never been based on the premise, fairly common in the neo-Stalinist critique of reform thinking in Eastern Europe, that reform economics is primarily a political movement of marginal intellectuals, disguised by pseudo-scientific argumentation, which uses understatements like 'decentralized planning' merely to sugarcoat the principles of *laissez faire* (cf. Kovács 1984, 1986, 1990a, b, 1991).

12 Cf. Bauer (1987), Bornstein (1979), Kowalik (1986), Nuti (1988) and Kovács (1990a). See also 'On Socialist . . .' (1989), and Bajt's, Davies's and Zhou's chapters in this book.

13 See, for instance, the following case studies: Batt (1988), Comisso (1979), Duff Milenkovitch (1971), Katsenelinboigen (1980), Kornai (1986), Kowalik (1986), Sutela (1984), Szamuely (1982, 1984), Wu (1988) and Zauberman (1976). In the history of socialist reformism there were quite a few legendary examples for semi-official reform packages (cf. the materials of the Varga Commission in Hungary in 1957 and of the Economic Council in Poland between 1956 and 1962, or the various reform blueprints made in the TSEMI in Moscow during the 1960s). For the lack of basic works in Hungarian economic science, see Kovács (1991).

14 For the place of Kornai's shortage theory in this interpretation, see Kovács (1991). Horvat's voluminous *Political Economy of Socialism*, published in 1982, rests on rather weak pillars in terms of empirical evidence. At any rate, the low-tide of practical reformism during the 1970s resulted in a general upswing of empirical research into the causes of the failure of reforms. The analytical processing of the new empirical facts, however, did not lead to a rejection of the reformist world-outlook as such. Of course, an important exception is China, where the first half of the 1980s witnessed a great upsurge of normative reformist thought (see Wu 1988 and Zhou's paper in this book).

15 Cf. Brus (1975, 1981, 1983, 1985), Brus and Laski (1989), Laski (1985, 1987), Nove (1983), Selucky (1979), Šik (1972, 1979, 1985, 1987). See also the works of Kosta and Levcik. Interestingly enough, the émigrés – while being more steadfast in their political critique of the Soviet-type systems – were not necessarily more radical than their colleagues at home in matters of privatization (cf. Brus's paper in this book).

16 For Kornai's changing attitude towards liberalism, see Kovács (1991).

17 It is the current dismantling of the Soviet-type system that provides the last opportunity to test the validity of the descriptive and analytical concepts which were used by the reformers in interpreting the economic behaviour of the *ancien régime* (cf. the notion of 'borderline-case economics' below).

18 Cf. Bauer (1984), Liska (1988, 1989), Siklaky (1985), Tardos (1972, 1982, 1986) and Tardos's paper in this book. For similar examples in other countries, see Kowalik's, Osiatynski's, Sutela's and Zhou's papers in this book.

19 Cf. Kornai's sceptical attitude towards normative economics and his critique of the main currents of Hungarian reformism (Kornai 1980a, b, 1986). In this volume Podkaminer calls for a widening of the knowledge of Eastern European economists in macroeconomics. For an important initiative to combine standard 'western' microeconomics with 'eastern' empiricism, see Galasi and Kertesi (1990).

20 See, for example, Bauer (1981) and Soós (1986). See also Brus (1986).

21 See Šik's idea of 'socialist commodity production' (1967), Brus's notion of a 'decentralized system' (1972), or Horvat's 'planning *cum* market' concept (1982). See also Popov's and Rakitskii's recent thoughts about the 'administrative' or 'barracks-like' system in the Soviet Union (Popov 1987; Rakitskii and Rakitskaia 1989). It is interesting to note that sometimes even empirical-minded economists got involved in rather speculative argumentation (cf. Bauer's 'neither-plan-nor-market' concept (1984) or Kornai's compromises between efficiency and socialist morals (1980b)). See also some recent attempts made by reform economists at defining the term of 'socialist market economy' ('On Socialist . . .' 1989).

22 Cf. Brus (1972), Horvat (1969), Lisichkin (1966), Péter (1956) and Šik (1967).

23 See, for example, the 1985 textbook of the Karl Marx University of Economics, Budapest (Hámori 1985). The first manual of microeconomics was published in Budapest only in 1988, twelve years after the first Hungarian translation of Samuelson's textbook. As regards the official economics manuals, the situation was not much more favourable in Belgrade and Warsaw either (cf. Vacic 1988). True, political economy in the university departments (which were in every socialist country traditionally more conservative than the research institutes of the government and the Academy of Sciences) could not resist 'secularization' as years passed. See also Sutela's paper in this book about the textbooks of socialist political economy in the Soviet Union.

24 Cf. Berend (1983), Brus (1985, 1986), Kowalik (1986), Nove (1983) and Szamuely (1982, 1984, 1986). See also Zhou's paper in this book.

25 See Antal *et al.* (1987), Balcerowicz (1987), Brus and Laski (1989), Gligorov (1991), Klaus and Jezek (1991), Kornai (1988), Kowalik (1986), Rumiantsev (1990, 1991), Rychard (1988), Szelényi (1989) and Winiecki (1987). See also Brus's, Comisso's, Davies's and Tardos's papers in this book.

26 See Kovács (1983, 1991).

27 For this 'indifference', see Bajt's, Grosfeld's, Leipold's and Dietz's papers in this book. See also Kovács (1991) on the historical gap between reformist thought in Hungary and economic science in the west. It is the misfortune of the Chinese, Hungarian and Polish, economists that the Yugoslav reform model offered better opportunities for examination by means of the standard analytical tools of mainstream economics. Now there are dozens of models of the 'Illyrian' firm in the literature, while the analytical patterns, different from what Lange proposed, of the 'Pannonian' or 'Polonian' ones are still lacking (cf. the works of Domar, Dreze, Estrin, Meade, Pejovich, Svejnar, Vanek and Ward). Duff Milenkovitch (1984) made a stimulating attempt to resist the magnetic attraction of the labour-managed economy.

28 Cf. Brus (1986), Lewin (1974), Madarász (1985) and Szamuely (1986).

29 Cf. Klaus and Ježek (1991) about the constructivist inclinations of the 'socialist

liberals' in Czechoslovakia, and Sutela (1984) about the lasting influence of the group of 'optimal planners' in the Soviet Union. See also Nuti (1988), Wagener (1985) and Davies's, Nove's and Zhou's papers in this book.

30 Cf. Kowalik (1986), Rychard (1988) and Kovács (1990a).

31 Cf. Bergson (1967), Brus (1972, 1985), Kornai (1986), Lavoie (1985), 'On Socialist . . .' (1989), Schüller (1988), and Balcerowicz's paper in this book.

32 Cf. Brus (1972), Horvat (1969), Lisichkin (1966), Šik (1967). This 'anti-apparatchik' approach has – understandably – prevailed in Soviet economic thought from Bukharin to Shatalin. See also Brus's paper in this book.

33 Ibid. For market failures, see Horvat (1982) and Šik (1985). See also Tardos (1972) on the competitive and non-competitive sectors in the state economy, and Wagener (1990a) about the impossibility of planning the market process.

34 Kornai's proposition about the 'whirlpool of bureaucratic restriction of the market' is a remarkable exception in the literature (Kornai 1984). See also Dietz's paper in this book.

35 See the popularity of concepts such as 'state-socialist redistribution', 'paternalism', 'administrative economy', and so on in the work of radical reform economists and sociologists (Brus and Laski 1989; Kornai 1988; Kowalik 1986; Lengyel 1989; Popov 1987; Szelényi 1989). See also Bajt's paper in this book.

36 For more about 'deformed liberalism', see Kovács (1990c, 1991).

37 Cf. Gligorov (1991), Klaus and Ježek (1991), Kolakowski (1978), Rakowski (1978).

38 See, for example, Brus and Laski (1989), Liska (1988), Nuti (1988), Tardos (1972).

39 Cf. Linder (1967)

40 See, for example, Buchanan (1979), Friedman (1984). Among the leading Eastern European economists Kornai was the least ready to accept this kind of discrimination. In criticizing general equilibrium theory, he did not cease to stress the similarity between the crucial problems of 'eastern' and 'western' economics. He even called repeatedly for the elaboration of a 'synthetical systems theory' or a 'political economy of co-ordination' (Kornai 1971, 1984). See also Knirsch (1987) on the (im)possibility of constructing a general – East-West – theory.

41 Cf. Madarász (1985), and Grosfeld's paper in this book. Needless to say, any less relativist requirement of scientific research (for example, those set by Popper or Lakatos) would call the scholarly credentials of reform economics even more into question. See also Brus (1981), Kosta (1987), Knirsch (1988) and 'On Socialist . . .' (1989).

42 The reader might wonder: aren't there relatively strict rules, based on the conventions in the reformist community, that govern the language of reform economics? If he were not convinced by the above demonstration of the amorphous nature of the plan-and-market concepts, I would recommend that he reflect on what 'planmarket' stands for in Liska's entrepreneurial model, or 'planning *cum* market' in Horvat's self-management scheme. It is also worth while studying why at a certain point 'decentralization', 'indirect control', 'marketization', and so on, became synonyms in the reformist discourse.

43 See Kolakowski (1978), Konrád and Szelényi (1979) and Rakowski (1978). According to Rakowski (that is, György Bence and János Kis) '. . . though the idea of "market socialism" remained Utopian, as an ideology it was nevertheless capable at certain moments of becoming a serious practical force and of having a real effect on social behaviour and attitudes'. Konrád and Szelényi recommend a revision of the term 'revisionism': 'We have to release the economic reformers of the 1960s in Eastern Europe from the accusation of revisionism, for we consider them the natural heirs of the rationalizing tendencies of Stalinist economic policy'.

44 This was exemplified by the fact that in the 1980s the doors of reform economics opened up not only before the historians and legal theorists, but also the sociologists and political scientists (cf. Aven's, Comisso's and Osiatynski's papers in this book). See also Comisso (1991), Gligorov (1991), Rychard (1988), Szelényi (1989) and Kovács (1990a, 1991).

45 Furthermore, can reform economics be excluded from among the subdisciplines of an overall (non-systemic) social theory of reform-making? I mean, a social theory that would explore the ways of transition between certain states of a given economic and political system. Cf. H.-J. Wagener (1990b) and Dietz's paper in this book.

46 See Kornai (1988) on the 'medium state'. The recurrent hesitation of the reform economists to choose between self-management and the market does not help clear up the theory either (cf. Balcerowicz 1987; Bauer 1984; Kowalik 1986).

47 This concept covered the maximum amount of reformism that the official ideology was capable of consuming in Hungary, Poland or the Soviet Union in the second part of the 1980s (cf. 'On Socialist . . .' 1989).

48 This 'clearing' function is, however, controversial. Although the establishment of economic reformism in countries like Hungary, Poland and Yugoslavia resulted in shattering the ideals of communism, the new mythology of market (self-managing) socialism blocked the road of rediscovering liberalism for a long time. Cf. Gligorov (1991), Kovács (1991).

49 For the dilemmas of reform thinking, see Kornai (1980) and Kovács (1984).

50 Cf. Konrád and Szelényi (1979).

51 See Brus (1986) and Szamuely (1982, 1984, 1986).

52 This 'partnership' may be illustrated by a long list of such names as Csikós-Nagy, Friss and Nyers in Hungary, Baka, Pajestka and Sadowski in Poland or Abalkin, Aganbegjan and Bogomolov in the Soviet Union. These 'moderates' were usually accompanied by 'radical' reform economists (like Tardos in the case of Nyers). See Katsenelinboigen (1980), Kurczewski (1990) and Kovács (1984, 1986).

53 Cf. Kovács (1990c, 1991)

BIBLIOGRAPHY

Antal, L. (1989) 'A debate on the crisis of the Hungarian reform in the 1970s', *Acta Oeconomica* 40, 105–63.

Antal, L. Bokros, L., Csillag, I., Lengyel, L. and Matolcsy, Gy. (1987) 'Fordulat és reform' ('Turnaround and reform'), *Közgazdasági Szemle* 34(b), 642–708.

Balcerowicz, Leszek (1987) 'Remarks on the concept of ownership', *Oeconomica Polona* 1, 75–95.

Batt, Judy (1988) *Economic Reform and Political Change in Eastern Europe*, London, Macmillan.

Bauer, T. (1979) 'The science of economics and the East European systems', in F. Silnitsky, L. Silnitsky and K. Reyman (eds) *Communism and Eastern Europe*, New York, 144–7.

Bauer, T. (1981) *Tervgazdaság, beruházás, ciklusok (Planned Economy, Investments, Cycles)*, Budapest, Közgazdasági és Jogi Könyvkiadó.

Bauer, T. (1984) 'The second economic reform and ownership relations', *Eastern European Economics* 22, 33–87.

Bauer, T. (1987) 'Reforming or perfectioning the economic mechanism', *European Economic Review* 31.

Berend, T. I. (1983) *Gazdasági utkeresés 1956–1965 (Seeking Directions for the Economy)*, Budapest, Magvetö.

Berend, T. I. (1989) 'A debate on the crisis of the Hungarian reform in the 1970s', *Acta Oeconomica* 40.

Bergson, Abram (1967) 'Market socialism revisited', *Journal of Political Economy* 5, 655–73.

Bornstein, Morris (1979), 'Economic reform in Eastern Europe', in M. Bornstein (ed.) *Comparative Economic Systems. Models and Cases*, Homewood, Ill., Irwin.

Bródy, András (1983) 'A gazdasági mechanizmus birálatának három hulláma' ('Three waves of the critique of the economic mechanism'), *Közgazdasági Szemle* 30, 802–08.

Brus, W. (1972) *The Market in a Socialist Economy*, London, Routledge & Kegan Paul.

Brus, W. (1975) *Socialist Ownership and Political Systems*, London.

Brus, W. (1981) 'Is market socialism possible or necessary?', *Critique* 14.

Brus, W. (1983) 'Political pluralism and markets in communist systems', in S.G. Solomon (ed.) *Pluralism in the Soviet Union*, London.

Brus, W. (1985) 'Socialism – Feasible and viable?', *New Left Review* no. 153, 43–63.

Brus, W. (1986) 'Institutional change within a planned economy', in M. Kaser (ed.) *The Economic History of Eastern Europe 1919–1975*, vol. 3, Oxford, Clarendon Press.

Brus, W. and Laski, K. (1989) *From Marx to the Market. Socialism in Search of an Economic System*, Oxford, Clarendon Press.

Buchanan, James (1979) *What Should Economists Do?*, Indianapolis, Liberty Press.

Comisso, E. (1979) *Workers' Control under Plan and Market*, New Haven, Yale University Press.

Comisso, E. (1991) 'Property rights, liberalism, and the transition from "actually existing" socialism', *Eastern European Politics and Societies* 5(1), 162–89.

Duff Milenkovitch, D. (1971) *Plan and Market in Yugoslav Economic Thought*, New Haven, Yale University Press.

Duff Milenkovitch, D. (1984) 'Is market socialism efficient?', in A. Zimbalist (ed.) *Comparative Economics Systems. An Assessment of Knowledge, Theory and Method*, Boston, Kluwer – Nijhoff Publishing, 65–109.

Friedman, Milton (1984) *Market and Plan*, London, Centre for Research into Communist Economies.

Galasi, Péter and Kertesi, Gábor (1990) 'Korrupció és tulajdon' ('Corruption and the property rights'), *Közgazdasági Szemle* 37, 389–425.

Gligorov, Vladimir (1991) 'The discovery of liberalism in Yugoslavia', *Eastern European Politics and Societies* 5(1), 5–26.

Hámori, Balázs (1985) *A szocialista gazdaság elmélete* (*The Theory of the Socialist Economy*), Budapest, Közgazdasági és Jogi Könyvkiadó.

Hoch, Róbert (1985) 'A folyamatosság és a változás dilemmái' ('The dilemmas of continuity and change'), *Világosság* 11, Appendix.

Horvat, B. (1969) *An Essay on Yugoslav Society*, White Plains, New York, International Arts and Sciences Press.

Horvat, B. (1982) *The Political Economy of Socialism*, Oxford, Martin Robertson.

Katsenelinboigen, Aron (1980) *Soviet Economic Thought and Political Power in the USSR*, Oxford.

Klaus, Václav and Ježek, Tomáš (1991) 'Social criticism, false liberalism and recent changes in Czechoslovakia', *Eastern European Politics and Societies* 5(1), 26–41.

Knirsch, P. (1987) 'Economics in East and West on the way to a general theory?', manuscript, Berlin, Freie Universität.

Knirsch, P. (1987) 'Economic reform between plan and market', manuscript, Berlin, Freie Universität.

Kolakowski, Leszek (1978) *The Main Currents of Marxism*, Oxford, Oxford University Press.

Compassionate doubts about reform economics   331

Konrád, Gyögy and Szelényi, Iván (1979) *The Intellectuals on the Road to Class Power*, New York, Harcourt Brace Jovanovich.

Kornai, J. (1959) *Overcentralization in Economic Administration*, London, Oxford University Press.

Kornai, J. (1971) *Anti-Equilibrium. On Economic System's Theory and the Tasks of Research*, Amsterdam–Oxford, North Holland.

Kornai, J. (1980a) *Economics of Shortage*, Amsterdam New York–Oxford, North Holland.

Kornai, J. (1980b) 'The Dilemmas of a Socialist Economy', *Cambridge Journal of Economics* 2, 147–57.

Kornai, J. (1984) 'Bureaucratic and market coordination', *Osteuropa Wirtschaft* 29, 306–15.

Kornai, J. (1986) 'The Hungarian reform process: visions, hopes and reality', *Journal of Economic Literature* 24(4), 1687–744.

Kornai, J. (1988) 'Individual freedom and reform of the socialist economy', *European Economic Review* 32 (2–3), 233–67.

Kosta, Jiri (1987) 'Can socialist economic systems be reformed?' *WIIW Forschungsberichte* Juli, no. 130.

Kovács, J.M. (1983) 'Bargaining, assimilation, bargaining', *Eastern European Economics* 3

Kovács, J.M. (1984) 'A reform-alku sürüjében' ('In the thick of reform-bargaining') *Valóság* 27, 30–56.

Kovács, J.M. (1986) 'Reform-bargaining in Hungary', *Comparative Economic Studies* 28, 25–42.

Kovács, J.M. (1990a) 'Reform economics: the classification gap', *Daedalus* 119 (1), 215–49.

Kovács, J.M. (1990b) 'Szocialista vagy szociális piacgazdaság?' ('Socialist or social market economy?') *Világosság* 31, 65–72.

Kovács, J.M. (1990c) 'Das Große Experiment des Übergangs' ('The grand experiment of the transition'), *Transit* 1, 84–107.

Kovács, J.M. (1991) 'From reformation to transformation (limits to liberalism in Hungarian economic thought)', *Eastern European Politics and Societies* 5(1), 41–73.

Kowalik, T. (1986) 'On crucial reform of real socialism', Research Report no. 122, The Vienna Institute for Comparative Economic Studies.

Kowalik, T. (1989) 'Towards a mixed socialist economy', manuscript, Warsaw.

Kurczewski, Jacek (1990) 'Power and wisdom: the expert as mediating figure in contemporary Polish history', in I. Maclean, A. Montefiore and P. Winch (eds) *The Political Responsibility of Intellectuals*, Cambridge, Cambridge University Press, 77–101.

Laski, K. (1985) 'Wirtschaftsreformen in Osteuropa als Gegenstand der Wirtschaftstheorie', *Vierteljahrshefte zur Wirtschaftsforschung* 2.

Laski, K. (1987) 'Marx-Sozialismus, Marktsozialismus und Wirtschaftsreformen des "real-existierenden Sozialismus"', Research Report no. 129, The Vienna Institute for Comparative Economic Studie.

Latouche, Serge (1985) 'Hibás elméletre alapozott receptek' ('Prescriptions based on a false theory'), *Tervgazdasági Fórum* 1, 31–41.

Lavoie Don (1985) *Rivalry and Central Planning. The Socialist Calculation Debate Reconsidered*, Cambridge, Cambridge University Press.

Lengyel, László (1984) 'A gazdasági mechanizmus reformjáról' ('On the reform of the economic mechanism'), *Valóság* 27, 88–96.

Lengyel, L. (1989) *Végkifejlet (End-Game)*, Budapest, Közgazdasági és Jogi Könyvkiadó.

Lewin, Moshe (1974) *Political Undercurrents in Soviet Economic Debates*, Princeton NJ, Princeton University Press.

Linder, Willy (1967) *Libermanismus ist nicht Liberalismus*, Siegen.

Lisichkin, *Gennadii* (1966) *Plan i rynok (Plan and Market)*, Moscow.

Liska, T. (1985) 'Liberális hatások a "szocialista vállalkozás" elméletére' ('Liberal impacts on the theory of "socialist entrepreneurship")', *Medvetánc* 2–3, 277–95.

Liska, T. (1988) *Ökonosztát (Econostate)*, Budapest, Közgazdasági és Jogi Könyvkiadó.

Liska, T. (1989) *Szent barmunk a politika alaprendje (Our Sacred Cow – the Political System)*, Budapest, Betüvetö.

Madarász, Aladár (1985) 'Uj paradigma felé?' ('Towards a new paradigm?'), in *Az uj Magyarország 4o éve*, Budapest, Kossuth.

Mandel, E. (1986) 'In defence of socialist planning', *New Left Review* 159, 5–39.

Mandel, E. (1988) 'The myth of market socialism', *New Left Review*, 169, 108–19.

Nove, A. (1983) *The Economics of Feasible Socialism*, London, Allen & Unwin.

Nove, A. (1987) 'Markets and socialism', *New Left Review* 161, 98–105.

Nuti, Mario (1988) 'Perestroika: the economics of transition between central planning and market socialism', Plan and/or Market project, Institut für die Wissenschaften vom Menschen, Vienna.

On Socialist Market Economy (1989) (Hungarian contributors: B. Csikós-Nagy, T. Földi, A. Hegedüs, R. Hoch, B. Kádár, F. Kozma, M. Laki, L. Lengyel, T. Nagy, L. Szamuely, M. Tardos; Foreign contributors: A. Bajt, L. Balcerowicz, Ch. Bettelheim, H.C. Bos, J. von Brabant, E. Comisso, K. Dyba, B. Horvat, P. Knirsch, M. Lavigne, G. Lisichkin, A. Nove, H–J. Wagener, *Acta Oeconomica*, 3–4.

Péter, György (1956) *A gazdaságosság és jövedelmezöség szerepe a tervgazdálkodásban (The Role of Efficiency and Rentability in the Planned Economy)*, Budapest, Közgazdasági és Jogi Könyvkiadó.

Popov, Gavril (1987) 'O romane A. Beka "Novoie naznachenie" ('About A. Bek's novel "New Appointment"') '*Nauka i zhizn*' 4, 54–65.

Rakitskii, Boris and Rakitskaia, G. (1989) 'Politicheskie predposylki perestroiki obshchestvennykh otnoshenii' ('Political preconditions for the transformation of social relations'), in A. Zavialova (ed.) *Postizhenie*, Moscow, Progress, 341–57.

Rakowski, Marc (Bence György and Kis János) (1978) *Towards an East-European Marxism*, London, Allison & Busby.

Rumiantsev, O. (1990) 'Authoritarian modernisation and the social-democratic alternative', *Social Research* Summer, 493–529.

Rumiantsev, O. (1991) 'From confrontation to social contract', *Eastern European Politics and Societies* 5(1), 113–27.

Rychard, Andrzej (1988) 'Social and political preconditions for and consequences of economic reform in Poland', Research Report no. 143, The Vienna Institute for Comparative Economic Studies.

Schüller, Alfred (1988) *Does Market Socialism Work?* London, Centre for Research into Communist Economies.

Selucky, Radoslav (1979) *Marxism, Socialism, Freedom*, New York, St Martin's Press.

Šik, O. (1967) *Plan and Market under Socialism*, White Plains, New York, International Arts and Sciences Press.

Šik, O. (1972) *Der dritte Weg (The Third Way)*, Hamburg, Hofmann & Campe.

Šik, O. (1976) *Das Kommunistische Machtsystem*, Hamburg.

Šik, O. (1979) *Humane Wirtschaftsdemokratie*, Hamburg, Knaus Verlag.

Šik, O. (1985) *Ein Wirtschaftssystem der Zukunft*, Berlin, Springer Verlag.

Šik, O. (1987) *Wirtschaftssysteme. Vergleiche – Theorie – Kritik*, Heidelberg.

Siklaky, István (ed.) (1985) *Koncepció és kritika. Vita Liska Tibor 'szocialista vállalkozási szektor' javaslatáról (Concept and Critique. A Debate on the Proposal by Tibor Liska of the 'Socialist Sector of Entrepreneurship')*, Budapest, Magvetö.

Soós, K. Attila (1986) *Terv, kampány, pénz* (*Plan, Campaign, Money*), Budapest, Közgazdasági és Jogi Könyvkiadó.
Sutela, Pekka (1984) *Socialism, Planning and Optimality. A Study in Soviet Economic Thought*, Helsinki, Finnish Society of Sciences and Letters.
Szamuely, L. (1982) 'The first wave of the mechanism debate in Hungary 1954–57', *Acta Oeconomica* 29, 1–24.
Szamuely, L. (1984) 'The second wave of the economic mechanism debate and the 1968 reform in Hungary', *Acta Oeconomica* 33, 43–67.
Szamuely, L. (1986) *A magyar közgazdasági gondolat fejlödése. Bevezetés* (*The Development of Hungarian Economic Thought. Introduction*), Budapest, Közgazdasági és Jogi Könyvkiadó. 9–57.
Szamuely, L. (1989) 'A debate on the crisis of the Hungarian reform in the 1970s', *Acta Oeconomica* 40.
Szegö, Andrea (1983) 'Gazdaság és politika – érdek és struktura' ('Economy and politics – interests and structure'), *Medvetánc* 2–3, 49–93.
Szelényi, Iván (1989) 'Eastern Europe in an epoch of transition: towards a socialist mixed economy?' in V. Nee and D. Stark (eds) *Remaking the Economic Institutions of Socialism*, Stanford, Stanford University Press, 208–32.
Tardos, M. (1972) 'A gazdasági verseny problémái hazánkban' ('The problems of economic competition in Hungary') *Közgazdasági Szemle* 19, 911–26.
Tardos, M. (1985) 'Development program for economic control and organization in Hungary', *Acta Oeconomica* 28, 295–315.
Tardos, M. (1986) 'The conditions for developing a regulated market', *Acta Oeconomica* 36 (1–2), 67–89.
Vacic, Aleksandar (1988) *Social Property, Market Economy and the Role of the State*, 'Plan and/or Market' Project, Institut für die Wissenschaften vom Menschen, Vienna.
Wagener, H. J. (1985) 'Allmacht oder Ohnmacht: Die Rolle des Staates im Sozialistischen Wirtschaftssystem', in *Jenseits von Staat und Kapital. Ökonomie und Gesellschaft* 3, 108–40.
Wagener, H. J. (1990a) 'The market and the state under perestroika', *Kyklos* 43, 359–83.
Wagener, H. J. (1990b) 'System, order and change (on evolution and transformation of economic systems)', manuscript, Groningen.
Winiecki, Jan (1987) 'Why economic reforms fail in the Soviet system? – A property rights-based approach,' IIES 374, Stockholm, January.
Wu, Jinglian (1988) The *Strategic Option of Reform and the Evolution of Economic Theories (An Analysis of China's Example)*, 'Plan and/or Market' Project, Institut für die Wissenschaften vom Menschen, Vienna.
Zauberman, Alfred (1976) *Mathematical Theory in Soviet Planning*, London, Oxford University Press.

Index

Wolf, C., 76
Wong, C., 204
work laws, 274–5
work quality, 276–7, 277–8, 278–9
workers' councils, 170, 172
working time, extraction of, 280–1
Wu, H., 105
Wu Jinglian, 199, 200
Wu Shuqing, 199

Yakovlev, A.N., 155
Yasin, E., 178
Young, D.R., 55
Yugoslavia: 72, 80, 151, 204, 223, 248, 312, 327; democratization, 240; food prices, 270; forced saving, 219; industrial hierarchy dismantled, 101; inefficiency, 212; labour migration, 242; marketization, 214, 216–17; monopolies, 234; political authority, 232–3; reform economists, 300; reforms compared with Hungary, 229–30; self-managed enterprises 225, Brus 139, 139–40, competition 86, 88, independence 222, 223; social waste, 92 state-owned banks, 236, 237

Zhang Yongjiang, 209
Zhang Zhouyuan, 199
Zhou Xiaochuan, 197, 199, 200
Zhuravlev, V.V., 148
Zienkowski, L., 258